AF560476

Gender and Public Policy

Gender and Public Policy

Dr. Anand Prakash

Gender and Public Policy

ISBN 978-93-5111-654-7

Published in 2015 in India by

RANDOM PUBLICATIONS

4376-A/4B, Gali Murari Lal, Ansari Road
New Delhi-110 002
Phone : +9111-43580356, 011-23289044, 011-43142548
e-mail: sales@randompublications.com,
info@randompublications.com, randomexports@gmail.com

Reprinted 2021

Type Setting by : Friends Media, Delhi-110089
Digitally Printed at : Replika Press Pvt. Ltd.

Preface

Gender is the often un-analyzed dimension of all public policies. From conflict resolution to economic development, public finance to public health, policies rest upon, are shaped by, and shape gender relations. Increasingly, international organizations, national and local governments, and private actors have recognized that gender must be explicitly taken into account if policy goals are to be attained.

Gender as a concept refers to masculinities and feminities, women and men, the relations between them, and the structural context that reinforces and creates these power relations. In practice, gender is taken nearly universally to refer to the social factors shaping realities of women and girls alone. Accordingly, researchers reviewed existing gender equality policies in each of the participating countries for ways that men and masculinities are considered, or not.

The specific policy areas covered in the analysis include civil and human rights, employment, income support and livelihoods, family life, health, education violence prevention and public security. The policy reviews conducted by partners in Brazil, Chile, India, Mexico and South Africa, with brief summaries on Norway and Tanzania, form the basis for the report. The country analyses- and additional policy examples from neglected policy areas- show the diversity of policy recipes needed.

Public policy as and government action is generally the principled guide to action taken by the administrative or executive branches of the state with regard to a class of issues in a manner consistent with law and institutional customs. In general, the foundation is the pertinent national and substantial constitutional law and implementing legislation such as the US Federal code. Further substrates include both judicial interpretations and regulations which are generally authorised by legislation. Other scholars define it as a system of "courses of action, regulatory measures, laws, and funding priorities concerning a given topic promulgated by a governmental entity or its representatives." Public policy is commonly embodied "in constitutions, legislative acts, and judicial decisions."

It is hoped that this book would provide to a wide cross-section of people an understanding of some of the issues on significant aspects of areas of concern.

I would like to thank my team for standing beside me throughout my career and writing this book. My special thanks go to "Random Publications" who have published the book.

– Dr. Anand Prakash

Contents

1

Socialization and Gender

INTRODUCTION

The several agents of socialization, including the family, peers, schools, the mass media, and religion. Such socialization helps boys and girls develop their gender identity. Socialization into gender roles begins in infancy, as almost from the moment of birth parents begin to socialize their children as boys or girls without even knowing it. Many studies document this process. Parents commonly describe their infant daughters as pretty, soft, and delicate and their infant sons as strong, active, and alert, even though neutral observers find no such gender differences among infants when they do not know the infants' sex. From infancy on, parents play with and otherwise interact with their daughters and sons differently.

They play more roughly with their sons—for example, by throwing them up in the air or by gently wrestling with them—and more quietly with their daughters. When their infant or toddler daughters cry, they warmly comfort them, but they tend to let their sons cry longer and to comfort them less. They give their girls dolls to play with and their boys "action figures" and toy guns. While these gender differences in socialization are probably smaller now than a generation ago, they certainly continue to exist. Go into a large toy store and you will see pink aisles of dolls and cooking sets and blue aisles of action figures, toy guns, and related items.

PEERS

Peer influences also encourage gender socialization. As they reach school age, children begin to play different games based on their gender. Boys tend to play sports and other competitive team games governed by inflexible rules and relatively large numbers of roles, while girls tend to play smaller, cooperative games such as hopscotch and jumping rope with fewer and more flexible rules. Although girls are much more involved in sports now than a generation ago, these gender differences in their play as youngsters persist and continue to reinforce gender roles. For example, they encourage competitiveness in boys and cooperation and trust among girls. Boys who are not competitive risk being called "sissy" or other words by their peers. The patterns we see in adult males and females thus have their roots in their play as young children.

Schools

School is yet another agent of gender socialization. First of all, school playgrounds provide a location for the gender-linked play activities just described to occur. Second, and perhaps more important, teachers at all levels treat their female and male students differently in subtle ways of which they are probably not aware.

They tend to call on boys more often to answer questions in class and to praise them more when they give the right answer. They also give boys more feedback about their assignments and other school work. At all grade levels, many textbooks and other books still portray people in gender-stereotyped ways. It is true that the newer books do less of this than older ones, but the newer books still contain some stereotypes, and the older books are still used in many schools, especially those that cannot afford to buy newer volumes.

Mass Media

Gender socialization also occurs through the mass media. On children's television shows, the major characters are male. On Nickelodeon, for example, the very popular SpongeBob SquarePants is a male, as are his pet snail, Gary; his best friend, Patrick Star; their neighbour, Squidward Tentacles; and SpongeBob's employer, Eugene Crabs. Of the major characters in Bikini Bottom, only Sandy Cheeks is a female. For all its virtues, *Sesame Street* features Bert, Ernie, Cookie Monster, and other male characters. Most of the Muppets are males, and the main female character, Miss Piggy, depicted as vain and jealous, is hardly an admirable female role model. As for adults' prime-time television, more men than women continue to fill more major roles in weekly shows, despite notable women's roles in shows such as *The Good Wife* and *Grey's Anatomy*. Women are also often portrayed as unintelligent or frivolous individuals who are there more for their looks than for anything else. Television commercials reinforce this image.

Cosmetic ads abound, suggesting not only that a major task for women is to look good but also that their sense of self-worth stems from looking good. Other commercials show women becoming ecstatic over achieving a clean floor or sparkling laundry. Judging from the world of television commercials, then, women's chief goals in life are to look good and to have a clean house. At the same time, men's chief goals, judging from many commercials, are to drink beer and drive cars.

Women's and men's magazines reinforce these gender images. Most of the magazines intended for teenage girls and adult women are filled with pictures of thin, beautiful models, advice on dieting, cosmetic ads, and articles on how to win and please your man. Conversely, the magazines intended for teenage boys and men are filled with ads and articles on cars and sports, advice on how to succeed in careers and other endeavors, and pictures of thin, beautiful women. These magazine images again suggest that women's chief goals are to look good and to please men and that men's chief goals are to succeed, win over women, and live life in the fast lane.

Religion

Another agent of socialization, religion, also contributes to traditional gender stereotypes. Many traditional interpretations of the Bible yield the message that women are subservient to men. This message begins in Genesis, where the first human is Adam, and Eve was made from one of his ribs. The major figures in the rest of the Bible are men, and women are for the most part depicted as wives, mothers, temptresses, and prostitutes; they are praised for their roles as wives and mothers and condemned for their other roles. More generally, women are constantly depicted as the property of men. The Ten Commandments includes a neighbour's wife with his house, ox, and other objects as things not to be coveted and many biblical passages say explicitly that women belong to men, such as this one from the New Testament:

- Wives be subject to your husbands, as to the Lord. For the husband is the head of the wife as Christ is the head of the Church. As the Church is subject to Christ, so let wives also be subject in everything to their husbands.

Several passages in the Old Testament justify the rape and murder of women and girls. The Koran, the sacred book of Islam, also contains passages asserting the subordinate role of women. This discussion suggests that religious people should believe in traditional gender views more than less religious people, and research confirms this relationship. To illustrate this shows the relationship in the General Social Survey between frequency of prayer and the view that "it is much better for everyone involved if the man is the achiever outside the home and the woman takes care of the home and family." People who pray more often are more likely to accept this traditional view of gender roles. Percentage agreeing that "it is much better for everyone involved if the man is the achiever outside the home and the woman takes care of the home and family."

BASIC SOCIOLOGICAL CONCEPTS

All societies are structured around relatively stable patterns that establish how social interaction will be carried out. One of the most important social structures that organizes social interaction is status—a category or position a person occupies that is a significant determinant of how she or he will be defined and treated. We acquire statuses by achievement, through our own efforts, or by ascription, being born into them or attaining them involuntarily at some other point in the life cycle.

We occupy a number of statuses simultaneously, referred to as a status set, such as mother, daughter, attorney, patient, employee, and passenger. Compared to achieved statuses occurring later in life, ascribed statuses are those immediately impacting virtually every aspect of our lives. The most important ascribed statuses are gender, race, and social class. Since a status is simply a position within a social system, it should not be confused with rank or prestige. There are high-prestige statuses as well as low-prestige statuses. In the United States, for example, a physician occupies a status ranked higher in prestige than a secretary.

All societies categorize members by status and then rank these statuses in some fashion, thereby creating a system of social stratification. People whose status sets are comprised of low-ranked ascribed statuses more than high-ranked achieved statuses are near the bottom of the social stratification system and vulnerable to social stigma, prejudice, and discrimination. To date, there is no known society in which the status of female is consistently ranked higher than that of male. A role is the expected behaviour associated with a status. Roles are performed according to social norms, shared rules that guide people's behaviour in specific situations. Social norms determine the privileges and responsibilities a status possesses. Females and males, mothers and fathers, and daughters and sons are all statuses with different normative role requirements attached to them. The status of mother calls for expected roles involving love, nurturing, self-sacrifice, home-making, and availability. The status of father calls for expected roles of breadwinner, disciplinarian, home technology expert, and ultimate decision maker in the household. Society allows for a degree of flexibility in acting out roles, but in times of rapid social change, acceptable role limits are often in a state of flux, producing uncertainty about what appropriate role behaviour should be.

People may experience *anomie*—normlessness—because traditional norms have changed but new ones have yet to be developed. For example, the most important twentieth-century trend impacting gender roles in the United Sates is the massive increase of women in the labour force. Although women from all demographic categories contributed to these numbers, mothers with preschool children led the trek from unpaid home-based roles to full-time paid employment roles.

In acting out the roles of mother and employee, women are expected to be available at given times to satisfy the needs of family and workplace. Because workplaces and other social institutions have not been modified in meaningful ways to account for the new statuses women occupy, their range of acceptable role behaviour is severely restricted. As a result, family and workplace roles inevitably collide and compete with one another for the mother-- employee's time and attention.

KEY CONCEPTS FOR THE SOCIOLOGY OF GENDER

As key components of social structure, statuses and roles allow us to organize our lives in consistent, predictable ways. In combination with established norms, they prescribe our behaviour and ease interaction with people who occupy different social statuses, whether we know these people or not. There is an insidious side to this kind of predictable world. When normative role behaviour becomes too rigidly defined, our freedom of action is often compromised. These rigid definitions are associated with the development of stereotypes—oversimplified conceptions that people who occupy the same status group share certain traits in common. Although stereotypes can include positive traits, they most often consist of negative ones that are then used to justify discrimination against members of a given group. The statuses of male and female are often stereotyped according to the traits they are assumed to possess by virtue of their biological makeup. Women are stereotyped as flighty and unreliable because they possess uncontrollable raging hormones that fuel unpredictable emotional outbursts.

The assignment of negative stereotypes can result in sexism, the belief that the status of female is inferior to the status of male. Males are not immune to the negative consequences of sexism, but females are more likely to experience it because the status sets they occupy are more stigmatized than those occupied by males. Compared to males, for example, females are more likely to occupy statuses inside and outside their homes that are associated with less power, less prestige, and less pay or no pay. Beliefs about inferiority due to biology are reinforced and then used to justify discrimination directed towards females. Sexism is perpetuated by systems of patriarchy, male-dominated social structures leading to the oppression of women.

Patriarchy, by definition, exhibits androcentrism—male-centered norms operating throughout all social institutions that become the standard to which all persons adhere. Sexism is reinforced when patriarchy and androcentrism combine to perpetuate beliefs that gender roles are biologically determined and therefore unalterable. For example, throughout the developing world beliefs about a woman's biological unsuitability for other than domestic roles have restricted opportunities for education and achieving literacy.

These restrictions have made men the guardians of what has been written, disseminated, and interpreted regarding gender and the placement of men and women in society. Until recently, history has been recorded from an androcentric perspective that ignored the other half of humanity. This perspective has perpetuated the belief that patriarchy is an inevitable, inescapable fact of history, so struggles for gender equality are doomed to failure.

Women's gain in education is associated with the power to engage in the research and scholarship offering alternatives to prevailing androcentric views. As suggested, see that such scholarship suggests that patriarchal systems may be universal, but they are not inevitable, and that gender egalitarianism was a historical fact of life in some cultures and is a contemporary fact of life in others.

DISTINGUISHING SEX AND GENDER

As gender issues have become more mainstreamed in scientific research and media reports, confusion associated with the terms *sex* and *gender* has decreased. In sociology, these terms are now fairly standardized to refer to different content areas. Sex refers to the biological characteristics distinguishing male and female.

This definition emphasizes male and female differences in chromosomes, anatomy, hormones, reproductive systems, and other physiological components. Gender refers to those social, cultural, and psychological traits linked to males and females through particular social contexts. Sex makes us male or female; gender makes us masculine or feminine. Sex is an ascribed status because a person is born with it, but gender is an achieved status because it must be learned.

This relatively simple distinction masks a number of problems associated with its usage. It implies that all people can be conveniently placed into unambiguous "either–or" categories. Certainly the ascribed status of sex is less likely to be altered than the achieved status of gender. Some people believe, however, that they were born with the "wrong" body and are willing to undergo major surgery to make their gender identity consistent with their biological sex. Sexual orientation, the preference for sexual partners of one gender or the other, also varies. People who experience sexual pleasure with members of their own sex are likely to consider themselves masculine or feminine according to gender norms. Others are born with ambiguous sex characteristics and may be assigned one sex at birth but develop a different identity related to gender. Some cultures allow people to move freely between genders, regardless of their biological sex. From a sociological perspective, this text is concerned with gender and how it is learned, how it changes over time, and how it varies between and within cultures.

Gender can be viewed on a continuum of characteristics demonstrated by a person regardless of the person's biological sex. Adding the concept of role to either sex or gender may increase confusion in terminology. When the sociological concept of role is combined with the biological concept of sex, there is often misunderstanding about what content areas are subsumed under the resultant *sex role* label.

Usage is becoming rapidly standardized, however, and most sociologists now prefer to employ the term *gender role* rather than *sex role* in their writing.

Gender roles, therefore, are the expected attitudes and behaviours a society associates with each sex. This definition places gender squarely in the sociocultural context.

SOCIOLOGICAL PERSPECTIVES ON GENDER ROLES

Sociologists explain gender roles according to several *theoretical perspectives*, general ways of understanding social reality that guide the research process and provide a means for interpreting the data. In essence, a theory is an explanation. Formal theories consist of logically interrelated propositions that explain empirical events. For instance, data indicate that compared to men, women are more likely to be segregated in lower-paying jobs offering fewer opportunities for professional growth and advancement.

Data also indicate that both in the United States and cross-culturally the domestic work of women performed in or near their homes is valued less than the work of men performed outside their homes. Because the issue of gender crosses many disciplines, explanations for these facts can be offered according to the theoretical perspectives of those disciplines. Biology, psychology, and anthropology all offer explanations for gender-related attitudes and behaviour. Not only do these explanations differ between disciplines, but scientists within the same discipline also frequently offer competing explanations for the same data, and sociology is no exception. The best explanations are those that account for the volume and complexities of the data. As research on gender issues accelerates and more sophisticated research tools are developed, it is becoming clearer that the best explanations are also those that are both interdisciplinary and incorporate concepts related to diversity. Sociological theory will dominate this text's discussion, but as suggested, also account for relevant interdisciplinary work and its attention to diversity issues. Sociological perspectives on gender also vary according to the level of analysis at which they operate.

Macrosociological perspectives on gender roles direct attention to data collected on large-scale social phenomena, such as labour force, educational, and political trends that are differentiated according to gender roles. *Microsociological* perspectives on gender roles direct attention to data collected in small groups and the details of gender interaction occurring, for example, between couples and in families and peer groups. Microsociological perspectives overlap a great deal with the discipline of social psychology. As suggested, see that theoretical perspectives may be differentiated according to macro- and microlevel of analysis, and perspectives from each level may be more or less compatible. When theoretical perspectives can be successfully combined, they offer excellent ways to better understand gender issues from a sociological perspective.

Early sociological perspectives related to gender roles evolved from scholarship on the sociology of the family. These explanations centered on why men and women hold different roles in the family that in turn impact the roles they perform outside the family. To a large extent, this early work on the family has continued to inform current sociological thinking on gender roles. The next parts will overview the major sociological perspectives and highlight their explanations regarding the gender–family connection.

FUNCTIONALISM

Functionalism, also known as "structural functionalism," is a macrosociological perspective that is based on the premise that society is made up of interdependent parts, each of which contributes to the functioning of the whole society. Functionalists seek to identify the basic elements or parts of society and determine the functions these parts play in meeting basic social needs in predictable ways. Functionalists ask how any given element of social structure contributes to overall social stability, balance, and equilibrium.

They assert that in the face of disruptive social change, society can be restored to equilibrium as long as built-in mechanisms of social control operate effectively and efficiently. Social control and stability are enhanced when people share beliefs and values in common.

Functionalist emphasis on this value consensus is a major ingredient in virtually all their interpretations related to social change. Values surrounding gender roles, marriage, and the family are central to functionalist assertions regarding social equilibrium.

Preindustrial Society

Functionalists suggest that in preindustrial societies social equilibrium was maintained by assigning different tasks to men and women. Given the hunting and gathering and subsistence farming activities of most preindustrial societies, role specialization according to gender was considered a functional necessity. In their assigned hunting roles, men were frequently away from home for long periods and centered their lives around the responsibility of bringing food to the family.

It was functional for women—more limited by pregnancy, childbirth, and nursing—to be assigned domestic roles near the home as gatherers and subsistence farmers and as caretakers of children and households. Children were needed to help with agricultural and domestic activities. Girls would continue these activities when boys reached the age when they were allowed to hunt with the older males. Once established, this functional division of labour was reproduced in societies throughout the globe. Women may have been farmers and food gatherers in their own right, but they were dependent on men for food and for protection. Women's dependence on men in turn produced a pattern in which male activities and roles came to be more valued than female activities and roles.

Contemporary Society

Similar principles apply to families in contemporary societies. Disruption is minimized, harmony is maximized, and families benefit when spouses assume complementary, specialized, non-overlapping roles. When the husband–father takes the instrumental role, he is expected to maintain the physical integrity of the family by providing food and shelter and linking the family to the world outside the home. When the wife–mother takes the expressive role, she is expected to cement relationships and provide emotional support and nurturing activities that ensure the household runs smoothly.

If too much deviation from these roles occurs, or when there is too much overlap, the family system is propelled into a state of imbalance that can threaten the survival of the family unit. Advocates of functionalist assumptions argue, for instance, that gender role ambiguity regarding instrumental and expressive roles is a major factor in divorce.

Critique

It should be apparent that functionalism's emphasis on social equilibrium contributes to its image as an inherently conservative theoretical perspective. This image is reinforced by its difficulty in accounting for a variety of existing family systems and in not keeping pace with rapid social change moving families towardss more egalitarian attitudes regarding gender roles. Often to the dismay of the scientists who developed them, scientific theories and the research on which they are based are routinely employed to support a range of ideologies.

Functionalism has been used as a justification for male dominance and gender stratification. In the United States, functional analyses were popularized in the 1950s when, weary of war, the nation latched onto a traditional and idealized version of family life and attempted to establish not just a prewar, but a pre-Depression, existence. Functionalism tends to support a white middle-class family model emphasizing the economic activities of the male household head and domestic activities of his female subordinate.

Women function outside the home only as a reserve labour force, such as when their labour is needed in wartime. This model does not apply to poor women and single parents who by necessity must work outside the home to maintain the household. It may not apply to African American women, who are less likely by choice to separate family and employment and who derive high levels of satisfaction from both these roles. Research also shows that specialization of household tasks by gender in contemporary families is more dysfunctional than functional. Women relegated to family roles that they see as restrictive, for example, are unhappier in their marriages and more likely to opt out of them. Despite tension associated with multiple roles and role overlap, couples report high levels of gratification, self esteem, status security, and personally enriched lives. Contemporary families simply do not fit functionalist models.

To its credit, functionalism offers a reasonably sound explanation for the origin of gender roles and demonstrates the functional utility of assigning tasks on the basis of gender in subsistence economies or in regions in which large families are functional and children are needed for agricultural work. Contemporary functionalists also acknowledge that strain occurs when there is too sharp a divide between the public and the private sphere particularly for women. They recognize that such a divide is artificial and dysfunctional when families need to cope with the growing interdependence called for in a global economy.

The "superwoman" who "does it all" in career achievement and family nurturance will be valued. Finally, neo-functionalism accounts for the multiple levels where gender relations are operative—biological, psychological, social, and cultural. A functionalist examination of their interdependence allows us to understand how female subordination and male superiority became reproduced throughout the globe.

CONFLICT THEORY

With its assumptions about social order and social change, the macrosociological perspective of conflict theory, also referred to as social conflict theory, is in many ways a mirror image of functionalism. Unlike functionalists, who believe that social order is maintained through value consensus, conflict theorists assert that it is preserved involuntarily through the exercise of power one social class holds over another.

Marx, Engels, and Social Class

Originating from the writings of Karl Marx conflict theory is based on the assumption that society is a stage on which struggles for power and dominance are acted out. The struggles are largely between social classes competing for scarce resources, such as control over the means of production and for a better distribution of all resources. Capitalism thrives on a class-based system that consolidates power in the hands of a few men of the ruling class, who own the farms and factories that workers depend on for their survival.

The interest of the dominant class is to maintain its position of power over the subordinate class by extracting as much profit as possible from their work. Only when the workers recognize their common oppression and form a *class consciousness* can they unite and amass the resources necessary to seriously challenge the inequitable system in which they find themselves. Marxian beliefs were acted out historically in the revolution that enveloped Russia, Eastern

Europe, and much of Eurasia, propelling the Soviets to power for a half a century of control over these regions. Friedrich Engels Marx's collaborator, applied these assumptions to the family and, by extension, to gender roles. He suggested that the master–slave or exploiter–exploited relationships occurring in broader society between the bourgeoisie and the proletariat are translated into the household. Primitive societies were highly egalitarian because there were no surplus goods, hence no private property.

People consumed what they produced. With the emergence of private property and the dawn of capitalistic institutions, Engels argued that a woman's domestic labour is "no longer counted beside the acquisition of the necessities of life by the man; the latter was everything, the former an unimportant extra." The household is an autocracy, and the supremacy of the husband is unquestioned. "The emancipation of woman will only be possible when women can take part in production on a large social scale, and domestic work no longer claims but an insignificant amount of her time".

Contemporary Conflict Theory

Later conflict theorists refined original Marxian assertions to reflect contemporary patterns and make conflict theory more palatable to people who desire social change that moves in the direction of egalitarianism but not through the revolutionary means outlined by classical Marxism. Today conflict theory largely asserts that social structure is based on the dominance of some groups over others and that groups in society share common interests, whether its members are aware of it or not.

Conflict is not simply based on class struggle and the tensions between owner and worker or employer and employee; it occurs on a much wider level and among almost all other groups. These include parents and children, husbands and wives, young and the old, sick and healthy, people of colour and whites, heterosexual and gay, females and males, and any other groups that can be differentiated as minority or majority according to the level of resources they possess. The list is infinite.

Gender and the Family

Conflict theory focuses on the social placement function of the family that deposits people at birth into families who possess varying degrees of economic resources. People fortunate enough to be deposited into wealthier families will work to preserve existing inequality and the power relations in the broader society because they clearly benefit from the overall power imbalance. Social class *endogamy* and inheritance patterns ensure that property and wealth are kept in the hands of a few powerful families.

Beliefs about inequality and the power imbalance become institutionalized—they are accepted and persist over time as legitimate by both the privileged and the oppressed—so the notion that family wealth is deserved and that those born into poor families remain poor because they lack talent and a work ethic is perpetuated. The structural conditions that sustain poverty are ignored. When social placement operates through patriarchal and patrilineal systems, wealth is further concentrated in the hands of males and further promotes female subservience, neglect, and poverty. Contemporary conflict theorists agree with Engels by suggesting that when women gain economic strength by also being wage earners, their power inside the home is strengthened and can lead to more egalitarian arrangements.

The conflict perspective is evident in research demonstrating that household responsibilities have an effect on occupational location, work experience, and number of hours worked per week, all of which are linked to the gender gap in earnings. Undesirable work will be performed disproportionately by those lacking resources to demand sharing the burden or purchasing substitutes. Because household labour is unpaid and associated with lack of power, the homemaker takes on virtually all domestic chores. The more powerful spouse performs the least amount of household work.

Critique

Conflict theory has been criticized for its overemphasis on the economic basis of inequality and its assumption that there is inevitable competition between family members. It tends to dismiss the consensus among wives and husbands regarding task allocation. In addition, paid employment is not the panacea envisioned by Engels in overcoming male dominance.

The gendered division of household labour does not translate to significant wage reductions for employed women outside the home or reduced in-home responsibilities. In the former Soviet Union women had the highest levels of paid employment in the world, but retained more household responsibilities than comparable women in other countries, and earned two-thirds of the average male income. In post–Communist Russia, there is no change in women's domestic work, but women now earn less than half of men's average earnings. Research unanimously concludes that even in those cultures where gender equity in the workplace is increasing, employed women globally take on a "second shift" of domestic work after returning home.

A conspiratorial element emerges when conflict theory becomes associated with the idea that men as a group are consciously organized to keep women in subordinate positions. A number of social forces, many of them unorganized or unintended, come into play when explaining gender stratification. Functionalism's bias against social change might be matched with conflict theory's bias for social change. Compared to functionalism, however, this bias is less of a problem for conflict theory once it is stripped of some Marxian baggage.

Contemporary conflict theory has made strong inroads in using social class to further clarify the gender–race–class link, suggesting that the class advantages for people of colour may override the race disadvantages. Most people are uncomfortable with sexism and patterns of gender stratification that harm both women and men. Women are denied opportunities to expand instrumental roles offering economic parity with men outside the home; men are denied opportunities for expanding expressive and nurturing roles inside the home. At the ideological level, sociological conflict theory has been used to support activities designed to reduce racism, economic-based disparity and sexism.

SYMBOLIC INTERACTION

Symbolic interaction, also called "the interactionist perspective," is at the heart of the sociological view of social interaction at the microlevel. With attention to people's behaviour in face-to-face social settings, symbolic interactionists explain social interaction as a dynamic process in which people continually modify their behaviour as a result of the interaction itself. Herbert Blumer who originated the term *symbolic interaction*, asserted that people do not respond directly to the world around them, but to the meaning they bring to it. Society, its institutions, and its social structure exist—that is, social reality is bestowed— only through human interaction. Reality is what members agree to be reality. People interact according to how they perceive a situation, how they understand the social encounter, and the meanings they bring to it.

Another important step in the interaction process involves how they think other people who are part of the interaction also understand the encounter. Each person's definition of the situation influences others' definitions. To illustrate symbolic interaction's emphasis on the fluidity of behaviour, I developed the concept of the end point fallacy, asserting that the negotiation of social reality is an ongoing process in which new definitions produce new behaviour in a never-ending cycle. The end point fallacy is an excellent way to explain the inconsistencies between people's behaviour as they move from setting to setting.

Social Construction of Reality

Symbolic interaction is a microlevel perspective, but it does take into account that social interaction is a process governed by norms that are largely determined by culture. Cultural norms offer general guidelines for role behaviour, but symbolic interactionists assert that we have latitude in the way we act out our roles. The context of the interaction is usually a key determinant of role performance. What is appropriate role performance in one context may be inappropriate in another. Cultural norms are modified whenever social interaction occurs because people bring their own definitions about appropriate behaviour to the interaction. These definitions shape the way people see and experience the world. Symbolic interactionists refer to this shaping process as the social construction of reality—the shaping of perception of reality by the subjective meanings brought to any experience or social interaction. Consistent with Herbert Blumer's view, every time social interaction occurs, people creatively construct their own understanding of it— whether "real" or not— and behave accordingly.

Doing Gender

Symbolic interactionists contend that concepts used to collectively categorize people—such as race, ethnicty, and gender—do not exist objectively but emerge through a socially constructed process. People called "females" or "males" are endowed with certain traits defined as feminine or masculine. Concepts such as gender, therefore, must be found in the meanings people bring to them. Gender emerges not as an individual attribute but something that is "accomplished" in interaction with others. People, therefore, are doing gender. In "doing" gender, symbolic interaction takes its lead from Erving Goffman who developed a dramaturgy approach to social interaction. Goffman maintained that the best way to understand social interaction is to consider it as an enactment in a theatrical performance. Like actors on a stage, we use strategies of impression management, providing information and cues to others that present us in a favorable light. Think about the heterosexual bar scene where men usually sit at the counter and operate from a script where they are expected to make the first move.

If a woman is with friends, she must disengage herself if she is "selected" by the man. It is probable that the women drove separately. Data from television also illustrate these concepts. Prime time television commonly depict traditionally scripted sexual encounters according to gender and beliefs about heterosexuality that sustain power differences between men and women and between heterosexual and homosexual men. Although there are many cultural variations, gender-scripted rules are laid out, negotiated, and acted upon in bars and meeting places for singles and witnessed by TV viewers across the globe.

Gender roles are structured by one set of scripts designed for males and another designed for females. Although each script permits a range of behaviour options, the typical result is that gender labels promote a pattern of between-sex competition, rejection, and emotional segregation. This pattern is reinforced when we routinely refer to those of the *other* sex as the *opposite* sex. Men and women label each other as opposite to who they are, then behave according to that label. The behaviour serves to separate rather than connect the genders.

Doing Difference

Research on men and women in various social networks— formed at school, work, and in volunteer activities. From early childhood these groups are usually gender segregated. Gendered subcultures emerge that strengthen the perceptions of gender differences and erode the common ground on which intimate, status-equal friendships between the genders are formed. Differences rather than similarities are much more likely to be noticed, defined, and acted on. When cross-gender social interaction occurs, such as in the workplace, it is unlikely that men and women hold statuses with similar levels of power and prestige.

Once the genders are socially constructed as different, it is easier for those with more power to justify inequality towards those with less power. Social difference is constructed into social privilege.

Critique

Symbolic interaction's approach to understanding gender role behaviour is criticized for its overall lack of attention to macrolevel processes that often limits choice of action and prompts people to engage in gendered behaviour that counters what they would prefer to do. Cultural norms may be in flux at the microlevel of social interaction, but they remain a significant structural force on behaviour. In some cultures, for example, women and men are dictated by both law and custom to engage in certain occupations, enter into marriages with people they would not choose on their own, and be restricted from attending school.

Larger social structures also operate at the family level to explain family dynamics. Men and women interact not only as individual family members but also according to other roles they play in society and the prestige associated with those roles. For example, a wealthy white man who holds a powerful position in a corporation does not dissolve those roles when he walks into his home. They shape his life at home, in the workplace, and in the other social institutions in which he takes part. Race, class, and gender offer a range of privileges bestowed by the broader society that also create a power base in his home.

Power and privilege can result in a patriarchal family regardless of the couple's desire for a more egalitarian arrangement. Others argue that symbolic interaction's emphasis on doing gender undermines its fluidity to recast gender norms in ways that benefit both men and women. Divorce allows for the "redoing" of gender—housework, parenting, and breadwinning roles are repudiated.

Traditional gender accountability may no longer apply in the post-divorce lives of former spouses and children. Research on social dancing and its highly sexualized "grinding" form demonstrates the ways females challenge scripts and may be redoing gender on the dance floor. In hip-hop clubs, young women of colour set the dance stage for negotiating sexual and emotional encounters.

These women challenge "hypermasculine" privilege by determining the form of dance, by taking the lead, by dancing with women, and by rejecting sexual groping by male partners. Other data suggest that young women of all races use social dance as escapism, fantasy, and compensatory sexuality, especially when dancing with acquaintances rather than friends.

Taking a step further, some argue that symbolic interaction's doing gender approach needs to be abandoned. If gender accountability assumes that inequality is inevitable, research on ways of "undoing gender" should be the focus of sociological analysis. Are the young women on the dance floor "redoing" or "undoing gender"? Gendered scripts invade their dance space even as they transgress its boundaries.

You buy into this scenario that.... we're all willing to pretend in this one place... that we're allowed to do things with each other that maybe you would think about doing off of first glance anyway.... it's kind of like a.... simulated closeness with people.

Sociological analysis of sexuality is beginning to explore the body not merely as a passive surface to be acted upon, but in its relationship to human agency. More research is needed to determine if in the micro-worlds of post-divorce homes or in dance clubs traditional scripts can be modified enough to say that gender is "undone."

FEMINIST SOCIOLOGICAL THEORY

By calling attention to the powerful impact of gender in the social ordering of our relationships and our institutions, the feminist theoretical perspective in sociology emerged as a major model that has significantly reshaped the discipline. By the research it spawned, feminist sociological theory is not only bridging the micro–macro gap, it has also illuminated the androcentric bias in sociology and in broader society. Disagreement remains on all elements that need to be included in feminist theory, but at a minimum, the consensus is that a theory is feminist if it can be used to challenge a status quo that is disadvantageous to women.

The feminist perspective provides productive avenues of collaboration with sociologists who adopt other theoretical views, especially conflict theory and symbolic interaction. The feminist perspective is compatible with conflict theory in its assertions that structured social inequality is maintained by ideologies that are frequently accepted by both the privileged and the oppressed.

These ideologies are challenged only when oppressed groups gain the resources necessary to do so. Unlike conflict theory's focus on social class and the economic elements necessary to challenge the prevailing system, feminists focus on women and their ability to amass resources from a variety of sources—in their individual lives and through social and political means. Feminists work through a number of avenues to increase women's empowerment—the ability for women to exert control over their own destinies. Symbolic interaction and feminist theory come together in research focusing on the unequal power relations between men and women from the point of view of women who are "ruled" by men in many settings.

For example, corporate women who want to be promoted need to practice impression management based on acceptable gender role behaviour of their corporate setting, but at the same time they need to maintain a sense of personal integrity. The feminist perspective accounts for ways to empower these corporate women by clarifying the relationship between the label of "feminine" and how these women are judged by peers and by themselves.

Linking Gender, Race, and Class

One of the most important contributions of the feminist perspective to sociology is its attention to the multiple oppressions faced by people whose status sets are disadvantaged due to distinctive combinations based on their gender, race, and social class. The gender–race–class linkage in analysing social behaviour originated with African American feminists in the 1960s, who recognized that an understanding of the link between these multiple oppressions is necessary to determine how women are alike and how they are different. For example, when the issue of poverty becomes "feminized," the issue is defined primarily by gender—women are at a higher risk of being poor than men.

A focus on the feminization of poverty ignores the link among race, social class, and marital status that puts certain categories of women—such as single parents, women of colour, and elderly women living alone—at higher risk than others. To explain poverty, racial and class oppression must be considered along with gender.

When white, middle-class feminists focus on oppression of women, they may not recognize the privileges that come with their own race and class. The attention to sociocultural diversity that originated with the gender– race–class link has reverberated throughout sociology and other disciplines, generating a great deal of interdisciplinary research.

It has opened new academic programmes in Women's Studies, Men's Studies, and Gender Studies and has increased dialogue between men and women. Feminist scholarship provides opportunities for men to view themselves as gendered beings and to make visible their concerns. With the gender–race–class link as a foundation, feminist researchers are identifying other sites of oppression that put people at risk both inside and outside their families, such as religion, sexual orientation, age, or disability.

Feminist Perspectives on the Family

Feminist scholars in the 1960s and 1970s viewed the traditional patriarchal family as a major site for the oppression of women. They asserted that when the patriarchal family is regarded as beneficial to social stability, it hampers the movement into egalitarian roles desired by both men and women. Feminist sociologists recognize that gendered family relations do not occur in a vacuum and that lives are helped or hurt by the resources outside the family that shape what is happening inside the family. In addition to gender, for example, single-parent African-American, Latino, and Native American women are disadvantaged by race when they seek employment necessary to support their families. Lesbians must deal with a system that represses same-sex relationships when they fight for custody of their children. The growing consensus of feminists in all disciplines is that women may be doubly or triply disadvantaged by their race, class, or sexuality, but they are not helpless victims. To some degree they possess agency—the power to adapt and sometimes to thrive in difficult situations.

Critique

With a view of gender, marriage, and the family focusing on oppression of women, the feminist perspective tends to minimize the practical benefits of marriages. This contention is that a marriage may be patriarchal, but it also includes important economic resources and social support that women in these marriages may view as more important in their daily lives than their feelings about subordination. Feminist scholars also find it difficult to reconcile research suggesting that women in traditional marriages are as satisfied with their choices as women in egalitarian marriages. Finally, emphasis on human agency may minimize situations in which women's victimization is condoned by custom and ignored by law. A key strength of the feminist perspective is its ability to provide bridges between sociological theories and account for social diversity in all its forms.

With its challenge to the patriarchal status quo and the androcentric bias inherent in much sociological research and theory, it has created dissent that may limit its acceptance by some sociologists. On the other hand, the feminist perspective may plant the seeds for building a truly integrative theory to draw together "conceptual pieces into a web of ideas that transcend patriarchal theory building". Feminist theory offers a powerful new perspective in sociology. Sociology will benefit from the intellectual ferment it has already created.

GENDER ROLES

Gender roles are both cultural and personal. These roles determine how males and females think, speak, dress, and interact within the context of society. Learning plays a role in this process of shaping gender roles. These gender schemas are deeply embedded cognitive frameworks regarding what defines masculine and feminine. While various socializing agents—educators, peers, movies, television, music, books, and religion—teach and reinforce gender roles throughout a child's life span, parents probably exert the greatest influence, especially when their children are very young.

Developmentalists indicate that adults perceive and treat female and male infants differently. Parents probably do this in response to having been recipients of gender expectations as young children themselves. Traditionally, fathers teach boys how to fix and build things; mothers teach girls how to cook, sew, and keep house. Children then receive parental approval when they conform to gender expectations and adopt culturally accepted and conventional roles. All of these lessons are reinforced by additional socializing agents, such as the media. In other words, learning gender roles always occurs within a social context, with the values of the parents and society being passed along to the children of successive generations.

THE COGNITIVE APPROACH

The theory proposes the interaction of mental schema and social experience in directing gender role behaviour. The cognitive approach focuses upon the child's 'understanding'. A child's understanding refers to the way he/she perceives and tackles a phenomenon. Information about gender is organized into sets of beliefs about the sexes, *i.e.*, gender schema Gender schema (plural schemata or schemas) is a mental framework that organizes and guides a child understands of information relevant to gender. Example: information about which toys are for girls and which toys are for boys forms schema that guides behaviour.

Example: If a child has seen women being respected in his family, he will perceive women as a respectable being; and if he has seen women being battered and maltreated he will perceive them as some low grade creature.

Lawrence Kohlberg's Cognitive Development Theory

Children understand gender just as they understand anything else. Children have experiences with people of both genders, they think about their experiences, having made sort of mental notes of what males and females do, and adopt behaviours performed by people of their own sex. Children do their own gender typing themselves. They make classifications of themselves and of others as male or female, and organize their behaviours around that classification. The gender roles that children adopt are organized around this classification. Behaviours consistent with their own gender are adopted. This is reflected in their use of language, clothes, toys, etc. According to Kohlberg, acquisition of gender roles results from gender constancy, *i.e.*, a child's understanding and awareness that his/her sex is permanent, constant, and will never change. Gender constancy is also known as sex category constancy in modern literature. Gender appropriate behaviours are adopted after the realization that sex is a permanent feature of personality. Gender constancy emerges somewhere between 3-7 years of age. Gender constancy is the key to gender typing, according to Kohlberg. Gender constancy is not a phenomenon that occurs at once, at one point in time. It takes place in three stages:

1. *Gender Identity*: Age 2-3 years; becoming aware of one's own gender, and that of others.
2. *Gender Stability*: Realization of boys and girls that they will grow up as men or women respectively, *i.e.*, gender is a fixed, permanent, quality and an integral feature of their personality. But at this stage they understand this on the basis of superficial, external appearances, and stereotyped behaviours.
3. *Gender Consistency*: The awareness that gender remains the same no matter what one wears, how one behaves, whatever hairstyle one has.

Although Kohlberg put forth the concept of gender constancy as a significant theme, there is not much solid research evidence supporting it. Different researches have yielded findings quite different from, and even contrary to, Kohlberg's hypothesis that gender constancy stage is the point where children actually learn gender roles and relevant appropriate behaviours. It has been seen that at 2½ years of age children begin to prefer the company of children of their own sex. Also, girls are more interested in dolls and boys in cars. Long before attaining the stage of gender constancy, children exhibit gender-typed preferences. Children can categorize activities and objects by gender, know a lot about what males and females do, and often acquire gender appropriate behaviours. Five-year old boys having reached gender constancy, or almost there, pay more attention to male characters on TV and watch more sports and action programmes in comparison to other age mates. Children tend to develop more complex beliefs about gender later on; also they tend to become more flexible in their views about gender roles.

Positionings in Gendered Relations

For the cognitive psychologist, theoretical interest is primarily centred on how automatic processes in the brain produce human knowledge and subsequent bodily activity in the social realm. For these theorists, the metaphor of the information processor, or computer, is most appropriate for understanding the functioning of the human brain. Cognitivists generally agree that the basic building block in the production of mental life is the schema. An individual's mental apparatus contains a variety of schemas, each helping to structure information into categories that are relevant to the person.

THE CONSTRUCTIVIST APPROACH

From the constructivist standpoint, gender schemas organize one's sense of personal identity, interpersonal behaviours, and social perceptions. Being classified as male or female is the critical first step in the categorization of a human after birth, and given the present state of technology, even months before. This category remains the prime distinguishing mark of our identity throughout life. By puberty, sexual orientation, whether we are heterosexual, homosexual or bisexual, is also regarded as a significant aspect of gender schemata critical to our social lives and interpersonal behaviours. These schemata—self, gender and sexual orientation—are of special relevance to psychologists who study gender issues, especially, feminist psychologists, who are interested in the political aspects of gender studies as well as the more traditional scientific concerns regarding theoretical orientations and empirical findings.

Enumerating the immense variety of theories and empirical research at the intersection of cognitive theories and gender is beyond the scope of this review. Two theoretical orientations that are of particular interest to this audience are those cognitive psychologists who would identify themselves as social constructivists of the Berger and Luckmann school, and those who are influenced by George Kelly's Personal Construct Theory. To varying degrees both of these perspectives has been influential in the development of a feminist psychology in the last two decades. However, most of the work in gender studies, while relying on the constructivist notions of constructs or schemas and the centrality of cognitive processes in the development of gendered self conceptions and social behaviours, has not directly acknowledged the contributions of Kelly or Berger and Luckmann to their theorizing or research.

Feminist Standpoint Theorists and Gender Differences

At the fringes of cognitive psychology are important feminist theorists from other specialties and disciplines, who have developed women-centred models of knowledge, which stress the cognitive aspects of sexual difference and personal experience. Representative of these many theorists are Jean Baker Miller, (1976), a psychologist, and Nancy Hartsock, (1983) and Dorothy Smith (1987), who are socialist feminists. These Feminist Standpoint theorists, as they have been called by philosopher Sandra Harding (1986), posit that the differentiated daily lives of men and women create differences in their cognitive development. Hartsock, for example, argues that women's roles as homemakers and mothers, across a variety of cultural settings, affect the development of their epistemological competencies. Through their personal experiences—rearing children, gathering food, and doing housework—women develop more refined cognitive capacities that yield more accurate depictions of the world than men acquire, with their distant relationship to daily material things.

Critiques/Limits of Cognitive Views of Gender

Common to all of these theoretical positions is the basic idea that internal cognitive mechanisms shape individual actions. One's knowledge of oneself as a man or a woman is deeply connected to these categories, which provide a strong controlling influence on other aspects of life. What are some of the limits to this form of theorizing about gendering? We would like to point up several interlocking arguments that lead to questioning the utility of this type of theoretical approach to understanding social behaviour.

To begin, a strong individualism is easily detected in this approach to understanding social behaviour. Alone by virtue of the inaccessibility of others to one's private mental world, each individual abstracts from experience—often via automated mechanistic processes—the meaning of that experience within the conceptual world. While social behaviour is most often conceived of as involving more than one actor, either other actors, or objects in a context, the theoretical focus tends to be entirely on the separated autonomy of the interacting units: perceiver and target. In the Deaux and Major model, for example, not only are there two separated units, they are each assigned separate functions within the model. Their two spheres of being and activity are influential as they are perceived and interpreted. There is no possibility for an emergent result, a joint action, or any truly mutual activity that could to be coded outside of an individualistic formulation. The level of analysis would have to be drastically changed to take account of such phenomena.

Social Constructionist Approach

In contrast to this constructivist view, a social constructionist approach emphasizes the social origins of linguistic patterns related to self, knowledge, and social activity. From this position, all aspects of 'reality', including personal identity—self, gender, sexual orientation, and points of view—are constructed interpersonally, and the emphasis in social constructionist theory is on the relational aspects of construction, not on the concomitant internal mechanisms that are coordinating the bodily affairs.

This theoretical position rejects the possibility of absolute truth and scientific objectivity. Thus, ways of talking about the world, including categories such as male and female, are constructed within social groups; the origins of categories of words are not natural, necessary or inevitable, but are created to serve ever shifting social ends. Feminist theorists of the social constructionist variety contend that these predominant gender constructions are often instantiated and retained to support patriarchal interests and viewpoints, which set women as opposed and 'other' to the major model of humanity—man.

While standpoint position feminists have tried to reverse the direction of the polarity, claiming for women the better part of the binary, this polarizing strategy has backfired in the sense that it has legitimated the system that validated the binary in the first place. From a social constructionist standpoint, rather than sustain the binary through the glorification of womanhood, it is possible to relativize the game of difference, perhaps at times, even calling it off, as other forms of linguistic categories are imagined.

RELATIONAL THEORY AS A FEMINIST APPROACH

A recent attempt to integrate these politically based concerns with a social constructionist emphasis on communal forms of sense-making is called relational theory. The goal of this theoretical endeavour is to move to the production of descriptive formulations that reifies processes of relatedness, that is to theorize units of meaning-making that extend beyond one actor, as an autonomous, separate entity, to relationships.

Relationships can extend beyond couples, to groups, and to relations between people and objects, or animals, or past conversations, visual displays, music and texts. By focusing on relatedness as furnishing the forestructure for the condition of our impulses to act into the on rushing demands of life, the process of mutual creations of meaning is sustained. Within this theoretical approach is the invitation to construct individual identities—the 'I' who speaks—subjectivities, and personal experiences as both outgrowths of relational process, and in a reflexive manner, as the producers of relational processes. The focus on a relational view suggests that we seek understanding of social life and the models for change in the generation of interactive conversation. When the relationship becomes the object of study, the originating point of action production is shifted, as is the need for new theoretical terms.

Using the metaphor of knitting with many balls of yarn at hand, one might envision relational processes as the creation of a multicolored argyle plaid, each of us a knitter, with many needles, producing from particular resources, in synchrony with one another.

Knitters coming and going, weaving an endless array of costumes... weaving up the knitted sleeve of care. We join together more or less easily, depending on our skills, our styles of doing, of the familiarity we have with the rest of the scene, and who we become within it. What we create in our illusory sweater is transformed with each moment of time, exists in our togethernesses, and from our past histories of knitting togethers, we know something of what we are trying to move towards. This knowing, however, is also a product of the moment and our being together.

In terms of our gendered identities, the relational approach suggests that gender comes into play as people in relation evoke the notion of sexual difference for specific purposes. Gender is significant, perhaps, when the caller begins the square dance, but becomes insignificant when lines are formed at the water fountain after a rigorous round. Sexual orientation, as well as sexual behaviours, may be important categories for reproductive purposes, but less so if one is interested in a sensual massage. By taking account of people-in-relationships the potential of describing behaviours as mutually produced is enhanced. From the social constructionist position, what happens in a social setting is more usefully or interestingly described as a dance, rather than as a field of abstract forces calling each actor from the depths of their private mental apparatuses and processes. People are responsive to each other in an ongoing, unthinking, spontaneous, yet regulated 'game'.

The novelty of the relational approach requires that much more be developed in order to enhance the utility of making this theoretical move. Some basis for its inception and proliferation can be found in the work of Ludwig Wittgenstein, whose poetic formulations suggest the possibilities of relationship as originary point for the construction of reality. Wittgenstein spoke of the 'order of possibilities' available 'from within our circumstances'. Instead of asking how we got here, our concern should be with 'now I know how to go on'. This remark focuses on the interaction as the mother of social life, of one thing following from another, which is the import of recognizable rituals of activity.

John Shotter has provided a theoretical option for filling out the relational sphere in his description of a third kind of knowledge, that is "a kind of knowledge one has from within a social situation, a group, an institution, or a society, and which exists only in that situation. We might call it a 'knowing-from-within'—meaning not within the person, or cognitively, but from within the situation. In this view, people as much 'act into' a set of future possibilities as 'out of' a set of past actualities, and in doing so, find their actions influenced just as much by the actions of the others around them as by any prior interests or desires. Thus in joint activity of this kind... novel possibilities for action are created beyond those available to any individual acting alone. Hence when diverse peoples come into contact with one another, there is always a possibility that through their differences, they might be able to fulfil in each other what singly they lack.

SOCIETY AND GENDER ROLES

Psychologists such as Sandra Bem, one cognitive process that seems nearly inevitable in humans is to divide people into groups. We can partition these groups on the basis of race, age, religion, and so forth. However, most of the times we split humanity on the basis of gender.

The first thing we instantly determine, when meeting someone new, is their gender. This process of categorizing others in terms of gender is both habitual and automatic. It's nearly impossible to suppress the tendency to split the world in half, using gender as the great divider. When we divide the world into two groups, males and females, we tend to consider all males similar, all females similar, and the two categories of "males" and "females" very different from each other. In real life, the characteristics of women and men tend to overlap. Unfortunately, however, gender polarization often creates an artificial gap between women and men and gender roles that are very difficult to change in time.

GENDER STEREOTYPES FOR MALES AND FEMALES

Stereotypes are representative of a society's collective knowledge of customs, myths, ideas, religions, and sciences. It is within this knowledge that an individual develops a stereotype or a belief about a certain group. Social psychologists feel that the stereotype is one part of an individual's social knowledge. As a result of their knowledge, or lack of knowledge, the stereotype has an effect on their social behaviour. Stereotypic behaviour can be linked to the way that the stereotype is learned, transmitted, and changed and this is part of the socialization process as well.

The culture of an individual influences stereotypes through information that is received from indirect sources such as parents, peers, teachers, political and religious leaders, and the mass media. In order to understand stereotyping, an individual must first be made knowledgeable about the definition of a stereotype. Stereotyping is how we perceive each other, especially individuals outside our group. What we believe to be "normal" is associated with who we are hanging out with.

Which are usually our friends and social networks. Gender stereotypes are related to cognitive processes because we have different expectations for female and male behaviour and the traditional gender roles help to sustain gender stereotypes, such as that males are supposed to be adventurous, assertive aggressive, independent and task-oriented, whereas females are seen as more sensitive, gentle, dependent, emotional and people-oriented. Here as suggested, deal with the opposite male dominance and feeling superior to women. Of course, not all men have power and arrogantly dominate women; indeed, according to Miller, many men are dominated by "the system" and considered disposable. Also, women are given certain advantages and "protected" in many ways that men do not enjoy. Clearly, each sex has and utilizes power in certain ways and we are getting more equal, but, clearly, the sexes aren't equal yet. The most recent suggestion to solve this problem is to completely disassociate gender from all personality traits. Within the two career families of today, the women-are-inferior attitude is muted and concealed, but the archaic sex role expectations are still subtly there.

The old rules still serve to "put down women and keep them in their place." By nature, men and women have some biological differences, but it is life experience that reinforces or contradicts those differences. The truth lies in differential socialization, which claims that males and females are taught different appropriate behaviours for their gender.

GENDER SOCIALISATION

Socialisation is the process, through which the child becomes an individual respecting his or her environment laws, norms and customs. Gender socialisation is a more focused form of socialisation, it is how children of different sexes are socialised into their gender roles and taught what it means to be male or female. Gender socialisation begins the moment we are born, from the simple question "is it a boy or a girl?".

We learn our gender roles by agencies of socialisation, which are the "teachers" of society. The main agencies in Western society are the family, peer groups, schools and the media. In respect with gender socialisation, each of the agencies could reinforce the gender stereotypes. Gender differences result from the socialization process, especially during our childhood and adolescence.

The classical example of gender socialisation is the experiment done with babies that were introduced as males to half of the study subjects and as females to the other half. The results are interesting and quite disturbing at the same time. The participants behave differently according to the sex they had been told. These findings show that other people contribute a lot to how we see ourselves only on the basis of gender.

THE FAMILY AS GENDERED RELATIONSHIPS: INFLUENCES ON GENDER SOCIALIZATION PROCESS

It is said before that parents are the primary influence on gender role development in the early years of one's life. With regard to gender difference, the family in fact, unlike other groups, is characterized by a specific way of living and constructing gender differences through a process that is surely biological, but also relational and social. The family is " the social and symbolic place in which difference, in particular sexual difference, is believed to be fundamental and at the same time constructed ". In particular, in the family the gender characterization reflects the individualities of the parents. The family is therefore a "gender relation".

In the family, the relation with the father and the mother assumes therefore one fundamental importance in the definition of the gender belonging, because it 's the first experience of relation with males and females. Gender identities and the expectations towardss male and female roles are socialized within the parents-children relationship; such expectations are today various and new compared with the past. The models from which fathers and mothers take inspiration need to be verified because "the crisis of the paternal authority has given more space to the father in shaping the educational relation with the child.

They think that the important thing is to converse and to build convincing representations of the world". The gender socialization inside the familiar relations evidences therefore also the temporal dimension of the transmission of styles and expectations between parents and children. The parents ' generation, in comparison with the child 's one, can highlight marked differences too. Parents today probably have different expectations from those their parents had, and their children have even more different expectations. We must go deeper into the matter on how transmission of gender differences happens today and how the gender belonging is constructed..

If such differences seem to diminish on the one side, on the other instead they move on different areas in comparison with the past. Between children in fact the sexual difference "produces various models of belongings and continuity", and they are today completely different from those of the previous generations. In the past, families had different educational demands for their sons and daughters after puberty, they then tended to differentiate them in the sense to promote the autonomy of the males and the dependency of the females.

It was implicit that the boy should realise himself, even if against familiar ties, while the girl had, in some ways, to accept and to conserve them. This difference has always favoured the fact that young women lived their desire of autonomy with a sense of guilt and of independency with intolerance.

A child's parents are the first socialization agents he or she will come into contact with. Parents teach stereotypes through different ways and behaviour : "the way they dress their children, they way they decorate their children's rooms, the toys they give their children to play with, their own attitudes and behaviour".

A RELATIONAL APPROACH TO GENDER ROLES SOCIALIZATION

The most important aspect of the sociological reflection is the ability to use the concepts elaborated in the theoretical debate at an empirical level, realizing "a hermeneutic" connection between the interpretative framework and social life. Gender socialization can be read like a "relational process". It is unavoidable that in the transformation a simplification is put into effect, a reduction of the complexity of the terms in game, because you need to lead back to the factors that explain a social phenomenon to one more rigid pattern of reality: in order not to fall into the trap of the merely casual interpretation it is necessary to always place, to the centre of attention, the relation between different factors that concur to see the phenomena from more points of view, in a multidimensional perspective. The relational model is assumed like the point of observation to verify the hypotheses in order to characterize those that are the gender socializing outcomes in the contemporary society. Within a risky society the relational model considers every phenomenon as the outcome of a process in which the challenges and the resources are put implicitly or explicitly in comparison.

The risk therefore is given from the relation of adequacy/inadequacy between challenges and resources. That appears clear if it is believed that every choice is linked to multidimensional situations, which are relational contexts, in which the phenomena are networks of phenomena and every node represents interlaces of challenges, ties and resources.

Speaking about challenges and resources in gender socialization simplifies reality and circumscribes a point of view from which to observe a phenomenon, but it always takes into account that is a relational phenomenon, in which more dimensions are intersected. Consequently the gender socialization process is divided into two orders of factors, one leads the challenges and the other the resources, in the hypothesis that behind every phenomenon there are however the intentions of the actors who arrange in a more or less balanced way, with reference to the context of options that delimits the action, objects to reach and strategies of participation.

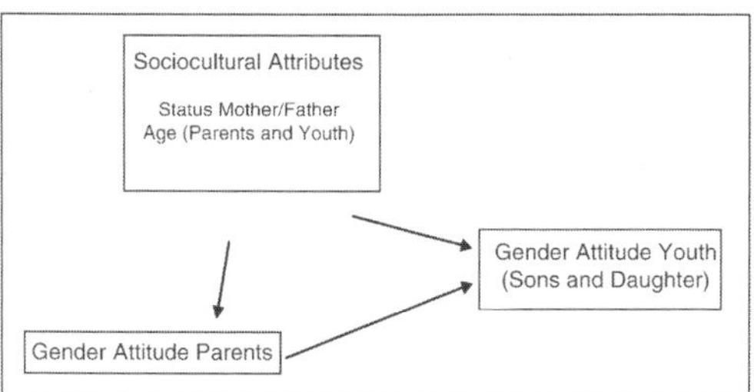

Fig. Analytical Framework for the Relationships between Soci-Demographic Attributes, Gender Attitude Parents and Gender Attitudes Youth.

A FINAL WORD ON THE SOURCES OF GENDER

Scholars in many fields continue to debate the relative importance of biology and of culture and socialization for how we behave and think as girls and boys and as women and men. The biological differences between females and males lead many scholars and no doubt much of the public to assume that masculinity and femininity are to a large degree biologically determined or at least influenced. In contrast, anthropologists, sociologists, and other social scientists tend to view gender as a social construction. Even if biology does matter for gender, they say, the significance of culture and socialization should not be underestimated. To the extent that gender is indeed shaped by society and culture, it is possible to change gender and to help bring about a society where both men and women have more opportunity to achieve their full potential.

GENDER AS A SOCIAL CONSTRUCTION

If sex is a biological concept, then gendergenderThe social and cultural differences a society assigns to people based on their biological sex. is a social concept. It refers to *the social and cultural differences a society assigns to people based on their sex*. A related concept, gender rolesgender rolesA society's expectations of people's behaviour and attitudes based on whether they are females or males., refers to *a society's expectations of people's behaviour and attitudes based on whether they are females or males*. Understood in this way, gender is a *social construction*.

How we think and behave as females and males is not etched in stone by our biology but rather is a result of how society expects us to think and behave based on what sex we are. As we grow up, we learn these expectations as we develop our gender identitygender identityIndividuals' beliefs about themselves as either females or males., or our beliefs about ourselves as females or males. These expectations are called *femininity* and *masculinity*. Femininity femininity Cultural expectations of girls and women, including gentleness and attractiveness. refers to *the cultural expectations we have of girls and women*, while masculinity Cultural expectations of boys and men, including toughness and bravery. refers to *the expectations we have of boys and men*. A familiar nursery rhyme nicely summarizes these two sets of traits:

- *What are little boys made of?*
- *Snips and snails,*
- *And puppy dog tails,*
- *That's what little boys are made of.*
- *What are little girls made of?*
- *Sugar and spice,*
- *And everything nice,*
- *That's what little girls are made of.*

As this nursery rhyme suggests, our traditional notions of femininity and masculinity indicate that we think females and males are fundamentally different from each other. In effect, we think of them as two sides of the same coin of being human. What we traditionally mean by femininity is captured in the adjectives, both positive and negative, we traditionally ascribe to women: gentle, sensitive, nurturing, delicate, graceful, cooperative, decorative, dependent, emotional, passive, and weak. Thus, when we say that a girl or woman is very feminine, we have some combination of these traits, usually the positive ones, in mind: she is soft, dainty, pretty, even a bit flighty.

What we traditionally mean by masculinity is captured in the adjectives, again both positive and negative, our society traditionally ascribes to men: strong, assertive, brave, active, independent, intelligent, competitive, insensitive, unemotional, and aggressive. When we say that a boy or man is very masculine, we have some combination of these traits in mind: he is tough, strong, and assertive. These traits might sound like stereotypes of females and males in today's society, and to some extent they are, but differences between men and women in attitudes and behaviour do in fact exist. For example, women cry more often than men do.

Men are more physically violent than women. Women take care of children more than men do. Women smile more often than men. Men curse more often than women. When women talk with each other, they are more likely to talk about their personal lives than men are when they talk with each other. The two sexes even differ when they hold a cigarette. When a woman holds a cigarette, she usually has the palm of her cigarette-holding hand facing upward. When a man holds a cigarette, he usually has his palm facing downward.

SEXUAL ORIENTATION

Sexual orientationsexual orientationPreference for sexual relationships with individuals of the opposite sex, the same sex, or both sexes. refers to a person's preference for sexual relationships with individuals of the other sex, one's own sex, or both sexes. The term also increasingly refers to transgendered individuals, those whose behaviour, appearance, and/or gender identity fails to conform to conventional norms. Transgendered individuals include transvestites and transsexuals. It is difficult to know precisely how many people are gay, lesbian, bisexual, or transgendered. One problem is conceptual. For example, what does it mean to be gay or lesbian? Does one need to actually have sexual relations with a same-sex partner to be considered gay? What if someone is attracted to same-sex partners but does not actually engage in sex with such persons? What if someone identifies as heterosexual but engages in homosexual sex for money or for power and influence?

These conceptual problems make it difficult to determine the extent of homosexuality. A second problem is empirical. Even if we can settle on a definition of homosexuality, how do we then determine how many people fit this definition? For better or worse, our best evidence of the number of gays and lesbians in the United States comes from surveys of national samples of Americans in which they are asked various questions about their sexuality. Although these are anonymous surveys, obviously at least some individuals may be reluctant to disclose their sexual activity and thoughts to an interviewer. Still, scholars think the estimates from these surveys are fairly accurate but that they probably underestimate by at least a small amount the number of gays and lesbians.

A widely cited survey carried out by researchers at the University of Chicago found that 2.8 per cent of men and 1.4 per cent of women identified themselves as gay/lesbian or bisexual, with greater percentages reporting having had sexual relations with same-sex partners or being attracted to same-sex persons. In the 2008 General Social Survey, 2.2 per cent of men and 3.5 per cent of women identified themselves as gay/lesbian or bisexual. Among individuals having had any sexual partners since turning 18, 2.2 per cent of men reported having had at least some male partners, while 4.6 per cent of women reported having had at least some female partners. Although precise numbers must remain unknown, it seems fair to say that between about 2 per cent and 5 per cent of Americans are gay/lesbian or bisexual. If it is difficult to determine the number of people who are gay/lesbian or bisexual, it is even more difficult to determine why some people have this sexual orientation while most do not have it. Scholars disagree on the "causes" of sexual orientation. Some scholars attribute it to unknown biological factor over which individuals have no control, just as individuals do not decide whether they are left-handed or right-handed. Supporting this view, many gays say they realized they were gay during adolescence, just as straights would say they realized they were straight during their own adolescence.

Other scholars say that sexual orientation is at least partly influenced by cultural norms, so that individuals are more likely to identify as gay or straight depending on the cultural views of sexual orientation into which they are socialized as they grow up. At best, perhaps all we can say is that sexual orientation stems from a complex mix of biological and cultural factors that remain to be determined.

THE DEVELOPMENT OF GENDER DIFFERENCES

What accounts for differences in female and male behaviour and attitudes? Do the biological differences between the sexes account for differences between these other differences? Or do these latter differences stem, as most sociologists think, from cultural expectations and from differences in the ways in which the sexes are socialized?

These are critical questions, for they ask whether the differences between boys and girls and women and men stem more from biology or from society. Biological explanations for human behaviour implicitly support the status quo. If we think behavioural and other differences between the sexes are due primarily to their respective biological makeups, we are saying that these differences are inevitable or nearly so and that any attempt to change them goes against biology and will likely fail.

As an example, consider the obvious biological fact that women bear and nurse children and men do not. Couple this with the common view that women are also more gentle and nurturing than men, and we end up with a "biological recipe" for women to be the primary caretakers of children. Many people think this means women are therefore much better suited than men to take care of children once they are born, and that the family might be harmed if mothers work outside the home or if fathers are the primary caretakers.

That more than one-third of the public agrees that "it is much better for everyone involved if the man is the achiever outside the home and the woman takes care of the home and family." To the extent this belief exists, women may not want to work outside the home or, if they choose to do so, they face difficulties from employers, family, and friends. Conversely, men may not even think about wanting to stay at home and may themselves face difficulties from employees, family, and friends if they want to do so. A belief in a strong biological basis for differences between women and men implies, then, that there is little we can or should do to change these differences. It implies that "anatomy is destiny," and destiny is, of course, by definition inevitable. Agreement or disagreement with statement that "it is much better for everyone involved if the man is the achiever outside the home and the woman takes care of the home and family."

This implication makes it essential to understand the extent to which gender differences do, in fact, stem from biological differences between the sexes or, instead, stem from cultural and social influences. If biology is paramount, then gender differences are perhaps inevitable and the status quo will remain. If culture and social influences matter much more than biology, then gender differences can change and the status quo may give way. With this backdrop in mind, let's turn to the biological evidence for behavioural and other differences between the sexes and then examine the evidence for their social and cultural roots.

2

Gender Equality

Gender equality, is also known as sex equality or sexual equality or equality of the genders which implies that men and women should receive equal treatment unless there is a sound biological reason for different treatment.

The concept based on the United Nations Declaration of Human Rights, and the ultimate aim is to provide equality in law and equality in social situations, especially in democratic activities and securing equal pay for equal work.

HISTORY

The movement towards gender equality, especially in Western countries, began with the suffragette movement of the late-19th century, which sought to allow women to vote and hold elected office. There have been substantial changes to women's property rights, particularly in relation to their marital status. In the 1960s, a more general movement for gender equality developed based on women's liberation and feminism. The central issue was that the rights of women should be the same as men.

Changes to attitudes to equality in education opportunities for boys and girls have also undergone a cultural shift. Over time, there have been significant changes in attitudes which have resulted in more just legislation. Some changes came about by adopting affirmative action policies. The change has also involved changes to social views, including 'equal pay for equal work' as well as most occupations being equally available to men and women, in many countries.

For example, many countries now permit women to serve in the armed forces, the police forces and to be fire fighters-occupations traditionally reserved for men. Although these continue to be male dominated occupations an increasing number of women are now increasingly active, especially in directive fields such as politics and occupy high positions in business.

Similarly, men are increasingly working in occupations which in previous generations had been considered women's work, such as nursing, cleaning and child care. In domestic situations, the biological differences between men and women in relation to activities related to child bearing are more commonly shared where possible, and the role of child rearing is not as widely considered to be an exclusively female role, so that a wife may be free to pursue her career after marriage and following childbirth.

Another manifestation of the change in social attitudes is the non-automatic taking by a woman of her husband's surname on marriage or combining names as in the Spanish naming customs. Many people consider that the objective of gender equality has not been fully achieved, especially in non-Western countries. A highly contentious issue relating to gender equality is the role of women in religiously orientated societies. For example, in Islam women have equal dignity, but not equal rights and in some Christian churches the practice of churching of women may still have elements of ritual purification and the ordination of women to the priesthood may be restricted or forbidden.

Not all ideas for gender equality have been popularly adopted. For example: despite Topfreedom the right to be bare breasted in public frequently applies only to males and has remained a marginal issue. Breastfeeding in public is more commonly tolerated, especially in semi-private places such as restaurants.

EFFORTS TO FIGHT INEQUALITY

World bodies have defined gender equality in terms of human rights, especially women's rights, and economic development. UNICEF describes that gender equality "means that women and men, and girls and boys, enjoy the same rights, resources, opportunities and protections. It does not require that girls and boys, or women and men, be the same, or that they be treated exactly alike." The United Nations Population Fund has declared that women have a right to equality. 'Gender equity' is one of the goals of the United Nations Millennium Project, to end world poverty by 2015; the project claims, "Every single goal is directly related to women's rights, and societies where women are not afforded equal rights as men can never achieve development in a sustainablemanner." Thus, promoting gender equality is seen as an encouragement to greater economic prosperity. For example, nations of the Arab world that deny equality of opportunity to women were warned in a 2008 United Nations-sponsored report that this disempowerment is a critical factor crippling these nations' return to the first rank of global leaders in commerce, learning and culture.

In 2010, the European Union opened the European Institute for Gender Equality (EIGE) in Vilnius, Lithuania to promote gender equality and to fight sex discrimination. It is also worthy to note that gender equality is part of the national curriculum in Great Britain and many other European countries. Personal, social and health education, religious studies and language acquisition curricula tend to address gender equality issues as a very serious topic for discussion and analysis of its effect in society.

'GENDER EQUALITY' AND 'THE MAINSTREAM'

Gender mainstreaming involves at least two different frames of reference:

one emanating from a 'gender equality' stance, and the other, the 'mainstream'. Thus at its heart gender mainstreaming is inevitably and essentially a contested process. Despite this intrinsic conflict there are usually moves within gender mainstreaming to focus on those areas where there might be commonality with the mainstream. The practice within gender mainstreaming is often one of looking for the points of overlap of the agendas of gender equality and of the mainstream, recognising that there are differences in the overall agendas but seeking to prioritise those areas of commonality, as a step in the right direction.

In policy practice the duality between gender equality and the mainstream can be sometimes be expressed as the holding of two aims simultaneously: first, the promotion of gender equality and gender justice as an end in its own right; and second, making mainstream policies more effective in their own terms by the inclusion of gender analysis. While the full reconciliation of these two aims is not regarded as a feasible short-term goal, there may already exist some points of overlap between the two agendas. One feature that is often included within definitions of gender mainstreaming is the practice of making visible the way that gender relations are significant in institutional practices where they had previously been seen as marginal or irrelevant, in order to facilitate the implementation of a strategy for both gender equality and for the improvement of the mainline policy.

It is important to note the frequent opposition to gender mainstreaming in order to understand the dualism between gender equality and mainstream agendas. Elgström suggests that new norms need to 'fight their way into institutional thinking' in competition with traditional norms. Other established goals may compete with the prioritisation of gender equality even if they are not directly opposed, such as that of economic growth. This means that the process is contested and often involves 'negotiation' and 'translation' rather than simple adoption or 'imitation' of new policies. Perrons provides a related account for opposition to gender mainstreaming.

She argues that, at least in the UK and perhaps more widely, the goal of the competitiveness of the economy takes precedence over equality considerations, thereby endorsing rather than tackling the low paid work so frequently found among women. The issue is not articulated as opposition to the goal of gender equality, but rather the prioritisation of some other goal. In this instance, the prioritisation of improving the competitiveness of the UK economy is seen to have indirect detrimental consequences for gender equality.

Indeed the reconciliation of the goals of gender mainstreaming and economic prosperity is widely found to be a contested process, despite several accounts which make a strong link, including Walby and Olsen on gender and productivity analysis, Elson on the essential role of the domestic sector of the economy for the provision of labour, Grosser and Moon on gender and corporate social responsibility, Dex and Dex, Smith and Winter on the business case for family friendly policies, and Vinnicombe on the business case for women directors. In these documents, the contribution of women to economic success is carefully made in diverse ways. Dex and Dex et al provide a strong evidential basis for the business case for family friendly policies, using data from the Workplace Employee Relations Survey to quantify the benefit to private sector organisations of such policies on their economic performance.

Vinnicombe and Singh and Vinnicombe demonstrate the links between the appointment of women directors and not only indicators of good corporate governance but also high market capitalisation. They suggest that this correlation is to be explained by the way that women directors act as good role models to women employees and help build companies' reputations in the market place, thereby attracting future employees.

The conceptualisation of this dualism between gender equality and the mainstream is central to many of the debates about gender mainstreaming. There are a variety of ways in which this mix of contestation and compromise can be analysed and outcomes assessed in multiple registers in several different theoretical vocabularies. These include the 'frames' of social movement theory; the 'discourses' of cultural studies/poststructuralism/Foucauldian analysis; the 'epistemologies' of Harding; and the paradigms of Kuhn.

The postulated end point of the process of mainstreaming can also be described using different theoretical vocabularies. One vision of gender mainstreaming is that it offers 'transformation', that is, neither the assimilation of women into men's ways, nor the maintenance of a dualism between women and men, but rather something new, a positive form of melding, in which the outsiders, feminists, changed the mainstream.

There are other ways to characterise the outcome. Jahan contrasts two possible outcomes as either 'agenda setting' or 'integration', as do also Lombardo and Squires , while Shaw makes a similar contrast between 'embedded' as compared with 'marginalised'. Verloo and Ferree refer to possibilities of 'frame extension' or 'frame bridging'. There are further parallel concepts in the field of ethnic politics, where some concepts represent asymmetrical processes, such as, 'assimilation', while others imply a more mutual accommodation, such as 'hybridisation'. These analogies may be illuminating for the gender context.

The distinction between approaches to gender mainstreaming that are either 'agenda setting' or 'integrationist' made by Jahan is used by several writers and a similar one by Shaw. Agenda setting implies the transformation and reorientation of existing policy paradigms, changing decision making processes, prioritising gender equality objectives and re-thinking policy ends. In this approach it is the mainstream that changes. Integrationist approaches are those that introduce a gender perspective without challenging the existing policy paradigm, instead 'selling' gender mainstreaming as a way of more effectively achieving existing policy goals. While this approach means that gender mainstreaming is less likely to be rejected, its impact is likely to be less substantial. Lombardo applies this distinction to events in the European Convention aimed at developing a European Constitution. While most of the feminists who sought to adopt a gender mainstreaming strategy preferred to be 'agenda setting', there was drift towardss one that was merely 'integrationist'.

The strategic framing of gender mainstreaming is an ongoing dilemma. In a similar vein, Shaw addresses the relationship of gender equality and the mainstream in relation to the proposed new EU Constitution asking whether gender mainstreaming is 'constitutionally embedded' or 'compreh-ensively marginalised'. She finds that while gender concerns are embedded in the Treaty framework, especially the Treaty of Amsterdam, they are less prominent in the politics of the Convention that was established to develop the Constitution and its ensuing white paper.

Frame theory is drawn on by both Verloo and Ferree to capture variations in the relationship between gender equality projects and the mainstream. Originating in the work of Goffman, and influentially articulated by Snow et al , frame theory has become a key influence in the theorisation of social movements in general and gender mainstreaming in particular. Frame theory provides a fluid vocabulary to engage with the contestations over and shifts in meaning that are key to the understanding of social movements and related civil society activities. Two terms in particular have been much used, those of 'frame extension' and 'frame bridging', which capture some of the ways in which social movements either modify and extend the dominant frame so as to include their own projects or find a way to link or bridge their project to the dominant frame.

Ferree and Verloo are critical of some features of frame theory, in particular, that it does not carefully enough distinguish among the available discursive structures and resources, the actors' strategic choices in this context, and the outcomes attained. As they develop it in their work, they include national structures of opportunity as well as the voices and activities of a range of actors as they re-work frames in complex ways. Further, Ferree links frame theory with comparative institutional histories so as to provide greater depth to the account of the resources on which feminist social movements draw.

A further issue in assessing the outcome of gender mainstreaming lies in how 'success' is to be defined. Gamson and the RNGS methodology suggest that it is important to differentiate between the inclusion of the policy goals and the inclusion of the actors. In most of the analysis here, however, the interest lies in the policy goals, rather than what happens to the specific actors. The outcome, then, depends on the specific understanding of the goal, in particular on the particular model of gender equality held by those seeking to mainstream gender, of which there are several possibilities.

This is further complicated by the possible change in the nature of the goal during the process of negotiation, since these are ongoing socially constructions in a changing context of what is perceived as possible. In such a context, both 'gender equality' and 'the mainstream' are likely to be changing simultaneously, both in response to each other and to other changes. It is important to be able to capture the continuously evolving nature of the interaction between feminist and mainstream conceptions. The conceptualisation developed by complexity theorists, of such processes being ones between 'complex adaptive systems' that are 'co-evolving' within 'changing fitness landscapes' captures these dynamics more adequately than simple one-way conceptions of 'impact'. This complexity theory informed approach goes beyond the more static concepts of agenda setting and integration, which tend to imply more stability in the alternative projects of gender equality and the mainstream than might be warranted.

CONTESTED VISIONS OF AND ROUTES TO GENDER EQUALITY

There are several different ways of understanding the variety of definitions of gender mainstreaming. Underlying these are three types of question. The first question is whether there can be identified a fundamental set of principles of gender mainstreaming, or whether it is more appropriate to conceive of it as always socially constructed. Second, is the question of whether the models of sameness and transformation are to be understood as alternative and mutually inconsistent visions of the end point of gender mainstreaming or as complementary political strategies. The third question concerns the implicit theory of the gender regime, in particular, the extent to which the different policy domains are seen as closely interconnected or as relatively independent, since this affects the extent to which 'sameness' may be held as a standard in one domain simultaneously with 'difference' in another.

The variety of definitions and practices of gender mainstreaming may be understood either as a result of confusion that can be resolved by attending to the difficult task of the development of an appropriate definition, or it may be understood as the result of essentially contested processes that inevitably produce varying outcomes in different contexts. One analytic strategy is to seek out underlying principles in an effort to abstract the essential characteristics of the phenomenon. For example, Rees identifies three underlying principles: regarding the individual as a whole person; democracy and participation; and justice, fairness and equity. Further she suggests that there are sets of tools that can be identified with each of these principles, including work/life balance, gender disaggregated statistics and gender budgeting. This is perhaps parallel to Nussbaum's neo-Arisitotelian approach to gendered well-being, which is grounded in notions of human needs and capacities and invokes a universalistic perspective.

In a contrasting analytic strategy, gender mainstreaming is seen as an 'empty signifier' which can be filled by an almost limitless variety of content, as a result of the social construction of this phenomenon. For example, Verloo focuses on the processes by which gender mainstreaming is socially constructed, which vary according to national political context. However, the contrast in approach is largely theoretical rather than substantive in that both approaches recognise that there is a diversity of approaches to conceptualisation of gender mainstreaming, and, in practice, both produce working definitions.

Although all accounts of gender mainstreaming imply significant changes to gendered institutions, a range of different visions or models of gender equality have been invoked. Three models of gender equality have often been identified as key. The first model is one in which equality based on sameness is fostered, especially where women enter previously male domains, and the existing male norm remains the standard. The second is one in which there is a move towardss the equal valuation of existing and different contributions of women and men in a gender segregated society. The third is one where there is a new standard for both men and women, that is, the transformation of gender relations. Rees describes the first, as 'tinkering' with gender inequality; the second as 'tailoring' situations to fit the needs of women; the third is 'transformation', in which there are new standards for everyone replacing the segregated institutions and standards associated with masculinity and femininity. There is question here as to whether the first two models actually constitute gender mainstreaming, because they retain the gender standards of the status quo. For Rees , only the third strategy constitutes gender mainstreaming and has the potential to deliver gender justice because this is the only strategy that involves the transformation of the institutions and the standards necessary for effective equality, while Booth and Bennett argue that all three are gender mainstreaming approaches.

While the elimination of gender inequality is the goal of the gender mainstreaming strategy, the extent to which this can mean accepting and valuing existing gendered differences is a key source of disagreement within gender mainstreaming theory and practice. This has been a debate within gender theory more generally. While all the definitions of gender equality include equality within each social domain, they vary as to whether a change in the balance of the domains, and the equalisation of any differential representation of women and men in each domain, constitute legitimate areas for intervention or not.

The most frequently cited definition of gender mainstreaming in the European literature is that devised by Mieke Verloo as Chair of the Council of Europe Group of Experts on Gender Mainstreaming:

- Gender mainstreaming is the (re)organisation, improvement, development and evaluation of policy processes, so that a gender equality perspective is incorporated in all policies at all levels at all stages, by the actors normally involved in policy making.

In contrast to Rees , the Council of Europe definition of gender equality implies that differences between women and men are not an essential obstacle to equality:

- Gender equality means an equal visibility, empowerment and participation of both sexes in all spheres of public and private life....Gender equality is not synonymous with sameness, with establishing men, their life style and conditions as the norm....Gender equality means accepting and valuing equally the differences between women and men and the diverse roles they play in society.

These discussions contain important aspects of the 'sameness/difference' debate that has taken place within feminist theory. This key analytic distinction, indeed often dichotomy, has been subject to much debate within feminist theory.

This is a multi-faceted debate, which is simultaneously normative, philosophical, theoretical, substantive, empirical and policy-relevant. Thus within an analysis of gender mainstreaming are the classical arguments within feminist theory about difference, universalism and particularism. Gender can be an example of difference, which has become a major issue in social theory. In particular, there are dilemmas in how to recognise difference, while avoiding the trap of essentialism and taking account of the global horizon. Postmodern ambivalence and the prioritisation of situatedness and fluidity may be contrasted with a new assertion of universal standards. Included within this is the question of whose standards and from or for which constituency?

It has often been argued that traditional equal opportunities policies are inherently limited because they mean that women can only gain equality with men if they are able to perform to the standards set by men. Can there be an effective route to gender justice in which existing separate gender norms/ standards are retained and become equally valued, or is it never really possible to be 'different but equal' because the differences are too entwined with power and resources? Some standards, such as equal pay for women and men, may already constitute standards that are already held by women as well as by men.

Some policy interventions, such as legislation on equal pay and government policy to improve child care, may be better conceived as contributions to gender mainstreaming rather than as mere equal treatment or special programmes, since they have the potential to transform the association of women with domesticated care. Is gender mainstreaming introducing new hybrid standards of gender justice for human beings, replacing the ostensibly more male oriented standard of the old equal opportunities policies, for instance, by beginning to transform the workplace so that it is organised around standards suitable for those who combine care-work and paid work? The Council of Europe specifies the need for the 'equal participation of women and men in political and public life' and the need for 'the individual's economic independence', and that 'education is a key target for gender equality.' This defines equal participation in political and public life, in education and the achievement of economic independence, as universal goals while other spheres remain sites of difference.

An underlying question here is that of the assumed degree of connection among the gender practices in different domains. If they are coupled tightly, it may not be possible to have equality through sameness in one domain and equality with difference in another. If the links are looser, this may be theoretically and practically possible.

This debate depends on an implied theory of gender relations that needs to be made explicit in order to understand the nature and degree of the postulated connections between different gendered domains and the implications of changes in one of them for the others.

There is a further question as to whether this three-fold distinction captures a trajectory of development from more minor strategies to larger strategies of gender equality, as is argued by Rees or whether these three models are in practice complementary, as is argued by Booth and Booth and Bennett. Underlying this disagreement is the issue of whether this threefold typology reflects different visions of gender equality, or instead a set of policy and political tactics. If it is the former, then they are more likely to be alternative approaches, if the latter then they are not necessarily mutually exclusive.

Booth and Booth and Bennett argue that each of these three approaches is actually essential for the successful conduct of the others; that they are complementary rather than mutually exclusive.

They challenge the compartmentalisation of different types of equality strategies, arguing that the 'equal treatment perspective', the 'women's perspective' and the 'gender perspective' are better conceptualised as components of a 'three-legged stool'. They are interconnected and each needs the other. If any of the three elements is weak, then the whole is weakened. They argue that the tendency to associate the gender mainstreaming approach only with the third perspective, the gender perspective, is mistaken, leading to limiting of the strategy's transformative potential.

An examination of documents from the European Commission and Council about gender equality finds that the European Commission recommends the use of all three gender equality strategies simultaneously. The European Commission in its 'Community strategy on gender equality' states first, that the 'principle of equal treatment for women and men' is a fundamental principle of Community law. Second, it notes that action should be continued 'combining integration of the gender dimension with specific action'. This approach, which appears to combine equal treatment, gender-specific actions and a wider gender dimension, is developed in the European Employment Strategy, the guidelines for the employment policies of member states put forward by the European Commission and Council. The European Employment Strategy notes two routes for gender equality, both 'gender mainstreaming' and 'specific policy actions', while the formulation of the policy implies a single standard for equality for women and men. The Council announces that:

- Member States will, through an integrated approach combining gender mainstreaming and specific policy actions, encourage female labour market participation and achieve a substantial reduction in gender gaps in employment rates, unemployment rates, and pay by 2010.

Thus in practice, the European Commission and Council, recommend all three strategies for gender equality. First, they posit a single standard of equality for women and men in employment that is based on minimizing gaps, that is achieving the same level of participation in employment, the same level of unemployment, and the same level of pay. This would appear to have significant similarities to the 'sameness' approach to gender equality. Second, there is reference to 'specific policy actions' and the naming of policy domains that are focused on women's activities, which emphasises difference. These include targets for increased childcare, agreed at the Barcelona European Council, so that this is available by 2010 to at least 90 per cent of children between 3 years and at least 33 per cent of children less than 3 years of age. Third, this is combined with a vision of transformed relations between care and employment:

- Particular attention will be given to reconciling work and family life, notably through the provision of care services for children and other dependants, encouraging the sharing of family and professional responsibilities and facilitating return to work after a period of leave.

The goal of the reconciliation of work and family life has the potential to constitute a transformation of gender relations. However, the implementation of the policy is open to varying interpretations. Indeed, Stratigaki argues that this policy has become less about sharing family responsibilities between women and men, and more about encouraging flexible forms of employment.

At least in the programmes of the EU, the three approaches to gender equality co-exist. What are the implications of three approaches to gender equality, that is, equal treatment, special programmes and gender mainstreaming, being adopted simultaneously by the European Union's governing bodies? Does it mean that the EU is incoherent on gender issues and has inconsistent policies that are in tension with each other? Or, does it mean, as Booth argues, that they are inherently complementary rather than mutually inconsistent? I believe instead that it is important to distinguish the use of these approaches as visions of the end point of gender equality from their use as policy and political tactics and strategy. If this distinction is made, then both the arguments by Rees and Booth can be sustained, since they are addressing different phenomena.

While some of the accounts have considered the whole range of social domains as if they were similar in regard to gender mainstreaming, others have suggested that different policy areas may have divergent practices with different visions and routes to gender equality. Underling this issue is the question as to whether the domains of a gender regime are closely coupled, or quite autonomous? How systematically inter-connected are the different domains of the gender regime? This issue can be explored both empirically and theoretically. The varied practices in regard to gender equality between different areas is implicit in the Council of Europe text, since it assumes that there can be a model of gender equality based on sameness in some domains, while equal valuation of different activities in other domains. Pollack and Hafner-Burton find differences in the implementation of gender mainstreaming between five issue areas of the European Union: Structural Funds, employment, development, competition, and science research and development. They explain these differences in terms of three factors: political opportunities, mobilizing structures and networks, and variations in strategic framing by advocates of gender mainstreaming.

Employment is perhaps the field where the development of similar standards, such as equal pay, is the most developed, while other areas, such as the care of children, are more likely to contain at least some elements that value differences between average men and women.

Employment is the arena that has been most fully addressed by the EU, because of the centrality of economic development to its core remit. It is in the domain of employment that the argument that the mainstream would benefit from attention to gender is perhaps most fully articulated. Here, the mainstream is understood as 'business' as in Dex , on the business case for family friendly policies because of its contribution to productivity, and in Vinnicombe , on the business case for women directors in terms of the benefits of diversity in the Boardroom for competitiveness and productivity. The mainstream can also be interpreted as the 'whole economy' as in Walby and Olsen , on the implications of gender relations in employment for the productivity of the UK economy.

Grosser and Moon extend this approach in their argument that the mainstreaming of gender benefits the corporate social responsibility agenda which is simultaneously good for both business and the wider society. They argue that the value of a company can be affected by its treatment of a wider range of stakeholders than is usually included. This is work that goes beyond the domains of the economy to that of governance, understood broadly especially in the work of Grosser and Moon and Vinnicombe. In this way, employment is not neatly compartmentalised from politics and governance., Further, a significant amount of the work on the EU and employment concerns the importance of the development of legally based regulations and of softer yet still politically-led changes through the development of the open method of policy co-ordination.

In the area of violence against women, there is a double move, involving not only mainstreaming gender into crime policy, but also the mainstreaming of the violence against women agenda across the breadth of policy arenas. This is a field which developed later than employment policy and which has not drawn so strongly upon the powers of the EU, not least because the competence of the EU in this area is more limited. Yet this does not mean that policy development is confined to individual countries. There has been much policy transfer as a result of global feminist networks and the development of the discourse of universal human rights.

Rather than generalising across all gendered domains within a country, it is important to consider the specificities of each domain, and the nature of its links to other domains in order to understand to development of gender mainstreaming. Each domain is likely to have its own institutional history and have been subject to different types of gender equality policy and politics. It is important both to distinguish between different domains and also to examine the nature of the connections between them so as to be able to understand whether changes in one domain are likely, ultimately, to have implications for other domains.

GENDER INEQUALITY

We have said that the women's movement changed American life in many ways but that gender inequality persists. Let's look at examples of such inequality, much of it taking the form of institutional discrimination, which can occur even if it is not intended to happen. We start with gender inequality in income and the workplace and then move on to a few other spheres of life.

INCOME AND WORKPLACE INEQUALITY

In the last few decades, women have entered the workplace in increasing numbers, partly, and for many women mostly, out of economic necessity and partly out of desire for the sense of self-worth and other fulfillment that comes with work. This is true not only in the United States but also in other nations, including Japan, where views of women are more traditional than those in the United States. In February 2010, 58.9 per cent of U.S. women age 16 or older were in the labour force, compared to only 43.3 per cent in 1970; comparable figures for men were 71.0 per cent in 2010 and 79.7 per cent in 1970. Thus while women's labour force participation continues to lag behind men's, they have narrowed the gap.

The figures just cited include women of retirement age. When we just look at younger women, labour force participation is even higher. For example, 76.1 per cent of women aged 35–44 were in the labour force in 2008, compared to only 46.8 per cent in 1970. Despite the gains women have made, problems persist. Perhaps the major problem is a gender gap in income. Women have earned less money than men ever since records started being kept. In the United States in the early 1800s, full-time women workers in agriculture and manufacturing earned less than 38 per cent of what men earned. By 1885 they were earning about 50 per cent of what men earned in manufacturing jobs. As the 1980s began, full-time women workers' median weekly earnings were about 65 per cent of men's. Women have narrowed the gender gap in earnings since then: their weekly earnings now are 80.2 per cent of men's among full-time workers. Still, this means that for every $10,000 men earn, women earn only about $8,002. To turn that around, for every $10,000 women earn, men earn $12,469. This gap amounts to hundreds of thousands of dollars over a lifetime of working. Although such practices and requirements are now illegal, they still continue. The sex segregation they help create contributes to the continuing gender gap between female and male workers. Occupations dominated by women tend to have lower wages and salaries. Because women are concentrated in low-paying jobs, their earnings are much lower than men's. This gender gap exists for all levels of education and even increases with higher levels of education. On the average, college-educated women working full-time earn almost $17,700 less per year than their male counterparts.

What accounts for the gender gap in earnings? A major reason is sex segregationsex segregationIn the workplace, the concentration of women into a relatively few low-paying clerical and service jobs. in the workplace, which accounts for up to 45 per cent of the gender gap. Although women have increased their labour force participation, the workplace remains segregated by gender. Almost half of all women work in a few low-paying clerical and service jobs, while men work in a much greater variety of jobs, including high-paying ones. This segregation is that socialization affects what jobs young men and women choose to pursue, and part of the reason is that women and men do not want to encounter difficulties they may experience if they took a job traditionally assigned to the other sex. A third reason is that sex-segregated jobs discriminate against applicants who are not the "right" sex for that job. Employers may either consciously refuse to hire someone who is the "wrong" sex for the job or have job requirements and workplace rules that unintentionally make it more difficult for women to qualify for certain jobs.

This fact raises an important question: why do women's jobs pay less than men's jobs? Is it because their jobs are not important and require few skills? The evidence indicates otherwise: women's work is devalued precisely because it is women's work, and women's jobs thus pay less than men's jobs because they are women's jobs. Studies of comparable worthcomparable worthThe idea that women's and men's jobs may be of roughly equal value and thus deserve the same pay, even though women's jobs typically pay less than men's jobs. support this argument. Researchers rate various jobs in terms of their requirements and attributes that logically should affect the salaries they offer: the importance of the job, the degree of skill it requires, the level of responsibility it requires, the degree to which the employee must exercise independent judgement, and so forth. They then use these dimensions to determine what salary a job should offer. Some jobs might be "better" on some dimensions and "worse" on others but still end up with the same predicted salary if everything evens out. When researchers make their calculations, they find that certain women's jobs pay less than men's even though their comparable worth is equal to or even higher than the men's jobs. For example, a social worker may earn less money than a probation officer, even though calculations based on comparable worth would predict that a social worker should earn at least as much.

The comparable worth research demonstrates that women's jobs pay less than men's jobs of comparable worth and that the average working family would earn several thousand dollars more annually if pay scales were reevaluated based on comparable worth and women paid more for their work. Even when women and men work in the same jobs, women often earn less than men and men are more likely than women to hold leadership positions in these occupations. Census data provide ready evidence of the lower incomes women receive than men even in the same occupations.

For example, female marketing and sales managers earn only 68 per cent of what their male counterparts earn; female human resource managers earn only 68 per cent of what their male counterparts earn; female claims adjusters earn only 83 per cent; female accountants earn only 72 per cent; female elementary and middle school teachers earn only 90 per cent; and even female secretaries and clerical workers earn only 86 per cent. When variables like number of years on the job, number of hours worked per week, and size of firm are taken into account, these disparities diminish but do not disappear altogether, and it is very likely that sex discrimination by employers accounts for much of the remaining disparity. Litigation has suggested or revealed specific instances of sex discrimination in earnings and employment.

In July 2009, the Dell computer company, without admitting any wrongdoing, agreed to pay $9.1 million to settle a class action lawsuit, brought by former executives, that alleged sex discrimination in salaries and promotions. Earlier in the decade, a Florida jury found Outback Steakhouse liable for paying a woman site development assistant only half what it paid a man with the same title. After she trained him, Outback assigned him most of her duties, and when she complained, Outback transferred her to a clerical position. The jury awarded her $2.2 million in compensatory and punitive damages. Some of the sex discrimination in employment reflects the existence of two related phenomena, the glass ceilingglass ceiling.

The invisible barrier facing women as they try to advance in the workplace. and the glass escalatorglass escalator. The smooth path afforded men in promotion in the workplace, especially in occupations primarily filled by women. Women may be promoted in a job only to find they reach an invisible "glass ceiling" beyond which they cannot get promoted, or they may not get promoted in the first place. In the largest U.S. corporations, women constitute only about 16 per cent of the top executives, and women executives are paid much less than their male counterparts. Although these disparities stem partly from the fact that women joined the corporate ranks much more recently than men, they also reflect a glass ceiling in the corporate world that prevents qualified women from rising up above a certain level.

Men, on the other hand, can often ride a "glass escalator" to the top, even in female occupations. An example is seen in elementary school teaching, where principals typically rise from the ranks of teachers. Although men constitute only about 20 per cent of all public elementary school teachers, they account for about 44 per cent of all elementary school principals. Whatever the reasons for the gender gap in income, the fact that women make so much less than men means that female-headed families are especially likely to be poor. In 2008, about 31 per cent of these families lived in poverty, compared to only 6.7 per cent of married-couple families. The term *feminization of poverty* refers to the fact that female-headed households are especially likely to be poor. The gendering of poverty in this manner is one of the most significant manifestations of gender inequality in the United States.

Sexual Harassment

Another workplace problem is sexual harassmentsexual harassmentUnwelcome sexual advances, requests for sexual favors, or physical conduct of a sexual nature used as a condition of employment or promotion or that interferes with an individual's job performance and creates an intimidating or hostile environment., which, as defined by federal guidelines and legal rulings and statutes, consists of unwelcome sexual advances, requests for sexual favors, or physical conduct of a sexual nature used as a condition of employment or promotion or that interferes with an individual's job performance and creates an intimidating or hostile environment.

Although men can be, and are, sexually harassed, women are more often the targets of sexual harassment, which is often considered a form of violence against women. This gender difference exists for at least two reasons, one cultural and one structural. The cultural reason centers on the depiction of women and the socialization of men. As our discussion of the mass media and gender socialization indicated, women are still depicted in our culture as sexual objects who exist for men's pleasure. At the same time, our culture socializes men to be sexually assertive. These two cultural beliefs combine to make men believe that they have the right to make verbal and physical advances to women in the workplace. When these advances fall into the guidelines listed here, they become sexual harassment.

The second reason that most targets of sexual harassment are women is more structural. Reflecting the gendered nature of the workplace and of the educational system, typically the men doing the harassment are in a position of power over the women they harass. A male boss harasses a female employee, or a male professor harasses a female student or employee. These men realize that subordinate women may find it difficult to resist their advances for fear of reprisals: a female employee may be fired or not promoted, and a female student may receive a bad grade. How common is sexual harassment? This is difficult to determine, as the men who do the sexual harassment are not about to shout it from the rooftops, and the women who suffer it often keep quiet because of the repercussions just listed. But anonymous surveys of women employees in corporate and other settings commonly find that 40 per cent–65 per cent of the respondents report being sexually harassed. In a survey of 4,501 women physicians, 36.9 per cent reported being sexually harassed either in medical school or in their practice as physicians. Sexual harassment cases continue to make headlines. In one recent example, the University of Southern Mississippi paid $112,500 in September 2009 to settle a case brought by a women's tennis graduate assistant against the school's women's tennis coach; the coach then resigned for personal reasons. That same month, the CEO of a hospital in Washington State was reprimanded after a claim of sexual harassment was brought against him, and he was also fired for unspecified reasons.

WOMEN OF COLOUR: A TRIPLE BURDEN

Earlier we mentioned multicultural feminism, which stresses that women of colour face difficulties for three reasons: their gender, their race, and, often, their social class, which is frequently near the bottom of the socioeconomic ladder.

They thus face a triple burden that manifests itself in many ways. For example, women of colour experience "extra" income inequality. Earlier we discussed the gender gap in earnings, with women earning 79.4 per cent of what men earn, but women of colour face both a gender gap and a racial/ethnic gap. We see a racial/ethnic gap among both women and men, as African Americans and Latinos of either gender earn less than whites, and we also see a gender gap between men and women, as women earn less than men within any race or ethnicity. These two gaps combine to produce an especially high gap between African American and Latina women and white men: African American women earn only 67.6 per cent of what white men earn, and Latina women earn only 60 per cent of what white men earn.

These differences in income mean that African American and Latina women are poorer than white women. We noted earlier that about 31 per cent of all female-headed families are poor. This figure masks race/ethnic differences among such families: 21.5 per cent of families headed by non-Latina white women are poor, compared to 40.5 per cent of families headed by African American women and also 40.5 per cent of families headed by Latina women.

While white women are poorer than white men, African American and Latina women are clearly poorer than white women.

SEXUAL ORIENTATION AND INEQUALITY

A recent report by a task force of the American Psychological Association stated that "same-sex sexual and romantic attractions, feelings, and behaviours are normal and positive variations of human sexuality". A majority of Americans do not share this opinion. In the 2008 General Social Survey, 52 per cent of respondents said that "sexual relations between two adults of the same sex" is "always wrong." Although this figure represents a substantial decline from the survey's 1973 finding of 74 per cent, it is clear that many Americans remain sharply opposed to homosexuality.

Not surprisingly, then, sexual orientation continues to be the source of much controversy and no small amount of abuse and discrimination directed towards members of the gay, lesbian, bisexual, and transgendered community. These individuals experience various forms of abuse, mistreatment, and discrimination that their heterosexual counterparts do not experience. In this respect, their sexuality is the source of a good deal of inequality.

For example, gay teenagers are very often the targets of taunting, bullying, physical assault, and other abuse in schools and elsewhere that sometimes drives them to suicide or at least to experience severe emotional distress. In 38 states, individuals can be denied employment or fired from a job because of their sexual orientation, even though federal and state laws prohibit employment discrimination for reasons related to race and ethnicity, gender, age, religious belief, and national origin. And in 45 states as of April 2010, same-sex couples are legally prohibited from marrying. In most of these states, this prohibition means that same-sex couples lack hundreds of rights, responsibilities, and benefits that spouses enjoy, including certain income tax and inheritance benefits, spousal insurance coverage, and the right to make medical decisions for a partner who can no longer communicate because of disease or traumatic injury.

HOUSEHOLD INEQUALITY

Someone has to do housework, and that someone is usually a woman. It takes many hours a week to clean the bathrooms, cook, shop in the grocery store, vacuum, and do everything else that needs to be done. The best evidence indicates that women married to or living with men spend two to three times as many hours per work on housework as men spend. This disparity holds true even when women work outside the home, leading sociologist Arlie Hochschild to observe in a widely cited book that women engage in a "second shift" of unpaid work when they come home from their paying job. The good news is that gender differences in housework time are smaller than a generation ago.

The bad news is that a large gender difference remains. As one study summarised the evidence on this issue, "women invest significantly more hours in household labour than do men despite the narrowing of gender differences in recent years". In the realm of household work, then, gender inequality persists.

DIVERSE INEQUALITIES

Gender equality and gender mainstreaming do not take place in isolation from other forms of inequality. The category 'woman' is internally divided by many other forms of difference and inequality. There has been increasing attention paid to the nature of the relationships between these diverse forms of inequality and their implication for the theory and practice of gender mainstreaming. On the one hand, attention to other inequalities may dilute the effort spent on gender mainstreaming if resources are allocated elsewhere, if there is loss of focus, if there is loss of appreciation of the specific structural causes of inequality, or if there is competition over the priority accorded to different forms of inequalities. On the other hand, the outcome of gender mainstreaming may be strengthened if there were concerted actions of previously separate communities and initiatives on agreed priorities for intervention and if it were to lead to a strengthening of procedures for deliberative democracy.

One result of the Treaty of Amsterdam is increasing legal recognition of diverse inequalities. When all the new regulations required by Article 13 of the Treaty come fully into effect by 2006, not only will gender, ethnicity and disability be legally recognised grounds on which to file complaints of discrimination, but religion, sexual orientation and age also will be. The implications for gender mainstreaming appear complex. Are the equality tools needed by diverse disadvantaged groups sufficiently similar that they can share institutional spaces rather than each needing their own?

Underlying the practical issues raised by the practical interconnection of gender mainstreaming with other forms of equality and diversity policies and politics is the question of the theorisation of difference and complex inequalities. Much debate in social theory has concerned these issues. To some extent, they overlap with the debates on sameness. While early concerns focused on the cross-cutting of gender inequalities by ethnicity and class, the inequalities and differences now considered are more numerous, extending at least to include sexuality, disability, religion, nationality and age. Indeed class is now more often treated implicitly, embedded within concepts of 'poverty', 'social exclusion' and 'pay', than as a focus of theoretical debate.

There are at least two major analytic strategies to address the conceptof gender within debates on difference. The first has been to disperse gender as a category, so that is understood always together with other complex inequalities rather than a category in its own right. Gender is always embedded within other social forms. Intersectionality with other complex inequalities is always present. In this approach the utilisation of the category of woman is criticised as problematically essentialising and homogenising. The second approach is to retain the concept of gender, while always noting that this is an abstraction since any practical category is always socially constructed. This approach has been supported by the revitalisation of realism as an approach in social theory, an approach that argues for greater depth in ontology, which can be better achieved by abstraction of specific categories that by their dispersal.

A range of strengths and weaknesses has been identified with the re-positioning of gender equality projects within a diversity framing. On the one hand, this potentially can strengthen and improve alliances to take forward particular issues; on the other hand, it can dilute the link of policy with a mobilized civil society grouping and distort the analysis of particular social structural causes of specific inequalities.

Squires suggests that in constructively addressing the diversity agenda, groups that are currently isolated from each other should be brought into dialogue. Such dialogue could help to resolve the tension between individual egalitarianism and the politics of group recognition that hold back the development of gender mainstreaming. Such dialogue could be understood to be a form of deliberative democracy that could develop new political projects that transcend old barriers.

Woodward contrasts the approaches to the relationship of gender equality and other complex inequalities in the US with those in the EU. In the US, early policies that named women and then gender as key categories have been replaced by policies focused on a new category of 'diversity'. Woodward explores the ambivalence about making women visible as a component of gender equality strategies. On the one hand this is essential if the specific social structural causes of gender equality are to be analysed and the effects of such policies are to be monitored and evaluated. On the other hand she recognises the tendency to then embed and entrench these categories as a consequence of the very policies that were intended to remove the inequalities. Woodward reports on the ambivalence reported by women in civil society that reflects these concerns, and the fear of the loss of affirmative action that some think may be entailed by gender mainstreaming. She concludes that the introduction of the concept of diversity into the equality policies of the EU could have detrimental consequences for the goal of gender equality, especially through the loss of the specific recognition of women as a category for policy.

Ferree addresses the inter-relationship of gender, race and class politics within the context of frame theory and comparative national institutional developments. The institutional history of each country sets the conditions shaping the development of different kinds of discursive construction of equality politics. In the US the history of struggles around race means that it is available as a metaphor for other kinds of equality politics. Further, in the US, race politics are positioned within a framing that is both liberal and democratic, but in which exclusion on the basis of 'natural' differences sets the terms of the debate.

Hence rights based arguments constitute a master frame for US social movements. By contrast in Germany, class struggle is the dominant motif of equality struggles, with a dominating continuum between Left and Right and a presumption of collective rather than individual articulation of claims. These different contexts provide different opportunities and obstacles for the development of gender equality projects, which are, accordingly, shaped by these conditions. In this analysis the co-existence of diverse equality projects is taken for granted, and the focus is on the way in which they influence each other in the context of the legacy of patterns of historic development. The meaning and potential of different gender equality projects is then specific to its context, and there can be no easy generalisation as to what is likely to be successful outside of this context.

The development of EU equality policy is currently shaped by the process of implementation of Article 13 of the Treaty of Amsterdam, which provides a legal basis for the removal of discrimination on at least six grounds: gender, ethnicity and race, disability, religion and belief, sexual orientation and age. This potentially repositions gender mainstreaming within a wider mix of equality and diversity issues.

For example, there is a question as to whether these regulations will entail the creation of more equality commissions, one for each of the strands, or whether existing equalities bodies are to be merged into a new body that addresses them all. Would the integration of the relevant governmental agencies entail the dispersal of expertise, loss of contact with the specific constituencies, and a diluted approach, or can it be an opportunity for levelling up to the best legislation for any one of the groups, more efficient deployment of resources, and a stronger approach?

The UK White Paper about the new Equality Commission for Equality and Human Rights proposes that all equalities issues together with human rights issues be addressed by a single body. This would replace the three existing Commissions for gender, race and ethnicity and disability and additionally address the inequalities associated with religion and belief, sexual orientation and age and human rights issues.

However, despite disparate legislation for each of these issues, there is no proposal for a single integrative act, merely modifications to existing acts, leaving different legal standards for complaints and interventions. There is a renewed commitment to the implementation of a duty on public bodies to promote gender equality, in a manner comparable to the existing duty in relation to race and the promise of one for disability. The implications of these proposed changes have yet to be seen. The relationship between gender inequality and other complex inequalities is an important but unresolved debate in both gender mainstreaming practice and in feminist theory. The dilemma of either abstracting and naming disadvantaged categories or of integrating with consequent loss of visibility and focus is common to both arenas. There is a two-way street in the exchange of ideas and analysis that makes this a fertile area for both theory and practice.

MULTIVARIATE ANALYSIS OF THE IMPACT OF GENDER INEQUALITY ON ECONOMIC GROWTH

GROWTH REGRESSIONS

All regressions have a high explanatory power and perform well on on specification tests. Regression confirms a number of known findings regarding conditional convergence, the importance of investment and openness for growth, the importance of initial levels of human capital as well as growth in human capital, the negative impact of population growth and the positive impact of labour force growth. The size of the coefficients on these variables are within the range of values observed in other studies. Some of the dummy variables for the various regions are significant suggesting that the growth regression is not picking up all effects that account for slower growth in these two regions. More interesting for our purposes is the finding that both the initial female-male ratio of schooling achievements as well as the female-male ratio of expansions in the level of schooling has a significant positive impact on economic growth.

Since I control for both investment as well as population and labour force growth, these results provide some support for the selection/distortion effect of gender bias in education as well as the 'direct' externality effect where lower gender inequality in education is associated with higher quality of education. The magnitude of the coefficient is also within the range of the possible. An increase in the female-male ratio of growth in schooling from 0.5 to 1.0 would raise the annual growth rate by about 0.4 per cent. Empirically, gender inequality in education also appears to be related to the health of the population.

When I include the under five mortality rate in 1960 or life expectancy in 1960 in the regressions, the direct effects of gender inequality in education on growth become smaller and the coefficients on child mortality and longevity are in the right direction, but not significant. As I show below that lower gender inequality in education seems to lower child mortality, this suggests that a third way lower gender inequality in education is promoting economic growth is through the effect it has on lowering child mortality and thus improving the health of the population. Regression 2 shows the determinants of investments and finds that higher investment rates are related to higher labour force growth, greater openness, and higher human capital. In addition, reduced gender inequality in education also appears to lead to higher investment rates, confirming the indirect linkage between gender inequality in education, investment, and economic growth postulated above. In particular, initial gender gaps in education appears to negatively affect investment rates. Regressions 3 and 4 also show that gender inequality in education has the expected impact on population growth and labour force growth so that the indirect linkage between gender inequality in education and economic growth via these two factors is also present. Regression 5 then shows the 'reduced form' estimate of the impact of gender inequality in education. Comparisons between regressions 1 and 5 indicate that the indirect effects of gender inequality in education are indeed sizable as the size of both coefficients, but particularly the one relating to initial gender inequality, have increased considerably.

This suggests that the initial level of gender inequality mainly affects growth indirectly, particularly through the impact it has on investment rates. In regressions 6 and 7, I add two possible measures of gender bias in employment to determine their effect on economic growth. The first one, the growth in the female share of the working age population that is employed in the formal sector has a large and significant impact on economic growth, while the other one, the growth in the female share of the labour force, also has a positive but insignificant impact on economic growth. These results should be treated with some caution. While they may be related to the selection effect and the measurement effect and thus show how greater access to employment for females boosts economic growth, it is also possible that the causality runs from economic growth to drawing females into the labour force.

Given the poor data on women's employment and wages, I am unable to come up with a good instrument that could address this issue. Thus the results on employment inequality remain suggestive and do indeed point to a possible effect of reduced gender inequality in employment on economic growth. I use the results from regressions 1-5 to determine to what extent growth in South Asia and Sub-Saharan Africa lagged behind growth in East Asia due to initial gender bias in education and gender bias in the growth of education. The numbers refer to the combined effect of initial gender gaps in education and gender gaps in the growth of education. In parentheses, I include the figures for the impact of the initial gender gap in 1960 and the gender gap in the growth of education, respectively. Using just the direct effect 0.45 per cent of the annual growth difference of 3.5 per cent between Africa and East Asia can be accounted for by differences in gender inequality in education, where most of the difference is due to differences in the gender bias in the *growth* of education.

The comparison between South Asia and East Asia is even more striking. Fully 0.69 per cent of the annual growth difference of 2.5 per cent can be accounted for by differences in gender inequality in education; here, about 2/3 of the difference can be accounted for by differences in gender bias in the *growth* of education, while 1/3 are due to differences in *levels* of gender inequality in 1960. Similarly, gender inequality in education appears to have slowed growth in the Middle East and North Africa by similar amounts to the ones observed in South Asia. In addition to the direct effects, the indirect effects can also account for some of the growth differences between South Asia and East Asia. Gender inequality in education can, via the effect on investment, account for a further 0.16 per cent of the growth difference between South Asia and East Asia. Gender inequality in education also accounts for 0.13 per cent of the growth difference between South Asia and East Asia via the impact on population growth. These indirect effects, esp. the one operating via the population and labour force growth rates, are somewhat smaller than expected.

Unless this is due to data issues, this suggests that the indirect effect, while present and significant, is of smaller magnitude than the direct distortionary effect of closing educational opportunities for promising female students and of reducing the positive externality of educated females on the quality of education of other household members. The total direct and indirect effects of gender inequality in education account for about 0.95 per cent of the growth difference between South Asia and East Asia, about 0.56 per cent of the growth difference between Sub-Saharan Africa and East Asia and about 0.85 per cent between the Middle East and North Africa and East Asia.

Since the initial level of gender inequality plays a larger role in the indirect effects than in the direct effect of gender inequality on economic growth, the total impact of gender inequality in education on growth differences between Africa and East Asia is due to 1/3 (55 per cent) to gender differentials in 1960, and 2/3 (45 per cent) due to gender differentials in the growth of education. Using the reduced form regression yields virtually identical estimates of the total size of the effects as well as their impact on the growth differences between developing regions. Thus gender inequality in education appears to have a sizable effect on economic growth.

It is important to emphasize that the results do not take into account the differences in *average* human capital between the regions, but just the gender *inequality* in education. From the regressions, it can be seen that differences in *average* human capital also matter a lot and can account for a further share of the growth differences between the developing regions. Based on regression 6, I also incorporate the effect of employment inequality on economic growth and find that it could account for about another 0.3 per cent of the growth difference between East Asia and South Asia, Sub Saharan Africa, and the Middle East, respectively. It is important to determine the robustness of the results.

First, it was mentioned that the estimates on gender inequality in education present an upper bound estimate as they implicitly assume that increases in female education could, *ceteris paribus*, have been achieved at no reduction in male educational enrollments. I present the regressions for the lower bound estimate, where I use the average level of human capital rather than the male level of human capital. As to be expected, the size of the coefficients on the gender gap in schooling is now smaller, but still sizable and, in most cases, significant. Calculations of the growth differences accounted for by this measure of gender inequality in education shows only small differences to the previous one.

Now the total effect of gender inequality in education can account for 0.77 per cent of the growth difference between South and East Asia, 0.44 per cent of the difference between Sub-Saharan Africa and East Asia, and nearly 0.7 per cent of the difference between East Asia and the Middle East. Adding the measure for employment inequality can again account for about another 0.3 per cent of the growth differences. Second, I need to worry about possible simultaneity issues; in particular, can it be the case that growth led to increases in the female-male ratio of schooling attainment rather than the other way around?

Regressions 10 and 11 are based on a panel analysis where the dependent and independent variables are split into three different time periods. As I only include initial levels of schooling and the initial female-male ratio of schooling in the regression, I avoid the simultaneity issue inherent in the educational growth variables. The results are very similar to the cross-section results which is very reassuring as often findings from cross-country regressions change in a panel setting. In fact, even the magnitude of the effects appears to be roughly similar to the cross-section regression. I estimate the impact of gender inequality in education using the panel regressions.

In the 1980s, in initial gender inequality in education accounted for some 0.3-0.5 per cent of the growth differences between East Asia and the other three regions. This is smaller than found in the crosssection regression, which is to be expected as we no longer consider the impact of further improvements in the gender gap in education that may have occurred after 1980. The panel regressions also show an interesting temporal pattern of the impact of gender inequality in education on economic growth. In 1960, East Asia did not exhibit much lower gender bias in education and the growth differences between it and the other regions were comparatively small.

By 1970 and also 1980, East Asia's gender gap was much lower than in the other regions and it was precisely then when growth differences really soared between East Asia o the one hand, and South Asia, Sub Saharan Africa and the Middle East on the other.

This confirms that the timing of gender gaps in education and economic growth suggest that reduced gender gaps in education did indeed play a significant role in furthering growth. To approach the simultaneity issue in another way, regression 12 presents a two stage least squares regressions where both the growth in average education and the female-male ratio of growth in average education are replaced by their predicted values using government spending on education, the total fertility rate in 1960, and the change in fertility rate between 1960 and 1990 as instruments.

Now the impact of the female-male ratio in the growth of education is still significant and considerably larger in magnitude. This lends further support to the contention that causality runs from gender bias in education to economic growth and not the reverse. In further analyses, I investigate whether the relationship between gender inequality and growth differs depending on which countries are included in the regression. While limiting the sample to more homogeneous groups of countries has the advantage of seeing whether the effects differ by region, it carries the disadvantage that some of the important variation that is needed to estimate these effects is thereby eliminated which may lead to less precise results.

Limiting the sample to 85 developing countries changes the results by very little. The impact of initial gender inequality is slightly larger than in the total sample, while the impact of gender bias in the growth of education is now smaller. Using these regressions to account for growth differences suggest that the gender inequality in education accounts for some 0.44 per cent of the growth difference between Africa and East Asia, and 0.81 per cent of the growth difference between South Asia and East Asia.

Adding gender inequality in employment adds another 0.4-0.5 per cent. Thus the effect of gender inequality on growth is as strong in developing countries as it is in developed countries. This findings differs from Dollar and Gatti who found gender inequality in education to have a significant impact only among countries with higher levels of female education. As the econometric methodology, time period considered, and some of the exogenous variables, including the human capital variables differ, it is not easy to determine what drives the differences in results. One thing I was able to determine is that the difference does not appear to come from the human capital variable used by Dollar and Gatti.

When I use their human capital variable and an amended version, it still is the case that gender bias hurts growth among poor and rich countries. Other than that, I can only point to the fact that I consider a longer time period in a cross-section or a three decade panel, while Dollar and Gatti limit the analysis to 75-90, that I model the gender gap in education differently to avoid multicollinearity problems, and that I include a few different independent variables to explicitly consider direct and indirect effects. Limiting the sample to African countries produces some interesting results. Now the impact of initial gender inequality in education is much larger and the impact of gender bias in the growth of educational attainment is slightly larger than in the overall regression. It thus appears that gender inequality in education appears to matter more in Africa than elsewhere. This may seem a bit surprising since one might expect growth in the largely agricultural African societies not to depend as much on education in general and female bias in particular. The regressions seem to suggest otherwise. They support a view that human capital is indeed very important also in Africa's agricultural societies.

Moreover, given the important role women play in African agriculture, their poor human capital appears to be a particularly important constraint for economic growth. To estimate the impact of gender bias in education in the African context, The contribution of gender inequality in education on the growth difference between Botswana, a country with low gender inequality in education, and Ghana and Niger, two countries with high gender inequality in education. The growth differences between the three economies are sizable, with Botswana having grown by more than 5.5 per cent, while Ghana and Niger grew by less than 0.3 per cent per year between 1960 and 1992. Gender inequality in education can account for a total of 1.59 per cent of the growth difference between Ghana and Botswana and a total of 1.82 per cent of the total growth difference between Niger and Botswana. These are very large effects indeed.

FERTILITY AND CHILD MORTALITY REGRESSIONS

I estimate models of fertility and child mortality to determine to what extent gender bias in education might hinder progress in reducing fertility and childhood mortality rates. Regression 16 estimates a model to predict total fertility rates in 1990. The regression reproduces findings from many other studies about the importance of female education for fertility.

Every year of female education reduces the total fertility rate by 0.23, while increases in male education raise the fertility rate. Higher child mortality promotes fertility while higher incomes lower fertility, both also as expected. Regression 17 then uses the measures of human capital used previously to make it compatible with the remaining parts of the document. It shows that average education makes little difference to the fertility rate, while the ratio of female to male achievement is highly significant. This clearly demonstrates that gender bias in education prevents reductions in fertility and thus harms women and their families in developing countries. Also here there may be direct and indirect effects.

In particular, income in 1990 and the under five mortality rate in 1990 may be influenced by gender gaps in education. Therefore I need to take into account those indirect effects and estimate a reduced form regression as well. Regression 18 shows that there is indeed a very large effect of gender bias in education on under five mortality, which is an important finding in its own right.

Even after controlling for income, *average* human capital, and other regional differences, gender bias in education has a huge impact on child mortality. If Sub Saharan Africa experienced the gender gap in education of Eastern Europe, the under five mortality rate would be about 45/1000 lower than it currently is. Thus gender bias in education leads to higher child mortality and thus prevents progress in this critical development achievement. Regression 20 then shows the reduced form regression of the fertility rate which demonstrates the sizable impact of gender gaps in education on fertility, both directly as well as indirectly via its impact on child mortality.

'EXPERTISE' OR 'DEMOCRATISATION'

Expertise and democracy are often treated as rival forms of governance. Democracy is usually contrasted favourably with expertise, which is regarded as associated with and contaminated by the dominant order. However, a different kind of contrast draws on the connotation that expertise is scientific and thereby politically neutral and mere sectional interest. Gender mainstreaming sits in the middle of such debates. Sometimes it is represented as if it were primarily a technical process and at others as primarily a political process.

On the one hand, it has been understood as a process of developing a more inclusive democracy, by improving gendered democratic practices. On the other hand, the process is represented as one of efficiency and expertise carried out by the normal policy actors with a specially developed toolkit. This issue raises larger questions about the changing nature of democracy in a gender unequal context and about the positioning of 'expertise' in debates on democracy. There is a question as to whether it is appropriate to polarise 'expertise' and 'democracy' as alternative models or interpretations of gender mainstreaming at all.

Beveridge et al make a distinction between the 'expert-bureaucratic' model, involving primarily experts and specialists, and the 'participatory-democratic' model involving a range of individuals and organizations. They suggest that these constitute real differences in the ways in which gender mainstreaming is implemented, not just perceptions of such processes. They consider that only the participatory democratic process can accomplish gender mainstreaming as agenda setting rather than integration.

Rai conceptualises gender mainstreaming as a process of gender democratisation, of including women and their own perceptions of their political interests and political projects into policy making processes. A range of different processes and practices are identified as involved, with a particular focus on the national gender machineries in the state and their relationship with civil society women's groups.

The accountability of the national machineries to a wider context that includes NGOs and women's groups is seen as essential to their effective operation. Gender mainstreaming is seen as a process by which various actors, previously outside the privileged policy arenas, get to have voice within them. This view appears to runs counter to the view that gender mainstreaming is done by the 'normal policy actors'. In the Council of Europe text, the definition of gender mainstreaming incorporates the notion that it is implemented 'by the actors normally involved in policy making'. This might be understood to imply that, once the political goal of mainstreaming gender equality has been set, the process can be effectively implemented by technocrats and bureaucrats within the policy and state machinery. This approach is further exemplified by that part of the discourse that prioritises the use of 'tools', such as those of gender disaggregated statistics, gender budgeting and gender impact assessments. Here the issue under discussion is focused on how, not whether, to mainstream gender equality. The focus then becomes the resources, such as expertise, that the technical experts have to do their jobs.

The relative significance of expertise or democracy may be an issue of context or one of interpretation. This issue resonates in the papers by Verloo and Woodward. Woodward argues for the importance of contextual factors in determining the success or otherwise of gender mainstreaming initiatives. In particular, the level of sophistication of the gender equality awareness within the political environment affects whether state functionaries can effectively implement gender mainstreaming. Where this is high, as in the case of the Netherlands, where some of Verloo's examples are based, then the normal policy actors may be effective in implementing gender mainstreaming. Where this is low, as is the case in Flanders in Belgium, then the normal policy actors are unlikely to carry out this process effectively. Woodward also draws attention to significance of experts who are outside of government. Further, Verloo makes clear that the political context, that is, whether there are political opportunities, strong mobilising networks within and outside the bureaucracy, and appropriate 'frames' available, should be expected to make a difference to the process and outcome of gender mainstreaming.

An alternative to polarising 'expertise' and 'democracy' is to see them as complexly entwined in contemporary practice. An example of this may be seen in the practice of gender budgeting. This is conventionally represented as a process invoking 'expertise' rather than one of 'gendering democracy' but in practice the process usually involves both..

Gender budgeting requires a specialised toolkit including gender disaggregated statistics, equality indicators and gender impact assessments. The use of statistics and economic data utilises an authoritative technical and abstracted mode of expressing the expertise. It is often presented as the efficient, neutral application of techniques to an already agreed agenda and set of policy goals.

However, gender budgeting is often more complex that this. First, it can include explicit statements about the importance of improving women's lives, that is, it can be situated within a wider framework that is not politically neutral. Second, the representation of the intervention as one that is based on expertise may itself be a political strategy. For example, the UK Women's Budget Group holds meetings with elected politicians, civil servants and wider civil society and knowingly positions itself as expert and technical, even as it also simultaneously uses democratic accountability to create pressure for change. There is a duality of expertise and participatory democratic working in this gender mainstreaming that is complementary rather than in contradiction.

These issues insistently raise the issue of the nature of democracy, in particular the inclusiveness of formal elected representation as well as the processes by which political projects are developed and support mustered. The traditional view of liberal democracy has centred on the formal election of representatives to national parliaments, so the narrow conventional definition of democracy focuses on free elections and free political parties in the context of a free civil society. However, recent debates highlight the nature and meaning of representation as well as the relevance of participation in deliberation about political projects.

Conventional liberal practices of electoral representation have not delivered equal numbers of women and men in elected positions, nor proportionate members of minority communities. There has been much discussion of the role of different kinds of political mechanisms in explaining variations in the representation of women. These discussions have given rise to a deeper consideration of what is meant by the 'representation' of women in both Parliament and other political arenas.

Is the presence of women essential to their democratic representation? Do women have collective political interests that might be represented electorally or are these either too individual or too diverse for this to be appropriate? Does 'identity' politics essentialise and stabilise the group at stake and underestimate the significance of differences within that 'group' in a politically problematic way? Does the concept of women's interests too readily assume that political interests can be read off from social structural location?

The investigations of associations between political preferences and location with the gender regime have found positive correlations, although these do not constitute a complete explanation of differences in political preferences. The development of feminist theories of the state and democratic representation drew attention to the plurality of arenas that are relevant to the representation of voices and political projects associated with perceived women's or gendered interests. These include not only the traditional focus on the elected representatives in parliaments and similar institutions, but also included consideration of the development of gender machinery and women's bureaus within the state and also the articulation of political projects by social movements and other civil society actors. The relationship between these three–gendered constituencies, elected representatives, women's units and civil society–has been shown to be important in explaining variations in the impact of feminist projects. Woodward demonstrates the importance of the 'velvet triangle' linking feminist bureaucrats, trusted academics and organized voices in the women's movement for the development of gender mainstreaming in the EU. The trio of relevant female players is slightly from those of Vargas and Wieringa , but the conception of alliances between differently positioned individuals and groups is common to both.

In Woodward's trio of allies there are academics, rather than elected representatives, suggesting the importance of expertise as a key component of these EU gender networks. The development of the analysis of gendered democracy has led to the consideration of the significance of alliances between those in different political arenas but engaged in complementary projects. The analysis of gender mainstreaming includes expertise, in the form of academics, as a key element.

The importance of expertise in the context of the gender machinery, elected politicians and academics for gender mainstreaming is addressed by Veitch in relation to the UK. The absence of information, knowledge and resources holds back gender mainstreaming by government officials.

The acquisition and utilisation of expertise is situated within the processes linking different parts of the gender machinery, other government departments, Ministers, MPs, academic researchers and the legal framework. In a related way, Zippel shows how governing bodies may have an interest in developing such expertise and working with such non-electoral networks.

'Accountability' is a concept within the repertoire of democratic practices, but is slightly off-centre. It has been used in several ways in relation to gender mainstreaming. Rai argues that national gender machineries should be accountable to civil society NGOs and women's groups. Grosser and Moon contend corporations need to be accountable to a wider range of stakeholders than shareholders if they are to deliver value. Accountability implies flows of information into the public domain and a willingness to engage in dialogue with those outside the organisation's boundary. Transformative gender mainstreaming often requires information be made public and input from actors external to the organisation because it is a practice that intrinsically goes beyond existing neatly bounded responsibilities.

Within democratic theory, an alternative focus to that on substantive representation is that of deliberative democracy, often drawing on the work of Habermas and his theories of communicative action, which is seen to offer the potential to address the resolution of initially conflicting priorities of diverse social groups and communities. Squires argues that it is essential in order to address gender mainstreaming in the context of diversity.

She argues that the debates on gender mainstreaming demand a resolution of the tension between liberal individual egalitarianism and the politics of group recognition. It is only when diverse groups bring to the public agenda their respective views and experiences and engage in democratic deliberation that gender mainstreaming can move forward.

One of the limitations of deliberative democracy, she notes, is that it depends on the institutional design of debate to ensure the inclusion of all groups, and how this will happen tends to be under-specified in the theoretical literature. Thus she concludes that the debates on gender mainstreaming and deliberative democracy have much to learn from each other.

Deliberative democratic theory has also produced new interest in the significance of expertise and argumentation. A conceptual vocabulary has developed that entwines expertise and democratic impulse. Those who have actively used expertise in pushing forward political projects have been variously conceptualised as 'epistemic communities' and as 'advocacy networks'.

An epistemic community is defined by Haas as 'a network of professionals with recognized expertise and competence in a particular domain and an authoritative claim to policy-relevant knowledge within that domain or issue-area...they have:

- A shared set of normative and principled beliefs...
- Shared causal beliefs, which are derived from their analysis of practices leading or contributing to a central set of problems in their domain...
- Shared notions of validity...
- A common policy enterprise.'

Here specific combinations of expertise and value commitment fuel new kinds of political interventions. In sum, while expertise and democracy have sometimes been seen as rival sources of legitimacy in governance, the case of gender mainstreaming suggests a strong inter-relationship. This may be conceptualised either as an alliance between individuals and groups or as a new integrated form of community or network in its own right.

These alliances, communities and networks often involve academics as well as more conventional political actors, such as elected politicians, civil servants and social movements. The analysis of gender mainstreaming thus involves a reconsideration of the nature of democracy, to consider not only the gender of the elected representatives, the institutionalisation of gendered interests in the gender machinery of the state and an active gendered civil society, but also the incorporation of expertise, especially from academics.

SOCIAL EQUITY MEASURES: THE EXPERIENCE

India has a long tradition of social equity and social assistance directed particularly towards the more vulnerable sections of society. The institution of self sufficient village communities, the system of common property resources, the system of joint families and the practice of making endowments for religious and charitable provided the required social equity and assistance to the needy and poor of the nation. In fact, the caste and religion based institutions also played significant role in providing the needed support to the weaker sections of the selected castes and group of people. These informal arrangements of social equity measures underwent steady and inevitable erosion in the wake of industrialisation and urbanisation.

During the British rule the policy was to provide assistance only to the employees of the company or the government, basically to promote the commitment and loyalty of the workforce and as a part of non-union strategy. Only during the postindependent period, the welfare dimension gained relevance and importance. However, even after independence, the State was concerned more with the problems of industrial workforce and neglected the rural labour force on social equity matters to a greater extent, till recent past. It is rightly true that when independent India's Constitution was drafted, social equity was specially included in List III to Schedule VII of the Constitution and it was made as the concurrent responsibility of the Central and State Governments.

A number of Directive Principles of State Policy relating to aspects of social equity were incorporated in the Indian Constitution. The initiatives in the form of Acts such as, the Workmen's Compensation Act (1923), the Industrial Dispute Act (1947), the Employees State Insurance Act (1948), the Minimum Wages Act (1948), the Coal Mines Provident Funds and Miscellaneous Provisions Act (1948), the Employees Provident Fund and Miscellaneous Provisions Act (1952), the Assam Tea Plantations Provident Funds/Scheme Act (1955), the Maternity Benefit Act (1961), the Seamen's Provident Fund Act (1966), the Contract Labour Act (1970), the Payment of Gratuity Act (1972), the Building and Construction Workers Act (1996), etc reveal the attention given to the organised workers to attain different kinds of social equity and welfare benefits.

Needless to state that the benefits arising through these initiatives are meant for (a) employees of the Central and State Governments, local bodies, including universities and aided educational institutions, (b) Public sector establishments, under both the Centre and States, including mines, railways, ports and docks, air corporations, banks, insurance companies, electricity Boards, road transport undertakings, manufacturing units, trading concerns, service industries, etc. (c) employees in organised private sector establishments in industries as in cotton textiles, jute, silk and art silk, cement, engineering, chemical, electronics, transport, construction, services and so on. Though it has been argued that the above Acts are directly and indirectly applicable to the workers in the unorganised sector also, their contribution is negligible to the unorganised workers.

Although not much has been done in providing social equity cover to the rural poor and the unorganised labour force, the country has made some beginning in that direction. Both the Central and State Governments have formulated certain specific schemes to support unorganised workers. The Old

Age Pension Scheme (OAPS) was introduced in all the States and Union Territories. Kerala was the First State to experiment with the pension scheme for the agricultural workers in the year 1982, followed by Tamilnadu (1982). Andhra Pradesh (1983) introduced the OAPS to the landless agricultural workers. The Government of Karnataka introduces the Asha Kiran Scheme (1983) to provide relief against death or loss of limbs due to accident to agricultural labourers and other labourers (aged 16-65) such as fishermen, beedi workers, washerman, cobblers, masions, goldsmiths, drivers of animal drawn vehicles, riksha pullers, etc. The Government of Maharashtra introduced a pension scheme in 1980 to support the physically handicapped and economically weaker sections of the society.

In addition to pension schemes, there were initiatives to provide death and retirement benefits for the artisans and skilled workers and insurance benefits to the unorganised sectors initiated in state level. In order to evolve comprehensive legislation for workers in the unorganised sectors, various commissions and study groups were appointed. The First National Commission on Labour (1969) defined the unorganised workers and recommended the Minimum Wages Act to cover unorganised workers too. In 1984, the Economic Administration Reforms Commission constituted a 6-member working group on social equity. The Working Group could not carry out detailed investigation. In August 1987, Government of India appointed a National Commission on Rural Labour to examine the national and regional problems pertaining rural labour in India. The Commission submitted its report in July 1991 and recommended old age pension, life insurance, maternity benefit, disability benefits and minimum health care and sickness benefits to all rural workers. The Second National Labour Commission constituted in 1999 submitted its report in 2002 and recommended an umbrella type legislation and drafted an indicative Bill also to provide protection to the workers in the unorganised sector. Based on the Commission's recommendations, the Government launched the 'Unorganised Sector Workers' Social Equity Scheme, 2004' on pilot basis in 50 districts.

The scheme provided three benefits such as, old age pension, medical insurance and accidental insurance. However, the scheme was not found viable as it had no statutory backing, it was voluntary in nature and the contribution from the employers was not forthcoming. Moreover, given the size of the unorganised sector the magnitude of the problem is huge and the resource requirements are quite large. The National Common Minimum Programme (NCMP) of the present government highlights the commitment of the government towards the welfare and wellbeing of all workers, particularly in the unorganised sector. The government constituted a National Commission for the Enterprises in the Unorganised Sector (NCEUS) under Chairmanship of Dr. Arjun Sen Gupta to examine the problems of enterprises in the unorganised sector and make recommendations to provide technical, marketing and credit support to these enterprises. The Commission was also to review the social equity system available for the unorganised workers and make recommendations for expanding their coverage. The Commission presented its report on the Social Equity for the unorganised sector workers in May 2006. Based on the committee's recommendations the government is in the process of enactment of Legislation (Bill) and formulation of social equity schemes. Poverty Alleviation Programmes (PAP) and Employment Oiented Programmes initiated in India are primarily focused on developing rural labour and unorganised workers.

These programmes improve the access of the poor to developmental programmes, use surplus labour for community asset formation and strengthen the position of the poor by providing assets and income. The first PAPs introduced were Small Farmers Development Agency (SFDA) and Marginal Farmers and Agricultural Labour Agency (MFAL). In 1980, Integrated Rural Development Programme (IRDP) was launched with the aim of helping the poor families to cross poverty line and enabling them to achieve sustain poverty eradication. Productive assets and inputs were provided through financial assistance by government subsidy and term credit from financial institutions.

The programme covered small and marginal farmers, agricultural labourers and rural artisans. In 1979, Training for Rural Youth for Self-Employment was introduced to provide technical and entrepreneurial skills to rural youth from families below poverty line to enable them to take up income generating activities. To develop women and children in rural areas with a cooperation of UNICEF a special programme named Development of Women and Children in Rural Areas (DWCRA) was started during 1982-83. As an effort towards employment equity National Rural Employment Programme (NREP) was launched during the sixth plan (1982-85).

In 1983, Rural Landless Employment Guarantee Programme (RLEGP) was introduced to ensure employment generation of hundred days in a year in the rural landless households. By replacing the NREP and RLEGP Jawahar Rozgar Yojana (JRY) was launched in 1989. In the same year Nehru Rozgar Yojana (NRY) also got launched with a target towards persons living below the poverty line in Urban areas. There are several other programme such as Drought Prone Area Programme (DPAP), Desert Development Programme (DDP), Hill Area Development Programme (HADP) and North-East Council (NEC) were also launched with similar objectives of developing weaker sections of selected areas. In addition to the Central assisted programmes, State-level initiatives for poverty alleviation and employment generation were initiated towards unorganised workers.

For instance in Tamil Nadu old age pension is available to (a) aged poor who are 65 year and above (b) destitute and physically handicapped, (c) destitute widows d) destitute agricultural labourers and (e) destitute/ deserted wives. Under the Annapurna Scheme, food grains are distributed to the destitute/ senior citizens covered under the National Old Age Pension Scheme. The beneficiaries are given 10 kgs. of rice per month at free of cost. The State of Goa has enacted the Goa Employment (Condiitons of Service) and Retirement Benefit Act, 2005. According to this act the employers is required to issue social equity cards to the workers engaged by him in both the organised and unorganised sectors.

West Bengal Government introduced a State Assisted Scheme of Provident Fund for unorganised workers in 2001. Tripura Government also introduced the similar Provident Fund programme in 2001. In the State of Punjab, in addition to old age pension scheme, financial assistance to women and destitute women, dependent children and disabled persons are also made available. Similar such State level initiatives are carried out in Kerala, Bihar, Uttar Prades, Madhya Pradesh, Haryana, Gujarat and other states. The involvement of Non-Governmental Organisations (NGOs) in the social equity of unorganised workers could not be ignored.

A large number of voluntary and people's organisations are directly involved in providing protective social equity to workers and their families in the unorganised sector. The services provided by the NGO's include access to microcredit, housing, preventive health care and employment. The NGO's support to unorganised workers is carried out in two ways. Firstly, the NGO's use their own funds and the aids obtained from other agencies (domestic and international donors) and implement several projects and schemes to the targeted people who are basically weaker and vulnerable sections of the community. Secondly, they serve as an intermediary between the formal provider (say, Government) and the community, and help in routing the services to the needy. In both the ways, it is expected that the services are reaching to the community with no delay, less cost and to the right ones. It is estimated that the NGO's could cover only 3 to 4 per cent of the total workforce in the unorganised sector.

SOCIAL EQUITY FOR THE UNORGANISED WORKERS: THE NEEDS

The foregoing discussion about the growing unorganised labourforce, their characteristics and the social equity initiatives of the Centre, State and NGO's indicated that the needs are much more than the supports provided and the efforts must be targeted and vast enough to cover the growing unorganised workers. In this context, it is worthwhile to list out the major equity needs of the unorganised workers. They are:

- Employment Equity: Unorganised workers are greatly affected by the seasonal nature of the employment opportunities. The problem of under-employment and unemployment persist to a large extent among unorganised sectors. There are several schemes such as Swarnajayanti Gram Swaeozgar Yojna (SGSY), Pradhan Manntri Gran Sadak Yojana (PMGSY), Sampoorna Gramin Rozgar Yojana (SGRY), National Food For Work Programme(NFFWP), Indra Awass Yojna (JAY), Integrated Wastelands (IWDP), Drought Prone Areas Programme (DPAP) and Desert Development Programme (DDP) initiated to generate employment opportunities in rural India. Further, the Government has recently enacted the National Rural Employment Guarantee Act to provide 100 days guaranteed employment to rural households. Though these initiatives have contributed in reducing the rural unemployment problem, the problem of employment insecurity needs to be addressed in a wider context and solved at.

- Food Equity: Food equity is considered as an important component of social equity. The rural workers and weaker sections of the community are badly affected during times of drought, flood and famine, and due to similar natural calamities. The DPAP largely confines itself in the provision of employment through rural works programme. What is required is to provide equity for food in times of difficulty and during normal times. The Public Distribution System (PDS) implemented in Indian States stand as a model attempt in this direction. It is through the PDS that the government endeavors to protect the real purchasing power of the poorer sections by providing them an uninterrupted supply of foodgrains at prices far below market prices. It is to be noted that the PDS was introduced only to the urban areas initially, but since 1970s rural areas are also covered
- Health Equity: Health equity can be described as ensuring low exposure to risk and providing access to health care services along with the ability to pay for medical care and medicine. Such health equity should be made available to all citizens. Several studies that examined rural health conditions and health care needs highlight that the inadequate and poor rural health infrastructure, growing health care needs and health care expenses. Establishing hospitals with required infrastructure in all the villages is a question of feasibility, viability and availability of inputs and resources. However, it is a matter of concern to consider the needs of the 70 per cent of the people living in villages. The poor do not treat for common illness and sometimes to major diseases that are unidentified by them, causing higher level of untreated morbidity. Similarly, the cost and burden of treatments are ever increasing and leading to difficulty for the poor and weaker sections of the community.
- Housing Equity: Housing is one of the basic needs of every individual

and family. The housing needs of the unorganised workers and the poor are ever increasing in the context of the decay of joint family system, migration and urbanisation. In urban areas, though housing is a major issue, the organised workers are supported by providing House Rent Allowances (HRA) or by providing houses through Housing Boards and by provising accommodation in the Quarters. There are several financing companies and commercial banks offering loans to organised workers to construct or purchase houses. These facilities are normally not available and could not be enjoyed by the unorganised workers. More over, the housing conditions of the rural poor are ‘really poor’ and there is scope for reconditioning, modification and reconstruction, in many. The rural housing programme implemented in Tamilnadu namely Samathuvapuram and construction of houses under Slum Clearance Board stand as examples for steps towards housing equity.

- Income Equity: Though income and number of days of employment are positively related, this relationship holds good mainly for organised workers. As for as unorganised workers are concerned, their income is highly influenced by nature of job, nature and type of products produced quantum of value addition, market value, competition, etc. To protect from the crop loss, Crop Insurance Scheme is available. But for various other self-employed enterprises and other jobs, there is no equity available to realise income for the efforts.
- Life and Accident Equity: The death of a worker in a family is a great loss to the entire family and it adds burden too. The death of a worker raises the question of survival of the family left behind due to the permanent loss of income to the family. Similarly, an accident is a major problem for an informal worker since it leads to loss of income and cost of treatment. If the accident leads to permanent or partial disability, the financial loss will be severe and unimaginable. By covering the unorganized workers under the Insurance schemes of individual, family and group could alone provide equity for life and accident.
- Nutritional Equity: It is not just ‘food’, but the nutrition is very important. The weaker sections of the community and the unorganised workers are not conscious about the nutrient intake. Particularly, the children and women, pregnant women and aged do not receive adequate nutrient requirements. Lack of nutrient leads to poor growth, poor health and sickness, poor performance and shorter life. There are certain initiatives by the states, local bodies and NGO’s to create awareness on health and nutrition and to ensure adequate nutrient intake for the targeted groups, particularly to children and women.

- Old Age Equity: The workers of the unorganised sector face the problem of insecurity when they reach to the life stage of aged when they could not work for themselves. The question of dependency is a major threat to the old age unorganised workers in the context of disappearing joint family system.

FEMINISM AND GENDER ISSUES

According to the American Census Bureau, by 2050 there would be 383 million people in the USA and about 195 million of them would be women. How many of them would be known as famous scientists, writers, doctors, etc.? How many of them will affect the national policy? Will the number of the women representatives in the government increase? At present there are 5 women in the US Government: Secretary of Agriculture, Secretary of the Interior, Secretary of Labour, Director of EPA and the last but not the least-National Security Advisor-Condoleeza Rice. Females are allowed to enter the Navy, the Air Force and Marine Corps. In 1990, 75 per cent of women received a high school diploma compared to 76 per cent men high school graduates. But there were times when a woman wasn't allowed to vote and the only priority she had in life was house and children. Women wanted more than that and understood they need to fight for their rights and they still continue doing it.

One of the donators to www.feminist.com described a feminist as each and every politically and socially conscious woman or man who works for equality within or outside the movement, writes about feminism, or calls her- or himself a feminist. Feminism stands for reproductive freedom (including access to safe, legal and accessible abortion), equality of rights with men, and is against sexism, representing woman as a sexual and maternity object only (an image created by media), domestic violence etc. So feminism is the movement for social, political, and economic equality of men and women.

Organized feminism did not really form until the first Women's Conference held in Seneca Falls (USA) in 1848. To begin with, the Women's Movement evolved out of social reform groups such as the Abolition of Slavery, the Social Purity and Temperance movements. Women began to realize that in order to transform society they would need their own organizations to do so. They campaigned upon a whole range of issues: guardianship of infants, property rights, divorce, access to higher education and the medical professions, equal pay, etc. In the 20th century, in 1963 was published a book by Betty Friedan, called *Feminine Mistique*. In it she attacked the injustices women had to deal with because of the passive roles of housewives and dependence on males. In 1966, the National Organization for Women was founded.

The time between 1920s and 1980s was the time of the second wave of the feminist movement, the time when the American females participated the most in the global feminist movement. It had its results: for instance, one of the most intensely developing segment of US Economy now is women-owned business, college enrolment of women is near that of men, etc. But still the gender issue is still very much a live issue in the USA today. An example of this may be the fact that women are not represented equally in all professions, the overall market remains sharply segregated by gender.

Originally, feminism was about giving a woman a perspective in social and any other area of life, from which she was excluded. But nowadays, many women who support the ideas of feminism do not want to be labelled as feminists. One of the main reasons for that lies in the 70s, when feminism came to be perceived as simply anti-family, anti-marriage, anti-children, and perhaps even anti-religion, not to mention anti-men. Feminism presented the family as a kind of prison, with a working career on the outside as a kind of freedom. Many feminist movement activists are trying to change that image. One of them is Angela McRobbie, who, in her book, said "the old binary opposition which put femininity at one end of the political spectrum and feminism at the other is no longer an accurate way of conceptualizing young female experience".

Of course, the whole body of the feminist movement doesn't solely consist of those somewhat rival groups—radical feminists and liberal feminists (so-called pod feminists). Besides them exists womanism, which distinct from feminism is often white-centred history, an alternative casting of the same basic beliefs about equality and freedom; few womanists would deny the link to feminism. Individualist Feminism (ifeminism as its often called) is a part of the feminist movement too. Theres also an interesting movement called Riot Girl which can be claimed a part of a feminist movement. Joanne Gottlieb and Gayle Wald, in their book '*Smells Like Teen Spirit: Riot Girls, Revolution and Women in Independent Rock* describe Riot Girl as: the introduction of self-conscious feminism into rock discourse and activity." In 1990s such bands as Bikini Kill and the Hole promoted an image of self-conscious, artistic and *also* attractive female on stage and fought with stereotypes of rock music as a genre ruled only by men. Nowadays the Riot Girl movement is on the wave again with bands like Sleater Kinney, Le Tigre, etc. There are many magazines devoted to the feministic movement (for instance, Chickfactor) and even a worldwide festival, called Ladyfest, where only the bands, supporting the philosophy of feminism, play.

Looking back, the American feminists may say how much they've achieved: women were given the equal rights with men and they are having high-paid jobs, conquering new fields. But still the attitude of the society towards working mothers, businesswomen, etc., is a subject to change. Although the rights were given, many men still see women as housewives. At the same time, due to the opened career possibilities, women delaying having kids and marriage which lowered the birth rate. But feminism has undoubtly achieved its main goal women now can decide what they want to do with their lives.

FEMINISM AND SEXISM

While Western feminists and Western theoretical models of feminism have done a commendable job of deconstructing several age-old binaries that have characterised dominant philosophical and political thinking on gender, what is remarkable is the continued existence and even valorisation of the dichotomy of the West and 'the Rest' in their discourse. Readers on feminist theories, even if they claim to give 'multicultural' or 'global' perspectives on women's studies, are still dominated by Western debates and taxonomies. Feminist perspectives from the global South, if included at all.

The implication is that there is uniformity or even agreement on what feminism means in these very diverse cultures of the global South. Different geographies and histories are conflated until difference is lost and one 'third world feminism' becomes interchangeable with another, collapsing into one theoretical model the multiple struggles of very different women under very different conditions. Even in collections that forefront non-Western feminisms, the incredible range, complexities and contested nature of 'feminisms' within different national histories is reduced to a singular unitary voice. Maitrayee Chaudhuri's collection Feminism in India challenges this reduction of local feminisms.

Tracing the history of the concept of feminism from colonial times to contemporary India, the anthology explores the infinite variety of Indian feminisms and their theoretical trajectories. As Chaudhuri says in her painstakingly thorough and methodical introduction, the articles chosen for inclusion outline the contours of feminist thought in India and its development into, if not one coherent framework, at least a dialogic body of work. The taxonomy of feminist theory usually deployed in the West delineates the categories of liberal, Marxist, socialist and black feminisms. Feminist writings in India can neither be pigeonholed into these categories nor be seen to follow the same developmental paths. Yet there has always been a continual engagement with Western theoretical positions not least because people in India have always lived in a world informed by Western reformist ideas such as liberalism and feminism. Thus, Chaudhuri rejects claims that feminism in India has been a Western import. Rather, she says, ideas about women's rights and gender construction have always been debated in India, but differently. Though there has been a great degree of variance in this theorising both historically and within different women's social movements today, one aspect that runs through all the work is the fact that feminism in India has always had to negotiate around and distinguish itself from Western discourses. As scholars and activists from different parts of the global South have argued, non- Western writers may choose to engage with non-Western thought and praxis.

But no such choice exists for those working and writing in the peripheries given that, to use Arundhati Roy's felicitous phrase, we are all subjects of empire. Hence, Chaudhuri flatly states 'There is no turning away from our engagement with the West'. This assertion is used by Chaudhuri to justify her inclusion in the anthology of writings from the late nineteenth-century onwards. Because feminism as we know it today, she argues, is a product of the modern entity of nation and nationhood, and because colonialism recast many of India's traditional hierarchies, she excludes any pre-colonial writing on gender from the text. This is one of the few flaws in this otherwise significant anthology.

As Tharu and Lalita's landmark collection of women writings in India has shown, there was a prolific exchange of ideas about gender construction and gender norms well before the late 1800s when Tarabai Shinde is supposed to have penned 'A Comparison of Men and Women.' Shinde included in the second section of Chaudhuri's book, is remarkable for its discussions of the construction of gender norms as a radical critique of patriarchy. Seen as India's pioneering feminist literary critic, Shinde draws links between colonialism and the commodification of women's bodies. In contrast to this polemical piece from an upper-caste Hindu woman is the position of the Oxford educated Parsi Christian reformer Cornelia Sorabji who saw education as the main means by which social transformation of women could be undertaken. Despite her legal training as a barrister in England, Sorabji argued that it was not law but education that could be the panacea sought by reformers attempting to end the practice of child marriage. Rokeya Sakhawat Hossain, a Bengali Muslim writer, very popular in her time. Her 'Sultana's Dream' is a feminist utopia which envisions a world where women are in charge of the public sphere. All three essays in this section work as significant counter-narratives to Orientalist historiography which posited brown women in the colonies as helpless and ignorant..

The third section of the book takes up the double engagement with national identity and the woman question. It is through reading the selections included here that one can surmise the difficult choices facing women during the period of the nationalist struggles: whether or not to join the national movement; whether or not to support freedom of religion or freedom of women – issues seen as antithetical to one another. Rather than give contemporary commentaries on nationalist texts, Chaudhuri lets historical documents speak for themselves. The 1931 'Karachi Resolution' on what 'swaraj' or 'self rule' in free India would entail, reads more impressively than the U.S. Bill of Rights. However, the gender issue is still marginalised as evidenced by the fact that only one of the resolutions expressly mentions protecting women's rights.

The 1947 report on 'Women's Role in a Planned Economy' is accompanied by a contextualised commentary by Leela Kasturi who lays out in great detail the lines along which a post-colonial India would dedicate itself to women's freedom and equality in a plural, multi-religious, multicultural society. Property rights, alimony, custody rights, and child maintenance were all detailed in this remarkable document. The largest and the most mainstream women's organisation in India at this time was the All India Women's Conference. Founded in 1927, it was many-layered and always attempted to reflect the regional diversity of the movement. What would constitute the nation? What would be the role of women in independent India? What would the role of women be in the process of nation-building itself ? These discussions were fraught with divisions that spoke to religious, caste and other fissures within Indian society. If feminist writing during twentieth century colonial India was characterised by societal hierarchies and a need to demarcate an Indian identity, feminist debates in post-colonial India dealt with ways in which feminist politics was practised. A section on 'Feminism in Independent India' includes some seminal essays that have interrogated both the connections and divergences within Left politics and feminist politics on issues such as agrarian land reform and workers' rights. Well known contemporary feminist thinkers and organisers like Gail Omvedt and Ilina Sen reiterate the need to re-theorise the fundamental causes of women's oppression in post-independent India. The sometimes complete disenfranchisement of the rural poor raises fundamental questions about gendered power relations in society. Sen's essay also discusses some of the Indian women's movements much celebrated in the West such as the environmental movement called 'Chipko' and the labour and cooperative credit movement called SEWA. Both these and other struggles challenged the fundamental tenets of the national developmental policy which was predicated on rapid industrialisation at the expense of communities whose lives and livelihoods depended on land and forests. These readings show that since independence much feminist activism and theorising has been geared at developing alternatives to existing state policy and redefining the enfranchisement and empowerment of women.

But what about the poorest sections of the society – the 'dalits'? The last essay in this section shows that the language of class cannot be ignored in any discussion of gender. Sharmila Rege concentrates on non-brahminical reconceptualisations of the feminist agenda in contemporary India. Her urging to reformulate the purely upper-caste historiographies could lead to more nuanced and dialectical understanding of gendered India. While this section is the thinnest, comprising only three essays, it is perhaps the richest for anyone wishing to learn about the key debates and concerns of grassroots feminist organising in contemporary India. This section of the book alone provides an excellent overview of the multiplicity of voices that introductory texts on global feminism ignore. Surprisingly, the next section of the book – 'Challenges to Feminism' – dealing with the impact of the politics of the Hindu Right, the Hindutva movement and of globalisation, is the least nuanced and least satisfactory section of the anthology.

Many of the five essays in this section deal with concerns of post-structuralist feminists, namely representations of gender and the gendered subject positions manufactured through available popular discourses. Women's studies and economics volumes have documented well the ways in which financial institutions such as the International Monetary Fund and the World Bank have actively appropriated and exploited both the language and agenda of feminism to further their goals of privatisation and marketisation. In reference to India, global economic policy documents have linked women's development and the nation's development in such a way that women are constructed as 'good' subjects because of their thrift and diligent labour. This, by contrast, pits them against those deemed 'bad' subjects by these international 'aid' agencies, namely their unruly men. This subject position created by discourses emanating from globalisation does not just interpellate rural women but also urban upper-class women, who are seen as liberated only if and when they entire the global market system as highly individualised conspicuous consumers.

Whether analysing the huge upsurge in public discourses selling the idea of beauty queens as liberated empowered femininity, print ads that co-opt the language of radical feminism or magazine editorials that equate modernity with conspicuous consumption, the selections all demonstrate the cooptation of the language of feminism by mainstream media and the coordinated backlash against genuine feminist positions. While the readings of popular vernacular press are useful in understanding how globalisation and its offer of a particular model of modernity are negotiated by women in contemporary India, I would have preferred the inclusion of at least one article based on reception studies or audience analysis. In other words, the issue of globalisation of culture is not just a matter of academic interest. It has impacted in real terms the ways in which women construct a political identity using cultural icons. How has the puncturing of cultural boundaries affected this process? How are hybrid identities disrupting the search for a peculiarly and specifically 'Indian' feminist identity? The impetus for the whole volume seems to be dictated by this search for the Indian roots of feminism and the possibilities of an 'authentic' or 'indigenous' feminism. The first and last sections of the book take up these concerns in innovative ways. While the essays in the opening pages of the book lay out the basics of feminism demonstrating the extent of feminist commitments in India and the need for the theorisation of sexuality within feminist formulations, they also provide an understanding of the 'anti-feminist' position and the reluctance of a vast number of Indians to use the 'F-word.' Madhu Kishwar's landmark essay 'Why I Do Not Call Myself a Feminist' is just one voice in the struggle for an indigenous feminism that has raged on in India from the colonial times.

The woman question in India historically has always been linked to anti-imperialist struggles whether for nationhood or an 'authentic' Indian identity. Much of theorising of Indian feminism has articulated the national question with the 'sanitised' image of Hindu upper-caste women. The construction of a nationalist rhetoric that erased internal differences has been tantamount to emptying India's history of all its internal conflicts. 'It is at once a claim for a distinct non-Western identity and a brushing away of internal differences,' Chaudhuri asserts.

In fact one of the most significant contributions of feminist theorising in the last two decades in India has been a sustained critique of essentialist notions of both the Indian nation and woman. This quest for indigeneity has opened up political possibilities to engage with tradition and that are antithetical to fundamentalist assertions. In the last section of the book, Vidyut Bhagat explores the concept of tradition and she uses Marathi folklore to open up radical possibilities for the future of Indian feminism. Her essay, useful as it is, reminded me of Frantz Fanon's warning that a return to 'tradition' paradoxically might also limit efforts at liberation because it re-inscribes an essentialist, absolute and fixed notion of culture and tradition. This caution is perhaps also expressed by Rajeshwari Sunder Rajan in her essay on goddess-inspired Hindu feminism. As she says, this tradition has not only marginalised and alienated women in minority communities, but has also opened by possibilities of further exploitation of these very communities by the Hindu Right and the demarcation of more restrictive and repressive cultural lines. All the essays in the opening and last sections speak to each other, contesting the assumptions of each writer in a truly dialogic way. The end result is a nuanced conceptualisation of Indian feminisms.

As Oyeronke Oyewumi has written in the context of African feminisms, much critical writing by feminist scholars from the global South has been appropriated and tokenised in Western academia. She and many others have pointed out that this 'objectification' is predicated on the silencing of third world voices in the articulation of their own realities; this despite the proliferation of 'multicultural,' 'multiracial' and 'transnational' sections in women's studies and feminist anthologies.

Maitrayee Chaudhuri's collection deconstructs this objectification of 'third world' feminisms and reconstructs a plural, contradictory, complex notion of what feminist paradigms mean in India. The anthology demonstrates that the heterogeneity of Indian experience and the ever-changing gender relations has necessitated the articulation of multiple feminisms and multiple theoretical frameworks striated with common concerns. These formulations have developed and transformed over time in response to the material realities of daily conditions of existence, ideological sensitivity to gender issues, the linguistic and political competencies, and historical events. Given that the articles are written, not by U.S.-based scholarly academics writing about India but, by activists and thinkers grounded in India and involved in its myriad feminist political battles, this book should be seen as a definitive work on gender scholarship in India.

PROBLEMS WITH THE SEX/GENDER DISTINCTION

An underlying metaphysical perspective on gender: *gender realism*. That is, women as a group are assumed to share some characteristic feature, experience, common condition or criterion that defines their gender and the possession of which makes some individuals women (as opposed to, say, men). *All* women are thought to differ from *all* men in this respect (or respects). For example, MacKinnon thought that being treated in sexually objectifying ways is the common condition that defines women's gender and what women *as women* share. All women differ from all men in this respect. Further, pointing out females who are not sexually objectified does not provide a counter example to MacKinnon's view. Being sexually objectified is *constitutive of* being a woman; a female who escapes sexual objectification, then, would not count as a woman.

One may want to critique the three accounts outlined by rejecting the particular details of each account. A more thorough-going critique has been levelled at the general metaphysical perspective of gender realism that underlies these positions. It has come under sustained attack on two grounds: first, that it fails to take into account racial, cultural and class differences between women (particularity argument); second, that it posits a normative ideal of womanhood (normativity argument).

PARTICULARITY ARGUMENT

Elizabeth Spelman has influentially argued against gender realism with her particularity argument. Roughly, gender realists mistakenly assume that gender is constructed independently of race, class, ethnicity and nationality. If gender were separable from, for example, race and class in this manner, all women would experience womanhood in the same way. And this is clearly false.

For instance, Harris and Stone criticise MacKinnon's view, that sexual objectification is the common condition that defines women's gender, for failing to take into account differences in women's backgrounds that shape their sexuality. The history of racist oppression illustrates that during slavery black women were hypersexualized and thought to be always sexually available whereas white women were thought to be pure and sexually virtuous. In fact, the rape of a black woman was thought to be impossible. So, (the argument goes) sexual objectification cannot serve as the common condition for womanhood since it varies considerably depending on one's race and class.

For Spelman, the perspective of white solipsism underlies gender realists' mistake. They assumed that all women share some golden nugget of womanness and that the features constitutive of such a nugget are the same for all women regardless of their particular cultural backgrounds. Next, white Western middle-class feminists accounted for the shared features simply by reflecting on the cultural features that condition *their* gender as women thus supposing that the womanness underneath the Black woman's skin is a white woman's, and deep down inside the Latina woman is an Anglo woman waiting to burst through an obscuring cultural shroud. In so doing, Spelman claims, white middle-class Western feminists passed off their particular view of gender as a metaphysical truth thereby privileging some women while marginalizing others. In failing to see the importance of race and class in gender construction, white middle-class Western feminists conflated the condition of one group of women with the condition of all.

Betty Friedan's well-known work is a case in point of white solipsism. Friedan saw domesticity as the main vehicle of gender oppression and called upon women in general to find jobs outside the home. But she failed to realize that women from less privileged backgrounds, often poor and non-white, already worked outside the home to support their families. Friedan's suggestion, then, was applicable only to a particular sub-group of women (white middle-class Western housewives). But it was mistakenly taken to apply to all women's lives a mistake that was generated by Friedan's failure to take women's racial and class differences into account.

Spelman further holds that since social conditioning creates femininity and societies (and sub-groups) that condition it differ from one another, femininity must be differently conditioned in different societies. For her, females become not simply women but particular kinds of women: white working-class women, black middle-class women, poor Jewish women, wealthy aristocratic European women, and so on.

This line of thought has been extremely influential in feminist philosophy. For instance, Young holds that Spelman has *definitively* shown that gender realism is untenable. Mikkola argues that this isn't so. The arguments Spelman makes do not undermine the idea that there is some characteristic feature, experience, common condition or criterion that defines women's gender; they simply point out that some particular ways of cashing out what defines womanhood are misguided. So, although Spelman is right to reject those accounts that falsely take the feature that conditions white middle-class Western feminists' gender to condition women's gender in general, this leaves open the possibility that women *qua* women do share something that defines their gender.

NORMATIVITY ARGUMENT

Judith Butler critiques the sex/gender distinction on two grounds. She critiques gender realism with her normativity argument; she also holds that the sex/gender distinction is unintelligible. Butler's normativity argument is not straightforwardly directed at the metaphysical perspective of gender realism, but rather at its *political* counterpart: identity politics. This is a form of political mobilization based on membership in some group (*e.g.*, racial, ethnic, cultural, gender) and group membership is thought to be delimited by some common experiences, conditions or features that define the group. Feminist identity politics, then, presupposes gender realism in that feminist politics is said to be mobilized around women as a group (or category) where membership in this group is fixed by some condition, experience or feature that women supposedly share and that defines their gender.

Butler's normativity argument makes two claims. The first is akin to Spelman's particularity argument: unitary gender notions fail to take differences amongst women into account thus failing to recognise the multiplicity of cultural, social, and political intersections in which the concrete array of women are constructed. In their attempt to undercut biologically deterministic ways of defining what it means to be a woman, feminists in advertedly created new socially constructed accounts of supposedly shared femininity. Butler's second claim is that such false gender realist accounts are normative. That is, in their attempt to fix feminism's subject matter, feminists unwittingly defined the term woman in a way that implies there is some correct way to be gendered a woman. That the definition of the term woman is fixed supposedly operates as a policing force which generates and legitimizes certain practices, experiences, etc., and curtails and delegitimizes others. Following this line of thought, one could say that, for instance, Chodorow's view of gender suggests that real women have feminine personalities and that *these* are the women feminism should be concerned about. If one does not exhibit a distinctly feminine personality, the implication is that one is not really a member of women's category nor does one properly qualify for feminist political representation.

Butler's second claim is based on her view that identity categories [like that of women] are never merely descriptive, but always normative, and as such, exclusionary. That is, the mistake of those feminists Butler critiques was not that they provided the incorrect definition of woman. Rather, (the argument goes) their mistake was to attempt to define the term woman at all. Butler's view is that woman can never be defined in a way that does not prescribe some unspoken normative requirements (like having a feminine personality) that women should conform to. Butler takes this to be a feature of terms like woman that purport to pick out (what she calls) identity categories. She seems to assume that woman can never be used in a non-ideological way and that it will always encode conditions that are not satisfied by everyone we think of as women. Some explanation for this comes from Butler's view that all processes of drawing categorical distinctions involve evaluative and normative commitments; these in turn involve the exercise of power and reflect the conditions of those who are socially powerful.

In order to better understand Butler's critique, consider her account of gender performativity. For her, standard feminist accounts take gendered individuals to have some essential properties *qua* gendered individuals or a gender core by virtue of which one is either a man or a woman. This view assumes that women and men, *qua* women and men, are bearers of various essential and accidental attributes where the former secure gendered persons' persistence through time as so gendered. But according to Butler this view is false: (a) there are no such essential properties, and (b) gender is an illusion maintained by prevalent power structures. First, feminists are said to think that genders are socially constructed in that they have the following essential attributes: women are females with feminine behavioural traits, being heterosexuals whose desire is directed at men; men are males with masculine behavioural traits, being heterosexuals whose desire is directed at women. These are the attributes necessary for gendered individuals and those that enable women and men to persist through time *as* women and men. Individuals have intelligible genders if they exhibit this sequence of traits in a coherent manner (where sexual desire follows from sexual orientation that in turn follows from feminine/masculine behaviours thought to follow from biological sex). Social forces in general deem individuals who exhibit *incoherent* gender sequences (like lesbians) to be doing their gender wrong and they actively discourage such sequencing of traits, for instance, via name-calling and overt homophobic discrimination. Think back to what was said above: having a certain conception of what women are like that mirrors the conditions of socially powerful (white, middle-class, heterosexual, Western) women functions to marginalize and police those who do not fit this conception.

These gender cores, supposedly encoding the above traits, however, are nothing more than illusions created by ideals and practices that seek to render gender uniform through heterosexism, the view that heterosexuality is natural and homosexuality is deviant. Gender cores are constructed *as if* they somehow naturally belong to women and men thereby creating gender dimorphism or the belief that one must be either a masculine male or a feminine female. But gender dimorphism only serves a heterosexist social order by implying that since women and men are sharply opposed, it is natural to sexually desire the *opposite* sex or gender.

Further, being feminine and desiring men (for instance) are standardly assumed to be expressions of one's gender as a woman. Butler denies this and holds that gender is really performative.

It is not a stable identity or locus of agency from which various acts follow; rather, gender is and instituted and through a *stylized repetition of* [habitual] *acts*": through wearing certain gender-coded clothing, walking and sitting in certain gender-coded ways, styling one's hair in gender-coded manner and so on. Gender is not something one is, it is something one does; it is a sequence of acts, a doing rather than a being. And repeatedly engaging in feminising and masculinising acts congeals gender thereby making people falsely think of gender as something they naturally *are*. Gender only comes into being through these gendering acts: a female who has sex with men does not *express* her gender as a woman. This activity (amongst others) *makes* her gendered a woman.

The constitutive acts that gender individuals create genders as compelling illusion[s]. Our gendered classification scheme is a *strong pragmatic construction*: social factors wholly determine our use of the scheme and the scheme fails to represent accurately any facts of the matter. People think that there are true and real genders, and those deemed to be doing their gender wrong are not socially sanctioned. But, genders are true and real only to the extent that they are performed. It does not make sense, then, to say of a male-to-female transvestite that s/he is *really* a man who only *appears* to be a woman. Instead, males dressing up and acting in ways that are associated with femininity show that [as Butler suggests] being feminine is just a matter of doing certain activities. As a result, the transvestite's gender is just as real or true as anyone else's who is a traditionally feminine female or masculine male. Without heterosexism that compels people to engage in certain gendering acts, there would not be any genders at all. And ultimately the aim should be to abolish norms that compel people to act in these gendering ways.

For Butler, given that gender is performative, the appropriate response to feminist identity politics involves two things. First, feminists should understand woman as open-ended and a term in process, a becoming, a constructing that cannot rightfully be said to originate or end and it is open to intervention and resignification. That is, feminists should not try to define woman at all. Second, the category of women ought not to be the foundation of feminist politics. Rather, feminists should focus on providing an account of how power functions and shapes our understandings of womanhood not only in the society at large but also within the feminist movement.

SEX CLASSIFICATION

Many people, including many feminists, have ordinarily taken sex ascriptions to be solely a matter of biology with no social or cultural dimension. It is commonplace to think that there are only two sexes and that biological sex classifications are utterly unproblematic.

By contrast, some feminists have argued that sex classifications are not unproblematic and that they are not solely a matter of biology. In order to make sense of this, it is helpful to distinguish object- and idea-construction: social forces can be said to construct certain kinds of objects (*e.g.*, sexed bodies or gendered individuals) and certain kinds of ideas (*e.g.*, sex or gender concepts). First, take the object-construction of sexed bodies. Secondary sex characteristics, or the physiological and biological features commonly associated with males and females, are affected by social practices. In some societies, females' lower social status has meant that they have been fed less and so, the lack of nutrition has had the effect of making them smaller in size. Uniformity in muscular shape, size and strength within sex categories is not caused entirely by biological factors, but depends heavily on cxcrcise opportunities: if males and females were allowed the same exercise opportunities and equal encouragement to exercise, it is thought that bodily dimorphism would diminish. A number of medical phenomena involving bones (like osteoporosis) have social causes directly related to expectations about gender, women's diet and their exercise opportunities. These examples suggest that physiological features thought to be sex-specific traits not affected by social and cultural factors are, after all, to some extent products of social conditioning. Social conditioning, then, shapes our biology.

Second, take the idea-construction of sex concepts. Our concept of *sex* is said to be a product of social forces in the sense that what counts as sex is shaped by social meanings. Standardly, those with XX-chromosomes, ovaries that produce large egg cells, female genitalia, a relatively high proportion of female hormones, and other secondary sex characteristics (relatively small body size, less body hair) count as biologically female.

Those with XY-chromosomes, testes that produce small sperm cells, male genitalia, a relatively high proportion of male hormones and other secondary sex traits (relatively large body size, significant amounts of body hair) count as male. This understanding is fairly recent. The prevalent scientific view from Ancient Greeks until the late 18th century, did not consider female and male sexes to be distinct categories with specific traits; instead, a one-sex model held that males and females were members of the same sex category. Females' genitals were thought to be the same as males' but simply directed inside the body; ovaries and testes (for instance) were referred to by the same term and whether the term referred to the former or the latter was made clear by the context. It was not until the late 1700s that scientists began to think of female and male anatomies as radically different moving away from the one-sex model of a single sex spectrum to the (nowadays prevalent) two-sex model of sexual dimorphism.

Fausto-Sterling has recently argued that this two-sex model isn't straightforward either. She estimates that 1.7 per cent of population fail to neatly fall within the usual sex classifications possessing various combinations of different sex characteristics. In her earlier work, she claimed that intersexed individuals make up (at least) three further sex classes: herms who possess one testis and one ovary; merms who possess testes, some aspects of female genitalia but no ovaries; and ferms who have ovaries, some aspects of male genitalia but no testes. Recognition of intersexes suggests that feminists (and society at large) are wrong to think that humans are either female or male.

To illustrate further the idea-construction of sex, consider the case of the athlete Maria Patiño. Patiño has female genitalia, has always considered herself to be female and was considered so by others. However, she was discovered to have XY chromosomes and was barred from competing in women's sports. Patiño's genitalia were at odds with her chromosomes and the latter were taken to determine her sex. Patiño successfully fought to be recognised as a female athlete arguing that her chromosomes alone were not sufficient to *not* make her female. Intersexes, like Patiño, illustrate that our understandings of sex differ and suggest that there is no immediately obvious way to settle what sex amounts to purely biologically or scientifically. Deciding what sex is involves evaluative judgements that are influenced by social factors.

Insofar as our cultural conceptions affect our understandings of sex, feminists must be much more careful about sex classifications and rethink what sex amounts to. More specifically, intersexed people illustrate that sex traits associated with females and males need not always go together and that individuals can have some mixture of these traits.

This suggest to Stone that *sex* is a cluster concept: it is sufficient to satisfy enough of the sex features that tend to cluster together in order to count as being of a particular sex. But, one need not satisfy *all* of those features or some arbitrarily chosen supposedly *necessary* sex feature, like chromosomes. This makes sex a matter of degree and sex classifications should take place on a spectrum: one can be more or less female/male but there is no sharp distinction between the two. Further, intersexes (along with trans people) are located at the centre of the sex spectrum and in many cases their sex will be indeterminate.

SEX AND GENDER DISTINCTION

In addition to arguing against identity politics and for gender performativity, Butler holds that distinguishing *biological* sex from *social* gender is unintelligible. For her, both are socially constructed: If the immutable character of sex is contested, perhaps this construct called 'sex' is as culturally constructed as gender; indeed, perhaps it was always already gender, with the consequence that the distinction between sex and gender turns out to be no distinction at all. Butler makes two different claims in the passage cited: that sex is a social construction, and that sex is gender. To unpack her view, consider the two claims in turn. First, the idea that sex is a social construct, for Butler, boils down to the view that our sexed bodies are also performative and, so, they have no ontological status apart from the various acts which constitute [their] reality. *Prima facie*, this implausibly implies that female and male bodies do not have independent existence and that if gendering activities ceased, so would physical bodies. This is not Butler's claim; rather, her position is that bodies viewed as the material foundations on which gender is constructed, are themselves constructed *as if* they provide such material foundations. Cultural conceptions about gender figure in the very apparatus of production whereby sexes themselves are established.

For Butler, sexed bodies never exist outside social meanings and how we understand gender shapes how we understand sex. Sexed bodies are not empty matter on which gender is constructed and sex categories are not picked out on the basis of objective features of the world. Instead, our sexed bodies are themselves *discursively constructed*: they are the way they are, at least to a substantial extent, because of what is attributed to sexed bodies and how they are classified. Sex assignment (calling someone female or male) is normative. When the doctor calls a newly born infant a girl or a boy, s/he is not making a descriptive claim, but a normative one. In fact, the doctor is performing an illocutionary speech act. In effect, the doctor's utterance makes infants into girls or boys. We, then, engage in activities that make it seem as if sexes naturally come in two and that being female or male is an objective feature of the world, rather than being a consequence of certain constitutive acts (that is, rather than being performative). And this is what Butler means in saying that physical bodies never exist outside cultural and social meanings, and that sex is as socially constructed as gender. She does not deny that physical bodies exist. But, she takes our understanding of this existence to be a *product* of social conditioning: social conditioning makes the existence of physical bodies intelligible to us by discursively constructing sexed bodies through certain constitutive acts.

For Butler, sex assignment is always in some sense oppressive. Again, this appears to be because of Butler's general suspicion of classification: sex classification can never be merely descriptive but always has a normative element reflecting evaluative claims of those who are powerful. Conducting a feminist genealogy of the body (or examining why sexed bodies are thought to come naturally as female and male), then, should ground feminist practice. Feminists should examine and uncover ways in which social construction and certain acts that constitute sex shape our understandings of sexed bodies, what kinds of meanings bodies acquire and which practices and illocutionary speech acts make our bodies into sexes. Doing so enables feminists to identity how sexed bodies are socially constructed in order to resist such construction.

However, given what was said above, it is far from obvious what we should make of Butler's claim that sex was always already gender. Stone takes this to mean that sex *is* gender but goes on to question it arguing that the social construction of both sex and gender does not make sex identical to gender. According to Stone, it would be more accurate for Butler to say that claims about sex *imply* gender norms. That is, many claims about sex traits (like females are physically weaker than males) actually carry implications about how women and men are expected to behave. To some extent the claim describes certain facts. But, it also implies that females are not expected to do much heavy lifting and that they would probably not be good at it. So, claims about sex are not identical to claims about gender; rather, they imply claims about gender norms.

The Sex/Gender Distinction Useful

Some feminists hold that the sex/gender distinction is not useful. For a start, it is thought to reflect politically problematic dualistic thinking that undercuts feminist aims: the distinction is taken to reflect and replicate androcentric oppositions between (for instance) mind/body, culture/nature and reason/emotion that have been used to justify women's oppression. The thought is that in oppositions like these, one term is always superior to the other and that the devalued term is usually associated with women. For instance, human subjectivity and agency are identified with the mind but since women are usually identified with their bodies, they are devalued as human subjects and agents. The opposition between mind and body is said to further map on to other distinctions, like reason/emotion, culture/nature, rational/irrational, where one side of each distinction is devalued (one's bodily features are usually valued less that one's mind, rationality is usually valued more than irrationality) and women are associated with the devalued terms: they are thought to be closer to bodily features and nature than men, to be irrational, emotional and so on.

This is said to be evident (for instance) in job interviews. Men are treated as gender-neutral persons and not asked whether they are planning to take time off to have a family. By contrast, that women face such queries illustrates that they are associated more closely than men with bodily features to do with procreation. The opposition between mind and body, then, is thought to map onto the opposition between men and women.

Now, the mind/body dualism is also said to map onto the sex/gender distinction. The idea is that gender maps onto mind, sex onto body. Although not used by those endorsing this view, the basic idea can be summed by the slogan Gender is between the ears, sex is between the legs: the implication is that, while sex is immutable, gender is something individuals have control over it is something we can alter and change through individual choices. However, since women are said to be more closely associated with biological features (and so, to map onto the body side of the mind/body distinction) and men are treated as gender-neutral persons (mapping onto the mind side), the implication is that man equals gender, which is associated with mind and choice, freedom from body, autonomy, and with the public real; while woman equals sex, associated with the body, reproduction, natural rhythms and the private realm.

This is said to render the sex/gender distinction inherently repressive and to drain it of any potential for emancipation: rather than facilitating gender role choice for women, it actually functions to reinforce their association with body, sex, and involuntary natural rhythms. Contrary to what feminists like Rubin argued, the sex/gender distinction cannot be used as a theoretical tool that dissociates conceptions of womanhood from biological and reproductive features.

Moi has further argued that the sex/gender distinction is useless given certain theoretical goals. This is not to say that it is utterly worthless; according to Moi, the sex/gender distinction worked well to show that the historically prevalent biological determinism was false. However, for her, the distinction does no useful work when it comes to producing a good theory of subjectivity and a concrete, historical understanding of what it means to be a woman (or a man) in a given society. That is, the 1960s distinction understood sex as fixed by biology without any cultural or historical dimensions. This understanding, however, ignores lived experiences and embodiment as aspects of womanhood (and manhood) by separating sex from gender and insisting that womanhood is to do with the latter. Rather, embodiment must be included in one's theory that tries to figure out what it is to be a woman (or a man).

Recently, Mikkola has argued that the sex/gender distinction, which underlies views like Rubin's and MacKinnon's, has certain unintuitive and undesirable ontological commitments that render the distinction politically unhelpful. First, claiming that gender is socially constructed implies that the existence of women and men is a mind-dependent matter. This suggests that we can do away with women and men simply by altering some social practices, conventions or conditions on which gender depends (whatever those are). However, ordinary social agents find this unintuitive given that (ordinarily) sex and gender are not distinguished. Second, claiming that gender is a product of oppressive social forces suggests that doing away with women and men should be feminism's political goal. But this harbours ontologically undesirable commitments since many ordinary social agents view their gender to be a source of positive value. So, feminism seems to want to do away with something that should not be done away with, which is unlikely to motivate social agents to act in ways that aim at gender justice. Given these problems, Mikkola argues that feminists should give up the distinction on practical political grounds.

SEX AND GENDER

Although the terms *sex* and *gender* are sometimes used interchangeably and do in fact complement each other, they non-etheless refer to different aspects of what it means to be a woman or man in any society. SexsexThe anatomical and other biological differences between females and males that are determined at the moment of conception and develop in the womb and throughout childhood and adolescence. refers to *the anatomical and other biological differences between females and males that are determined at the moment of conception and develop in the womb and throughout childhood and adolescence*. Females, of course, have two X chromosomes, while males have one X chromosome and one Y chromosome.

From this basic genetic difference spring other biological differences. The first to appear are the different genitals that boys and girls develop in the womb and that the doctor and parents look for when a baby is born so that the momentous announcement, "It's a boy!" or "It's a girl!" can be made. The genitalia are called primary sex characteristicsprimary sex characteristicsAnatomical and other biological differences between females and males that begin developing in the womb., while the other differences that develop during puberty are called secondary sex characteristicssecondary sex characteristicsBiological differences between females and males that emerge during puberty. and stem from hormonal differences between the two sexes. In this difficult period of adolescents' lives, boys generally acquire deeper voices, more body hair, and more muscles from their flowing testosterone. Girls develop breasts and wider hips and begin menstruating as nature prepares them for possible pregnancy and childbirth. For better or worse, these basic biological differences between the sexes affect many people's perceptions of what it means to be female or male, as we shall soon discuss.

BIOLOGY AND GENDER

Several biological explanations for gender roles exist, and we discuss two of the most important ones here. One explanation is from the related fields of sociobiology and evolutionary psychology and argues an evolutionary basis for traditional gender roles. Scholars advocating this view reason as follows. In prehistoric societies, few social roles existed. A major role centered on relieving hunger by hunting or gathering food. The other major role centered on bearing and nursing children. Because only women could perform this role, they were also the primary caretakers for children for several years after birth. And because women were frequently pregnant, their roles as mothers confined them to the home for most of their adulthood. Meanwhile, men were better suited than women for hunting because they were stronger and quicker than women. In prehistoric societies, then, biology was indeed destiny: for biological reasons, men in effect worked outside the home while women stayed at home with their children. Evolutionary reasons also explain why men are more violent than women. In prehistoric times, men who were more willing to commit violence against and even kill other men would "win out" in the competition for female mates.

They thus were more likely than less violent men to produce offspring, who would then carry these males' genetic violent tendencies. By the same token, men who were prone to rape women were more likely to produce offspring, who would then carry these males' "rape genes." This early process guaranteed that rape tendencies would be biologically transmitted and thus provides a biological basis for the amount of rape that occurs today. If the human race evolved along these lines, sociobiologists and evolutionary psychologists continue, natural selection favored those societies where men were stronger, braver, and more aggressive and where women were more fertile and nurturing.

Such traits over the millennia became fairly instinctual, meaning that men's and women's biological natures evolved differently. Men became, by nature, more assertive, daring, and violent than women, and women are, by nature, more gentle, nurturing, and maternal than men. To the extent this is true, these scholars add, traditional gender roles for women and men make sense from an evolutionary standpoint, and attempts to change them go against the sexes' biological natures. This in turn implies that existing gender inequality must continue because it is rooted in biology. As the title of a book presenting the evolutionary psychology argument summarizes this implication, "biology at work: rethinking sexual equality". Critics challenge the evolutionary explanation on several grounds. First, much greater gender variation in behaviour and attitudes existed in prehistoric times than the evolutionary explanation assumes. Second, even if biological differences did influence gender roles in prehistoric times, these differences are largely irrelevant in today's world, in which, for example, physical strength is not necessary for survival. Third, human environments throughout the millennia have simply been too diverse to permit the simple, straightforward biological development that the evolutionary explanation assumes. Fourth, evolutionary arguments implicitly justify existing gender inequality by implying the need to confine women and men to their traditional roles. Recent anthropological evidence also challenges the evolutionary argument that men's tendency to commit violence, including rape, was biologically transmitted. This evidence instead finds that violent men have trouble finding female mates who would want them and that the female mates they find and the children they produce are often killed by rivals to the men.

The recent evidence also finds those rapists' children are often abandoned and then die. As one anthropologist summarizes the rape evidence, "The likelihood that rape is an evolved adaptation extremely low. It just wouldn't have made sense for men in the to use rape as a reproductive strategy, so the argument that it's preprogrammed into us doesn't hold up". A second biological explanation for traditional gender roles centers on hormones and specifically on testosterone, the so-called male hormone. One of the most important differences between boys and girls and men and women in the United States and many other societies is their level of aggression. Simply put, males are much more physically aggressive than females and in the United States commit about 85 per cent–90 per cent of all violent crimes. Why is this so? This gender difference is often attributed to males' higher levels of testosterone.

To see whether testosterone does indeed raise aggression, investigators typically assess whether males with higher testosterone levels are more aggressive than those with lower testosterone levels. Several studies find that this is indeed the case. For example, a widely cited study of Vietnam-era male veterans found that those with higher levels of testosterone had engaged in more violent behaviour. However, this correlation does not necessarily mean that their testosterone increased their violence: as has been found in various animal species, it is also possible that their violence increased their testosterone. Because studies of human males can't for ethical and practical reasons manipulate their testosterone levels, the exact meaning of the results from these testosterone-aggression studies must remain unclear, according to a review sponsored by the National Academy of Sciences.

Another line of research on the biological basis for sex differences in aggression involves children, including some as young as ages 1 or 2, in various situations. They might be playing with each other, interacting with adults, or writing down solutions to hypothetical scenarios given to them by a researcher. In most of these studies, boys are more physically aggressive in thought or deed than girls, even at a very young age. Other studies are more experimental in nature. In one type of study, a toddler will be playing with a toy, only to have it removed by an adult.

Boys typically tend to look angry and to try to grab the toy back, while girls tend to just sit there and whimper. Because these gender differences in aggression are found at very young ages, researchers often say they must have some biological basis. However, critics of this line of research counter that even young children have already been socialized along gender lines, a point to which we return later. To the extent this is true, gender differences in children's aggression may simply reflect socialization and not biology. In sum, biological evidence for gender differences certainly exists, but its interpretation remains very controversial.

It must be weighed against the evidence, to which we next turn, of cultural variations in the experience of gender and of socialization differences by gender. One thing is clear: to the extent we accept biological explanations for gender, we imply that existing gender differences and gender inequality must continue to exist. This implication prompts many social scientists to be quite critical of the biological viewpoint. As Linda L. Lindsey notes, "Biological arguments are consistently drawn upon to justify gender inequality and the continued oppression of women." In contrast, cultural and social explanations of gender differences and gender inequality promise some hope for change. Let's examine the evidence for these explanations.

CULTURE AND GENDER

Some of the most compelling evidence against a strong biological determination of gender roles comes from anthropologists, whose work on preindustrial societies demonstrates some striking gender variation from one culture to another. This variation underscores the impact of culture on how females and males think and behave. Margaret Mead was one of the first anthropologists to study cultural differences in gender. In New Guinea she found three tribes—the Arapesh, the Mundugumor, and the Tchambuli—whose gender roles differed dramatically. In the Arapesh both sexes were gentle and nurturing. Both women and men spent much time with their children in a loving way and exhibited what we would normally call maternal behaviour. In the Arapesh, then, different gender roles did not exist, and in fact, both sexes conformed to what Americans would normally call the female gender role. The situation was the reverse among the Mundugumor.

Here both men and women were fierce, competitive, and violent. Both sexes seemed to almost dislike children and often physically punished them. In the Mundugumor society, then, different gender roles also did not exist, as both sexes conformed to what we Americans would normally call the male gender role. In the Tchambuli, Mead finally found a tribe where different gender roles did exist.

One sex was the dominant, efficient, assertive one and showed leadership in tribal affairs, while the other sex liked to dress up in frilly clothes, wear makeup, and even giggle a lot. Here, then, Mead found a society with gender roles similar to those found in the United States, but with a surprising twist. In the Tchambuli, women were the dominant, assertive sex that showed leadership in tribal affairs, while men were the ones wearing frilly clothes and makeup. Mead's research caused a firestorm in scholarly circles, as it challenged the biological view on gender that was still very popular when she went to New Guinea. In recent years, Mead's findings have been challenged by other anthropologists. Among other things, they argue that she probably painted an overly simplistic picture of gender roles in her three societies. Other anthropologists defend Mead's work and note that much subsequent research has found that gender-linked attitudes and behaviour do differ widely from one culture to another. If so, they say, the impact of culture on what it means to be a female or male cannot be ignored. Extensive evidence of this impact comes from anthropologist George Murdock, who created the Standard Cross-Cultural Sample of almost 200 preindustrial societies studied by anthropologists.

Murdock found that some tasks in these societies, such as hunting and trapping, are almost always done by men, while other tasks, such as cooking and fetching water, are almost always done by women. These patterns provide evidence for the evolutionary argument presented earlier, as they probably stem from the biological differences between the sexes. Even so there were at least some societies in which women hunted and in which men cooked and fetched water. More importantly, Murdock found much greater gender variation in several of the other tasks he studied, including planting crops, milking, and generating fires.

Men primarily performed these tasks in some societies, women primarily performed them in other societies, and in still other societies both sexes performed them equally. The gender responsibility for yet another task, weaving. Women are the primary weavers in about 61 per cent of the societies that do weaving, men are the primary weavers in 32 per cent, and both sexes do the weaving in 7 per cent of the societies. Murdock's findings illustrate how gender roles differ from one culture to another and imply they are not biologically determined. Anthropologists since Mead and Murdock have continued to investigate cultural differences in gender. Some of their most interesting findings concern gender and sexuality. Although all societies distinguish "femaleness" and "maleness," additional gender categories exist in some societies. The Native Americans known as the Mohave, for example, recognize four genders: a woman, a woman who acts like a man, a man, and a man who acts like a woman. In some societies, a third, intermediary gender category is recognized. Anthropologists call this category the berdache, who is usually a man who takes on a woman's role. This intermediary category combines aspects of both femininity and masculinity of the society in which it is found and is thus considered an androgynousandrogynousContaining aspects of both femaleness and maleness, or of both femininity and masculinity. gender. Although some people in this category are born as intersexed individuals, meaning they have genitalia of both sexes, many are born biologically as one sex or the other but adopt an androgynous identity.

An example of this intermediary gender category may be found in India, where the hirja role involves males who wear women's clothing and identify as women. The hirja role is an important part of Hindu mythology, in which androgynous figures play key roles both as humans and as gods. Today people identified by themselves and others as hirjas continue to play an important role in Hindu practices and in Indian cultural life in general. Serena Nanda calls hirjas "human beings who are neither man nor woman" and says they are thought of as "special, sacred beings" even though they are sometimes ridiculed and abused. Anthropologists have found another androgynous gender composed of women warriors in 33 Native American groups in North America.

Walter L. Williams calls these women "amazons" and notes that they dress like men and sometimes even marry women. In some tribes girls exhibit such "masculine" characteristics from childhood, while in others they may be recruited into "amazonhood." In the Kaska Indians, for example, a married couple with too many daughters would select one to "be like a man." When she was about 5 years of age, her parents would begin to dress her like a boy and have her do male tasks. Eventually she would grow up to become a hunter. The androgynous genders found by anthropologists remind us that gender is a social construction and not just a biological fact. If culture does affect gender roles, socialization is the process through which culture has this effect. What we experience as girls and boys strongly influences how we develop as women and men in terms of behaviour and attitudes. To illustrate this important dimension of gender, let's turn to the evidence on socialization.

3

Public Policy

INTRODUCTION

Public policy as and government action is generally the principled guide to action taken by the administrative or executive branches of the state with regard to a class of issues in a manner consistent with law and institutional customs. In general, the foundation is the pertinent national and substantial constitutional law and implementing legislation such as the US Federal code. Further substrates include both judicial interpretations and regulations which are generally authorised by legislation. Other scholars define it as a system of "courses of action, regulatory measures, laws, and funding priorities concerning a given topic promulgated by a governmental entity or its representatives." Public policy is commonly embodied "in constitutions, legislative acts, and judicial decisions."

In the United States, this concept refers not only to the result of policies, but more broadly to the decision-making and analysis of governmental decisions. As an academic discipline, public policy is studied by professors and students at public policy schools of major universities throughout the country. The U.S., professional association of public policy practitioners, researchers, scholars, and students is the Association for Public Policy Analysis and Management.

Shaping public policy is a complex and multifaceted process that involves the interplay of numerous individuals and interest groups competing and collaborating to influence policymakers to act in a particular way. These individuals and groups use a variety of tactics and tools to advance their aims, including advocating their positions publicly, attempting to educate supporters and opponents, and mobilizing allies on a particular issue. As an academic discipline, public policy brings in elements of many social science fields and concepts, including economics, sociology, political economy, programme evaluation, policy analysis, and public management, all as applied to problems of governmental administration, management, and operations. At the same time, the study of public policy is distinct from political science or economics, in its focus on the application of theory to practice.

While the majority of public policy degrees are master's and doctoral degrees, several universities also offer undergraduate education in public policy. Policy schools tackle policy analysis differently. The Harris School of Public Policy Studies at the University of Chicago has a more quantitative and economics approach to policy, the Heinz College at Carnegie Mellon uses computational and empirical methods, while the John F. Kennedy School of Government at Harvard University has a more political science and leadership based approach. The Indiana University School of Public and Environmental Affairs provides traditional public policy training with multidisciplinary concentrations available in the environmental sciences and non-profit management.

The Jindal School of Government and Public Policy in India offers an interdisciplinary training in public policy with a focus on the policy making processes in developing and BRIC countries. In Europe, the School of Government of LUISS Guido Carli offers a multidisciplinary approach to public policy combining economics, political sciences, new public management and policy analysis. Traditionally, the academic field of public policy focused on domestic policy.

However, the wave of economic globalisation, which ensued in the late 20th and early 21st centuries, created a need for a subset of public policy that focuses on global governance, especially as it relates to issues that transcend national borders such as climate change, terrorism, nuclear proliferation, and economic development. Consequently, many traditional public policy schools had to tweak their curricula to adjust to this new policy landscape.

DECISION METHODS FOR POLICY ANALYSIS

Displaying the impacts of policy alternatives can be done using a policy analysis matrix (PAM). As shown, a PAM provides a summary of the policy impacts for the various alternatives and examination of the matrix can reveal the tradeoffs associated with the different alternatives. Once policy alternatives have been evaluated, the next step is to decide which policy alternative should be implemented. At one extreme, comparing the policy alternatives can be relatively simple if all the policy goals can be measured using a single metric and given equal weighting. In this case, the decision method is an exercise in benefit cost analysis (BCA).

At the other extreme, the numerous goals will require the policy impacts to be expressed using a variety of metrics that are not readily comparable. In such cases, the policy analyst may draw on the concept of utility to aggregate the various goals into a single score. With the utility concept, each impact is given a weighting such that 1 unit of each weighted impact is considered to be equally valuable (or desirable) with regards to the collective well-being. Weimer and Vining also suggest that the "*go, no go*" rule can be a useful method for deciding amongst policy alternatives ^ 8. Under this decision making regime, some or all policy impacts can be assigned thresholds which are used to eliminate at least some of the policy alternatives.

In their example, one criterion "*is to minimize SO_2 emissions*" and so a threshold might be a reduction SO_2 emissions "of at least 8.0 million tons per year". As such, any policy alternative that does not meet this threshold can be removed from consideration. If only a single policy alternative satisfies all the impact thresholds then it is the one that is considered a "go" for each impact. Otherwise it might be that all but a few policy alternatives are eliminated and those that remain need to be more closely examined in terms of their trade-offs so that a decision can be made.

CASE STUDY EXAMPLE OF RATIONAL POLICY ANALYSIS APPROACH

To demonstrate the rational analysis process, let's examine the policy paper "Stimulating the use of biofuels in the European Union: Implications for climate change policy" by Lisa Ryan where the substitution of fossil fuels with biofuels has been proposed in the European Union (EU) between 2005–2010 as part of a strategy to mitigate greenhouse gas emissions from road transport, increase security of energy supply and support development of rural communities.

Considering the steps of Patton and Sawicki model, this chapter only follows components 1 to 5 of the rationalist policy analysis model:

1. Defining The Problem—the report identifies transportation fuels pose two important challenges for the European Union (EU). First, under the provisions of the Kyoto Protocol to the Climate Change Convention, the EU has agreed to an absolute cap on greenhouse gas emissions; while, at the same time increased consumption of transportation fuels has resulted in a trend of increasing greenhouse gas emissions from this source. Second, the dependence upon oil imports from the politically volatile Middle East generates concern over price fluctuations and possible interruptions in supply. Alternative fuel sources need to be used and substituted in place of fossil fuels to mitigate GHG emissions in the EU.
2. Determine the Evaluation Criteria—this policy sets Environmental impacts/benefits (reduction of GHG's as a measure to reducing climate change effects) and Economical efficiency (the costs of converting to biofuels as alternative to fossil fuels and the costs of production of biofuels from its different potential sources)as its decision criteria. However, this chapter does not exactly talk about the social impacts, this policy may have. It also does not compare the operational challenges involved between the different categories of biofuels considered.

3. Identifying Alternative Policies—The European Commission foresees that three alternative transport fuels: hydrogen, natural gas, and biofuels, will replace transport fossil fuels, each by 5 per cent by 2020.
4. Evaluating Alternative Policies—Biofuels are an alternative motor vehicle fuel produced from biological material and are promoted as a transitional step until more advanced technologies have matured. By modelling the efficiency of the biofuel options the authors compute the economic and environmental costs of each biofuel option.
5. Select The Preferred Policy—The authors suggest that the overall best biofuel comes from the sugarcane in Brazil after comparing the economic and the environmental costs. The current cost of subsidising the price difference between European biofuels and fossil fuels per tonne of CO_2 emissions saved is calculated to be □229–2000. If the production of European biofuels for transport is to be encouraged, exemption from excise duties is the instrument that incurs the least transactions costs, as no separate administrative or collection system needs to be established. A number of entrepreneurs are producing biofuels at the lower margin of the costs specified here profitably, once an excise duty rebate is given. It is likely that growth in the volume of the business will engender both economies of scale and innovation that will reduce costs substantially.

SETTING THE POLICY AGENDA

Your organisation has limited resources – time, money, people, etc. Whatever your company's intent, whatever its objectives and strategy, you can only do so much. Your policy agenda is a concession to the scarcity of resources. What resources you have, you manage well and you prioritise. The smaller the organisation, the easier it is to set a policy agenda, generally. It's with large organisations that we see more intense competition to politicise an agenda – to get preferred items on the agenda because they serve localised interests, which are easier to understand and deal with, rather than those of the entire company.

WRITING POLICY

A policy has to be easy to understand and implement. Policy statements have to be written clearly, concisely, and directly. Policies should not be open to interpretation, though this isn't always possible, especially with high-level policies. In that case, the company must identify policy experts who will be readily available to interpret policy and resolve differences. Policy writing has to be an iterative process. Policy drafts should be reviewed by a representative sample of the group or groups who will be responsiblc for implementing the policy on a daily basis.

IMPLEMENTING POLICY

People have to know that a policy exists if they're to be held accountable for it. Not only do they need to be aware of it – they should also know why the policy exists. People generally view policies as restrictions and unless it's clear where and why the policy originated – that there's a valid reason for it and that the organisation benefits – compliance will be a problem. Policies have to be communicated effectively and there needs to be a suitable introductory period to ensure compliance. People should have plenty of advance notice – give them time to learn the policy, discuss it with others, understand it, and submit their comments. When people feel like they've had a say in policy, they're more likely to comply.

ENFORCING POLICY

Given that policies are often developed in response to problems, how do you make sure the problem doesn't recur? Well, you try not to do what a lot of governmental bodies often do – you don't make policy that's unenforceable. The U.S., Congress has been doing this for years with respect to food safety, writing more laws for the FDA to enforce while hampering its ability to conduct inspections by slashing its budget. Policy has to be clear on what constitutes compliance and what happens in the event of non-compliance. There has to be a clear responsibility for ensuring compliance and imposing penalties.

REVIEWING AND UPDATING POLICY

Policies are often changed only because a noticeable event or trend occurred which forced the organisation to respond. A notable example of that is the proliferation of smartphones; so many individuals have purchased smartphones and incorporated them into their daily routines so quickly that the company can't keep up. The majority of company policies, once written and implemented, are rarely looked at again. Yet, all policies have to be reviewed on a regular basis to ensure that they reflect the business realities of the moment. A good example of that is some automakers' infatuation with the SUV, based on a policy of maximizing profit rather than giving customers what they need. Even if $140 barrels of oil and the decline in SUV sales weren't a strong enough signal to them, the automakers should have been reevaluating their policy periodically with an eye to updating it. Their hundred-year-plus histories should have told them – you either change or you have change forced on you.

PUBLIC CAMPAIGNS AND ADVOCACY

TYPICAL ACTIVITIES

Some approaches to policy influencing target large numbers of individuals, or the political debate on an issue, through public messaging and campaigning.

They might try to build up public support for a new policy, using public meetings and speeches to communicate the rationale for a proposed reform, or using television and radio to raise public awareness of an issue. This is about trying to influence change from the 'outside' track, rather than in closed meetings with decision-makers. An organisation might work through messaging in the media, public events, speeches and meetings and building national and sub-national coalitions. Such approaches often mobilise a number of initiatives at the same time.

This type of approach to policy influence has been undertaken by civil society groups worldwide for decades, working to influence national policy debates and public will. There is also a wealth of experience in public communication campaigns aimed at individual behaviour change and 'public education'. There are many ways to solicit relevant information for the running of these campaigns, but it is not easy to ascertain the precise amount of influence that a particular programme has had. With factors as multifaceted as the public dialogue on an issue, and for outcomes such as 'public attitudes and beliefs', which are affected by so many factors, distinguishing the effects of one single campaign is still extremely difficult, and there are few rigorous methods for this.

TOC, OUTCOMES AND TOOLS

In general, public campaigns hope to achieve influence either through delivering messages directly to an audience, or through placement in the media.

The importance of monitoring and understanding target audiences cannot be underestimated for this sort of work, and is crucial for the planning of a project, for strategic adaptations during the project, and for evaluation afterwards. Based on various models of behaviour change and public interest in political issues, a number of outcomes may be of relevance: awareness of an issue or campaign, perception of saliency or importance of an issue, attitudes, norms and standards of behaviour, and actual behaviour.

There are a number of ways to ascertain this information:

- *Surveys* can be used to gauge attitudes of particular audiences, and to make judgements about how these change over time and the influence of a project over them. Because of the large number of people targeted by campaigns, quasi-experimental methods can sometimes be used, given the large number of people targeted by campaigns. This would include, for example, cases where the same people are targeted a number of times, where a campaign has a staged implementation or roll-out, or where there is a clear way to determine the exposure of segments of the population. Rolling sample surveys, where a random selection of people in the target audience are surveyed at regular intervals, are another way to keep track of changes ovcr time.

- *Focus group discussions* are a key tool for under-standing the perspectives of a target audience on an issue, idea or event, and what drives that audience. If facilitated effectively, they can provide richer and deeper information than surveys, although with less information about 'coverage'. While there are less sophisticated methods to determine influence or attribution, attitudes can be assessed at different points in time, or groups could be asked for their specific opinions about a campaign.
- *Direct responses and informants* represent a 'light touch' way to track influence on a target audience. One method is to track the number of enquiries received from the audience, or the number attending public meetings. Another could be to interview individuals who are judged to be 'well placed' to assess a particular target audience.

It is often crucial to monitor the media. Increased coverage in the media is likely to help messages to get through to the target audience more consistently or more frequently, and there are a number of ways to measure this. In addition, the way in which the media presents or discusses certain issues can be crucial, as this is thought to be a strong determinant of the public attitudes on the issue.

The following tools may be useful:

- *Media tracking logs* can be simple forms that allow project staff to record how campaigns or issues are covered in the media quickly and easily. This could mean keeping quotes, newspaper cuttings, and information about date and time of reference, for example.
- *Media assessments* are more proactive, assessing the extent to which an issue/campaign is covered. This could involve tracking column inches in newspapers, air time on television or radio, or monitoring hits on a web site. These could be combined with additional information to get a richer understanding of the influence on the media, such as calculating the estimated audience figures for a programme that features the campaign, or the amount of money column inches would have cost if paid for through advertising.

Understanding the link between the information presented in the media and the effect on the target audience is an extremely difficult area. This is about understanding how people receive information in their everyday lives or in their jobs, and what determines how it affects them. There is plenty of social science theory in this area, such as Tversky and Kahneman's 'framing theory', which shows how the way in which the media communicates information triggers certain meanings and interpretations, but it is difficult to test these causal links and processes robustly.

The possible approaches include:

- *Exposure*: measuring exposure means looking at the degree to which the target audience has encountered a campaign, how many times they were exposed, and whether they paid attention. Interviews and surveys could be used to see whether people recall a particular message or campaign, and simple figures about readership of thesiss, and ownership of televisions/radios can be a useful guide.

- *Framing analysis*: this means looking at how issues are presented or discussed, by reviewing the key themes, metaphors, arguments and descriptions in a given media. This is based on framing theory, which indicates that these issues are a key component of the way in which peo-ple are influenced by the media. This can then be compared to the campaign's take on an issue, and the language it uses, and the change in framing over time can give important M&E information. Aside from exposure and framing analyses, there are very few tools that can give information about the link between media coverage and public attitudes.

LOBBYING APPROACHES

TYPICAL ACTIVITIES

The primary means of influencing policy is often direct interaction with decision-makers, allies and other key players. This might include participation in negotiations or meetings, direct communications with government ministers, or informal discussions with partners and other contacts. Teams will work to influence through persuasion, negotiation and lobbying. In more formal spaces this may be conducted through evidence-based dialogue, while in other channels this will require more informal discussions and debate. Projects will draw on the relationships staff have with various contacts, and will use budget support and other material incentives to influence proceedings directly or, more often, indirectly. It has long been recognised that this sort of activ-ity is crucial to shape the course of policy. Some research has found that face-to-face personal interaction is the strongest factor in facilitating the use of particular policy ideas or evidence. However, there is little literature on M&E for this interaction. There are, in general, strong incentives against the sharing of good practice in this area, as well as obstacles to recording related knowledge and information. However, some guidance can be drawn from professional lobbyists and negotiators, and 'good practice' for systematically managing work in these fields. While M&E tends to be carried out informally, if at all, this work relies on seeking out and reacting to information on some key factors. Expectations about what kind of M&E can be carried out in these contexts need to be adjusted accordingly.

TOC, OUTCOMES AND TOOLS

ToCs for this kind of influencing activity are based on actors, the relationships between them, and the institutions within which they work. One review of successful lobbying has found that, in addition to clear and focused policy goals, the key strategic capacities required are identifying natural allies, developing relationships and credibility with policy actors, and understanding the nature of the policy process and institutional access. McGrath, however, argues that the lobbyist's key working tools are: the monitoring of key players and decision-makers, including their personal history, perspectives and interests; and building coalitions and alliances around particular policy goals.

Another example comes from Gladwell, who argues that the spread of influence relies on three types of people: connectors—networkers who know who to pass information to and who are respected enough to influence key players; mavens—information specialists, who acquire information and educate others; and salespeople—powerful, charismatic and persuasive individuals who are trusted, believed and listened to.

Therefore, keeping systematic track of the various actors, their interests, ideologies, capacities, their alignment with programme goals, and their relationships with other players, and how all of these change, is central to managing this type of influencing, and should be the basis for measuring and understanding one's influence. And understanding the key institutions and spaces, and how they affect decision-making is also crucial—different spaces may shape what kind of policy outcome will occur, based on the structure and rules of dialogue and decision-making.

It is not easy. This work takes place in highly fluid contexts, based very much on tacit knowledge and experience, and split-second subjective judgements about, and reactions to, people's attitudes, emotions, positions and perspectives. Expectations about how formalised and standardised M&E can be in such situations must be duly adjusted, and determining attribution is simply not feasible in these contexts.

Having said this, there are some tools and approaches that can help:

- *Recording observations from meetings and negotiations* is a useful and low-cost activity. This could be done simply by storing e-mails, meeting minutes or back-to-office reports, or using meeting observation checklists to record how particular issues are covered, or how different actors behaved. For a slightly more in-depth analysis, an 'after action review' could be carried out with the project team to discuss what happened, why, and what can be learned.
- *Tracking people and relationships* and the project's interactions with them is another key area. Literature on policy networks shows the importance of 'policy champions' and 'opinion leaders' who can facilitate the uptake of certain policies. Simple tracking forms could be used to record what actions have been taken with them and when. Tracking the quality of relationships and access to such people provides important information for managing

influencing work as well as indications about the credibility and influence of the project. A more comprehensive approach could be to keep spreadsheets or a database on various key actors including political intelligence information about their job, their position in decision-making processes, and their perspectives and interests, as well as recording interactions with them.

- *Interviewing informants*. Building up an 'information network' is seen as essential to effective lobbying and is a useful avenue for understanding a project's influence on policy. Interviewing people with knowledge about the institutions and processes, or particular actors with whom the project is working, can provide invaluable guidance. These could be people with technical expertise on an institution, who have years of experience with a particular individual or organisation, or who are well-placed in terms of their role in decision-making processes. Identifying who may be able to provide information relevant for the project should be done as early as possible, and relationships built up, as the project may need to rely on them to be their 'eyes and ears' in many situations where knowledge is quite politicised. Natural allies in lobbying efforts could be used this way, and tools for 'horizontal evaluation' may be effective or simply surveys about advocacy efforts.
- *In-depth analysis*: a variety of tools could provide richer information about the influence of lobbying efforts: the alignment-interests-influence matrix synthesises perspectives and evidence on different actors' relationship to project goals. Social network analysis could function as a way of measuring and understanding actors' relationships with each other and how they share information or resources. And power analysis or political economy analysis provides tools to look into the workings of decision-making institutions. Three promising tools that have been used in the EU context could provide interesting avenues here: process tracing, which attempts to uncover the steps through which meetings and other events led to, and caused, outcomes; attributed influence, where observers of key spaces in the policy process are surveyed on their judgement of the influence of a particular actor or action; and preference attainment, where the influence of actors is judged by the extent to which final policy outcomes reflect their 'ideal' positions.

ENHANCING CAPACITIES TO FORMULATE POLICY—CRITICAL FACTORS AND KEY ISSUES

The three country studies reveal a number of key factors which influenced the process through which the policies on cost-sharing in the education sector were formulated. These factors are presented in this stage in the context of the three components of governance—the institutional environment, the core process of policy formulation, and the involvement of civil society. The identification of these factors provides a base on which to signal key issues to consider when developing a programme to enhance capacity for policy formulation. The study confirms that the policy process is indeed complex. Any programme to enhance capacity must be multi-pronged and tailored to the specific institutional environment.

INSTITUTIONAL ENVIRONMENT

Characteristics of the broader institutional environment, shown to influence policy formulation include:

- The extent to which the environment may facilitate or constrain the policy formulation process
- The political nature of the process, reflected in issues of timing
- The level of external agency involvement in the policy process

A Facilitating Environment

The need for a facilitating environment at all levels is made clear in all the reports. While there are some specific characteristics relating to the political, economic, social and cultural realities of individual countries, many characteristics of an institutional environment may be common to most situations. What the Ghana study makes clear is that one essential pre-requisite for achieving this facilitating environment is the existence of mutual trust between the various actors. This immediately brings to the fore the importance of two of the characteristics identified with governance — transparency in decision-making, and accountability of the executors of policy to the concerned sections of civil society. It also highlights the need for government and civil society to interact fully.

Like so much else about institutional issues, it is much easier to agree on the need for a facilitating environment than to achieve it. In many instances, achieving it calls for farreaching changes involving a new administrative culture on the one hand and raised awareness by non-governmental actors and stakeholders of their potential contributions to policy formulation on the other. The current recognition of the wider governance environment supports this. It underlines the importance of setting policy in its proper environmental context, of having the institutional means to ensure that the views of interested groups can be ascertained and that they can be kept informed of the reasons why certain policy option have been chosen.

In the past, the top-down and centralised approach to policy-making practised in many African countries did not provide a positive environment in which participatory policy formulation could flourish. However, since the policy decision studied in this exercise was made, there have been many political changes on the African continent that have helped to create institutional environments that favour more decentralised and open policy-making. The increasing number and openness of elections is helping to develop a political awareness among the general public while African governments have moved away from the doctrines of central control.

Currently most public service reform programmes in Africa have a large decentralisation component. But decentralisation is a means to an end rather than an end in itself. It needs a sustaining environment to operate effectively. A recent thesis identifies a number of "environmental" conditions important for the successful introduction of decentralisation. It states that the country must have a strong national identity, with mutual respect between local and central levels, so that "local levels feel that the centre speaks for them, and national identity comprises central and local elements." There must also be political commitment which is "reflected in the diffusion of human and economic resources to the periphery." It is also necessary to put in place the institutional provisions required to make the system work. There must be clear definitions of the roles, missions and responsibilities of each of the levels of government and of the individual organisations at each level. For many African countries, realisation of these conditions requires a large degree of institutional readjustment. All three studies support decentralisation, but do not underestimate the size of the task involved.

Implementation of the twin policy of ministerial restructuring and decentralisation in Ghana, for instance, would transform the central Ministry of Education into what is essentially a planning, budgeting and monitoring and evaluation organisation able to coordinate the policies, programmes and budgets of all the agencies in the education sector. Implementation responsibilities would be transferred to the Education Services and its regional and district offices. The reorganised Service would have to contend with possible vested interests of existing organisations which might be adversely affected by the proposed changes. The process of creating space for wider participation therefore calls for highly capable leaders and managers.

Key Issues for Enhancing Capacity:

- Any programme to enhance the capacity of government to formulate policy needs to assess the institutional environment within which administrative processes take place. Such an assessment provides a basis on which to identify constraints and opportunities in the environment which could affect the viability of proposed capacity building activities.
- Moves towards more pluralistic systems of governance, and towards decentralisation are expected to create a more faciliative environment for policy management, albeit one that is more institutionally complex.

This will require more attention to the design of organisational structures and systems to facilitate coordination and consultation, clearer role and mission definition, and means for identifying, recruiting and retaining capable managers and leaders.

The Time Dimension

A significant factor in the policy formulation process identified explicitly in both the Ghana and Uganda reports was the timing of the policy decision — both in terms of when it was introduced and the duration of the process. The Ghana report illustrates how, for a policy issue that materially affects the public, timing the introduction of a policy is primarily influenced by political considerations. The delay of ten years in introducing a policy of cost-sharing can be attributed to such considerations. The Uganda study states that the decision to introduce cost-sharing was both timely and justified. It was widely accepted that something had to be done about funding education and it needed to be done quickly. However, there was less agreement on what needed to be done. Almost all those interviewed suggested that the solution proposed would have been relevant and appropriate if the government had been able to introduce the whole new education policy at the same time, or at least the part that contained measures to accommodate students with financial problems. It was timely, but the timing of its introduction ahead of other policy provisions to deal with the situation which produced the serious reactions was not good.

Another aspect of timing is the question of the duration of the process. Here, the judgement of the politicians and officials involved must play a large part. If there is acute urgency, it may be necessary to move quickly although this may mean curtailing the time available to consult and evaluate several possible courses of action. In Ghana, the decision to introduce the policy took ten years; in Uganda, it was an element of a national education policy still being processed at the time of introduction of the cost-sharing initiative. In Ghana, it was claimed that the long lapse of time had allowed the population to be sensitised to the need to adapt the policy of free primary education. In Uganda, the main dissatisfaction with the policy was the ad hoc nature of the decision to go ahead, before interactions with other parts of the main policy had been thoroughly examined. Some were of the opinion that the action was not warranted by the relative urgency of the problem if this was viewed within the overall economic situation in the country.

Key Issues for Enhancing Capacity:

- Political considerations can be a major factor influencing the timing of policy decisions and the overall duration of the process. It is therefore important that programmes to enhance capacity take account of the overtly political nature of policy formulation. The strategic importance of time should be more fully explored so that those involved in the process can take cognisance of any likely hostile reactions on the political front and highlight how these might be ameliorated or removed.

The 'Donor' Dimension

The studies give a mixed picture of the perceived influence of outside agencies on the policy formulation process. Only in Uganda was it acknowledged to have been significant in determining policy content and then more with regard to the overall review of education policy than the specific element of cost-sharing. In Ghana, external pressures related to provision of finance brought the government to the point of implementing a policy they had long recognised as necessary, but had hesitated to apply because of fears that it would be politically unwise. Tanzania did not consider there had been any external influence. There was, however, considerable reliance on external technical assistance, and the country report suggested that the line between support and influence might on occasion be so fine as to disappear.

From the study, three forms of donor influence emerge: conditionality; use of external agencies by national governments to introduce a desired policy likely to carry a high political risk if introduced by the government alone; and influence by default, for example, through the use of expatriates in advisory and operational positions where they necessarily became involved in the policy process.

The extent to which donors directly influence policy will vary with the level of political stability and institutional capacity within a country. However, even where a recipient country has its own highly competent and experienced personnel, the strength of some external agencies and the traditional relationship that characterises donor-recipient relations often results in donors having a greater influence than might be desired. The task of building institutional capacity is a long one. As widely admitted, approaches to achieving it during the first 25 to 30 years of independence were not particularly successful in the holistic sense, though they did produce some highly qualified personnel. How to capitalise on the availability of this resource, and build up the confidence as well as the competence of African personnel so that they can negotiate on an even playing field with the funding agencies is now a major task.

Another aspect of donor involvement relates to coordination, both between several donors, and between separate projects supported by the same donor. Just as it is necessary for ministries to have internal consultation on policy proposals, donors should ensure that separate initiatives in a single country are complementary. The case of the Planning, Budgeting, Monitoring and Evaluation Unit and a Project Management Unit in the Ministry of Education in Ghana is a good example. Both were funded by the same donor and introduced a degree of overlap of roles as well as competition for expert staff.

Key Issues for Enhancing Capacity:

- External agencies can be both actors and stakeholders in the development process. The country reports suggest that they influence the policy formulation process in both direct and indirect ways. Programmes to enhance capacity need to take account of the donor dimension. Measures to enhance institutional capacity, as identified in this study, should necessarily reduce such external influence, but it is a long-term process. In the short to medium term, more specific attention might focus on:
  - Strengthening overall coordination of national development within which to evaluate the relevance, utility and longer-term benefits and costs of externally resourced programme offers
  - Building negotiating skills to enable more effective operation at the international level
  - Assuring that donors have up-to-date understanding and appreciation of the political, economic and social realities within which policies are to be applied
  - Ensuring that donor projects and programmes are mutually consistent.

CORE PROCESS OF GOVERNMENT

The country reports identified three fundamental action instruments which support the policy formulation process within government administration:

- Information gathering,
- Information analysis, and
- Consultation.

The studies show that the extent to which these are used in the formulation process influences policy outcomes. Programmes to enhance capacity for policy management have focused largely on the first two of these. They have led to the development of systems and structures such as modern computerbased management information systems and policy analysis units, and have provided technical and professional training. The fact that the benefits which might have been expected from these programmes have not been fully realised underlines the importance of the institutional environment - the culture of the administration and the capacity to recruit and retain effective personnel.

Information Gathering

The studies confirmed the importance of better and more accessible information, as well as its wider use. Defining the issue presents an interesting example of the complexity of the policy path. There is a common perception that databases are weak in most African countries. However, this is not uniformly so. In most countries, coverage of the formal sector is adequate.

Outside this, there is a scarcity of dependable data in the traditional quantified meaning of the word.

However, this raises the issue of what constitutes data and information. Is it a question of better systems to collect and process non-quantifiable but available data ? What Harris Mule refers to as "casual empiricism" - the views of those with long experience and knowledge handed down from generation to generation, by farmers for example may well be a source of information to be used in policy analysis. It would, of course, need to be organised in a way that makes it useful as a base on which to build policy options. Those accustomed to quantified data may find this less than satisfactory. There are risks in using such information; it would certainly need to be assessed by experienced policy-makers. But then, using econometric or mathematical techniques to arrive at conclusions on the basis of incomplete statistics may not enable decision-makers to come up with the right policy. Indeed, there may be an additional risks if the result is wrong; information backed up by quantitative data tends to appear reliable, even if the data itself is unreliable.

Agreeing on the need to improve the quality and availability of information is closely interlinked with the perception by policy analysts and decision makers of the importance of information to policy formulation. An ECDPM workshop identified something of a vicious circle here. Because there was a lack of appreciation of the importance of accurate data and information for good policy formulation at the early stages of independence, gathering it was not a very prestigious job; so the best people did not want to be involved in it; so the information was not very good; so policy makers did not tend to use what was available; so there was no tradition of calling on such services as statistics because of the distrust of them; so they did not improve.

Key Issues for Enhancing Capacity:

- Enhancing the generation and utilisation of information in the policy process is an essential component of enhancing capacity. It is generally acknowledged that the provision of structures and systems to facilitate the collection and use of data and information will not guarantee their use, unless accompanied by measures to raise awareness of the value of information at different stages of the process. Civil servants need sensitisation in this respect. Account must also be taken of the importance of culture in influencing perceptions on the role of information, and on the potential value of different types of information, such as indigenous knowledge sources.

Information Analysis

Making good use of information demands the availability of good analytical capacity. This capacity is needed to define issues, determine the criteria for choice, generate alternative policy options and appraise political feasibility. As the country reports demonstrate, the way in which the issue of cost recovery was addressed was substantially influenced by how it got onto the policy agenda — who brought it forward as a matter to be addressed urgently at that time. In each case, there was little analysis applied to its definition. The extent to which development of alternative options was undertaken is not clear from the information available. Even in Uganda where options were elaborated for the overall education policy, there did not appear to be any such study in relation to the issue of cost-sharing. The Tanzanian study went so far as to say that there was no other option than to go to the parents for the additional money required. The fact that, in the event, large numbers of parents did not pay suggests that, farther down the line, some other option would need to be sought.

The studies also revealed a lack of attention paid to the design of implementation strategies. Some of the less fortunate consequences of the policy choices in each of the three countries was imputed to the lack of proper consideration as to how the policy should or might be implemented. Such consideration would also have helped the announcement and promulgation stage. There was no evidence available to the study teams to suggest that much attention had been given to this in any of the three countries. What is clear from all three studies is that, at the time the decisions were taken, there was little capacity within the central administration devoted exclusively to analysis and little, if any, constructive relationship between the administration and possible sources of such capacity outside it. Steps were, however, being taken at the time of the field work to address this deficiency. The setting up of the Planning, Budgeting, Monitoring and Evaluation units in Ghana is one example. So is the decision in Tanzania to provide similar capacity.

The optimal location of analytical capacity within government administrations is debatable. It could be argued that it should be located in each ministry. Such a solution might, however, fragment already scarce analytical capacity. If this is the case, the capacity might be more appropriately located in a central or core ministry such as planning. In any event, it is not sufficient to have good policy analysis capacity in specialised units. It is necessary to consider how to develop and strengthen the management capability of an organisation as a whole, such as a ministry, to contribute to and support the policy process. It is, for instance, essential for line managers to understand and appreciate the importance of the policy analysis and planning processes. Here, as in so much else related to the development of institutional capacity, the solution will have to be adapted to local institutional circumstances.

Capacity for policy analysis does not have to be completely internalised within the public service. Indeed, there is a very strong case to be made that some of this capacity is best located outside the formal government organisation.

Universities, independent research institutes or advisory bodies are often better placed than civil servants to provide objective analysis and review of policy options. Also, they would be less likely to have a commitment to previous policy decisions not having been involved in their final selection or implementation. However, as is clear from the study findings, the existence of such organisations does not guarantee either their effectiveness or their use by governments. Africa, like many other parts of the world, seems to have a 'glass wall' between researchers and practitioners. They see each other but cannot hear in any real sense what are each other's needs. To be effective contributors to the policy analysis process, non-governmental organisations would require access to requisite information from government sources. Their functions vis-a-vis government and the channels of communications between themselves and government would have to be clearly identified.

Two things may be said in general. First, whatever the solution adopted, it is essential that those responsible for the final proposals and the ultimate decision appreciate the vital importance of the process of policy analysis and the signal contribution that well executed analysis can make to policy decisions. This will increase demand which will, in turn, stimulate the supply of valid and reliable information. Secondly, no institutional options, whether within or outside government, will be successful unless financial resources are provided and sustained to enable analytical capacity to be maintained at the requisite level.

Key Issues for Enhancing Capacity:

- The study points up the weakness of the available analytical capacity. Some of the difficulties in implementing the selected policies may be attributed to this weakness. The enhancement of analytical capacity must begin by creating awareness of the value of good policy analysis, and of the consequences of adopting policies which have not been rigorously analysed.
- Having generated demand, actions need to be taken to develop the personnel, structures and systems to support and deliver policy analysis. A key issue is where best to locate the capacity. Within the government administration, the relative merits of centralised coordinating units or sector specific units needs consideration in the context of available resources. The potential value of capacity outside of government and of how to promote the development of such non-governmental capacity needs also to be examined.

Consultation

A factor closely related to the generation of information and analytical capacity is the need for adequate intra and interministerial consultation. Interministerial consultation serves to identify components of policies of other ministries that may be relevant to the policy issue under consideration. It also provides an opportunity to draw on existing relevant information and expertise in those ministries. Within a ministry also, there are likely to be several departments or units involved in the formulation or implementation of a particular policy. As is clear from the Uganda study, there may be different perceptions of the objectives of a given policy. These perceptions may determine the internal support for the policy measures decided on and may, in some cases, give rise to conflict at the policy implementation stage if the perceived objectives differ from the real ones.

A culture of internal consultation is, moreover, essential to the proper functioning of policy analysis unit. This raises the issue of clarity of roles of organisations and of units within them. It is also very important to consult with the Ministry of Finance so as to have accurate information on financial constraints within which the policy will have to operate.

For example, the situation which gave rise to the need for the policy of costsharing might not have arisen at all, or at any rate not have constituted such a break with previous policy, if the political wish to offer free education had been closely examined in the light of its likely costs relative to the available funding.

Such a culture must be consciously fostered. Dealing with requests from other ministries as part of a consultation process must be perceived as a legitimate part of the work of civil servants and their political masters. Otherwise, the response may not get the required attention and therefore is unlikely to be of a quality which is useful to the requesting ministry.

Key Issues for Enhancing Capacity:

- The study indicates that while inter and intraministerial consultation would have helped the quality of the policy decision, this was generally weak. The promotion of a culture of consultation is thus an important element of any capacity development initiative. Appropriate mechanisms to facilitate the consultative process will also need to be identified. But, developing a culture of consultation is likely to call for changes in the behavioural and attitudinal characteristics of civil service administrations. This is, and should be recognised as a long-term process.

INVOLVEMENT OF CIVIL SOCIETY

The study points to instances of the participation of non-state actors and stakeholders in the policy formulation process, and to instances where such involvement did not occur but would clearly have been advantageous. Each of the three countries acknowledged that the policy formulation process could have benefited from more active involvement of civil society.

Two critical factors which affect participation are:

1. The overall awareness of the value of civil society contributions, and
2. The availability of institutional mechanisms to facilitate participation.

Awareness of t11he Value of Civil Society Contributions

The discussions at the in-country review workshops showed that participants from both the civil service and from civil society had little appreciation of the potential value of consultation between them in the policy formulation process.

On the side of civil society, the views varied from scepticism that anything they said or did would have an effect on the eventual outcome to disbelief that they could have anything of interest to offer. Some were very surprised to learn that their experience and knowledge were of value to the work of the people they saw as the policy-makers. From the discussions, it evident that teachers could have suggested modes of implementation of the policy better suited to the situation on the ground than those developed without their input. One teacher attending the Tanzanian workshop remarking on the fact that the teachers did not have a lot to say in the plenary sessions mentioned that they had never realised that what they had to say might be listened to 'on high'. She said that this was the first time any of them had been involved in such an exercise. They did not really know what to expect but, if given the opportunity again, would hope to make a larger contribution. It is noteworthy that they had plenty to say in the small group discussions during the workshop — where the fact that the language used was Swahili may also have helped.

Other civil society participants - mainly some NGOs who had, from time to time, been asked for comment on policy proposals - were more cynical. As reported earlier, the cynicism arose from being asked for comments when the matter was already at Cabinet level or having their advice ignored in the final decisions.

They felt that such consultation was 'window-dressing'. This reaction was further vitiated by the fact that many of the non-governmental actors - especially those who were members of representative bodies - appeared to be unclear about their roles in relation to policy formulation. These factors had an effect not only on what they could do to influence policy but, more perniciously, on their own attitudes towards their involvement in policy formulation activities. Equally, civil servants were surprised at the richness of the largely untapped source of data, ideas and practical suggestions that was available among the non-governmental actors and stakeholders. Lack of a culture of consultation on policy matters was in part responsible for this remaining unexplored and un(der)utilised. Apprehension among civil servants that drawing the stakeholders on them would risk delay and special pleading may also have been a factor. They feared that non-government stakeholders might not differentiate between policy at national level and the needs of their individual organisations or perhaps not be willing to do so. It was clear from the level and content of the discussions at the review workshops that this is a misjudgement in relation to both the capacity and attitude of these groups.

Key Issues for Enhancing Capacity:

- Two issues arise in the context of this critical factor. The *first* is the need to sensitise government decision makers to the benefits to be gained from consultation with non-governmental actors and stakeholders in seeking to formulate sustainable policies. The *second* is how to make civil society aware of its own potential on the one hand so that it will participate in the policy formulation process and, on the other hand, of the responsibilities accompanying such participation.
- The current moves towards more transparency and accountability in the governance environment increase the importance of these issues in seeking to enhance overall institutional capacity for policy formulation.

An Infrastructure for Consultation with Civil Society

The study shows the importance of inputs from actors and stakeholders outside as well as inside the government structure for the development of achievable and sustainable policies. Effective access to these inputs does not happen by chance; it needs functioning institutional machinery. For example, there was no evidence in the study that ignoring non-governmental actors and stakeholders was a conscious decision. Rather, it reflected a lack of institutional infrastructure for such consultation. Civil society organisations, where they existed, were weak and were not clear on their roles. Civil servants - often operating against tight deadlines - had to maintain ongoing policies as well as develop policies to deal with emerging issues.

They had no time to review this element of the policy process and create mechanisms for consultation. The lack of an effective institutional infrastructure is both an outcome of lack of appreciation of the importance of consultation with non-governmental groups and a cause of their non-involvement. When the policy decisions being studied were taken, there was an absence or discouragement of organised political opposition, independent trade unions, interest groups, and free media. The Ghana study, for example, makes specific reference to the scarcity of journalists specialising in political and economic matters which stood in stark contrast to expertise available in sports journalism. Involvement in the policy formulation process was, as a result, largely restricted to the upper echelons of the political and bureaucratic system. Even where some formal consultation structure existed, the system did not seem to work satisfactorily — in part because of the feeling among civil society members that no notice was taken of their submissions.

Addressing the institutional infrastructure issue involves both the government and civil society. The government can take a lead in creating the governance environment in which public debate can flourish. Civil society has to gear itself up to benefit from such a climate. It has to understand the context in which policy is formulated, to be able to take account of the broader picture within which policy at national level is framed and to appreciate the most useful inputs which it can contribute. It may well be a 'chicken and egg' situation with the various elements of civil society reluctant to spend time, energy and resources on activities and the development of skills which they cannot effectively use. However, until they are able to contribute effectively to the policy debate when asked, they are unlikely to be invited to do so.

Key Issues for Enhancing Capacity:

- Consultation with civil society as an integral element of the policy formulation process calls for procedures for such consultation within government which are effective and are used. It also requires that there are aware and informed 'focal points' in civil society capable of making or responding to opportunities to participate. The study highlights the need to develop trust on the part of civil society that with it consultation is real.
- Timing is a key element of any effective process for consultation. It must ensure contact at a sufficiently early point in the formulation process to show that the consultation is in good faith. It must also ensure that realistic time is allowed for reaction - realistic in the context of the communications infrastructure of the country.

Endpiece

This study aims to increase knowledge and understanding of the actual policy formulation process within the broader context of policy management in sub-Saharan Africa. It seeks to provide insights into the roles of, and the interactions between, the various actors and stakeholders in the decision-making process, and to identify factors critical to the effectiveness of the process.

There is no universally applicable recipe for creating policy management capacity. Understanding the process as it occurs in real life in sub-Saharan Africa helps to identify where there are capacity gaps. This is a first step to taking action to enhance the capacity. But the findings are not only relevant to the countries of the region or to their citizens. As was said at the beginning of this report, many of the issues identified in the study can be found in countries with ostensibly more advanced institutional infrastructures. The factors emerging as significant will also be of interest to agencies that fund programmes of public service reform or of the development of institutional infrastructures to ensure that civil society can be and is involved in the formulation, monitoring and adaptation of national policy.

The potential contribution of civil society to the process stands out in each of the country studies. So, too, does the lack of appreciation of its value, both by government and, at least in some cases, by civil society itself. While consultation is time-consuming and expensive, the value of uncovering possible pitfalls and ways to avoid them at the policy formulation stage makes it worthwhile to give these matters sufficient attention early in the process.

Such interactions between central government service and civil society may increase the iterative nature of policy formulation. The resulting policy formulation process becomes less and less a linear path, more and more a maze, with routes to information potentially relevant to the decision at hand crossing and running parallel. The way through a maze from "entry" to "exit" is not often, perhaps is never, the shortest line between two points. However, knowing that the process is complex and messy is itself a help. Having a menu of potential sources of information, a map showing where they are located, and an effective system of signposting or signalling to remind the traveller will, at the end of the journey, make the journey through the process much smoother and the resulting policy more effective.

This study has tried to help travellers on the journey from identification of a policy issue to the formulation and promulgation of a policy. It signals some of the possible pitfalls on the journey. Many of them are generic, but their precise nature and impact is situation-specific. By paying attention to the policy process, and by anticipating how obstacles will be met and overcome, participants in policy-making can have much more confidence in the quality, relevance, and acceptability of their product.

POLICY ANALYSIS IN PRACTICE

There are certain aspects of policy analysis and development which are particularly relevant to administrative capabilities, resource utilization and the implementation of public programmes. Better understanding of the relevant concepts can enable administrators to play a more effective role in national development, and increase the relevance of public activities to national goals. An important concept to emerge from the policy analysis process is policy design. In many cases, policies are piecemeal, fragmented and even contradictory. Perceptions of a policy problem may also sharply differ among various individuals and organizations involved in the process. By promoting a better definition of the problem, it should be possible to come up with more consistent and viable policies. Another important contribution of the policy analysis process is the stress it places on the search for alternatives, and the pursuit of optimal policies.

Some countries use special commissions and committees to carry out policy analysis and development. For a variety of reasons, the effectiveness of such commissions remains limited. The appointment of a commission can be as much a device to get action on a pressing problem, as a device for delaying it. At one point it was found that a particular country had almost thirty commissions working on major issues including education, law, energy, agriculture, labour, public administration, corruption, and the press. The membership of commissions has also influenced their success. Normally, the members come from the same groups which may be part of the problem, or have a vested interest in the outcome.

Finally, the problem-solving methods of such commissions are usually limited to existing frameworks and modalities. The output of commissions can be greatly improved by changing their composition and work methods. They should also be exposed to the major ideas put forward in the policy sciences. All of this assumes, however, that the appointing authority is genuinely interested in their input to the policy process. The practice of appointing special policy staffs in the office of the chief executive has not generally caught on in developing countries. Some developed countries have discontinued the practice altogether. Nonetheless, a strong case can be made for permanent policy units, especially for important sectors where policy issues involve many competing interests.

A major drawback in many public organizations is the lack of policy orientation. Many organizations think in terms of tasks rather than policy objectives. There is a need to reorient public organizations and their management structures towards thinking in terms of policy goals. The national institutes of public administration and management can play a useful role in this regard by running training programmes on policy-oriented topics and the policy process more generally.

THE POLICY CYCLE

Too little is known about the policy process of developing countries. For analytical purposes, it can be divided into a number of stages. These include problem identification and formation, policy formulation, adoption and legitimization, policy implementation and policy monitoring/evaluation. Each stage requires careful analysis to give policy relevance to genuine issues. For example, a problem may be the perception of a vested interest rather than a society-wide problem. The prevalence of interest groups is a fact of life in most developing countries, even though their organization, activities and methods of operations may significantly differ.

Externalities also affect the policy cycle. A good example is the way many problem definitions and policy initiatives may come from outside the country. Often local people and even the political leadership may not perceive the problem or the proposed course of action in the same way as those coming from outside the country. In some instances, the policy as proposed is perceived by many to be the problem. This situation often arises over environmental issues, particularly in matters such as land use, pollution and the preservation of forests or certain species.

The formulation of policy proposals also causes problems because the process does not normally exhaust all the policy alternatives. This frequently happens with the work of commissions as described earlier. Sometimes, it is due to lack of resources, or the way in which resources are deployed. Frequently, it is due to lack of familiarity with different possibilities. This shortcoming could be eliminated through wider participation and the encouragement of innovative thinking. The adoption and legitimization of policies occur through legislation, executive orders, judicial actions or other relevant instruments. Unfortunately, the dissemination of policy decisions is not always given much attention beyond publication in official gazettes or memoranda to the relevant public organization. Thorough dissemination of policy decisions, as well as the rationale, benefits and target groups can significantly increase acceptance of the policy in society and enhance its successful implementation.

Implementation is the weak link in the policy process of many developing countries. Announcement of a policy is often equated with implementation. Policy implementation almost always involves the redeployment of human, physical, organizational and financial resources. It may also entail new relationships among citizens groups, or between them and the Government. Sometimes changes in existing rules and regulations are required. Many implementation plans fail because they ignore important resources or linkage relationships.

The evaluation of policy outputs is a neglected aspect of the policy cycle. While policies launched with assistance from abroad may undergo evaluation, the exercise is more likely to happen on specific projects. Thorough programmatic reviews are rare. Similarly, some analysis may also be carried out on locally developed policies, but the reports in all such cases are likely to remain limited in scope, circulation and use. The practice of designing a feedback system to correct the course of a specific policy or to improve the policy process generally is uncommon in most countries. An analysis of policies in areas such as land reform, transportation and industrial relations could produce excellent case studies to understand the dynamics involved at different stages of the process.

ETHICS IN PUBLIC LIFE

We come next to my second point about the changing role of ethics in public life. It is the assertion that while ethics has been used to domesticate and humanize power, we now live in a world where ethics is power. Many speak of the United States as a marriage of Jerusalem, Athens and Rome. They argue, quite correctly, that the strength of America has been its moral strength. According to Gertrude Himmelfarb, long before the founding of the American republic," those concerned with morality explained that "Virtue is the distinctive characteristic of a republic, as honour is of monarchy, and moderation of an aristocracy." I would now say much the same thing about values. We cannot long preserve the public ethos of America's founding without the simple understanding that while we used ethics in much of the twentieth century to domesticate and humanize power, in the twenty first century ethics is power.

We hear much these days about American military strength and American economic power, but there is very little discussion of the many ways the international system is changing and the implications for American power and influence. Many foreign policy analysts are appalled by the lack of realism in the allocation of our national budget and the lack of emphasis in our national security strategy on what is increasingly called soft power. In a July 1999 article in the Foreign Affairs journal, Professor Joseph Nye, who heads the Kennedy School at Harvard, made an important distinction between "hard power" and "soft power." Hard power refers to the use of military might or economic muscle to influence and even coerce. Soft power refers to the ability to attract and influence through the flow of information and the appeal of social, cultural and moral messages. Hard power is the ability to get others to do what we want. Soft power is the ability to get others to want what we do. The former is based on coercion while the latter is based on attraction.

Military power in the world is unipolar, with the United States outstripping all others states. Economic power is multipolar, with the United States, Japan and Europe accounting for two-thirds of the world's production. Soft power is more widely dispersed. It crosses borders and is not dependent on military or economic power. A compelling message from a disaster area, a gross human rights violation, a military conflict or a story of hope and healing conveyed by the Internet or television can easily catapult new priorities into a nation's foreign policy. And that is why values may be the most fundamental and the most significant source of soft power.

The power that comes from being a "city on the hill" does not provide the coercive capability with which presidential candidates and most Americans identify, but in the new age of national security it can sometimes be the most influential. While greater pluralism in the mobilization and use of soft power may diminish the ability of the United States to impose its will through the use of hard power, the attractiveness of our institutions, the openness of our society and the values we espouse should continue to give us an edge in the new world of soft power; providing our people and our leaders recognize that while American military and economic advantages are great, they are neither unqualified nor permanent. The impact of soft power first hand during my tenure as United Sates Ambassador to South Africa; for Nelson Mandela represented the epitome of soft power. His moral standing and political stature in the world went far beyond that suggested by the size of the military or the Gross Domestic Product of South Africa. His influence came from the power of his humanity and the elegance of his spirit. His influence came from his message of reconciliation and the moral instinct embodied in his spirit of forgiveness and reconciliation. He is the prototype of the leader whose influence comes not from military or economic might, but from the power of ideals and the ability to capture the minds and hearts of people in all corners and colours of the universe. Among the many lessons we should have learned from the life and legacy of Nelson Mandela is the fact that diplomacy increasingly depends on a moral ecology that can not be found in military or economic power.

UNDERSTAND THE ETHICS POWER

It is not only governments that must come to understand that ethics is power. The same is true of multinational business. The Reverend Leon Sullivan, who authored the principles used in South Africa by those American corporations operating under the apartheid system, has been conferring with international organizations and businesses to come up with a global set of principles. He has been in conversation with multinational corporations from three continents, business associations, non-governmental organizations and national governments.

While several hundred companies have signed on, there are those who reject this exercise as fruitless or an attempt at self-aggrandizement or publicity, but there are others who feel strongly that signing and affirming these principles is not only right but in their company's self-interest. Many of these groups have pledged to develop and implement policies, procedures, training and internal reporting structures to ensure integrity and responsibility in the operation of business corporations. Here's what they are asking their colleagues in business to do:

- Express support for universal human rights and, particularly, those of their employees, the communities in which they operate, and the parties with whom they do business.
- Promote equal opportunity for their employees at all levels of the company with respect to issues such as colour, race, gender, age, ethnicity or religious beliefs, and operate without unacceptable worker treatment such as the exploitation of children, physical punishment, female abuse, involuntary servitude, or other forms of abuse.
- Express support for the voluntary freedom of association of their employees.
- Compensate employees at a level that enables them to meet at least their basic needs and provide the opportunity to improve their skill and capability in order to raise their social and economic opportunities.
- Provide a safe and healthy workplace; protect human health and the environment; and promote sustainable development.
- Promote fair competition including respect for intellectual and other property rights, and not offer, pay or accept bribes.

- Work with communities in which they do business to improve the quality of life in those communities-their educational, cultural, economic and social well being-and seek to provide training and opportunities for workers from disadvantaged backgrounds.
- Promote the application of those principles by those with whom they do business.

ENFORCEMENT MECHANISMS

These are voluntary principles without any enforcement mechanisms except for the positive images enjoyed by those who sign them. Why, it might be asked, should a company bother? Given my own experience in international business and my service as an advocate for American business abroad, We are convinced that a sound set of principles can have an affect on the bottom line in at least five ways:

- They build trust within the company and within the community. That trust translates into loyalty, consistency and greater productivity.
- They demonstrate that companies are only as good as its people and its policies. A company is what it rewards. It is not so much what it says in its mission statement or code of conduct as it is what it rewards its people for being. The performance review and reward system must reflect the values the company affirms.
- Customers and consumers increasingly take note of company values. They like to know that they are doing business with a company that not only produces an excellent product or provides excellent service, but it is committed to fairness, honesty, integrity and the larger community. As international competition increases, companies that do things ethically, and are seen doing them, may have a competitive edge in some countries.
- More and more shareholders also care about company values. The socially responsible movement, once laughed at and dismissed as a minor nuisance, is now a $650 billion movement and growing. According to Rush Kidder of the Global Ethics Institute, socially conscious investments now account for some ten per cent of invested funds in the United States.

Does responsible behaviour affect the bottom line? I am convinced that it does and I believe that in the years ahead you will see increasing evidence that principles affect profits and have a powerful, practical and immediate impact on the bottom line.

SOCIAL ETHICS

We come now to my third point about the changing role of ethics in public life. Social ethics at the dawning of the nation-state helped us understand the obligations of the citizen to the state. We now need public values that will help us cope with an interdependent world that is integrating and fragmenting at the same time. A major contribution of social ethics at the birth of the nation state was to help citizens understand the implication of freedom from tyranny, particularly the social obligation of citizenship and the limits of freedom.

Consider for a moment, the evolving vision of citizenship. The earliest vision of democracy was that the people have the power. The evolving vision is that the people have the vote, which is no longer the same as having the power. The awakening of the sense of citizenship as obligation to a larger community came with the French and American revolution when the word signified in theory, but not in practice, the equal participation of everyone in a social contract. The notion of citizen is still evolving, but we can draw lessons for enlarging the meaning of citizenship from the almost unknown civic traditions of some of the groups that are transforming our national life.

Long before Alexis deTocqueville became the most quoted (and probably the least read) authority on American civic life, Benjamin Franklin had become so enamoured with the political and civic culture of the Native Americans he met in Pennsylvania that he advised delegates to the 1754 Albany Congress to emulate the civic habits of the Iroquois. Long before Martin Luther King wrote his Letter From A Birmingham Jail, African American's had come to believe that the primary passion of the patriot should be the passion for justice, and that justice is often a precondition to order-where a people feel a stake in a community they are more likely to work for order and value tranquility. Long before Robert Bellah wrote Habits of the Heart, Neo-Confucians in the Chinese community were teaching their children that a community without benevolence invites its own destruction.

All of these traditions now join our evolving vision of public values, but understanding our obligations as citizens also requires an understanding of what it means to be members of a public. We need to keep in mind that instead of a well-defined, distinct public, many publics exist, and the idea of public good frequently depends on which public is defining the good. It is only in the broadest sense that we are able to speak of a mass public. In the recent presidential campaign, we were reminded often that there is a voting public, which is all too often only a small fraction of the mass public and there are issue publics who hold strong opinions and are often seeking influence.

We need students, graduates and faculty who are willing to be a voice for those publics who are poor, weak or marginalized; all those whom someone powerful might deem inconvenient or outside the circle of care. We need politicians who are willing to seek power to disperse it rather than simply concentrate it. We need community leaders who can, by example, convey the message that doing something for someone else-making the condition of others our own-is a powerful force in building community. When you experience the problem of the poor or troubled, when you help someone to understand the human condition through theatre or dance, when you help someone to find meaning in a museum or creative expression in a painting, when you help someone to find housing or regain his health, you are far more likely to connect on a deeper level, and you are likely to gain a sense of self-worth in the process.

Robert Putnam, who writes about the declining role of social capital in a democracy, Amitai Etzioni, who argues that shared values are essential for social solidarity and community and Robert Bellah, who wrote about his fears of a democracy without citizens, are all pointing to the importance of what Alexis deTocqueville once described as the habits of the heart of the American people; the tendency to form voluntary groups to meet social needs and to solve social problems. We now know that when neighbours help neighbours and even when strangers help strangers both those who help and those who are helped are transformed. When that which was "their" problem becomes "our" problem, a new relationship is established and new forms of community are possible.`

And here we can learn a lot from the South African people about building community. Their emphasis on reconciliation may be at the heart of our search for public values appropriate for a world that is integrating and fragmenting at the same time. To live together in community is to be constantly engaged in connecting or re-connecting with those who differ not simply in race or religion, but tradition and theology as well as politics and philosophy. Where there is diversity, there is likely to be alienation and separation. Conflicts are inevitable and social relationships are constantly threatened and broken.

Reconciliation, thus, becomes as highly prized a value in the age of interdependence as freedom was in the scramble for independence. Reconciliation has to do with re-establishing or sustaining a connection to a wider community. There is an implicit notion of brokenness, a relationship that needs to be built or rebuilt. But the estrangement individuals and communities face can be moral as well as social and political. In South Africa, reconciliation is both a public value and a public process. It is fused into the political culture of those who govern, the theology of those who claim a new moral authority and the ancestral tradition of those who now have the lead in building a new society. The commitment to a reconciling society has deep roots in the African experience. In the worse days of apartheid, the African National Congress wrote into its charter that South Africa belongs to all who live in it. These words also found their way into the new constitution.

There is among black South Africans a traditional concept of community called ubuntu. It assumes that all of humanity is bound together into a relationship that is bigger than any individual or group. This notion of community is best expressed in the Xhosi proverb Archbishop Tutu likes to quote, "People are people through other people." It follows that to deny the dignity or seek to diminish the humanity of another person is to destroy one's own. This is the message so badly needed in a world where the more interdependent we become the more people are turning inward to smaller communities of meaning and memory. This may, at first glance, appear to be reason for anxiety and even despair, but I am increasingly convinced as I travel around the world that the search for beginnings, the focus on remembering and re-grouping, may simply be a necessary and natural stage of the search for common ground. People are demanding respect for their primary community of history and heritage before they can more fully embrace a larger community of function and formality.

With so much happening in so many places, with so many pressing needs within the American borders and beyond, and with so many conflicts still to be resolved, many Americans still feel the tug of separateness, of ultimate loyalties devoted exclusively to their own group. Yet, while it is only natural to feel an affinity with those whom we share a special heritage and a special history, it is time that we learn to see ourselves and our group, not through the haze of parochial emotions, but against the backdrop of a larger vision and as part of a larger community.

So let me conclude by suggesting that we can not understand nor appreciate the changing role of ethics in public life without trying to understand the many voices urging a return of respect for the spiritual dimension, without trying to understand why religion is playing such a large role in public life. Many people, whether they are Buddhist, Muslim, Christian, Jew or some other expression of a spiritual connection, are coming to believe that we are not here alone, that we do not exist for ourselves alone, that we are a part of something bigger and more mysterious than ourselves.

It is not yet clear what role religion will play in the search for either common ground or public values, but there are many reasons to believe that the search for a higher level of being is a reflection of the human condition. And it may be that it is the common search, rather than our different answers, that will provide the basis of our unity. And that is why I am so pleased to have been given this opportunity to address the subject of the changing role of ethics in public life.

As we look to the future, it is clear that the ethical issues with which policymakers now struggle are tame compared to some of the issues on the horizon. It is now reliably predicted, for example, that within five years either a U.S. government agency or a private corporation (perhaps both) will have in a desktop computer the entire human gene decoded. Policy analysts and ethicists will then be arguing over the implications of extending the human life span for Americans beyond 150 years, at the same time that the AIDS virus and other infectious diseases devastate populations in Africa and elsewhere. We hope that the emerging community of leadership educators, the institutes they develop and the students they teach, will be prepared to handle the new generation of public policy issues as well as the old.

But even more fundamentally, We hope the new leadership industry is prepared to handle the diversity that will characterize leadership in the new millennium. Although the present leadership climate may appear at first glance to be a leadership vacuum, it is more likely that we have simply been looking in the wrong places for leadership. If we have learned anything from those who are building new societies in Eastern Europe, Southern Africa and Central America, it is that the next generation of leaders is not likely to fit the traditional mold, nor are those leaders likely to be found in traditional places.

The days of looking for leaders with the right endorsements and the right credentials as defined by an established elite are hopefully nearing an end. The leaders of the future are not likely to come riding out of the sunset on white charges-heroes without heroism. Many will instead be ordinary people with extraordinary commitments. Their styles will be different. Their accents will be different and so will their colour and complexion. We do not yet know much about these emerging leaders, but we know enough about the changing role of ethics in public life to suggest at least these four conclusions:

- The demographic changes are creating a demand for a new group of leaders who seek power in order to disperse it rather than simply hold it. The demand is for leaders who understand what it means to share power rather than simply dominate it. Those who seek power to concentrate it may ultimately lose it to those who seek it only to diffuse it.
- Tomorrow's leaders must be able to use their values not simply to affirm absolutes but also to cope with ambiguities. During times of rapid change, there is always a revival of religion. Zealots emerge claiming one truth and one theology. As people search for something to hang on to, they tend to respond to those who provide answers rather than those who point to ambiguities. No religion, however, offers absolute clarity and self-evident truth; hence no vision of the present-let alone the future-can be accepted as final; no institution can be accepted as complete; no ideology can be accepted as closed. In matters of faith and morals, the right question is usually more important than the right answer to the wrong question.
- It is imperative that leaders develop the capacity for humility. Our world desperately needs leaders who are open to the possibility of error in themselves and human wisdom in unlikely places. I remember my early days in a new administration in Washington. The euphoria of victory after long months of struggle produced a climate in which it was easy to believe that the rascals had been thrown out and intelligence and foresight had finally come to government. In fact, some rascals had probably been thrown out, but in every group of people there are likely to be a few who share a commitment to the

same goals. The challenge of leadership is to identify them and make them allies rather than adversaries.

- It is the involvement with the needs of others that provides the social cement that binds people together in community.

Much attention has been given to individualism and "lone ranger" leadership in American history. It remains a major theme of historical analysis and self-understanding. But leadership scholars and educators may need to acknowledge and affirm another tradition that goes back to John Winthrop's notion of a city on a hill. Those who seek "to make the condition of others their own" will find that the effect of doing something for some else is powerful. When by trying to help you experience the problems of those economically disadvantaged or politically disenfranchised, you are far more likely to find common ground. And you are likely to gain a sense of self-worth, personal satisfaction and meaning in the process. Once the potential leader discovers the ability make a difference, the leadership impulse-which may start out as a very personal and solitary drive-is likely to be transformed into a larger commitment to making the concern for others, to making some form of civic engagement on behalf of others, a part of the human journey.

4

The Process of Public Policy

Democracy is not a spectator sport. So, let's shift gears and look at how elective bodies go about making policy and how an individual can impact that process. Think of elected bodies as large stadiums. In the arena are the *policymakers* who are armed with a tool called the *vote.* Each day the policymaker goes into the arena and struggles, debates, persuades, and eventually votes on the public *policy.* The process is very open and participatory. Each day the legislature and the Congress publicise the issues that will be considered on that day. One can observe this process on cable television (*e.g.*, C-SPAN) and see the reporting of the results through the traditional news media. What is not so obvious is the power and influence of other people who participate in the policymaking while sitting in the stands.

THE ACTORS

Basically, there are three sets of actors or warriors who also participate in the policymaking process.

SPECIAL INTEREST GROUPS

First are the special interest groups. These groups generally represent a specific interest, business, or point of view. They are represented by sophisticated lobbyists who are armed with weapons as well. The lobbyist provides expert information that can be used to persuade policymakers to agree with their point of view. That information is also used to educate and inform the public of their point of view. Lobbyists also have enormous power because they have money to buy policymakers lunch, to entertain, to persuade, and to influence campaigns.

State Government Departments

The second set of warriors sitting in the balcony are the departments of state government. Each department has a "legislative liaison" whose job it is to follow the process and educate the policymakers and the public. The departmental legislative liaison's powerful tool is expert information, which is supposed to be neutral, not self-serving, and in the best interest of the entire community.

Consumers, Citisens, and Taxpayers

The third set of warriors are the consumers, interested citisens, and the taxpayers. Some groups are organised and sophisticated, like Common Cause, the National Rifle Association, and the senior citisen network, AARP. All kinds of citisens groups organise to follow, observe, and participate in the policymaking process. The power of this warrior group is seen in their ability to generate large numbers of people who are informed, get actively involved in the policy process, and vote regularly.

POLICY INTO LAW

When all three groups agree—the special interest groups, the department liaison, and the consumer groups—their power coalesces around the policy, and it becomes law. It is good politics and generally good policy if all three of these groups are in agreement. Unfortunately, these groups don't always agree nor get along with each other; they are often at odds. An effective policymaker will work to get at least two of the three groups to support the evolving consensus or compromise policy. The politics are to at least get the special interests and the consumers on the same page.

The departments and the expert "neutral" information they represent do not carry the same weight as the well-financed lobbyists representing the special interest and the powerful influence of organised consumers who vote. Power is the bottom line! The most important point that can be made is that the democratic process is a participatory process; it works best when all of the interests are involved and engaged and part of the process. If consumers and taxpayers get discouraged—give up and walk away from the policymaking process—power goes by default to the special interests. Thomas Jefferson once said that "The best cure for an ailing democracy is more democracy." Democracy is best served by getting people involved, organised, and focused.

THE POLICY FORMULATION PROCESS

Participants at the Planning Workshop identified seven 'stages' in policy formulation that represent nodal points in an effective policy formulation process. While the stages can be placed in a linear sequence, the process is not normally an orderly progress from one to the next. It is likely to require a good deal of doubling back to adjust earlier stages in the light of fresh information. In other words, it is an iterative process.

The stages identified were:

- Issue/Problem Identification;
- Specification of Objectives;

- Development of Possible Options;
- Choice of Preferred Option;
- Policy Decision Making;
- Design of Implementation Strategy;
- Policy Review and Reformulation.

They also identified three "action instruments" which animate the process and provide inputs at each of the various stages: information gathering, information analysis, and consultation. Resulting from the inputs supplied by these instruments, the journey along the path from issue identification through policy decision-making to review and eventual reformulation takes on much of the appearance of a journey through a maze.

While there is some artificiality in making a distinction between the stages and the instruments, such a distinction was judged to provide a useful framework within which to examine the findings of the case studies in this stage.

STAGES IN POLICY FORMULATION

Identification of the Policy Issue

It seems a truism to state that the starting point for policy formulation is to have a clear and detailed definition of the issue to be addressed. While this is easy to state in principle, the reality is far more complex. It is often difficult to decide precisely what the issue is that needs to be addressed. In particular, the distinction between the symptoms and the real causes of a problem is often not sufficiently analysed.

A number of factors affect the articulation of the issue. To begin with, there is the question of how the agenda is set, how an issue comes to light. The power to decide what will or will not be a policy issue has a significant impact on the evolution of the policy process. Identifying an issue, bringing it to attention, and then mounting pressure to have action taken are important political tactics. Equally, keeping attention away from certain issues is as important. "Non-decision making" occurs when influential individuals or groups, or the political system itself, prevent the emergence of challenges to the dominant values or interests in society.

Then there is the nature of the policy issue. It may be an issue which has been chosen; one which arises out of a normal process of monitoring and review; or one which is thrust on government by a crisis. It has been argued that the process of policy formulation tends to unfold differently depending on whether policy elites perceive they are dealing with a crisis situation or with orderly progress of a political agenda. Pressures for reform, stakes involved in change, the level of decision-makers involved, the degree of change considered and the timing of reform all influence the process. The institutional environment within which a specific issue arises will also affect the way in which it is expressed. The immediate issue may be relatively narrow but the 'ripple effect' in the policy 'pool' may be wide-ranging. For instance, the issue for this study raises fundamental philosophical and political issues related to the objectives of education policy in low income countries. Germane too are issues of social equity; of the importance of education to economic growth and to the alleviation of the poverty of the most disadvantaged members of society.

At a more mundane but equally important level of consideration, are issues of budgetary policy within the constraints of macro economic management, particularly in situations of financial crisis. The background to policy initiation in relation to cost-sharing was strikingly similar in all three study countries. At independence, each of the countries wanted to radically review the education system inherited from the British. In Ghana, the Government decided, as a matter of national policy, that primary education should be free and compulsory. In Tanzania, the government had committed itself to primary education for all as early as 1964. Following the Arusha Declaration, Government committed itself to achieving the goal of Universal Primary Education by 1989. In 1974, however, the Party directed, in the Musoma resolution, that UPE should be accelerated and reached by the end of 1977. Uganda gave priority to higher education, with a view to producing sufficient highly qualified civil servants. Tertiary level education would be free and, in addition, students would be paid several allowances.

The level of investment in education implied in each of the policies proved to be unsustainable. This spurred the need for policy change. Proposals for cost-sharing were a clear response in all three countries to a severe financial crisis resulting from a mismatch between societal demands and previous government policy on the one hand and available government resources on the other. Thus, budgetary provision became the framework within which remedies would be sought. The experience in Tanzania illustrates the complexity of the issue. The political environment was one where the decision to undertake UPE had already been taken and the political leadership was committed to its realisation. Thus, the issue of cost recovery could be construed as incremental in the context of UPE. But, the decision taken at Musoma to cut the original timespan for realising UPE by about half may be described as bold or idealistic — but unrealistic.

The issue arose in the first place from problems related to effective implementation of the existing policy and the perceived need to correct those problems without changing in any substantial manner the goals and content of UPE. The big increase in school attendance in the framework of UPE was not matched by an increase in budget allocation for school materials. This led to public complaints over the deteriorating quality of education. The matter was raised in Party meetings as well as in the press and other media. A question was put to the Minister in the National Assembly as to the cause of shortage of exercise books in primary schools. The Treasury articulated the problem by identifying scarce financial resources as the main constraint. The policy objective, then, was how to get more finance. Subsequent policy analysis was more concerned with this than with addressing the problem in a broader frame of analysis of the delivery of an education service.

Cost recovery proposals also constituted a significant departure from the previous policy and practice, *i.e.* of the Government's commitment to finance primary education. It was a high profile issue related to a central government policy and affecting society at the broadest level. This made the policy issue in itself a critical one.

Specification of Objectives

Just as the policy path should have a beginning - the issue to be addressed — it should also have, from the start, at least a general idea of a destination — the objective to be achieved. As soon as the issue to be addressed is identified, it is necessary to agree a statement of the objective. The objective at this stage will be tentative.

It may, indeed almost certainly will, be modified in the light of information gathered on the way. But an initial statement of the issue and of the objective will help to determine the nature of the information required and the actors and stakeholders who need to be brought into the process. Moreover, it is essential that there is a clear policy objective at the end of the formulation process, one that can provide a basis for useful monitoring, evaluation and review of policy implementation. Without a clear ex-ante statement of objectives of the policy eventually agreed, no serious ex-post evaluation can be made.

Often, there may be different understandings among the several actors and stakeholders involved of what this objective means. The Tanzanian and Ugandan studies, in particular, give some insights into how these differences can arise. They highlight the need for clarity at this stage of the process.

In Tanzania, parents and pupils as well as the wider public were the first to recognise and react to the imperfections of the existing primary education situation. They perceived the issue as a shortage of education materials, particularly exercise books. Getting the issue on the policy agenda was precipitated by public outcry about shortages of education materials. This prompted responses and reactions from the various actors, but each of these in their turn had different perceptions of the specific issue. Regional and district authorities were more concerned with the quality of the immediate service being delivered as a consequence of the lack of thesis and other school materials. The Ministry of Education was primarily concerned with the quality of education in general. The Treasury, was worried about the rising demand of primary education on the public purse. The political leadership was concerned to achieve the goal of UPE, as well as to contain public dissatisfaction.

The non-governmental stakeholders were motivated by interest in a single issue which affected them and their families in a very real and personal way. But, the various ministries responded to the issue within their broad institutional mandates and obligations. Their perception was inevitably influenced by their role in relation to the achievement of what was a major policy aim—Universal Primary Education. The Treasury took the first step in officially setting the issue on the policy agenda when it put a question to the Minister of Education on financing of education policy proposals. The Ministry of Finance was sensitive to the seriousness of the unrest and identified the problem as being able to meet the financial implications of a major part of the education policy of the country. So, the initial issue emerged as a symptom of the real problem rather than the problem itself. Variations in the perception of the objectives also appeared at an early stage in Uganda. There, a general review of education policy was in train and, due to the general shortage of funds, the issue of cost-sharing was taken out of a broader policy discussion. The general objective of the policy change was to diversify sources of finance for tertiary education through cost-sharing and by containing unit costs to government.

From the outset, however, different actors within the Ministry of Education saw the policy as having different objectives. For instance, the Department for Higher Education assumed that resources raised would be used to increase the quality of tertiary education, while the department dealing with primary and secondary education expected a reallocation of resources in its favour. It was interesting to see how the way in which the issue was finally identified and the objective set influenced the thinking on how the matter should be dealt with.

Development of Options and Process of Choice

Choice is at the heart of policy formulation. Choice between different options with differing resource requirements and differing impact on perceived problems. What might achieve one objective might be of no use, or even be disastrous, for the achievement of other objectives. The role of policy analysis is to help formulate the policy options from which a choice can be made. In theory, each option would be given a different weighting based on its advantages and disadvantages in relation to realising the objectives of the policy. It would set out, for instance, who would gain and who would lose from each option. Under a linear model of policy formulation, officials set out all the options along with all the advantages and disadvantages of each in terms of the objectives to be achieved. In some instances and in some administrations, they might recommend a particular option; in all cases, they would leave politicians to decide which option to adopt. However, the more realistic iterative model of policy formulation recognises that, at an early stage in policy analysis, there is likely to be interaction between technical and political considerations. Thus, the elimination of certain options as politically unacceptable and the modification of other options to make them more politically acceptable, takes place during the analytical process. The final decision on policy from a sometimes very limited range of options will be made at the political level at a late stage in the process.

The need to articulate options for the government was implicitly included in the terms of reference given to the consultative commissions and committees that were set up in both Ghana and Uganda to review education finance. However, in Ghana, the Consultative Committee did not articulate options but made a single proposal, namely a cost-sharing partnership between Government and parents on a 50/50 basis. This proposal was rejected by the Government on the grounds that "as far as practicable, primary education should be free." Yet another Commission suggested "devolution of responsibility" to local communities with the understanding that "when genuine help was needed it will be forthcoming."

This may have been a useful principle to guide policy action, but could hardly be considered to have resulted from an analysis of options. In fact, the country report says that it found no evidence of multiple options having been analysed within the Ministry of Education or within the related institutions and thus it found no evidence of any process of choice having been undertaken. The delay in introducing a policy which had been on the stocks for over a decade had certainly given time for the population to become somewhat accustomed to the idea of having to pay something for education. It had not produced a strategy for implementation which was likely to meet with an acceptable level of success. The Uganda study asserts that "lack of reliable data and overall inadequacy of the information base did not enable the identification of cost-sharing policy options." Important aspects of the envisaged policy were not analysed before decision making. For instance, no proper study of the income profile of students or of their parents was done. While the Education Policy Review Commission did identify options, it did not provide information on the process of their selection and the report is silent on options considered but not recommended.

The Tanzania report presents an interesting contrast. No evidence was found of any real identification of options having been undertaken. Government was committed to achieving UPE and this was seen as having an irreversible social and political momentum. It was a 'given' and so eliminated any consideration of options which would alter it. As a consequence, financing options were rigidly constrained. There was no need for consideration of options. The "only option was to find a source of additional funds and the only available source was some kind of cash contribution from parents". Whether this was, in fact, the only option may be open to question but the fact is that what was seen as the higher imperative of a basic policy of the politicians led to the adoption of this line. Having a large quantity of data may itself present a problem for analysis almost as great as having too little. The review of previous implementation experience becomes part of the analytical process and of the identification of options. The experience of the personnel involved becomes a very important component. Time, too, or more often the lack of it, is always a dimension in the policy formulation process. It is probably unrealistic, even naive, to assume that if a vast amount of data and information were available to policy analysts they could anticipate all the effects which would flow from given policy options including the political, personal and other reactions.

Even the most sophisticated of analytical work could hardly do this. Nevertheless, ex ante review of options should still be adequate to avoid the need for a complete volte face of the type that occurred in Uganda where the introduction of cost-sharing led to student and faculty riots including deaths, to the closing of Makerere University for eight months and to the policy being reconsidered in its totality. In the event, the ensuing review of policy led to a package of measures which was far more acceptable to all parties involved. These measures, for instance, established a special fund for "needy students", introduced a Book Bank Scheme to compensate for the abolition of book allowances, and partly reversed the abolition of all travel allowances. Similarly in Tanzania, the achievement of UPE within three years was declared as a political objective without any consideration of its feasibility or implications. Civil servants were left in complete disarray and were invariably forced to modify the original policy objectives as resources rarely permitted the attainment of the ambitious targets set by the politicians.

These experiences point to the need to spend as much effort as possible in analysing the likely results of different options so as to avoid problems. The decision in Uganda to impose cost recovery measures in tertiary education which were part of a wider policy proposal in advance of the completion of the global education sector study, was, certainly in retrospect, far too precipitate and inadequately considered. The ten year delay in Ghana between the initial recommendation by the National Consultative Committee that parents should pay 50 per cent of the cost of text-books and stationery supplied to primary school children, and the eventual decision of the government to introduce some cost recovery measures may be questioned, even though the intervening period was well used to sensitise parents to the need for such measures. It must be recognised that the process of analysis is time consuming and, particularly in the context of financial crises, can be carried to excess.

Policy Decision-making

In all three countries, the policy was decided at very high level. As a result, it was not easy to get much information on the considerations that eventually informed the policy decision. It is common experience in most administrations that the nearer decisions are to the apex of the policy pyramid, the more the process involves confidential discussion. Often only decisions are recorded and everywhere, for researchers and practitioners alike, it is difficult to get access to what really happened during cabinet meetings.

In both Ghana and Tanzania, the political sensitivity towards introducing or increasing parental contributions to primary education meant that these decisions were made at the highest levels of government. Background documentation and advice for the decisions would have come not only through the civil service and ministerial channels but also, and perhaps mainly, through the internal consultative processes of the ruling parties. The advice was not necessarily of the objective genre presumed to be produced by the administrations on which those of the countries in the study were modelled at least initially. The advice would almost certainly have had at least a leaven of what the decision makers wanted to hear.

In Uganda, a somewhat different path was followed. As already noted, the cost recovery measures were part of a comprehensive education sector policy report which had been prepared by the Government and submitted to the Cabinet by the Minister of Education. From its package of recommendations on financing tertiary level education, the Cabinet singled out a few measures for immediate implementation. The Cabinet, including the President who is also chairman of the ruling party, the National Resistance Movement made the final decision although, given the sensitivity of the matter, it could have been expected that the final decision would have been made by the highest body, namely the National Resistance Council.

Design of Strategies for Implementation

Promulgation and dissemination of a decision among the actors and stakeholders emerged as a significant element of the policy formulation process though it was not identified explicitly as a stage at the planning workshop. It may be regarded as the bridge between formulation and implementation and is thus treated in this section.

The way in which the policy was announced and promulgated was raised explicitly in all the reports as having a significant effect on the implementation of the policy. "Managing the message" is increasingly recognised as necessary for effective realisation of policy goals. In Tanzania, for instance, great care was taken at the highest levels to ensure that the decision on cost-sharing was not interpreted as any weakening by the government of its commitment to UPE or to its implementation.

The President reiterated this commitment. One report in a Government owned newspaper stated that the President warned parents who kept their children from attending school because of the new policy that they would be dealt with severely. He also added that "no pupil shall bc turned away from school if his parents fail to pay the contribution." This ambiguity appears to have led some people to believe that the payment was not obligatory. The country report argues that this ambiguity gave rise to the situation in which, even after several years, there was still a low level of compliance with the policy.

In Uganda, evidence suggests that the Government underestimated the importance of this stage of the process. The decision was passed to the Ministry of Education where it was simply signed by a Permanent Secretary and then circulated to the appropriate educational institutions for implementation.

The letter of transmittal gave neither an implementation strategy nor a monitoring and evaluation procedure. Most of those interviewed criticised not the policy as such but the piecemeal and ad hoc basis on which a single element of a larger policy package was introduced and the fact that there was no real effort to popularise the decision. The abrupt method of policy announcement was consistent with the top-down way in which the Government had handled earlier stages of the policy formulation process when no effective consultation had taken place. The result, however, was that key actors and stakeholders were taken by surprise sparking the resistance and rioting already noted.

In Ghana, the study report also judged that managing the message was inadequately handled. Despite the fact that the policy was introduced a long time after it had been recommended for the first time and the efforts of the government during that period to sensitise the population to the rationale of the policy, the consensus building that was essential to the effective implementation of the policy had not been achieved.

ACTION INSTRUMENTS

Three main action instruments provide links between the stages in the policy process. Their use means that the process cannot be represented as a straight sequential line, but rather as a web or maze with the analyst having to double back to review earlier stages in the process in the light of events or information occurring at a later stage.

These action instruments are:

- Information Gathering;
- Information Analysis;
- Consultation.

Information Gathering

The importance of having adequate provision for information gathering has already been highlighted in the section concerned with the administrative dimension of the institutional environment.

Both the Ghana and Uganda reports saw the quality of the information base as a critical factor in the process of policy formulation. They also referred to several weaknesses. The main reason for the observed gap in data provision was said to be the hostile political and economic environment in which, for instance, salaries and morale of civil servants were low, and the basic means of state functioning could be lacking or in short supply. Another contributing factor, was a 'confidentiality syndrome' within the bureaucracy. This hampered the free flow of information both within the ministry primarily involved and between it and other ministries. The Ghana study also reveals the possibility that data were often 'enhanced'. The fact that head teachers had an incentive to present favourable enrolment figures to the Ministry of Education was said to be one reason for enhancing data.

One consequence of this lack of reliable data was that external agencies felt obliged to collect data themselves. This sometimes resulted in a situation where field offices of external agencies were much better informed about the local situation than the local administrations.

In the case of Uganda, the problem faced by the Education Policy Review Commission established specifically to provide background for the intended policy change on cost-sharing, was reported to be "not a lack of cooperation with government officials in getting information but the absolute lack of detailed, up-to-date and reliable data."

There were comprehensive and regular reporting arrangements between Regional and District Education Officers and the Ministry of Education, including a regular flow of information about the payment of parental contributions to education costs. These arrangements were, on the whole, judged to be adequate by the study team though it was not possible to ascertain the precise use that was made of the information during the process of policy formulation.

However, reference in the report to a belief that District Committees were diverting some of the funds to other purposes under their responsibility suggests gaps in the nature and quality of the information available. The report somewhat provocatively makes the point that because the shortcomings of the education system were sufficiently known to policymakers and to the public, there was hardly any need for data to be used in monitoring and evaluation.

The failure to correct deficiencies was said not to be a matter of information but almost entirely a matter of lack of funding. This would seem to bear out the truth of Gulhati's point referred to earlier that there has not been much demand for policy relevant studies by those making policy decisions. They believe they know the score already! Closely linked to the issue of demand for such studies is that of the extent to which analytical capacity to produce them exists.

Information Analysis

An effective process of policy formulation has to include the capacity not only to generate and analyse new policy options but also to monitor, evaluate and review ongoing policies as a basis for their modification or discontinuance. In all three countries the capacity to undertake these tasks was both weak and underutilised.

Many of those involved considered that the weakness of the information base was not so much a result of lack of information but of lack of the institutional capacity for adequately processing and analysing this information. Several factors contributed to this problem.

First has been either the absence of policy analysis units in government or, where they formally exist, their widespread under-utilisation. A World Bank study of education policy in Africa, "lack of staff and other resources had reduced central policy and planning units to the status of statistics offices, concerned primarily with meeting the information needs of external funding agencies. Such units are not able to generate a range of policy options for review or to monitor and thus to learn from the implementation of policy decisions".

The country reports for the three studies show that this has been the case in Ghana and Uganda where institutions for policy analysis and advice to government existed but were allowed to decay. Once created, they were left on their own; their roles were not clearly spelt out and understood; and they were not given adequate financing and support. In Ghana, for instance, the budget of the Education Commission dried up and vacancies in its membership were left unfilled.

In Tanzania, the report noted that lack of policy analysis capacity at ministerial level badly affected sound policy formulation including the review of ongoing policies. Policy analysis units have been established in a number of central ministries. While this represents a move to create analytical capacity, it still leaves unresolved the issue raised by a senior Tanzanian civil servant, who points out that even if these units were universally established it "may not be easy to find people who have the necessary expertise" to staff them.

Secondly, the absence of any significant analytical capacity in government had been aggravated by the existence of few applied research studies undertaken by independent research institutions. At the Ghana review workshop, for instance, it was noted that despite "a long-standing tradition of community participation in financing education... its main features have never been analysed." Yet, the relevance of experience with this tradition in the context of the decision to introduce cost-sharing schemes was obvious.

This reflects a chronic mismatch between the demand for and the supply of applied research. Researchers are seldom asked to develop alternative policy options. Decision-making on research priorities is often an arbitrary process with few attempts to link specific applied research assignments to the priority needs of policy-makers. Boards of research institutes were perceived to act as mere rubber stamps for government policies. Participants in the Ghana workshop attributed this to the fact that board members were usually not aware of their institutional roles in the process of policy formulation. A third factor was the often simultaneous existence of several units with the same or closely related policy functions. For example, in Ghana, the decision to establish Planning, Budgeting, Monitoring and Evaluation units was a move by government to strengthen the capacity for policy formulation within the ministries. However, in the case of the Ministry of Education, before the PBME was established, a Policy Management Unit had been set up on an ad-hoc basis with support from a major external agency to oversee one of its projects. Some claimed that these two units had complementary functions. Others acknowledged that the similarities of functions of the two would lead to overlapping though they were of the view that any confusion of role and functions would gradually fade away as the PMBE increased its capacity to fulfil the different aspects of its mandate and thus to take over.

At the time of the study, the PMU had not faded away. Partly this may reflect that the PMU had been first in existence and had, therefore, marked out its functional 'territory'; that it had access to external financing; or even, that, like the Marxian state, once established, institutions never fade away. But it also reflects a view of the people involved in the PMU that PBME, as a regular unit of the Ministry competing for resources with the rest of the organisation, might face a deeper problem to develop greater analytical capacity and move beyond mere statistical descriptions of the system.

Consultation

Consultation has several forms and functions and it is relevant to many of the stages of the policy path. It may be used to secure expert views, to determine the relationship and interaction between the policy in question and other policies of the same or other ministries, or to garner the views of stakeholders in the broader societal environment. It can contribute to data collection and to the processing and analysis of these data in the national context.

Two main groups may be included in the consultation process — public bodies including ministries and agencies of central government, and civil society. Active linkages are required between ministries in order to draw on the technical and specialist knowledge of other ministries, to ensure that the interests of these other ministries are included in the policy formulation process, and to seek their cooperation when this is required to implement a policy proposal. The interdependent nature of much public policy makes linkages all the more necessary. In many cases there may be several policy groups considering similar or related issues simultaneously. Given the relative scarcity of policy formulation capacity, it is important to avoid any overlapping of functions leading to waste or underutilisation of existing resources. To ensure the necessary consultation, institutional mechanisms need to be in place and in working order. It is too late to begin setting them up when a policy issue, particularly if it is critical, urgent or controversial, demands it. In many countries, the need for intra-governmental consultation is recognised, at least in principle, even though it may come at too late a stage. Consultation with civil society is not so clearly part of the process with often unfortunate consequences at the implementation stage.

Consultation Mechanisms

In all three countries, lack of adequate inter-ministerial linkages was seen as a major defect in the policy formulation process relating to education and specifically to the cost-sharing policy. In two of the countries, Ghana and Tanzania, there was recognition that Finance as well as Education was involved in the policy under study. In each of these countries, the Finance Ministry was very much aware of deteriorating conditions in schools.

In fact, in the case of Tanzania, it was the Treasury which initiated the policy process in relation to cost-sharing with its request to the Ministry of Education for a "lasting solution" to the budget problems of primary education. From the beginning, therefore, there was an explicit linkage between the two ministries. Likewise in Ghana, the Ministry of Finance and Economic Planning was closely involved. In fact, the Ministry was aware that some parents were prepared to buy text-books. Its officials felt that there was no valid reason why parents should not, in the spirit of community participation, share the costs of education.

Thus, they discussed the issue with their counterparts at the Ministry of Education. But the issue was considered to be so sensitive politically that the proposed action was greatly delayed and had been weakened long before the dialogue with the World Bank took place. The Uganda case provides an interesting contrast. Here the role of the Ministry of Finance was limited. It was not represented in the Education Policy Review Commission nor in the White Paper Committee despite the obvious financial implications of the various policy options. At a general level, it is typical to establish inter-ministerial working groups where policies cross ministerial responsibilities. In Ghana, such working groups had in effect been established at the level of the Provisional National Defence Council Committee of Secretaries and, ultimately, in the PNDC itself. The researchers were given to understand that policy proposals submitted for decision to PNDC were scrutinised to ensure that inter-ministerial linkages had been made. If this was not the case, the submission would be referred back for further review. A similar structure existed in Tanzania where the Principal Secretaries, assisted by the Cabinet Secretariat, constituted an Inter-Ministerial Technical Committee. This committee scrutinised all policy proposals before submission to Cabinet. Neither report provides any indication as to the extent to which these procedures operated in relation to the introduction of cost-sharing in education.

It has to be recognized that major constraints exist to effective inter-sectoral policy formulation. The prevailing administrative culture favours a mechanistic, routinized approach to policy management. The administration is generally vertically organized into sectoral or functional ministries and departments and information flows tend to be vertically structured. Notwithstanding the multi-sectoral composition of the Cabinet, inter-sectoral linkages may neither be recognized nor managed at that level because issues are usually presented from a narrow sectoral perspective. They are also, of course, difficult to manage both technically and politically. Battles of competence and mandate at the bureaucratic level are not to be excluded. It is interesting to note that none of the three reports refers to an active role of central planning function in the policy process under review. This possibly may well have reflected the withering away of planning in favour of finance - a widespread phenomenon throughout sub-Saharan Africa.

Tools for Consultation

All three country studies indicate that there was extensive use of appointed Commissions and White or Green Papers to inform policy formulation. Commissions may be either interministerial or public. They may also have several subcommittees. Organised groups as well as interested citizens can be invited to give evidence to them and the former at least may have representatives on commissions and any sub-committees. To be credible, such consultation must take place at a stage when the output can be taken into account in arriving at policy decisions. It emerged on a number of occasions during the field studies that it is important to keep those consulted informed of progress including, if their recommendations do not appear in the final decision, some indication of the considerations which led to their omission. There was some cynicism about the degree to which such consultations could be regarded as genuine with an effective input to the process of policy formulation. One participant in the in-country workshop cited his experience of receiving a request for views and comments after the closing date for receipt of responses as supporting the suspicion that his potential impact was limited!

Some interviewees considered Commissions useful in terms of gathering data and analysing policies in general terms, but others saw them as window dressing or a delaying tactic by government. This latter was a perception which was reported in Uganda. Several macroeconomic and sectoral studies were made on educational policies. In particular, in 1987 an Education Policy Review Commission was appointed to review and appraise the education system at all levels and to formulate policy recommendations.

Extensive reviews of experience in other countries around the world were undertaken and the final report was a comprehensive study of the sector with concrete proposals for action. After receiving the report, the Minister appointed yet another consultative group to examine the report of the previous Commission. The costs of such duplication of efforts as compared with any possible benefits to the policy-making process can certainly be questioned. In Ghana, there was institutional provision for consultation in the process of policy formulation in the field of primary education and the report stated that it had been used, in the main, satisfactorily. Following a long-standing tradition of committees on education policy, a National Consultative Committee on Educational Finance was established which had no less than 54 members drawn from a very wide spectrum of relevant knowledge and interest groups. In March 1984, the Education Commission was appointed. Between then and 1988, it produced four reports. Nevertheless, there was still widespread concern among the stakeholders with what was seen as lack of adequate consultation.

Consultation with Civil Society

While this might be considered part of the consultation process, it emerged as such a significant but under-recognised factor and is so central to governance that it is dealt with separately. Consultation is at the centre of studying the role of actors and stakeholders outside of government in the policy formulation process. Policy is not made in a vacuum but within the socio-economic complexity of the country. It has earlier been emphasised that a more realistic and more effective concept of the process of policy formulation has, inter alia, to include the role of actors and stakeholders in this process. This is consistent with the current emphasis on adopting a "governance approach" in addressing issues of policy management.

Government has a major initiating role to play if civil society is to be effectively included in the policy formulation process. First, government has to recognise the need to stimulate public debate on policy issues, through the media for example, thereby encouraging more participatory forms of policy formulation. This would provide a channel through which to identify, publicise and influence policy issues. It would also pass part of the responsibility for ensuring that stakeholders are involved in the policy formulating process to the stakeholders themselves and to the leaders of their associations. The policy formulation process would be able, thus, to take account of bottomup views and ideas while, at the same time, helping to increase the political awareness of the population.

To tap the opinions of civil society, especially through formally constituted groups, specific mechanisms need to be put in place. As with interlinkages with other government bodies, they need to be developed independently of any specific policy issue so that they can be mobilised quickly when necessary and be part of the accepted institutional infrastructure. As is evident from some of the remarks made in relation to tools for consultation, there is critical need to ensure that involvement does not appear to be artificial to have a mechanism for keeping civil society informed or in the loop. While Ghana was found to have a good provision for consultation, people and institutions outside of formal structures often felt that no consideration had been given to their evidence and proposals if these did not feature in the final policy choice. There was also a belief among officials that objective comment was unlikely from members of the public who had a vested interest in the policy issue. Also, the Ghana study makes the point that no consultation with parents took place on the basis that "parents who had not previously been required to pay anything for their children's education could not be expected to agree to the introduction of any charge."

The Tanzania study found no evidence of any prior consultation between decision-makers and other actors or stakeholders. However, the Tanzania Parents' Association asserted that extensive consultation had in fact taken place within the ruling Party structures "from local branch up to the national Executive". The study could not confirm the extent or content of this consultation or whether the details of this consultation process had been made available to the Government officials dealing with the specific subject of cost-sharing for primary education. It may be assumed, however, that while there were certainly parents of children still in the education system in the Party structures, they were not there primarily in that capacity. The more likely reason for the paucity of consultation was that it simply was not part of the process. The richness of what they had missed because of the lack of consultation which emerged during the review workshop amazed senior officials.

In Uganda, the Education Policy Review Commission solicited views from individuals, groups and institutions. However, as a consultative mechanism it was seen to have two significant weaknesses. First, there was major criticism of its membership. It was asserted that the Commission was much too narrowly based thus excluding major actors and interest groups from participation directly in its deliberations. Out of the 28 members, 22 were from the Ministry of Education; one was from a party; the rest were from other government organisations. Cynics understandably wondered what was the point in setting up a Commission with this membership in the first place.

Moreover, there was deep concern, as in the case of Ghana, that those people and institutions that gave evidence to the Commission had no idea of what consideration had been given to suggestions that they had presented. There was no standing mechanism for communication and no feedback had been given.

This encouraged the sense that neither the Government nor the Commission was serious in undertaking a consultation process with actors and stakeholders in civil society. The levels of trust, confidence and openness between the government and civil society actors and stakeholders were low. Actions taken by the government further eroded the existing low level of trust.

Some actors and stakeholders felt that being asked to comment a year and a half after the publication of the report of the Commission, when a White Paper based on its contents was already before the Cabinet for decision, did not suggest a genuine interest in their views or any likelihood that they would be taken into account. All this is likely to have contributed to the fact already noted, that they did not perceive themselves to be involved in a process of policy formulation.

In all three countries, it was believed that effective policy formulation would benefit from increased participation of the various actors and stakeholders. The Ghana and Tanzania studies suggest that the levels of participation were better than in Uganda. However, participation was confined within the structures of the one party system in the case of Tanzania, and participation was held to have had only limited impact on final decision-making as in the case of Ghana. Much of the frustration, particularly in Ghana and Uganda, derived from the failure of governments to communicate regularly and effectively with them, including the almost complete absence of feedback when they had previously been asked for their advice. When no explanations were given as to why a particular policy option had been rejected or another had been adopted, there was a disposition to assume that no attention had been given to their own input into the process. While it is easy in these circumstances for people to be cynical over the genuineness of the government's consultation process, it is quite possible that the situations arose simply out of the sluggishness or incompetence of the bureaucratic machinery of government rather than of anything more politically sinister. Whatever the case, attention should be directed to improving the process of communication both within and outside of government. This can, of course, be costly but it is unlikely to approach the costs arising from an inefficient and often ineffective policy formulation process.

REFORMING INSTITUTIONAL STRUCTURES AND PROCESSES

This part of the chapter proposes a set of reforms in institutional structures and processes.

The proposed measures are grouped under three broad areas:

1. Reduction in fragmentation.
2. Separation of policy-making from implementation and de-centralising implementation authority.
3. Widening and enhancing the knowledge base used in policy-making and promoting integration and synthesis.

Reduction in Fragmentation

It was observed that, *a priori*, there are both benefits and drawbacks from fragmentation. Broadly, the benefit is specialised knowledge while the demerit is weaker coordination and integration. Having concluded that the present level of fragmentation is excessive, the question that arises is, how to go about reducing it. Applying the principles described earlier, the first reform would be to achieve a progressive decrease in fragmentation as one goes up the hierarchy. This would mean that fewer Secretaries, each of whom would handle more than one of the existing sectors. The result would be that coordination and integration will be achieved far more smoothly.

When deciding which portfolios to "broadband", the second principle— the degree of interconnection and overlaps between sectors—would be the guide. Figure is a schematic diagram of the proposed structure; Figure (the existing structure) is repeated for ease of comparison.

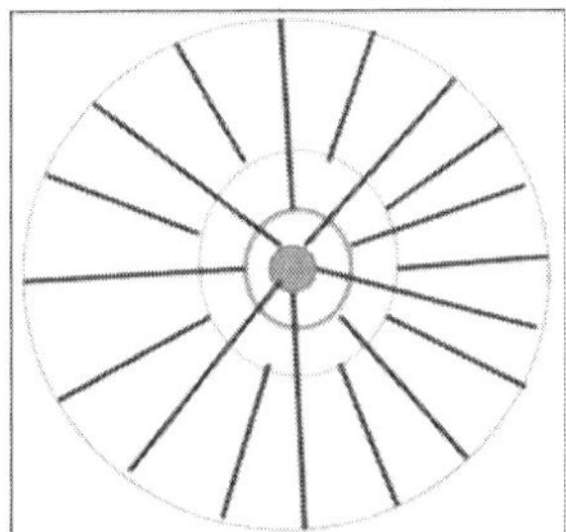

Fig. Proposed Structure.

In figure at the higher levels of government, there is a progressive reduction in the number of "compartments"—denoted by *fewer radial lines.*

Separating Policy-making from Implementation and Decentralising Implementation Authority

The proposal to reduce fragmentation invites the question: How will the Secretaries cope with such enhanced responsibilities, when they are already overworked ? It is true that senior level civil servants in the Government of India appear to be constantly overworked.

But this is mainly because of:

- The heavy burden of day–to-day administrative (implementation) work, which occupies far more time than thinking on policy issues.
- The high degree of centralisation of administrative powers.

The proposed reform is that the implementation responsibilities should be entrusted to Boards and Agencies, headed by a Director-General, in the rank of Joint Secretary or Additional Secretary. While his primary responsibility would be implementation, he would also provide essential inputs for policy making. He would, thus, be a bridge between policy and implementation.

The Secretary will be responsible for policy-making and have no implementation responsibilities. He would only get feedback on the progress of implementation, largely to aid future policies or to correct existing policies. Files on individual implcmentation decisions will not go to the Secretary, nor will he attend meetings on implementation issues. This will not only release

Secretaries from their excessive routine workload, but also give policy-making the focus it deserves. This change is depicted in figure: the thin lines separating policy and execution are replaced by thicker lines, denoting a much stronger separation of execution and policy-making. However there are pitfalls in completely isolating the Secretary from implementation.

The flow of information and policy-relevant ideas can be weakened if the policy-maker is not also the implementer. Secondly, lack of authority over current implementation can, in the real world, lead to a perception of diminished "power" with an attendant downgrading of the importance of the policy-making function. There is a way around this: the Director-General's annual performance appraisal should be carried out by the Secretary. This should ensure that the Secretary continues to have access to information and that the policy-making role is not seen as a secondary or unimportant one. Such restructuring could pose a problem in accommodating a large council of ministers. For dealing with this, the Boards/ Agencies could have a political executive at the top, in the rank of Minister of State or Deputy Minister. Cabinet ministers may head policy-making broadband ministries. Accountability for policies would rest with the Cabinet Minister and for implementation with the Minister of State/Deputy Minister. In fact, such separation of the policy advice function from the implementation or service delivery function has been a key ingredient of governance reforms in the UK, Australia, New Zealand, Malaysia and other countries.

Improving Integration and the Flow of Knowledge from Outside Government

The third broad reform would be to create structures which ensure the availability to policy-makers of non-Governmental inputs and subject matter expertise. To this end, each Ministry or Department should have a "Policy Advisory Group".

This would consist of:

- Selected top civil servants, covering related sectors. To ensure that the groups do not become one more bureaucratic mechanism without clout, only Secretary-level officers should be on these groups.
- Stakeholder/ Industry representatives.
- Academics with expertise in the field.

These Policy Advisory Groups should cut across departmental viewpoints, and offer integrated policy suggestions. Consultation of the Policy Advisory Group and a consideration of the Group's views would be mandatory on all policy matters, before a proposal is placed before the Cabinet.

STAGES IN THE DECISION-MAKING PROCESS

Decision-making can be regarded as the mental processes resulting in the selection of a course of action among several alternative scenarios. Every decision-making process produces a final choice. The output can be an action or an opinion of choice. Human performance in decision terms has been the subject of active research from several perspectives. From a psychological perspective, it is necessary to examine individual decisions in the context of a set of needs, preferences an individual has and values they seek. From a cognitive perspective, the decision-making process must be regarded as a continuous process integrated in the interaction with the environment. From a normative perspective, the analysis of individual decisions is concerned with the logic of decision making and rationality and the invariant choice it leads to.

Yet, at another level, it might be regarded as a problem solving activity which is terminated when a satisfactory solution is reached. Therefore, decision making is a reasoning or emotional process which can be rational or irrational, can be based on explicit assumptions or tacit assumptions.

One must keep in mind that most decisions are made unconsciously. Jim Nightingale, Author of *Think Smart-Act Smart*, states that "we simply decide without thinking much about the decision process." In a controlled environment, such as a classroom, instructors encourage students to weigh pros and cons before making a decision. However in the real world, most of our decisions are made unconsciously in our mind because frankly, it would take too much time to sit down and list the pros and cons of each decision we must make on a daily basis.

Logical decision making is an important part of all science-based professions, where specialists apply their knowledge in a given area to making informed decisions. For example, medical decision-making often involves making a diagnosis and selecting an appropriate treatment. Some research using naturalistic methods shows, however, that in situations with higher time pressure, higher stakes, or increased ambiguities, experts use intuitive decision-making rather than structured approaches, following a recognition primed decision approach to fit a set of indicators into the expert's experience and immediately arrive at a satisfactory course of action without weighing alternatives. Recent robust decision efforts have formally integrated uncertainty into the decision making process. However, Decision Analysis, recognized and included uncertainties with a structured and rationally justifiable method of decision making since its conception in 1964.

A major part of decision-making involves the analysis of a finite set of alternatives described in terms of some evaluative criteria. These criteria may be benefit or cost in nature. Then the problem might be to rank these alternatives in terms of how attractive they are to the decision-maker when all the criteria are considered simultaneously. Another goal might be to just find the best alternative or to determine the relative total priority of each alternative when all the criteria are considered simultaneously. Solving such problems is the focus of multi-criteria decision analysis also known as multi-criteria decision making. This area of decision making, although it is very old and has attracted the interest of many researchers and practitioners, is still highly debated as there are many MCDA/MCDM methods which may yield very different results when they are applied on exactly the same data. This leads to the formulation of a decision-making paradox.

PROBLEM ANALYSIS VS DECISION-MAKING

It is important to differentiate between problem analysis and decision-making. The concepts are completely separate from one another. Problem analysis must be done first, then the information gathered in that process may be used towards decision making.

Problem Analysis:

- Analyse performance, what should the results be against what they actually are
- Problems are merely deviations from performance standards
- Problem must be precisely identified and described
- Problems are caused by some change from a distinctive feature
- Something can always be used to distinguish between what has and hasn't been effected by a cause
- Causes to problems can be deducted from relevant changes found in analysing the problem
- Most likely cause to a problem is the one that exactly explains all the facts

Decision-Making:

- Objectives must first be established
- Objectives must be classified and placed in order of importance
- Alternative actions must be developed
- The alternative must be evaluated against all the objectives
- The alternative that is able to achieve all the objectives is the tentative decision
- The tentative decision is evaluated for more possible consequences
- The decisive actions are taken, and additional actions are taken to prevent any adverse consequences from becoming problems and starting both systems all over again
- There are steps that are generally followed that result in a decision model that can be used to determine an optimal production plan.

EVERYDAY TECHNIQUES

Some of the decision-making techniques people use in everyday life include:

- Pros and Cons: Listing the advantages and disadvantages of each option, popularized by Plato and Benjamin Franklin

- Simple Prioritization: Choosing the alternative with the highest probability-weighted utility for each alternative
- Satisficing: using the first acceptable option found
- Acquiesce to a person in authority or an "expert", just following orders
- Flipism: Flipping a coin, cutting a deck of playing cards, and other random or coincidence methods
- Prayer, tarot cards, astrology, augurs, revelation, or other forms of divination
- Taking the most opposite action compared to the advice of mistrusted authorities

DECISION-MAKING STAGES

Developed by B. Aubrey Fisher, there are four stages that should be involved in all group decision making. These stages, or sometimes called phases, are important for the decision-making process to begin:

- *Orientation stage*—This phase is where members meet for the first time and start to get to know each other.
- *Conflict stage*—Once group members become familiar with each other, disputes, little fights and arguments occur. Group members eventually work it out.
- *Emergence stage*—The group begins to clear up vague opinions by talking about them.
- *Reinforcement stage*—Members finally make a decision, while justifying themselves that it was the right decision.

DECISION-MAKING STEPS

Each step in the decision-making process includes social, cognitive and cultural obstacles to successfully negotiating dilemmas. Becoming more aware of these obstacles allows one to better anticipate and overcome them.

Pijanowski developed eight stages of decision-making based on the work of James Rest:

1. *Establishing community*: Creating and nurturing the relationships, norms, and procedures that will influence how problems are understood and communicated. This stage takes place prior to and during a moral dilemma
2. *Perception*: Recognizing that a problem exists
3. *Interpretation*: Identifying competing explanations for the problem, and evaluating the drivers behind those interpretations
4. *Judgement*: Sifting through various possible actions or responses and determining which is more justifiable
5. *Motivation*: Examining the competing commitments which may distract from a more moral course of action and then prioritizing and

committing to moral values over other personal, institutional or social values

6. *Action*: Following through with action that supports the more justified decision. Integrity is supported by the ability to overcome distractions and obstacles, developing implementing skills, and ego strength
7. *Reflection in action*
8. *Reflection on action*

When in an organization and faced with a difficult decision, there are several steps one can take to ensure the best possible solutions will be decided.

These steps are put into seven effective ways to go about this decision-making process:

- *The first step* - Outline your goal and outcome. This will enable decision-makers to see exactly what they are trying to accomplish and keep them on a specific path.
- *The second step* - Gather data. This will help decision-makers have actual evidence to help them come up with a solution.
- *The third step* - Brainstorm to develop alternatives. Coming up with more than one solution ables you to see which one can actually work.
- *The fourth step* - List pros and cons of each alternative. With the list of pros and cons, you can eliminate the solutions that have more cons than pros, making your decision easier.
- *The fifth step* - Make the decision. Once you analyse each solution, you should pick the one that has many pros and is a solution that everyone can agree with.
- *The sixth step* - Immediately take action. Once the decision is picked, you should implement it right away.
- *The seventh step* - Learn from, and reflect on the decision-making. This step allows you to see what you did right and wrong when coming up, and putting the decision to use.

COGNITIVE AND PERSONAL BIASES

Biases can creep into our decision-making processes. Many different people have made a decision about the same question and then craft potential cognitive interventions aimed at improving decision-making outcomes.

Here a list of some of the more commonly debated cognitive biases:

- *Selective search for evidence*—We tend to be willing to gather facts that support certain conclusions but disregard other facts that support different conclusions. Individuals who are highly defensive in this manner show significantly greater left prefrontal cortex activity as measured by EEG than do less defensive individuals.
- *Premature termination of search for evidence*—We tend to accept the first alternative that looks like it might work.

- *Inertia*—Unwillingness to change thought patterns that we have used in the past in the face of new circumstances.
- *Selective perception*—We actively screen-out information that we do not think is important. In one demonstration of this effect, discounting of arguments with which one disagrees was decreased by selective activation of right prefrontal cortex.
- *Wishful thinking or optimism bias*—We tend to want to see things in a positive light and this can distort our perception and thinking.
- *Choice*—supportive bias occurs when we distort our memories of chosen and rejected options to make the chosen options seem more attractive.
- *Recency*—We tend to place more attention on more recent information and either ignore or forget more distant information. The opposite effect in the first set of data or other information is termed Primacy effect.
- *Repetition bias*—A willingness to believe what we have been told most often and by the greatest number of different sources.
- *Anchoring and adjustment*—Decisions are unduly influenced by initial information that shapes our view of subsequent information.
- *Group think*—Peer pressure to conform to the opinions held by the group.
- *Source credibility bias*—We reject something if we have a bias against the person, organization, or group to which the person belongs: We are inclined to accept a statement by someone we like.
- *Incremental decision-making and escalating commitment*—We look at a decision as a small step in a process and this tends to perpetuate a series of similar decisions. This can be contrasted with zero-based decision-making.
- *Attribution asymmetry*—We tend to attribute our success to our abilities and talents, but we attribute our failures to bad luck and external factors. We attribute other's success to good luck, and their failures to their mistakes.
- *Role fulfillment*—We conform to the decision making expectations that others have of someone in our position.
- *Underestimating uncertainty and the illusion of control*—We tend to underestimate future uncertainty because we tend to believe we have more control over events than we really do. We believe we have control to minimize potential problems in our decisions.
- Framing bias is best avoided by using numeracy with absolute measures of efficacy.

COGNITIVE STYLES

Influence of Briggs-Myers Type

A person's decision-making process depends to a significant degree on their cognitive style. Myers developed a set of four bi-polar dimensions, called the Myers-Briggs Type Indicator. The terminal points on these dimensions are: *thinking* and *feeling*; *extroversion* and *introversion*; *judgement* and *perception*; and *sensing* and *intuition*. She claimed that a person's decision making style correlates well with how they score on these four dimensions. For example, someone who scored near the thinking, extroversion, sensing, and judgement ends of the dimensions would tend to have a logical, analytical, objective, critical, and empirical decision making style. However, some psychologists say that the MBTI lacks reliability and validity and is poorly constructed. Other studies suggest that these national or cross-cultural differences exist across entire societies. For example, Maris Martinsons has found that American, Japanese and Chinese business leaders each exhibit a distinctive national style of decision-making.

Optimizing vs. Satisficing

Herbert Simon coined the phrase "bounded rationality" to express the idea that human decision-making is limited by available information, available time, and the information-processing ability of the mind. Simon also defined two cognitive styles: *maximizers* try to make an optimal decision, whereas *satisficers* simply try to find a solution that is "good enough". Maximizers tend to take longer making decisions due to the need to maximize performance across all variables and make tradeoffs carefully; they also tend to more often regret their decisions.

Combinational vs. Positional

Styles and methods of decision-making were elaborated by the founder of Predispositioning Theory, Aron Katsenelinboigen. In his analysis on styles and methods Katsenelinboigen referred to the game of chess, saying that "chess does disclose various methods of operation, notably the creation of predisposition—methods which may be applicable to other, more complex systems."

In his book Katsenelinboigen states that apart from the methods and sub-methods, there are two major styles—positional and combinational. Both styles are utilized in the game of chess. The two styles reflect two basic approaches to the uncertainty: deterministic and indeterministic. Katsenelinboigen's definition of the two styles are the following.

The combinational style is characterized by

- A very narrow, clearly defined, primarily material goal, and
- A programme that links the initial position with the final outcome.

In defining the combinational style in chess, Katsenelinboigen writes: The combinational style features a clearly formulated limited objective, namely the capture of material. The objective is implemented via a well-defined and in some cases in a unique sequence of moves aimed at reaching the set goal. As a rule, this sequence leaves no options for the opponent. Finding a combinational objective allows the player to focus all his energies on efficient execution, that is, the player's analysis may be limited to the pieces directly partaking in the combination. This approach is the crux of the combination and the combinational style of play.

The positional style is distinguished by

- A positional goal and
- A formation of semi-complete linkages between the initial step and final outcome.

"Unlike the combinational player, the positional player is occupied, first and foremost, with the elaboration of the position that will allow him to develop in the unknown future. In playing the positional style, the player must evaluate relational and material parameters as independent variables. The positional style gives the player the opportunity to develop a position until it becomes pregnant with a combination. However, the combination is not the final goal of the positional player—it helps him to achieve the desirable, keeping in mind a predisposition for the future development. The Pyrrhic victory is the best example of one's inability to think positionally."

The positional style serves to:

- Create a predisposition to the future development of the position;
- Induce the environment in a certain way;
- Absorb an unexpected outcome in one's favour;
- Avoid the negative aspects of unexpected outcomes.

Katsenelinboigen writes:

- "As the game progressed and defence became more sophisticated the combinational style of play declined.... The positional style of chess does not eliminate the combinational one with its attempt to see the entire programme of action in advance. The positional style merely prepares the transformation to a combination when the latter becomes feasible."

NEUROSCIENCE PERSPECTIVE

The anterior cingulate cortex, orbitofrontal cortex are brain regions involved in decision-making processes. A recent neuroimaging study found distinctive patterns of neural activation in these regions depending on whether decisions were made on the basis of personal volition or following directions from someone else. Patients with damage to the ventromedial prefrontal cortex have difficulty making advantageous decisions.

A recent study involving Rhesus monkeys found that neurons in the parietal cortex not only represent the formation of a decision but also signal the degree of certainty associated with the decision. Another recent study found that lesions to the ACC in the macaque resulted in impaired decision making in the long run of reinforcement guided tasks suggesting that the ACC may be involved in evaluating past reinforcement information and guiding future action.

Emotion appears to aid the decision-making process: Decision-making often occurs in the face of uncertainty about whether one's choices will lead to benefit or harm. The somatic-marker hypothesis is a neurobiological theory of how decisions are made in the face of uncertain outcome. This theory holds that such decisions are aided by emotions, in the form of bodily states, that are elicited during the deliberation of future consequences and that mark different options for behaviour as being advantageous or disadvantageous. This process involves an interplay between neural systems that elicit emotional/bodily states and neural systems that map these emotional/bodily states.

Although it is unclear whether the studies generalize to all processing, there is evidence that volitional movements are initiated, not by the conscious decision-making self, but by the subconscious.

INDIVIDUAL PROCESSES OF MOTIVATIONAL THEORY

What makes us do the things we do? Why would two individuals, in similar circumstances, choose two different options? The answer, in part, is motivation. Motivation drives behaviour; it is the force behind an individual's decision to commit or not commit to certain acts or behaviours. The elements that make up what we call motivation are complex, unique for each individual, and generally dynamic through time.

Handy suggests that motivation is the intersection of assessed need and the likelihood or nature of results. An individual calculates an "E" (energy, enthusiasm, effort) the product of need, and prediction for likelihood of achieving the desired results. When a person enters into a contract with an organization some calculation will be made in regards to the individual's "E" put forth. Organizations also put forth an "E", either by resources alone (salary), or by other items such as prestige and stature. This exchange sets the limits of a physical and "psychological contract" between the organization and the person. The psychological contract can be defined as the shared and unshared expectations between the individual and the organization based on initial agreements and the individual's motivation calculations. When both parties see the psychological contract clearly, (*i.e.*, when it is fully understood and acknowledged by both parties), the motivation of the individual becomes transparent.

Motivation theory tells us a few things about managing groups of people. First, in order to find successful ways to change people's behaviours in an organization you must understand the terms of the psychological contract for those individuals. When you understand the terms by which a person joins an organization, you can better secure meeting that demand and hopefully sustain an "E" input over time. If, however, an organization changes its "E", or increases demands on the individual, "E" will change according to the person's motivation calculation. Management must carefully consider how to maintain or adjust the psychological contract in order to keep that person a productive member of the team. This may mean an increase in salary or manpower and/or increased managerial responsibilities.

ROLE OF THEORY

The roles we carry shape the way we see ourselves and help to define the behaviours we should exhibit, and those we should not. Roles also help us to communicate responsibilities and set expectations for appropriate responses from others. In an organization roles can help to clearly define boundaries between individuals and locis of power.

Adjusting to or meeting role expectations can however create problems. Role ambiguity is one such problem. Role ambiguity occurs when either the focal person or others around him/her are unclear about the nature or expectations of a role. Role ambiguity can plague employees endeavouring to successfully attain and maintain new responsibilities or goals. On the other hand, a person may not reach role objectives due to overloading of responsibilities or under utilization of talents and abilities. Role conflict may arise when two roles intersect creating tension or difficulty fulfilling one or both roles. For example, when a mother returns to work and attempts to maintain breast-feeding. Management may not support the amount of time taken during the day to pump milk, leaving the mother at a hazard of not meeting both role expectations fully. Role incompatibility may occur when the expectations/nature of the role is clear but is incompatible with other roles or a person's sense of self.

Organizations need to acknowledge that its employees manage many roles and that problems or conflicts can arise since role conflicts create tensions that can change the ability of the individual to reach their goals. Organizations should be sure to support their team members in meeting new roles by giving time for transition, or offering training and support. In addition, when role conflict arises the organization can nurture employee's ability to relieve tension by allowing time to devote to caring for roles outside the office. An example of this may be support for a breast pumping station in the office and management support of breaks for pumping.

PERSONALITY AND UNIQUE THEORY

Personality is the unique and enduring traits, behaviours and emotional characteristics in an individual. Personality can either aid or hinder meeting work goals dependent on fit. For example, perhaps the best well know personality types are Type A vs. Type B. Type A personalities are competitive, impatient, seekers of efficiency and always seem to be in a hurry. Type B personalities are laid back and possess more patience and emotional stability, but tend to be less competitive. In a work environment Type A's tend to be more productive in the short term and pursue more challenging work. However, they also have a greater tendency towards health risks and are less likely than Type B's to be in top executive positions.

The later fact might be surprising. Why would Type A's tend to be in top executive positions more frequently than Type B's? Daniel Goleman might suggest that the difference in performance by classic Type A vs. Type B personalities is less due to fixed personality traits as they are for propensities to grasp the concept of emotional intellect (EQ). Unlike IQ, EQ is the "capacity for recognizing our own feelings and those of others, for motivating ourselves, and for managing emotions well in ourselves and our relationships."

Another possibility is that these trends are less the product of an innate character as it is the interaction of experience, personality and circumstance. If this is the case, a person's ability to work in groups or propensity for certain types of work may be task and time dependent, but can be changed with motivation and effort. Organizations can play a role in developing their staff for success. Workshops, seminars, even book clubs that focus on developing EQ an strengthen organizational success. Allowing for a diverse set of experiences, with appropriate support can maximize and expand the capabilities of each employee.

SIGNIFICANT OF ORGANIZATIONAL THEORY

Do motivation, role theory and personality factor into our day-to-day experiences in an organization in a significant way? Three theorists would suggest individual processes are very important to the success of any organization. The Human Resource Model, as developed by the contributions of Likert in 1967, McGregor in 1960 and Argyris in 1957, proposes that the individual is the most important, indeed the central consideration for maximizing the success of an organization.

According to The Human Resource Model each employee as an untapped well of creativity, talent and motivation, and the success of an organization depends on how well human resources are tapped. As an employee is placed in an environment where they becomes the originator and leader of their work, the organization's goals and their individual goals become one. When organization goals are internalized the individual's satisfaction increases, as well as the amount of motivation to be efficient and productive. Therefore the motivation of the employee is key because talent and creativity flows when the person is motivated to do so by internalization of organizational goals. According to the human resource model, the challenge of growth and productivity in an organization is the challenge of assisting human resources in reaching their maximum potential. The multiple dimensions of individual processes, the calculation of motivation, role development and development of innate talent and abilities, are all factors that must be considered seriously and channelled appropriately for achieving success.

GROUP PROCESSES

Power and Influence

One needs only to superficially examine the tabloids and other media outlets to see the action of power and influence: Movie stars promoting everything from prostate exams to weight reduction pills or popular health guru's preaching cures for all ills. These individuals, and others like them, wield great power and influence. Within the walls of an organization, power and influence also make an impact on individuals and groups. Although one may often think of power and influence in terms of how it is abused, it can also be used to do positive work within an organization to drive production and to meet goals. To that end we will consider its role within organizations and implications for change.

Influence is the action or force by an individual that modifies another person's activity or behaviour. Power is the force behind influence to make it effective. There are three fundamental principles regarding power. First, for power to be wielded it must have an identifiable and credible source; power would have no bearing on individuals without evidence to show that it can be used. Sources of power are those substances, physical or not, that can be mobilized to have influence. There are at least five broad sources of power: resource, position, expert, personal and negative power. Resource power derives from the control of wealth and resources: for example, the boy who owns the soccer ball gets to say if there will be a game. Position power is the power identified with fulfilling certain roles. A Chief Executive Officer easily wields decision-making power because it stems from his appointment responsibilities. Expert power is the power arising from knowledge and experience. Personal power is the innate charisma a person may possess, a type of magnetism. Finally negative power is the ability to *not* do something, and in so doing prevent another person(s) from gaining what they want.

Second, power is a balance between both parties. Both the person commanding influence and the person on whom the power is being exerted commands power, the later commanding at least negative power. Finally, power is relative. Power can be exerted only when those to whom you are trying to wield power recognize the source of it. Take for example the conundrum a professor of the arts would be in trying to guide decisions made by a Medicare policy review board. His credibility as leader is diminished because the professional source of power stems from expertise in the arts not public policy.

Once a power source (or sources) are established, influence must be communicated through recognizable methods. Each method chosen predisposes individuals to certain types of responses. Depending on how individuals respond, their new behaviour may or may not be sustainable over time. Influence methods include, but are not limited to: the use of force and coercion, rules and procedures, exchange (bargaining, negotiating), persuasion/logic, and ecology. An example of ecology would be changing the environment people are in. Chatty employees moved to different floors will quickly influence their behaviour by changing the amount of talking that can be done in the workday.

If the goal of power and influences is to increase productivity and the quality of services delivered by changing employee behaviour, then the central measurement of outcome success is individual response. Depending on sources of power, certain individual responses are more desirable for organizational strategy because of the way they correlate with sustainability of the response over time. Compliance is the agreement to a behaviour because of force – the "I have to" response. This implies the lack of self-initiated behaviour because the person "has to" rather than "wants to". Generally compliance will be the result of methods of force, rules and procedure and sometimes exchange methods, and must be maintained with continual supervision. Unlike compliance, identification and internalization have some degree of acceptance of the new behaviour, however the sustainability of the behaviours are not the equal. Identification is a behaviour adopted out of a desire to please or admiration for the person wielding the power. The manager exerting this type of power has great magnetism but must constantly be present for the behaviour to continue. The organization becomes dependent on the power figure, making the employee action not sustainable independently. Internalization is for most situations the most desirable response because it is independent of the source of influence and is self-sustaining.

WORKING IN GROUPS

In the 1930's and 40's a set of experiments were done at the Western Electric's Hawthorne plant. The initial round of experiments involved a select group of female employees, whom constructed telephone equipment, placed in a variety of environments (changes in lighting, quota demands, rest period frequent and duration) in order to measure their effect on productivity. To their astonishment, the research team found that the environment had little to no effect on productivity. In all simulated environment changes the level of productivity increased, and once back in their original environments the production level of the employees continued to remain at higher than pre-experiment levels. The team hypothesized that the major cause for increased productivity was the relationships formed between the employees and between the employees and the management.

A second round of experiments were conducted on male employees that involved in wiring and smouldering of telephone equipment at the same plant.

No change of environment was made as in the first experiment, except to place the men under observation. The research team found what they called the "Hawthorne Effect": Regardless of quota set by the company, the employees neither under nor overproduced. In addition, work output was equal for all members of the group. The research team hypothesized that the workers created informal groups between themselves and their superiors, which tightly regulated production in order to maintain a group identify where no man excelled beyond the others. This well-known experiment demonstrated for the first time in a controlled setting the role of informal groups on productivity, and that the effects of group culture in work environments could have positive or negative consequences.

Outside of the informal groups created by employees, administrators form groups in order to meet organization goals. The nature of these types of groups also deserves some discussion. Motivation for utilizing groups may include: (1) improved decision-making, (2). More risk taking, (and therefore presumably more innovation), and (3). Satisfying the need of individuals to be in a group.

Groups, like children, go through stages of growth. According to Handy, there are four stages of growth: forming, storming, norming and performing. As managers you must be sensitive to the needs of the group at each stage in order to help the group reach its goals successfully. In the forming stage relationships are being built through the establishment of goals, role definition and time-line formation. Quickly groups move into the storming phase, where roles, procedures and goals are questioned. It is vital at this stage that conflicts be resolved effectively and efficiently. In the third phase, norming, members establish a formal or informal set of rules and procedures for group members to incorporate into their work. Open communication is vital for the norms defined to be accepted and uniformly applied. Only when the forming, storming and norming phases are completed will groups be able to move into a performing stage of growth.

A few thoughts on groups remain. The group, leaders can motivate activities according to the stages the group is in. During the forming and storming stages leaders should assist group members by encouraging participation and viable communication. Leaders are key in maintaining group stability through effective negotiation during the storming phases. As the group matures, reaching the norming phase the leaders should practice foresight, promoting the next level of action by introducing effective evaluation methods and standard setting adjustments as necessary. Perhaps one of the greatest challenges for working in groups is the element that can be its greatest strength, diversity. Those who have studied groups acknowledge that diversity in certain combinations can be key to success. RM Belbin agrees, finding that teams do not need brilliance but balance for success.

GOALS OF MEETING ORGANIZATION

Working in groups are building blocks for meeting organization goals. Managers should consider ways to develop leadership in team members. Training for versatility in leadership styles through workshops could encourage this growth. Encouraging self-growth through concepts of EQ or even Covey's *Seven Habits of Highly Effective People* can also provide the groundwork for leadership growth by mastering interpersonal skills. Managers should also be pro-active about identifying and cultivating talent of his/her staff. When committees must be formed managers can help select individuals to create groups that have the balance of personalities and talents to maximize the likelihood of success.

Each manager must also consider diversifying their own talents by analysing spheres of social competence and goals though which to improve these abilities, but also seeking to diversity sources of power and methods of influence. For example in an environment that is strictly managed with rules and procedures, implementing a democratic process can broaden influence by example. This method however would require a great deal of time, effort and must be approached with focused investment.

ORGANIZATIONAL PROCESSES

ORGANIZATIONAL STRUCTURE AND DESIGN

If we were to look at any organization from a bird's eye view we could observe its structure and design. In the biological sciences structure defines function, so too for human organizations. Important concepts to consider in the studying of organizational structure are the flow of information and sources of power.

The challenge for all managers will be to balance the need for uniformity with the demands for diversity. Uniformity guarantees ease of control and supervision, ease of integrating work of multiple subgroups or teams (such as between offices) and economy since it is easier to pay for and maintain one system rather than many (one type of form verse multiple forms). However the environment in which the organization is based, and for which the product is being delivered, is constantly changing making it unpredictable. Organizations must than manage responses to these changes-diversifying their processes and thinking.

Organizations may tend to seek too much uniformity, following the classic futile fight against the law of entropy-that all things move towards greater disorder. An organization should recognize the many demands for diversity classify their importance and decide on which to pursue, maximizing the cost of diversity with the achievement of goals carefully. Open Systems Theory (OST) has integrated these conflicting pressures. According to OST organizations live within dynamic environments and are shaped by them. The organization is an organism with external (resource availability, changes of needs and demand) and internal (employee characteristics, adaptation to organizational change teams and individuals) environmental influences. The organization evolves according to the pressure exerted by these sources and therefore is evolving by successful adaptation within this dynamic, changing and an open system. The challenges to managers are to identify appropriate sources of influence by prioritizing them, and to guide successful adaptation by the organization.

ORGANIZATIONAL CULTURE

Organizational culture is "a cognitive framework consisting of attitudes, values, behavioural norms, and expectations shared by the organization's members." Organizational cultures help to establish a sense of identity for employees within the organization and therefore can facilitate comfort and a greater likelihood of internalizing organization goals. Organizational culture also provides a status quo and maintains stability in processes, communication and role interaction.

Culture is enforced in a number of ways, such as by ceremony, symbols and language. Ceremonies that commemorate employees demonstrating "excellence" as evidenced by exemplifying organizational values demonstrate in front of a large audience those values to be celebrated while also reinforcing them. Symbols, such as mission statements or encouragement slogans can constantly reinforce the vision the organization wants each individual to be guided by. Special language can also help to define a culture and allow an individual to identify with it.

The presence of culture demands uniformity. Managers must consider the consequence of paradigm shifts and plan in detail implementing changes. Implement new paradigms require the complete support of the administration, and should be able to address the needs of the employee working body.

MAJOR ORGANIZATIONAL PROCESSES

The two major organizational processes do not stand diaposed end of organizational theory in practice. In fact, organizational structure and culture must reflect one another in order to reinforce the goals and mission of the organization.

Imagine an international refugee mission seeking to initiate programmes for maternal child wellness in which people at the front lines aren't in the community with the individuals diving the resources. Although the goal of the organization values may be to respond to the needs of the community, administers, isolated from certain staff (organizational structure) leads to the inability to reach goals.

5

Public Policy in Administration

POLICY, AND APPROACHES TO INFLUENCING IT

This thesis looks at how to monitor and evaluate activities that aim to influence policy. A starting point, then, is to look at what 'policy' is, and how to understand change in policy. Rather than seeing policy as one single, discrete decision, it is important to broaden one's view, so that policy is understood as a series of documents and decisions that are best described as a set of processes, activities or actions.

Jones and Villar, for example, draw on the 1998 study by Keck and Sikkink on transnational advocacy and the policy process to highlight five key dimensions of possible policy impact:

1. *Framing debates and getting issues on to the political agenda*: this is about attitudinal change, drawing attention to new issues and affecting the awareness, attitudes or perceptions of key stakeholders.
2. *Encouraging discursive commitments from states and other policy actors:* affecting language and rhetoric is important to, for example, promote recognition of specific groups or endorsements of international declarations.
3. *Securing procedural change at domestic or international level*: changes in the process whereby policy decisions are made, such as opening new spaces for policy dialogue.
4. *Affecting policy content*: while legislative change is not the sum total of policy change, it is an important element.
5. *Influencing behaviour change in key actors*: policy change requires changes in behaviour and implementation at various levels in order to be meaningful and sustainable.

There is a very wide variety of activities to influence policy. One way to categorise them is to distinguish between approaches that take the 'inside track', working closely with decision-makers, versus 'outside track' approaches that seek to influence change through pressure and confrontation. There is also a distinction between approaches that are led by evidence and research versus those that involve, primarily, values and interests. The approaches and tools used to manage and measure 'outside track' influencing are relatively similar to each other, so we can simplify this to three main types of approaches to influencing policy. The three types of policy influencing activity are: evidence and advice, public campaigns and advocacy, and lobbying and negotiation. These correspond, roughly, to 'advisory'. Each of these typically involve certain sets of activities carried out in certain spaces and through certain channels.

TACKLING THE CHALLENGES OF M&E OF POLICY INFLUENCE

Monitoring and evaluation are widely recognised as being crucial elements of managing and implementing projects, programmes and policies in both public and private sector organisations. The production and use of M&E information during and after an intervention is generally seen as a central plank in systems for reporting and accountability, in demonstrating performance, and/or for learning from experience and improving future work. Monitoring and evaluating policy influencing work, however, presents some particular challenges and complexities. These challenges are, in general, integral to policy influencing work and not specific to one particular sector or approach to policy influence.

Although they have been well documented and described elsewhere, they provide a useful starting point for looking at approaches to the M&E of policy influence.

- *First*, there are a range of conceptual and technical challenges. It can be very difficult to determine the links between policy influencing activities and outputs, and any change in policy. Policy change is highly complex and proceeds in anything but a 'linear' or 'rational' fashion, with policy processes shaped by a multitude of interacting forces and actors. This makes it almost impossible to predict with confidence the likely consequences of a set of activities on policy, and extremely difficult to pin down the full effect of actions even after the event.
- This is about a difficulty in establishing causality, and is known as the 'attribution problem', which has a long history in the field of evaluation. Methodologies such as experimental and quasi-experimental impact evaluation that can function to analyse attribution in other circumstances are unsuitable for policy influencing work because it is difficult to establish a plausible counter-factual. Some have argued that there are additional problems in measuring both inputs and outputs of many influencing activities, such as research communication.
- *Second*, the nature of policy influencing work presents further challenges to more traditional M&E approaches. 'Outright success' in terms of achieving the specific changes that were sought is rare, with some objectives modified or jettisoned along the way. There is an element of subjectivity in whether gains were significant, consistent

with the wider goals of an organisation or campaign, or co-opted. In other words, the policy context is likely to change of its own accord, and influencing objectives may need to be altered in reaction to this or to other external forces. This means that objectives formulated at the outset of influencing work may not be the best yardstick against which to judge its progress. Policy changes tend to occur over long timeframes that may not be suitable to measurement in the usual rhythms of projects and evaluations in aid agencies. In addition, much influencing work and advocacy is most effective when carried out in alliances, coalitions and networks, which presents difficulties in judging the specific contribution of one organisation to a change.

- *Third*, there are further practical problems that constrain the production and use of knowledge about influencing activities. Staff carrying out influencing work rarely have the time or resources to conduct robust M&E, and there tend to be further problems of M&E capacity at the individual and institutional level in many organisations that work in advocacy and other influencing activities. This can also result in objectives and goals that are not clearly defined or communicated from the outset. Policy influencing involves political and sometimes highly conflicting processes, leading to difficulties in determining how best to solicit or interpret the accounts of different actors. Influencing work is often unique, rarely repeated or replicated and, even worse, there are incentives against the sharing of 'good practice'. If one lobby found, for example, some kind of 'magic bullet' to influence policy, it would be nullified if they shared the technique publically. Equally, policy-makers are unlikely to be happy with claims that their decisions can be attributed to the influence of another actor.

These challenges present serious difficulties for strategic decisions, for the adaptation of implementation, and for reporting to funders about where their money has gone. There are, however, a number of frameworks and approaches to help users overcome the conceptual and technical difficulties. The vast majority of these involve, either explicitly or implicitly, developing a 'theory of change'. This is referred to in various ways, such as a 'logical model', 'programme theory' or 'roadmap', but it is, basically, a model of how the policy influencing activities are envisaged to result in the desired changes in policy or in people's lives.

A ToC is an essential tool for the M&E of policy influence, not only for improving policy influencing projects and enhancing decision-making, but also for accountability and reporting to stakeholders external to the programme.

IMPROVING PROJECTS

Improving projects literature on planning and M&E in complex settings highlights the importance of M&E to test and reflect on a project's ToC. This is, for example, a key principle of adaptive management, in which projects or programmes are seen as 'experiments', examining hypotheses about problems and how they can be addressed, with ongoing cycles of evaluation, assessment, and adjustment of change models and activities. M&E activities must, therefore, focus on 'making sense' of the available information and data. Sense-making is defined as 'a motivated continuous effort to understand connections in order to anticipate their trajectories and act effectively'. Evidence shows that this key activity runs alongside action for contexts and circumstances that are complex, uncertain and ambiguous.

In complex situations project and programme managers face ambiguity, with available knowledge and information supporting several different interpretations at the same time. This means that teams need to come together to question their models of change, their underlying assumptions and the relevance of their goals. It is important to discuss the framing of an issue explicitly, and question whether interpretations truly follow from available data, and what is missing or uncertain.

ACCOUNTABILITY AND REPORTING

Once a ToC is completed it lays out a number of dimensions and intermediate outcomes against which the project's influence can be measured. Providing a clear statement of strategy and direction is a central element of accountability practices, and is even more important for policy influencing, where making objectives and strategies explicit is a key ingredient of success. Evaluating strategy and direction, and analysing a project's expectations for change is, then, an important part of evaluating that project.

Evaluators often have to construct the ToC from the assumptions and ideas implicit in a project's conception and implementation if none has already been constructed, but this is not ideal as implementing teams miss out on potential strategic benefits.

DEVELOPING A THEORY OF CHANGE

The ToC, often presented in a diagrammatic fashion or a table serves as a basis for future planning and M&E activities, as well communication about such activities with partners and funders. It is best to develop such a theory explicitly to cover all aspects of one's influencing work before undertaking the work, but this is not always possible.

Sometimes, teams must react to emerging circumstances by acting in ways that they had not anticipated and that take them outside the original plans. In other situations whole influencing initiatives are carried out without an explicit ToC being constructed. In the former situation it is best for teams to collect whatever information seems relevant to be incorporated into an improved ToC at a later date. However, this is a challenge in the latter situation, where theories must be reconstructed from available project documents and other sources.

There are three common types of ToC:

1. *Causal chain*: Perhaps the best-known kind of ToC, which describes a succession or 'chain' of elements and the logical or causal connections between them. This usually involves a set of inputs, activities, outputs, outcomes and impact, with each element causing or leading to the next one, depending on certain assumptions. For example, a log frame that sets out this sort of chain can be the basis for a ToC, identifying a series of intermediate outcomes that can be measured as determinants of progress or success. The downside is that the actual theoretical content and hypotheses about causal links can remain implicit, rather than explicit.
2. *Dimensions of influence*: This approach looks at the different dimensions of change. This involves a set of areas of outcomes, each of which is presumed to be important in contributing towards policy influence. For example the 'context-evidence-links' framework developed by the RAPID team at ODI specifies four key areas that are crucial in shaping the influence of evidence or researchers on policy: the political and policy context, the nature of the evidence, the key actors and the relationships and networks between them, and external factors, such as social structures or international forces. These represent various changes that, taken together, help create the conditions for policy change. Again, they highlight areas that can be monitored or evaluated.
3. *Actor-centred theories*: Some frameworks focus on the behaviour change of different actors. Actors are seen as the key driving force for change, with policy-making largely dependent on policy actors and networks, their behaviour, relationships, perspectives and political interests. Gearing ToCs around actors provides a clear, concrete focus for M&E activities, namely the behaviour changes of those actors. One framework that structures M&E in this way is Outcome Mapping, which focuses M&E activities on the behaviour of a programme's 'boundary partners'—'those individuals, groups, and organizations with whom the programme interacts directly to effect change'. Another is Rick Davies's 'Social Framework', which combines elements of the 'causal chain', mapping out a pathway to change through a series of actors and their relationships to each other.

There are various ways to combine different ideas about ToCs. The straightforward 'causal chain' model may be too linear or simplistic for understanding policy influence, and may force M&E into a straightjacket that does not reflect the dynamics of the specific context. Patricia Rogers provides a wealth of guidance about how to fit ToCs to complex challenges, such as incorporating simultaneous causal strands or alternative causal strands.

Another area for elaboration is the interaction with various different contexts. Both Pawson and Tilley argue that evaluation must consider how a programme may function by various different causal mechanisms which would interact with various potential contexts in order to produce an outcome. For example, the literature shows that the influence of research on policy will play out in very different ways depending on whether the government happens to have an interest in the issue, or capacity to respond. The emphasis should not be on making things highly intricate, but on trying to provide a realistic and intuitive model that clearly sets out a team's assumptions and ideas about change. There are two important considerations for developing a ToC. *First*, start with a picture of what drives change in the 'target'. A good ToC should, where possible, draw on a realistic understanding of what forces tend to affect the desired target audience or outcome. This is an important opportunity to incorporate social science theory into the planning and M&E of policy influencing, but also crucial to establish realistic expectations about what can be achieved, and what degree of influence a particular programme may have exerted.

Stachowiak presents six theories of policy change:

1. *'Large Leaps' or Punctuated Equilibrium Theory*, like seismic evolutionary shifts, significant changes in policy and institutions can occur when the right conditions are in place.
2. *Coalition' Theory or Advocacy Coalition Framework*, where policy change happens through coordinated activity among a range of individuals with the same core policy beliefs.
3. *'Policy Windows' or Agenda Setting*, where policy can be changed during a window of opportunity when advocates successfully connect two or more components of the policy process: the way a problem is defined, the policy solution to the problem or the political climate surrounding their issue.
4. *'Messaging and Frameworks' or Prospect Theory*, where individuals' policy preferences or willingness to accept them will vary, depending on how options are framed or presented.
5. *'Power Politics' or Power Elites Theory*, where policy change is made by working directly with those with power to make decisions or influence decision-making,
6. *'Grassroots' or Community Organising Theory*, where policy change is made through collective action by members of the community who work to change the problems affecting their lives.

Second, link into this the way that the project aims to influence the target. A causal chain, or 'pathway' can then be linked into the model of what affects the target audience or outcome, to specify how the project or programme hopes to influence it. This could flow from the project outputs, to a chain of intermediate outcomes, to the wider and longer-term outcomes. Alternatively, coming to a case ex-post, the process would try to trace the key chains of events that lead towards final decisions or outcomes. It is likely that certain outcomes required for success are beyond the direct control of the individual project, programme or organisation.

While the project team is in charge of the inputs and resources, local actors will often become involved in activities and outputs, and any policy influencing activity is likely to be only one of a multitude of factors that influence outcomes and impact. It is also desirable for projects and programmes to gradually reduce their control over changes as the causal chain progresses, as change needs to be owned locally, rather than externally, to be sustainable, especially if these are questions of politics and policy. In these situations, it may be wise to focus a good deal of the data collection, and accountability measures, on the sphere within which the project/programme has a direct influence when developing a ToC, to provide more useful guidance for reporting and decision-making. Outcome Mapping, for example, focuses on the influence on partners with whom an organisation works directly.

FORMULATION PROCESS OF PUBLIC POLICY

Current development thinking suggests that the policy framework is critical in determining the performance of firms, farmers, households, public sector bodies, and other economic units. By extension therefore, the economic development of a country depends on the quality of this policy framework, the decisions taken, and the processes involved in formulating each decision. It is clear also that countries throughout the world - developed and developing - vary considerably in their ability, and perhaps their willingness, to formulate and implement policies that will generate improved development performance.

At the outset, it should be emphasised that weaknesses in the policy formulation process are not exclusive to Africa, nor indeed, to the developing world. They can be found, to a greater or lesser extent, in all administrations. Examples abound where lack of attention to implementation strategies during policy formulation results in shortages of required resources or an underestimation of the complexity of the policy. In countries that have better developed and equipped institutional arrangements, unforeseen difficulties can often be addressed, through additional resource allocations for example. This is in contrast to most developing countries where capacity shortages, especially in the area of policy formulation, pose serious problems. African countries seem to have had particular difficulty in this respect. The development record of sub-Saharan African countries since they became independent some thirty years ago is generally recognized to have been disappointing. Many reasons for this have been advanced. In some cases, the causes have been outside the control of national governments. Natural disasters and global economic factors have been particularly significant. While national governments can do little to remove the causes of such economic and natural shocks, ill-conceived, inadequate and poorly implemented national policies have undeniably been a factor in reducing the ability of countries to deal with them.

Concern about this distressing experience within Africa itself, within the donor community, within research organisations, and within NGOs, has tended to focus on shortcomings in the *content* of economic policies pursued by most African countries. Thus, increased emphasis has been given to the role of the private sector, the role of the state, the importance of prices and markets, the contributions of primary education and health in reducing poverty, and a whole series of other issues which represent the 'content' of development policy. In fact, policy-makers and researchers have reached considerable agreement regarding the range of policy measures needed to achieve sustained economic growth and poverty alleviation. However, knowing what to do is not the same as knowing how to do it. The problem now is to discover how policies can best be implemented.

The emphasis on the content of development policy is in sharp contrast to the lack of attention to how policies can be made operative within a national policy framework. Without any clear understanding of the institutional processes needed to make policy formulation effective, knowledge of the needed policy measures is of little use. Much needs to be done to correct this imbalance; to ensure that effective policy formulation processes exist — processes which would allow appropriate development policies to be introduced and implemented with some degree of confidence. This study contributes to addressing this imbalance.

But why has this imbalance arisen? First, policy formulation capacity has been seen as "a residual that has to be created after technical prescriptions have been formulated", and its creation and enhancement is still one of the least understood aspects of institutional capacity. Doubtless, the fact that it is conceptually an untidy subject, arising in every sector of national interest, yet with no single discrete disciplinary boundary, loaded with political connotations and heavily determined by the surrounding environment, contributes to this. Essential questions such as how public policy is generated within the political system, how organisations and processes handle demands generated in the institutional environment, and how different actors behave in the policy-making process, remain largely unanswered — encapsulated in a "black box".

Second, not only is the enhancement of institutional capacity a complex and inadequately understood topic; it is also a slow process. In this respect, once again, it stands in sharp contrast to decisions. These may have a long lead time - the process of formulation - but the actual decision taking is generally quick. It can, equally, change a situation very quickly. For instance, decisions to raise incentive prices for farmers or to devalue the currency are likely to produce perceptible short-term economic changes. By contrast, enhancing institutional capacity by developing personnel with the requisite knowledge and skills and by developing enabling organisational structures and systems often takes quite a long time.

There are no quick fixes. Operationally, the development of institutional capacity requires that both governments and external agencies take a long-term view and sustain their commitment and support to measures required to strengthen this capacity. However, such long-term perspectives are rare. Several studies of technical assistance to strengthen African institutional capacity report the failure to recognize the need for a sustained commitment. Statements by some major agencies indicate that this is now recognised in principle. However, a lot of adaptation is needed, by both the external agencies and the countries working with them, to ensure that development cooperation programmes are designed with this in mind.

Finally, there has been a fundamental defect in the conceptual framework within which the policy-making process is examined, and within which programmes to improve it are formulated. This process has typically been seen as a linear model within which the complexities of policy-making are reduced to a sequence of steps, each with an identifiable beginning and an end. In this model, policy formulation is seen as a rational outcome of detailed data analysis with choices optimised to suit existing circumstances. It assumes that decisions are made centrally in a 'top-down' manner and on the basis of analysis by highly trained personnel.

These decisions are then announced to the public and handed down to subordinate agencies for implementation according to predetermined schedules and procedures. The mechanistic view of policy formulation processes has major flaws. It draws an artificial line between the process of policy formulation and the process of policy implementation. It fails to evoke or even to suggest the distinctively political aspects of policy-making, its apparent disorder, and the strikingly different ways in which policies emerge. It provides little understanding of the process of designing policy alternatives, nor of the politics, rules and intergroup competition that influence policy-making.

In practice, a strikingly different picture of the policy formulation process emerges. It is typically "an iterative, often haphazard and highly political process". At the top, it inhabits a grey and sensitive area at the frontiers of the administrative and political worlds. Policies are often made on the basis of perception, stored conventional wisdom, and attitudes of particular interest groups or bureaucratic interests, to which some partial technical analysis and information, whenever available, are added in the form of a brief technical memorandum written hurriedly at very short notice. Policy-makers often decide on matters without first having obtained full and detailed knowledge of the possible consequences of their decisions. They start running and take the consequences as they occur. In this respect, they come close to the "motivation outruns understanding" style of policy-making. Policy decisions emerging from such a process are likely to set off a chain of unanticipated actions which, in turn, lead to a swift policy reversal. As will be seen later, the country studies illustrate the truth of this observation. In short, the journey between identifying a policy issue and promulgating a policy decision - far from being a well-signposted path across level playing fields, more closely resembles movement through a maze.

THE GOVERNANCE FRAMEWORK FOR THE STUDY

It was from a recognition of the complexity and multi-dimensional nature of the process of policy formulation at the national level that this study began. It was not seen as just an issue of academic interest. On the contrary, it was and remains a matter of profound importance for designing programmes to address institutional weaknesses that constrain policy management. In particular, the study was anxious to understand why so many previous efforts by governments and external agencies to improve the capacity for policy formulation in African countries had such disappointing results.

Most of these efforts were based on the belief that improvements to policy formulation could be achieved by simply strengthening the technical-economic capacity of central governments. Staff training and the use of expatriate advisers were thought to be the most effective instruments to build up a critical mass of policy analysts and managers in the public sector. However, the outcomes of these efforts show that this was insufficient. By concentrating on only one aspect of the problem - personnel - they paid less attention to other parts of the governance framework within which national policy has to be formulated and implemented.

It was a serious oversight. This study looks at the process of policy formulation by and for government within the context of the broader institutional environment in which a policy is introduced and implemented. It relates primarily to the capacity of a government to design, formulate and implement policies and to discharge its functions - one of three elements of the governance environment. The study identified three main components as forming this element of governance: the institutional environment, the core policy formulation process within government, and the involvement of civil society. *First*, the study recognised the need to consider policy formulation processes within the context of the national institutional environment — political, economic, cultural and social. It is frequently overlooked that, in sub-Saharan Africa as a whole, policy formulation has had to take place in environments where governments have been pre-occupied with nation-building and with the complex social and political problems inherited from their colonial past. In addition, development policy issues have normally been addressed by governments that have been almost continually confronted by financial crises. These pressures have been particularly significant in shaping the ability of African states to formulate indigenous policies that reflect local needs and priorities. Very often it has been external organisations that have set the pace and direction of development policies, adding an international dimension to national policy-making processes.

Second, a core policy formulation process within government was identified. This comprises the identification of the policy issue, specification of policy objectives, the development of policy options, decision-making, promulgation, and implementation. It also includes the gathering, processing and analysing of data in connection with each of these activities. Thus stated, this internal process seems to conform with traditional presentations of policy formulation as a linear process. However, as already stated, this is not so. Instead, it is a complex process, without clear beginnings and ends, involving a varying group of people, with many seemingly unsystematic steps, and that some elements may be missed out completely.

Third, the approach recognised the importance of the roles and involvement of non-governmental actors and stakeholders - civil society - in policy formulation. Civil society is not a passive element in policy-making. Its members have vested interests in the outcomes of the process of national policy formulation. It includes all those people and institutions who assume, based on their expertise and specialist knowledge and the significance the policy will have for them, that they have as much right to be part of the policy formulation process as those within government.

THE INSTITUTIONAL ENVIRONMENT FOR POLICY FORMULATION

The critical importance of the institutional environment within which policies are formulated cannot be overstated. This environment is the source of the demands to which policy-makers must respond. It is also the main source of constraints on what can be done by the policy-makers. Since state boundaries in sub-Saharan Africa often owe more to colonial rule than to natural frontiers, this has sometimes given rise to weak national allegiances and strong attachments along ethnic lines. Most of the countries have suffered from political instability. In many countries, prevailing poverty was exacerbated by vulnerability to external economic shocks — shocks which increased in intensity after the early 1970's. Levels of formal education among the general population are still generally low. Public sector employees work in a context where expectations constantly exceed what can realistically be attained. Add to this the critical financial situation with which most countries had to deal and one can see why environmental factors are often said to be more of a constraint to effective policy management in Africa than elsewhere.

Environmental constraints to effective policy formulation were addressed in all three country studies. Each concluded, explicitly or implicitly, that adequate enabling institutional environments for policy formulation did not exist. All three countries shared a culture of governance based on centralised and bureaucratic decision-making. Little 'political space' was made available for inputs in policy formulation from sources other than the state. All have experienced severe economic crises, and in two of the countries there have been periods of political instability. In all three, wider issues of governance emerge from the studies as having a central importance for policy formulation.

THE POLITICAL DIMENSION

In Ghana and Uganda, arguably among the brightest hopes on the African continent at independence, political turmoil seriously diminished organisational capacity for policy management.

Uganda at the time of independence had the best expectations for economic growth, for institutional strengthening, and for human development of any country in sub-Saharan Africa. Shortly after, however, it became a victim of chronic political instability, war and civil strife that brought the whole human, economic, and institutional framework of the country to collapse. When a new administration took office in 1986, political stability and security were gradually restored and a reversal of the downward spiral of political chaos and economic decline began to emerge. However, beyond this, the policy environment was still extremely fragile and highly centralised at the time the cost recovery policy was introduced. The party structure still extended down to the village level. There was still no distinction between the powers of the Executive and the Legislature.

The Ghana case makes the point that the country at independence was relatively better endowed than most other African countries in terms of its institutional capacity for policy management. However, this capacity could not be sustained in the 1960's and 1970's when the acceptance of, and support for, a rational approach to policy formulation were seriously undermined by the combined effects of political instability and economic decline. Existing institutions decayed; the scope for wider participation in policy-making declined, and a tremendous exodus of skilled people took place.

During the 1980's, the Government sought to create a general institutional environment for policy formulation which would be more conducive to wider consultation. Major structural changes were introduced in the functioning of the state machinery. The changes centred on twin programmes: *First*, to decentralise government and to increase popular participation. *Second*, to restructure the ministerial structure and give ministries the capacity to coordinate policies. The Ghana study reports that these structural changes gradually allowed a more participatory approach to policy formulation to emerge. Increased political stability helped. Yet, the need for some cost recovery policy in education was recognised by the National Consultative Committee for over a decade before government felt strong enough to take action. This indicates that political stability was still perceived to be a fragile plant. Even when the policy was introduced, it was the externally promoted and supported Economic Reform Programme which was the main catalyst for action on this sensitive issue.

While Tanzania enjoyed relative political stability, its institutional capacity to formulate policy was highly constrained. For most of the period since independence, Tanzania had a single party system with a constitution that established the supremacy of the Party in the national policymaking. The Party had a highly organised structure from the local branch to the national level. It embraced a number of mass organisations which participated in the deliberations at various levels. Some assumed that this was sufficient to provide a genuine basis for consultation with intended beneficiaries.

Even before the end of the one-party state, some changes had been introduced into government. For example, as early as 1984, local government was re-established as part of a drive towards more efficient role division in which local authorities financed and managed primary education through, for instance, the collection of parents' contributions. It is not clear, however, to what extent these authorities played a direct role in policy formulation. Another change was the establishment of a Policy Unit in the Cabinet Secretariat of the President's Office and of parallel Policy Analysis and Review Units in the Prime Minister's Office and in the Civil Service Department. While these units were designed as 'think-tanks' to advise policy-makers, it was difficult to find the expertise necessary to staff these units, as well as those planned in other ministries.

THE ECONOMIC DIMENSION

The three studies identify the economic crisis as the main environmental issue to constrain effective policy formulation processes. Policy-making was reduced to *ad-hoc* responses to urgent problems, leaving little room for more fundamental and long-term policy analysis, consultation, design of effective implementation strategies, monitoring, and evaluation. There has also been little time to develop effective cross-sectoral linkages. While it is generally considered that effective policy formulation is most needed in situations where resources are scarce, all three studies demonstrate that short-term crises tend to receive top priority and this leads to grossly inadequate political, analytical and administrative effort being given to development policy formulation.

Aggravating these features of the institutional environment, African countries have confronted difficulties in dealing with both the "pressing nature and the low degree of understanding of problems". Most African countries have had to formulate policy in situations in which immediate financial crises have inevitably taken precedence over policy issues with more long-term, strategic and development-oriented objectives. In such conditions, policymaking is often a question of slipping from one expedient to another without tackling underlying problems. The inevitable result of these *ad-hoc* responses is policy decisions that may be well-intentioned but, in many cases, are ill-conceived.

THE ADMINISTRATIVE DIMENSION

Another feature of the institutional environment has been the centralisation of policy decision-making. Since independence, top-down policy-making based on one-party systems and the absorption of independent institutions by the state was the norm. The Tanzanian and Ugandan studies exemplify this.

In Tanzania, overall responsibility for policy formulation was given to weak central government agencies. The system, in practice, amounted to equating 'policy management' with 'control of everything and everyone'. The Uganda study notes that "authority is concentrated in the hands of the Minister of Education. District Education Officers routinely request intervention by the Minister on issues that should be resolved at lower levels. But despite this highly centralised system, the central administration does not have the ability to ensure that its policies are implemented. It lacks adequate resources, including finances, to monitor what is happening at lower levels let alone to control the finances that are collected at that level. The capacity to deliver high quality work is hampered by the lack of motivation and of basic skills at the support level. Because of inflation, civil servants get very low salaries and are forced to do other things to supplement their incomes."

The centralised, top-down approach has usually confined policy formulation to a narrow elite. In the absence of organised political opposition, independent trade unions, interest groups, and free media, involvement in policy-making is largely restricted to upper echelons of the political and bureaucratic system. This small circle "tends to make decisions on the basis of intuition, ideology or a process of give and take. They have little appreciation of how technical policy analysis can feed into the decision-making process. Consequently the ruling circle has not articulated much demand for policy relevant studies".

The country studies illustrate the narrowness of the inner policy formulation circle; the paucity of institutional provision for policy analysis; and the general underutilisation of what is or can be made available. One result of this has been the failure to create institutional capacity for policy analysis inside or outside of government. A second has been a failure to provide opportunities for non-governmental actors and stakeholders to contribute to the process of policy formulation. The lack of demand from decision-makers for analysis is a very important point in accounting for the disappointing outcome of past efforts to improve the policy-formulation capacity of governments through training, and by the deployment of expatriate advisers. It has become increasingly clear, even though it should perhaps be obvious, that it is of little or no use to improve the capacity of the 'supply side' of policy formulation if there is virtually no action to improve the 'demand side'. "No significant improvements will be forthcoming in the generation and processing of information unless greater efforts are made to inculcate into policy-makers a greater sense of information awareness".

Some commentators, including an FAO adviser on an early warning systems project in Zambia, do not perceive the problem as a lack of information. "A lot more statistical information exists than is often assumed and, with appropriate strategies, the usefulness of this information for policy analysis and decision-making can be considerably enhanced". It is interesting that similar points were highlighted by a senior Kenyan civil servant - Harris Mule - six years earlier.

An adequate and appropriate information base is a precondition for effective policy formulation. In the case of education, this must include data on such obvious and basic matters as enrolment rates, the numbers of children of different age groups and their geographical distribution, the numbers of teachers and their age profiles, the current accommodation, school equipment and supplies situation and future needs. In the case of the policy proposal to introduce cost-sharing measures, information on parental and student incomes is also required if policy formulation is to have a realistic information base.

However, building a reservoir of data and knowledge, no easy task in itself, is even more complicated if it is to be presented in a 'user-friendly' form accessible to those involved in the process of policy formulation. In the western world, there may often be too much data available for it to be adequately accessed, processed and analysed in the time available. On the other hand, Kiregyera notwithstanding, the general perception is that most countries of Africa suffer from a shortage of detailed, up-to-date and reliable data. The scarcity of data usually reflects technical and organisational problems at the level of collection, analysis and dissemination of information. In some cases, the problem is not lack of data but poor management of information flows, with data production exceeding the institutional capacity to target it appropriately to potential users and in general to process it in a user-friendly way.

Stanley Please in his editorial for the DPMN Bulletin special issue on information points to another problem. This is the failure of decision-makers to identify the kind of guidance they want from policy analysts and to put in place procedures that will ensure that the analysts are provided with the necessary data in a timely and reliable manner. The present situation with regard to information in African countries on the whole has led some to argue that African governments are data rich but information poor.

The absence of any significant demand by governments for technical policy analysis pervasively negative effect on bureaucratic behaviour. This was brought out in a study of bureaucracies in Southern Africa in which the author concluded that policy issues occupied only a minor part of the work of permanent secretaries in the civil service. They did little strategic analysis. Work aimed at adapting their organisation's mission to the changing environment was much less prominent than might have been expected. Bureaucrats tended to respond defensively when confronted with policy questions, believing instead that policy came to them from the party political process rather than from processes within the civil service. Moreover there is hardly any room for feedback from experience with policy implementation. "Whatever is being fed back at the top is in the form of praise rather than critique." There may also be cultural elements at play. In the case of Ghana, for instance, it was observed that respect for elders and reverence for authority may inhibit subordinates from contributing to policy formulation.

The counter-productive behaviour of the bureaucracy was also a problem in at least one of the three countries, but possibly more generally. Withholding of information and failure to coordinate with units working in related fields were identified as problems. More worrying was mention of the poor commitment of officials to the common good, lack of transparency in proceedings and even mention of corrupt practices.

THE EXTERNAL DIMENSION

The extensive involvement of external agencies in sub-Saharan Africa represents a further environmental factor which impacts on the process of policy formulation. Economic dependency on the outside world has become the rule rather than the exception, with many countries becoming almost completely dependent on external sources for their development finance. During the 1980's, the functioning of several African States was only made possible by external aid flows of a level relative to GNP rarely seen in other parts of the developing world. Donor conditionalities - explicit or assumed - as well as actual availability of resources, affect policy at both the macro and the sector levels.

The lack of sufficient institutional capacity to cope with the scale and strength of external intervention increases the impact of this intervention on policy formulation, in some cases to a point where "the state as a nerve centre for national policy-making may risk collapse". What the Economic Commission for Africa describes as "the growing influence of officials of international institutions and donor agencies on policy design, implementation and monitoring, without any accountability to the people of Africa" leads, in the view of that organisation, to "a gradual erosion of sovereignty." But how dependent, in fact, on outside influences has policy formulation been in the three study countries? The picture conveyed by the studies is mixed. In Ghana, external agencies appear to have led the government, as part of the Economic Recovery Programme, to adopt policies which had been recommended by the National Consultation Committee ten years earlier but which the government had been unwilling for political reasons to implement. In addition, external agencies insisted on the need for government to address long-standing problems of policy management in the education sector - *e.g.* the inadequacies in the information and data base and in its capacity to undertake monitoring and analytical work.

Recognizing these institutional weaknesses, a Planning, Budgeting, Monitoring and Evaluation Division was set up in the Ministry of Education. The aim was to provide a division inside the ministry to generate policy relevant data and information. The belief was that by establishing such a division, policy planning and formulation would be separated from implementation. This would enable the Ministry to concentrate on its primary function of policy planning and allow it to be the central coordinating agency for the educational sector. However, evaluation revealed major weaknesses in the functioning of the PBME. Part of the problem arose from unclear definitions of its functions and links with other units of the Ministry. The existence of a Project Management Unit supported by external finance was also a contributing factor.

In Tanzania, the evidence suggests that external agencies did not play a very significant role in the formulation of the cost-recovery policy in education, and that this was largely consistent with the intentions of government. The study team found "no evidence that external agencies exerted any influence in respect of this particular policy decision." Local representatives of donor agencies saw their role as being ready to assist the country; they did not consider that it should be part of their role "to attempt to influence policy which they fully accept to be the prerogative of the Government."

The report, however, recognises that, in some cases, the distinction between assisting and influencing policy may be a very fine line. This is the case, for instance, when a donor agency offers or is invited to undertake the management of a programme because there is no local capacity to do the job. This may result in an external agency becoming so deeply involved in management details as to become virtually a part of the system. Only in Uganda, does it appear that policy was provided virtually as a package by the donors to the government. The basic studies which recommended policies for the education sector as a whole and tertiary level education in particular were carried out by donors. The latter were instrumental in identifying the problems, in setting objectives and in the analysis of options. This may have led to an underestimation by government of the interdependence of the several elements of the policy. Because national personnel had not been centrally involved in its formulation, they had not brought a critical eye to bear on likely national reactions to the specific element of the overall policy — cost-sharing. To use a somewhat overworked word, they did not feel ownership of the policy. In this context, the ensuing political difficulties were, perhaps, inevitable.

PUBLIC ADMINISTRATION IMPROVEMENTS IN OECD COUNTRIES

Government expanded substantially in most OECD countries after World War II, and by the mid-1970s had become overextended and unaffordable. The resulting fiscal pressure prodded public administration reforms, which occurred in two broad waves from the late 1970s. The first wave—"less government"—consisted of reforms to control the growth of government spending. The second wave—"better government"— comprised reforms to improve services and relations with citisens. Currently, a "third wave" may be ongoing, to correct some of unforeseen side effects generated by the earlier reforms, and to reconcile the advantages of greater managerial autonomy with the need to preserve cohesion and integrity in the public administration. The *first wave* of reforms included efforts to both control aggregate expenditure and make government more efficient.

Helped by the stimulus provided by the fiscal discipline requirements of the European Union, by the end of the century these efforts had been successful in restoring fiscal stability in most OECD countries. The goal of expenditure reduction required greater selectivity in government intervention as well as some downsising of the government apparatus.

Most OECD governments responded to this challenge by withdrawing from commercial activities, while maintaining their general commitment to social protection. Downsising, too, was achieved largely by attrition and redeployment rather than by outright staff cutbacks. The specific content of personnel management reforms varied. Some countries went as far as trying to establish a single public/private labour market with fixedterm contracts for public employees and maximum mobility from one sector to the other, while other countries have retained the traditional features of the lifetime career civil service. In most countries, however, managers have been given greater flexibility to make individual personnel decisions and to evaluate the performance of their staff.

The preservation of the social protection compact, in the face of more limited resources, required also efforts to make government more efficient. In most OECD countries, such efficiency improvements were attempted through corporatisation of public enterprises; some regulatory streamlining; arrangements to contract out service delivery to private entities; and giving more authority to managers. Corporatisation was largely successful in improving efficiency in public enterprises, but regulatory simplification was neither universal nor very far-reaching on most OECD countries, and contracting out is subject to severe limitations and risks.

Much of the hoped-for efficiency improvement in government rested on the assignment of greater responsibility to managers to manage their budgets and staff. However, managers' flexibility has been limited by the need to preserve the newly restored fiscal discipline and assure uniform treatment of government employees across all agencies. In many OECD countries, therefore, improvements in public administration efficiency were generally not as significant as the substantial improvements that were achieved in the aggregate fiscal situation.

The *second wave* of reforms—better government—was stimulated by the increasing pressure from the public for improved services and for a more responsive administration acting to serve the citisens rather than dictate to them. The two broad directions of reform consisted of moving closer to the citisens and assuring stronger accountability. The former entailed mainly efforts to improve administrative responsiveness and service quality, and bringing the responsibility for some services closer to the users by decentralisation. In turn, better service quality called for improving transparency in administration, opening up channels for participation, addressing client requirements, and increasing accessibility. Enhanced accountability is the counterweight to providing more autonomy and flexibility to public managers.

However, even when effectively counterbalanced by internal accountability, the greater autonomy of public managers carries the risk of diluting the accountability of the executive as a whole to the legislature. This raises issues such as whether top public managers should report directly to the legislature, or whether legislative bodies are adequately equipped to oversee results, and similar difficult questions. One solution in some OECD countries has been to separate accountability for operational matters from accountability for policy. In any event, greater autonomy for public managers has entailed in most countries the need for stronger external audit and evaluation.

The speed and methods of administrative reform have been mostly country specific, but three approaches can be identified among OECD countries. A few countries shifted to a private sector approach in government, through introducing quasimarket mechanisms, splitting policy from implementation, adopting commercial accounting, etc. Other countries added new solutions to existing models, for example by giving more responsibilities to the voluntary sector. A third group of countries preferred *ad hoc*, pragmatic responses to specific problems, while maintaining their framework of rules and procedures. Common issues have emerged, however, and mainly the difficulties of measuring performance; ethical tension between delegation of authority and protection of integrity; risk of fragmentation and confusion in state intervention; demoralisation from authoritarian introduction of topdown reforms; and uncertainty from never-ending change transformed into an end in itself. As noted, therefore, many OECD countries are now in what may be called *third stage* reforms—to preserve the good innovations of the previous years while jettisoning the ones that have proven to be too costly or counterproductive.

GOVERNMENT EMPLOYMENT AND COMPENSATION POLICIES

The goal of government employment and wage policy is neither to minimize employment nor to compress wages but to achieve a workforce with the size, motivation, professional ethos, and accountability needed to provide quality public services; reduce transaction costs for the private sector; design and implement economic policy; execute budgets and investment projects; and preserve the key assets of society. A skilled, motivated, and efficient civil service with a professional ethos is one of the key requirements for good government. While such a civil service is not sufficient to produce good governance, experience shows that a very bad civil service is sufficient to produce bad governance.

Worldwide, general government civilian *employment* averages around 5 per cent of the population. Government employment is relatively largest in industrial countries, and relatively smallest in sub-Saharan Africa and East Asia. During the last two decades, not including teachers and health personnel, local government employment has grown to almost the same size as central government administration. Generally, the size of government employment is positively correlated with per capita income—confirming the so-called "Wagner's Law" —and negatively correlated with average wages. Concerning *wages*, the central government wage bill absorbs about 5 per cent of GDP, and general government about 8 per cent of GDP. The heaviest fiscal weight of government wages is in the Middle East and North Africa, which have the highest average public wages. Worldwide, public sector wages are about 70–80 per cent of comparable wages in the private sector. This is broadly justified by the greater security of employment. However, vast differences in wage adequacy exist between regions, with Asian government employees at the higher end and civil servants in anglophone African countries at the lowest end of the spectrum.

In the last two decades, major changes in employment and wages have occurred:

- Central government employment has contracted by about 40 per cent. This reduction was partly offset by growth in local government, primarily in Latin America, but general government employment declined overall.
- A smaller but significant relative decline has occurred in government wages as well.
- Consequently, the weight of the government wage bill has declined on both counts in most countries.

Concerning employment policy, an assessment of the right size of government employment must be country-specific and consider the functions assigned to the state, the organisational structure of government, the degree of administrative centralisation, the availability of resources and information technology, and the constraints on staff mobility.

There is no hard and fast rule on the right size of government, and any staff retrenchment should normally be a part of a comprehensive civil service reform programme.

When the civil service is badly overstaffed, or the wage bill is unsustainable, retrenchment by itself may be inevitable. Even so, it is essential to design it correctly, to avoid deskilling the government, demoralising employees, and risking social conflict. Experience shows that it is cost-effective to take the time and resources needed to tailor severance compensation to employee characteristics, avoid seniority-targeted retrenchment and seniority-weighted compensation, and put in place strong measures to prevent the recurrence of overstaffing.

Concerning wage policy, the key objectives are:

- Equal pay for equal work,
- Differences in pay should be related to differences in responsibilities and qualifications,
- Comparability of government pay and private pay, and
- Periodic revision of the government compensation structure.

Identifying non-wage benefits is a major problem, particularly because they tend to proliferate during times of fiscal stringency. Salary inequalities between men and women are also persisting, and are widest in developing countries. Salary compression has been another chronic problem of civil service compensation.

Because wage reduction has entailed in practice larger cuts at higher levels, incentives have been eroded, and decompressing the wage structure is a normal component of civil service reform programmes. In any event, the worse response to inadequate salaries is grade inflation and *ad hoc* remedies. In recent years "performance pay" has been introduced in some countries. The evidence shows that performance pay schemes have been at best marginally effective, and at worst have reintroduced political control over the civil service and heightened ethnic tensions in plural societies. Nevertheless, greater merit orientation in the compensation system is a must, including non-monetary incentives such as public recognition, national honours, and career development options.

Managing Government Personnel

The management of government personnel is influenced by the circumstances and social values of a country. Moreover, countries vary widely in their personnel management practices. But all government personnel systems, regardless of the country, must fulfill four functions: planning, recruitment, development, and sanction/discipline. Personnel planning is needed to monitor the growth of government employment, ensure the effective use of staff, and implement the staff recruitment and development strategies of the government. Planning starts with the identification of the personnel requirements of the government. Jobs can be classified according to the rank-in-person criterion, by which the employee's rank is independent of his specific duties, or the rank-in-post criterion, which assigns a specific rank to each position.

Each system has its advantages and disadvantages. Rank-in-person systems tend to become inbred and top-heavy, while rank-in-post systems hamper mobility and recognition of individual performance. However, all job classification exercises are timeconsuming and costly. If data are weak or the process is subject to manipulation, personnel requirements may be better defined through simple demand and supply forecasting. In any event, it is critical to establish a simple but reliable personnel database and keep it up to date. Recruitment in the public service should be based on the principles of merit and non-discrimination, modified as appropriate by social goals such as redressing past discrimination or assuring regional equity or including minorities and women. Recruitment procedures can be somewhat different in different countries.

However, the best way to assure merit and non-discrimination in recruitment is through open competition based on clear criteria and transparent procedures. Advancement, too, requires non-discrimination and the recognition of merit through performance appraisal. Merit and performance assessments, however, can be manipulated. In countries with governance weaknesses, seniority must retain a major role in advancement decisions to insulate government employees from political interference and avoid a perception of favouritism and discrimination.

The issue is not whether to evaluate employees' performance, but how to do so fairly, reliably, and without compromising the effectiveness of the work group. When country and agency circumstances do permit a fair and reliable evaluation, formal performance appraisal should cover only observable behaviour, entail a dialogue between manager and staff, and rest on frequent informal feedback rather than an isolated annual exercise. Generally, the more complex performance appraisal techniques do not produce benefits commensurate to their cost and the disruption they create.

In performance appraisal, simpler is better, provided that the system always includes confidential feedback from the individual's coworkers and subordinates. Merit-based personnel systems can include an elite cadre, usually called the senior executive service, whose members have higher managerial or professional responsibilities, enjoy better pay but less job security, and can be deployed wherever they are needed. Elite cadres are common in Asian countries, especially those in the British administrative tradition, but are also present in the French civil service and have been introduced more recently in other developed countries such as the US.

In an SES of the closed or mandarin type, the members are recruited at a relatively young age through a centralised agency; are groomed, trained, and socialised as a group; and become eligible for eventual leadership positions in a variety of government agencies. In an SES of the open type, recruitment is flexible, decentralised, and market-oriented.

Each government agency sets its qualification standards, and applicants from both within and outside the career civil service can enter horizontally into the SES at any age. In both open and closed elite systems, the greater mobility of the senior staff permits developing broad policy-making skills and spreads the available expertise. The personnel system should be neither fully centralised nor fully decentralised.

Good personnel management must not only conform to the overall strategies of the government but also meet the needs of individual ministries and agencies. Generally, the individual agency defines its own personnel needs; has the major role in individual recruitment decisions; and is responsible for managing the employees, once they are recruited. The central personnel unit sets personnel procedures for recruitment, promotion, and discipline and monitors their application; assists the government agencies in recruitment, normally by administering central examinations; provides a means for redress of grievances; and maintains the government personnel database. In many countries public service commissions play the central role in protecting merit and non-discrimination in all aspects of government personnel management, while respecting other legitimate concerns, and responding to the personnel needs of the individual government agencies.

Too often, unfortunately, such bodies have become a source of red tape, unnecessary rigidities, and bureaucratic delays, which lead government agencies to take shortcuts in recruitment and reduce the transparency of the entire system. In those cases, the solution is not to move to a wholly decentralised personnel system but to improve the functioning of the public service commission. The rights of government personnel are constrained by obligations stemming from the nature of public service, such as neutrality, impartiality, and equal treatment of all citisens and sectors.

Subject to reasonable restrictions related to those obligations, employee rights are mainly:

- Job protection and due process;
- Equal opportunity and non-discrimination;
- Freedom of speech;

- Privacy; and
- Right of association.

Most countries protect these rights through special procedures for grievance redress, but enforcement is often weak. An inefficient administrative apparatus for grievance redress coupled with weaknesses in the judicial system may deprive civil servants of an effective recourse against arbitrary treatment. In other countries, in contrast, civil service unions are such a strong political force that taking disciplinary action can be very complicated even when fully warranted, and necessary reforms in government employment and compensation can become difficult to implement.

THE DYNAMICS OF ADMINISTRATIVE DECISION-MAKING

Administrative decision-making is hierarchical. Decisions at the lowest levels may be more structured and amenable to few options. Administrators at higher levels make decisions with more discretion. However, there are strong linkages among the decision-making levels, although the nature and scope of the decision may be different. The recognition of these linkages is important to improve both the formulation and implementation of decisions. Promoting interaction between various levels in terms of goals and objectives, rather than cases and transactions, is critical for improving the overall decision-making process.

Administrators need a better understanding of how the structure of organizations impinges upon decision-making authority. In addition to hierarchical linkages, there are lateral ones. Most substantive decisions involve the commitment or redeployment of personnel, financial and logistical resources which may be situated in different units. Operating managers have to interact with these units to make realistic decisions. While the value systems and criteria used by various units may differ significantly, strategies have to be developed to build consensus.

Administrative decision-making at the higher levels almost always involves interdepartmental and inter-organizational collaboration. Arrangements to promote collaboration may be extremely difficult, as the different entities involved may have competing and conflicting interests. At a minimum, higher-level decision-making involves planning, finance and personnel agencies. Other substantive agencies may also have a stake in the decision.

On organizational and institutional imperatives, examines the complexities involved in organizing for different functions, making the point that typically a large number of agencies have an interest in a particular subject (for example, water). The target groups or beneficiaries of decisions are often overlooked. However, most decisions have short-or long-term impacts on the governance patterns that develop between State and society. When decisions are made in the name of the people, they are likely to be ignored. Thus, it is important to include the concerns of affected groups in the decision-making process Administrative decisions generally fall into four categories.

- Decisions about organizational survival, maintenance and discipline;
- Operational decisions based on the function of an agency;
- Decisions that affect the maintenance of linkages with the environment, including client groups and individuals, and beneficiaries;
- Development related decisions which may be linked to one of the other categories, or required by the changing priorities of society.

Each category entails different dynamics and relationships for decision-making. Sometimes there is a tendency to concentrate on one category of decisions, to the exclusion or neglect of other categories. The costs of doing so can be high not only in terms of substantial progress, but also for organizational survival. Of course, most of the decisions in public administration have to be made within the framework of relevant laws, rules and regulations.

Developing countries exhibit many contradictions in this regard. For instance, decision-making parameters may be highly structured or routinized for some functions through a multiplicity of rules, regulations, conventions and precedents. Alternatively, there may be a complete absence of rules on emerging functions. Administrators need to be aware of these contradictions, and order their decision-making processes accordingly.

Administrators may have their decisions challenged by their superiors. They may be taken before administrative tribunals or courts of law, although this is more likely in cases where decision parameters are explicitly stated. The point worth underlining is that the decisions of administrators are not exclusively administrative. They can equally become matters for judicial cognizance. When administrative decisions negatively affect persons and groups who may also happen to have political clout, the issue can become politicized. The need to act within decision parameters, therefore, becomes imperative.

Finally, few administrators evaluate and assess the impact of their decisions. The reasons for not doing so vary: there may be no motivation to do so; the requisite skills and techniques for monitoring and evaluation may be poorly understood or absent; superiors and political leadership have concluded for their own reasons that assessments are inappropriate; or the long-term impacts or consequences of decision-making may not be appreciated when there are intense pressures to take immediate action on an issue. Governments can lose perspective and public administration can become irrelevant when there are no feedback loops in the decision-making process. Many developing countries continue to struggle with this issue.

IMPROVING PERFORMANCE

In the last analysis, nothing can take the place of integrity in decision-making. While individual administrators may have their own style and personal biases, it is important to question the motives behind particular decisions. Administrators must be concerned with the philosophical and ethical dimensions of making good decisions. While it may be difficult to explicitly define goodness in some cases, it is usually possible to examine its broad connotations. For instance, every developing country at least formally defines the concept of goodness through the constitution, statutes and official pronouncements. The problem lies in making the concept operational. Administrators have a moral and professional responsibility to promote the realization of formally declared values through strict adherence to the principle of integrity in decision-making. It is the only way to bring honesty and sincerity into the administrative decision-making process and eliminate the dichotomy between pronouncements and practice in public administration.

DEFINITION OF PUBLIC ADMINISTRATION

It is proper to begin by defining exactly what constitutes "public administration." James Skok defines public administration as "the carrying out of policies established by the political (or policy making) elements of the government." For the purposes of this chapter, this definition will be used. The implications of using this definition include a sharpening of the politics-administration dichotomy and accepting the assumption that public administration itself does not influence the policy-making process.

The politics-administration dichotomy represents the idea that politics and administration are two separate entities that should be mixed as little as possible. The major benefit of using this definition are its broad base and its emphasis on implementation as a key factor. The chief criticism of this approach lies in the idea that it oversimplifies the dichotomy itself. The logical place to begin the application of Rosenbloom is with the executive branch.

DEFINITIONS

One scholar claims that "public administration has no generally accepted definition", because the "scope of the subject is so great and so debatable that it is easier to explain than define". Public administration is a field of study (*i.e.*, a discipline) and an occupation.

There is much disagreement about whether the study of public administration can properly be called a discipline, largely because of the debate over whether public administration is a subfield of political science or a subfield of administrative science". Scholar Donald Kettl is among those who view public administration "as a subfield within political science". The North American Industry Classification System definition of the Public Administration sector states that public administration "... comprises establishments primarily engaged in activities of a governmental nature, that is, the enactment and judicial interpretation of laws and their pursuant regulations, and the administration of programmes based on them". This includes "Legislative activities, taxation, national defence, public order and safety, immigration services, foreign affairs and international assistance, and the administration of government programmes are activities that are purely governmental in nature".

From the academic perspective, the National Centre for Education Statistics (NCES) in the United States defines the study of public administration as "A programmes that prepares individuals to serve as managers in the executive arm of local, state, and federal government and that focuses on the systematic study of executive organization and management. Includes instruction in the roles, development, and principles of public administration; the management of public policy; executive-legislative relations; public budgetary processes and financial management; administrative law; public personnel management; professional ethics; and research methods."

THE EVOLUTION OF PUBLIC ADMINISTRATION

An ordinary citizen of an ordinary modern democracy fortunate enough to undertake a journey backwards in time is likely to find meaningful similarities between public administration of our era and administrative systems of old cultures. The foundations of modern public administration can be discerned thousands of years ago, across cultures and in various nations around the globe.

The Bible mentions a variety of hierarchical and managerial structures that served as prototypes for the governance of growing populations. Ancient methods of public labour distribution were expanded by the Greeks and the Romans to control vast conquered lands and many peoples. The Persian and Ottoman empires in the Middle East, like imperial China in the Far East, paved the way for public administration in the modern age, wherein European Christians, and later Christians of the New World, were in the ascendant. All these, as well as other cultures, used a remarkably similar set of concepts, ideas, and methods for governing and administrating public goods, resources, and interests. They all employed professionals and experts from a variety of social fields. They all used authority and power as the cheapest control system for individuals, governmental institutions, and processes. All of them faced administrative problems close in type and in nature to problems of our own times: how to achieve better efficiency, effectiveness, and economy in government, how to satisfy the needs of the people, and how to sustain stable political hegemony despite the divergent demands and needs of sectorial groups. Not surprisingly, all the above cultures and nations also used similar managerial tools and methods aimed at solving problems of this kind.

They all used, fairly effectively, division of labour, professionalism, centralization and decentralization mechanisms, accumulation of knowledge, coordination of jobs, complex staffing processes of employees, long-range planning, controlling for performance, and so on. Intuitively, one feels that nothing has really changed in the managerial and administrative process of public organizations for centuries, possibly millennia, but this feeling is of course exaggerated. Some major changes have taken place in recent centuries to create both a totally different environment and new rules to which rulers and citizens must adhere and by which they must adjust their operation. In fact, a new kind of governing game has taken shape in which public administration plays a central role. Despite basic similarities, public administration of our times is an organism entirely different from public services in the past. It is larger than ever before, and is still expanding.

It is more complex than in the past, and is becoming increasingly so by the day. It has many more *responsibilities* to citizens, and it still has to cope with increasing demands of the people. It is acquiring more *eligibilities*, but more than ever before it must restrain its operation and adhere to standards of equity, justice, social fairness, and especially accountability.

Moreover, modern public administration is considered a social *science*, a classification that carries high esteem but also firm obligations and rigid constraints. For many individuals who decide to become public servants it is also a *profession* and an *occupation* to which they dedicate their lives and careers. Most important, however, public administration is one of the highly *powerful institutions* in modern democracies. It wields considerable strength and influence in policy framing, policy making, and policy implementation, hence it is subject to growing pressures of political players, social actors, and managerial professionals.

An overview of the relatively short history of modern public administration reveals that the field is far more eclectic than might be thought. The science of public administration was born towards the end of the nineteenth century when the business of the state started to attract social academic attention. The revolution that turned public administration into an independent science and profession is traditionally related with the influential work and vision of Woodrow Wilson (1887) and Frank J. Goodnow (1900). These scholars were among the first who advocated the autonomy of the field as a unique area of science that drew substance from several sources.

In the first years, law, political theory of the state, and several hard sciences such as engineering and industrial relations were the most fundamental and influential mother disciplines. Over time these fields strongly influenced the formation and transition of public administration, but the extent and direction of the influence were not linear or consistent.

Kettl and Milward argued that traditional public administra-tion as advocated by the progenitors of the discipline consisted in the power of law. Representatives of the people make the law and delegate responsibility to professional bureaucrats to execute it properly. Highly qualified bureaucrats, supported by the best tools and resources, are then expected to discharge the law to the highest professional standards, which in return produce good and accountable managerial results that best serve the people. According to Rosenbloom (1998), the legal approach views public administration as applying and enforcing the law in concrete circumstances and is infused with legal and adjudicatory concerns. This approach is derived from three major interrelated sources:

- Administrative law, which is the body of law and regulations that control generic administrative processes,
- The judicialization of public administration, which is the tendency for administrative processes to resemble courtroom procedures, and
- Constitutional law, which redefines a variety of citizens rights and liberties.

Several legal definitions argue that public administration is law in action and mainly a regulative system, which is government telling citizens and businesses what they may and may not do. Over the years, however, it has become obvious that law in itself does not maintain satisfactory conditions for quality public-sector performance to emerge. Constitutional systems furnish platforms for healthy performance of public administration, but do not account for its effectiveness or efficiency. Stated differently, good laws are necessary but insufficient conditions for creating a well-performing public service.

One such important contribution came from the classic hard sciences of engineering and industrial relations. In its very early stages public administration was heavily influenced by dramatic social forces and long-range developments in the western world. The ongoing industrial revolution in the early 1900s, which was accompanied by political reforms, higher democratization, and more concern for the peoples welfare, needed highly qualified navigators.

These were engineers, industrial entrepreneurs, and technical professionals who guided both markets and governments along the elusive ways to economic and social prosperity. Various fields of engineering, the subsequent evoking area of industrial studies, and other linked disciplines, such as statistical methods, became popular and crucial for the development of management science in general and were also gradually found useful for public arenas. The link between general management and public administration has its roots in understanding complex organizations and bureaucracies, which have many shared features.

With time, dramatic changes occurred in the nature, orientation, and application of general organizational theory to public administration of modern societies. A major transition resulted from the exploration of the Hawthorn studies in the 1920s and 1930s, conducted by a well-known industrial psychologist from Harvard Business School, Elton Mayo. A behavioural apparatus was used to drive a second revolution, beyond the revolution that originally produced the theory, which swept the young science into its first stages of maturity. Today, trends and developments in the public sector cannot be fully understood without adequate attention to behavioural, social, and cultural issues, which are also an essential part of the present volume.

These aspects conjoin with questions of policy making and policy evaluation, as well as with managerial, economic, and organizational contents, to better illuminate public systems. The human and social side of public organizations became central and critical to all seekers of greater knowledge and comprehension of the states operation. People and groups were placed at the heart of the discussion on organizational development and managerial methods. The human side of organizations was made an organic part of the art of administration. It is still an indispensable facet of the craft of bureaucracy. All who are interested in the healthy future and sound progress of public organizations and services both as a science and as a profession have to effectively incorporate humanistic views into their basic managerial ideology.

Major transitions still lay ahead, however. International conflicts during the 1930s and the 1940s forced immense changes in national ideology and democratic perspectives in many Western societies, consequently public administration and public policy had to be transformed as well. During the Second World War theoretical ideas were massively supported by advanced technology and higher standards of industrialization. These were pioneered by professional managers and accompanied by new managerial theories.

Ironically, the two world wars served as facilitators of managerial change as well as accelerators and agents of future developments and reforms in the public sector. The political leaders and social movements of the victorious democracies were convinced that the time had come for extensive reforms in the management of Western states. The assumed correlation of social and economic conditions with political stability and order propelled some of the more massive economic programmes in which the state took an active part. The rehabilitation of war-ravaged Europe involved governmental efforts and international aid, most of it from the United States. Major attention was dedicated to the creation of better services for the people, long-range planning, and high-performance public institutions capable of delivering quality public goods to growing numbers of citizens. To build better societies was the target. A larger and more productive public sector was the tool.

In many respects the utopian vision of a better society generated by the postwar politicians and administrators in the 1940s and 1950s gradually crumbled and fell during the 1960s and 1970s. A large number of governments in the Western world could not deliver to the people many of the social promises they had made.

The challenge of creating a new society free of crime and poverty, highly educated and morally superior, healthier and safer than ever before, remained an unreachable goal, so during the 1970s and 1980s, citizens trust and confidence in governments and in public administration as a professional agent of governments suffered a significant decline. The public no longer believed that governments and public services could bring relief to those who needed help, and that no public planning was good enough to compete with natural social and market forces. The promises of modern administration, running an effective public policy, seemed like a broken dream. Political changes took place in most of the Western states, most of them stemming from deep frustration in the public and disapproval of government policies. By the end of the twentieth century the crises in public organizations and mistrust of administrators were viewed both as a policy and managerial failure. In addition, this practical uncertainty and disappointment with governments and their public administration authorities naturally diffused into the scientific community.

Theoretical ideas for policy reforms in various social fields, which once seemed a key for curing malaise in democracies, proved unsuccessful. Within the last decade the search for new ideas and solutions for such problems has reached its peak, and premises originally rooted in business management have been increasingly adapted and applied to the public sector. Among these ventures are re-engineering bureaucracies, applying benchmarking strategy to public services, reinventing government, and the most influential movement, of New Public Management (NPM).

These receive growing attention, accompanied by large measures of skepticism and criticism.

IMPLEMENTATION OF PUBLIC ADMINISTRATION

At its core, the study of public administration is a study of implementation; it is an evaluation of whether policy can be put into practice. The chief architects of theories concerning implementation of bureautically-derived policies are Jeffrey Pressman and Aaron Wildavsky. Wildavsky defines implementation by the dictionary definition, "to carry out, accomplish, fulfil, produce, complete." Writing in the 1970s, the two used the federal government intervention in Oakland as a classic example of how policy enacted in Washington frequently fails to affect the individual on the street.

In 1966, the newly-created Economic Development Administration (EDA) was seeking a target destination for its endowment of $23 million dollars. The EDA was under the Department of Commerce, and until the mid 1960s, the agency had concentrated its aid in rural areas, which was its jurisdiction. Its authorizing act was the Public Works and Economic Development Act, passed into law on August 26, 1965.

This legislation was created to stimulate economic development and aid recovery in areas of the country which were suffering through depletion of a natural resource, like gold or timber, or an area that was shifting from reliance on one natural resource to another. Suddenly, the agency did an about-face and selected Oakland, California as the first site where it would try to rebuild cities, eliminate poverty, and quell racial tensions by redressing unemployment. The agency ignored its original directive and chose to implement its own policy.

Douglas Murray McGregor claims that "non-compliance tends to appear in the presence of perceived threat." Herbert Kaufman concurs, and argues that "people who calculate that they will be worse off under the proposed changes than they would be under the status quo often will not cooperate with them." The political process often results in a serious misallocation of resources. Logically, other cities like Chicago, Los Angeles, or New York, which already had suffered riots, would be first in line to receive funds. Still, Eugene Foley, the Assistant Secretary of Commerce and the head of EDA, choose to spend the EDA's funds in Oakland rather than another large city because it had a Republican administration, and if there had been quarrels with a mayor in the city chosen, Foley "did not want some Democratic mayor—like Daley—to be able to pick up the phone and call President Johnson." Even more appalling, the agency had too much free rein in determining which business enterprises were eligible for funds. Because of a tight time schedule, and the pressure imposed by the Watts riot in Los Angeles, the EDA's hands were tied.

Tension and foreboding were combined with stringent budgetary requirements. Funds were available in the 1965 budget, but if they were not used within four months, the money would be lost. The end result was that, three years later, only $3 million had been spent, and most of that was spent on one highway overpass and architect's fees. Jobs created were largely temporary, and very small in number.

The implementation is found indirectly within his legal and political approaches. The view of the individual emphasizes procedural and substantive due process, placing the interests of the individual above society. Organizations under the legal approach focus on individuals, who are guaranteed basic rights, which include certain rights of obstruction. Public administration under the political approach values responsiveness,representativeness, and accountability. Clearly, the political approach led to the selection of Oakland as a beneficiary of EDA funds.

EDA directors, alarmed by the riots that had been taking place in the inner cities, thought they could make a contribution by diverting their funds to a city with the right preconditions for a riot.

Oakland was an obvious target. The fact that Oakland city government was viewed as non-hostile led to the realization that a plan to hire minorities would promote political pluralism, another key concept embedded in the political approach of Rosenbloom. Not surprisingly, Rosenbloom claims that this approach has been widely denounced as making government "unmanageable, costly, and inefficient."

Therefore, McGregor's idea that managerial strategies can induce commitment may actually be dangerous in circumstances such as these. Instead, should one desire to change policy, it is wiser to approach the problem by using no coercive techniques to push the bureaucrat down the desired road. Leonard White lists several, including educational campaigns and compliance through publicity.

Kenneth Meier takes a more extreme view. He remarks that "zero-base budgeting, management by objectives, reform in the civil service structure, reinventing government, and planned programmed budgeting systems are "efforts to convince us that bureaucracy is the problem with governance in the United States."

The real problem, according to Meier, is that good policy can be political suicide in the short run. For example, because the government has a limited supply of funds, Congress deals with the Social Security system by creating an "intergenerational transfer of wealth," which creates intergenerational conflict that Congress failed to address. Meier.

Congress, in essence, has failed as a deliberative body, and gridlock is the major reason American public administration is worse off than its European counterpart. To resolve this problem, which is the exact problem Rosenbloom cites as his "political approach," Meier advocates redesigning the political system to eliminate some checks and balances, making United States government more like British or Canadian government. Tacitly, this admits that the Rosenbloom approach is correct, based on Meier's willingness to scrap the monkey wrenches in the system cited by Rosenbloom.

Next, Meier wants to lengthen the time frame for public policy making and manipulate the system to favour a long-term, rather than a short-term policy approach, through the use of longer terms for elected officials. Conceivably, this would allow executives to be better managers, as they would not need to be quite as responsive to the whims of a changeable electorate. In fact, Meier fails to recognize one other aspect of this point. The European bureaucracies he champions all have elected executives with terms longer than that of the United States President.

In Great Britain, the Prime Minister serves a term up to five years, and in France, the President serves a seven year term. Both are re-electable at least once, and in Britain, the shorter term is compensated for by a greatly shortened election process compared to the United States. Executives in these Western European democracies can concentrate on long-term contingency planning, without fear of upsetting the electorate or engaging in reelection campaigns that in the United States seem to begin shortly after inauguration. Since it is unlikely that we will adopt the British model, Rosenbloom is helpful in clarifying how the United States system combines political and legal insights in the pursuit of efficiency.

BUDGETING

Meier hinted that intimately related to the troubles of implementation is the problem of budgeting. A budget is "a document, containing words and figures, which proposes expenditures for certain items and purposes." At best, budgets can be a tool to help achieve the objectives of an organization. At worst, budgets create unfair expectations, obstruct the process by dictating how money will be spent, and create resentment that leads an agency to backlash and devote itself to causes other than its original mission, as we have seen occurred in Oakland with EDA.

Budgets are measured both quantitatively and qualitatively. James Q. Wilson points out, "bureaucracies are often prepared to accept less money with greater control than more money with less control." Wilson provides the example of Robert McNamara, the Secretary of Defence under Presidents Kennedy and Johnson, whose budget was considerably higher than his predecessors and successors, including Melvin Laird, who despite having a smaller budget, was a far more popular secretary of defence among the military services. The reason for this discrepancy is that McNamara embraced a PPBS, or planned, programmed budgeting system. McNamara saw the budget as a tool to achieve goals, whereas Laird, when he took office, slashed the budget but allowed the individual services to determine where the savings would come from. Laird cut the budget twenty-eight per cent during his tenure, resulting in the loss of army divisions, ships, and total personnel.

Still, each service continued its own projects; the Navy was free to continue developing its high-performance, pricey F-14 fleet defence fighter, and the army was permitted to continue research into technological communications breakthroughs. This is an example of the coordination of Rosenbloom's managerial and political principals. The amount of leverage given to individual agencies is a managerial question typical of what Frederick Mosher labels the "political challenge."

The product of egalitarianism, knowledge expansion, and management, the political challenge represents the fact that politics is the enemy of career systems, and that many systems, including the military, actually grew up in opposition to politics. Knowing that the military services function as one of these enemies eliminates the ability to use the budget as a tool to achieve specific objectives. True, budgets can achieve overall goals; but it must be accepted that when dealing with career systems agencies, it is best to not force specific tactics. Hence, the politics of coercion and the price paid for enforcing that coercion play a major role in the calculations of bureaucrats like Laird. McNamara, as a Washington outsider, could not or would not recognize this fact.

PUBLIC ADMINISTRATION AND SOCIETY

Throughout history and in many traditional societies today, critical information has been closely held by a relatively small number of individuals. In premodern times the possession and control of information belonged largely to government officials, scribes, and some scholars, priests, or magi. The authority of information was identified with the authority of the governing classes, secular and religious. The mass of people had practical folk knowledge about matters directly affecting their work in trades or agriculture, but little information of affairs beyond their direct experience or communal consensus.

In the more simple societies and tribal groups, in which the great majority of people had substantially equal access to practical information, the differences between what the elders, shamans, or governors knew and what those they governed knew could be relatively marginal. When knowledge increased and administrative institutions developed in royal and imperial states, the distribution of knowledge and information affecting the state became more concentrated. Unlike the smaller tribal communities, in which authority tended to depend on popular assent, in larger and more complex societies authority moved to the top of the political and ecclesiastical hierarchies and the information gap between governed public and government administration widened.

When the authority of knowledge merged with the authority of princely and priestly status, information itself became an instrument of power and governance. Karl A. Wittfogel provides examples of closely held information and royal and priestly political power in his book *Oriental Despotism: A Comparative Study of Political Power* (1957). Foreknowledge of hydrological cycles enabled a ruling elite to control peasant agriculture dependent upon irrigation or cycles of rainfall and the flow of rivers. Insofar as knowledge was regarded as official, it acquired an authoritative status. Challenge to the veracity of that knowledge could be regarded as foolishness, insubordination, or heresy. When Copernicus proposed a new model of the solar system, he contradicted the attitudes prevailing at the Vatican, in effect challenging the authority of the Roman Catholic Church, regardless of the demonstrable veracity of its claims. This historical background is introduced here only to illustrate the progressive vulnerability of official knowledge (*i.e.*, opinion) to advances in science and the dissemination of information, from the discovery of printing to the new electronic technology.

In societies characterized by high information levels, information as a social resource becomes largely independent of the traditional institutions of governance. Official authorities can no longer indefinitely contain the extent of information spreading throughout society. The Internet, for example, has created a medium of communication wherein large quantities of information can be rapidly transmitted around the world and used for a variety of political and social purposes. Beyond its service to political power, knowledge in the form of information is ever more essential to multitudinous public activities today. Governments need information, particularly scientific information, and since the seventeenth century they have become major patrons of science and technology, particularly in relation to military and economic affairs. Government was the sponsor of the informative science of statistics, yet in promoting the expansion of knowledge, government weakens the effectiveness of its control over information, and so to some extent loses *control* of information as an instrument of political power. For example, the American Freedom of Information Act in 1966 and the Government in the Sunshine Act in 1976 opened public access to official documents and administrative proceedings.

Rapid growth and dissemination of information, especially from science derived knowledge, has resulted in more information available in society than its present institutions, popular attitudes, and political agendas seem able to use effectively. Rising levels of information result in heightened awareness of risks and problems that scientific knowledge and methods might more effectively address if the means and will to do so were available. Governments and their administrative agencies have been made responsible for dealing with many of these problems, but much of the information and skill needed for their administration lie outside the structure and information of official government, hence the unprecedented recourse to official expert consultants and involvement of other non-governmental organizations.

Moreover, whereas scholarly knowledge is organized discretely into disciplines, the complex issues of our times require interdisciplinary approaches for effective response. Multidisciplinary public research institutes and private issue-focused institutions as clearing houses for information are responses to these needs. New sciences, such as informatics, have also been responses to the need to integrate information into the decision-making structures of modern governance public and non-governmental.

The so-called social lagthe gap between advancing knowledge and conventional belief and behaviour is common among modern societies. When knowledge and its interpretation outrun social conventions, levels of tension arise among knowers, actors, and believers. Believers wrath has often fallen on dedicated knowers whose zeal for mass enlightenment and social reform outrun tolerance for change.

Institutional and behavioural changes regarded by the best-informed persons as desirable (even necessary) are often tacitly rejected or ignored by an uninformed and indifferent multitude and its leaders. Their minds remain unchanged because they have not yet been reached or have become hostile because the new information threatens their personal status, beliefs, and behaviours. Moreover, large numbers of people in the developed countries are addicted to commercialized entertainment and have no interest in learning about the impacts of population growth and modern society destructive impact upon the natural environment of the Earth.

Public administrators must somehow take account of these conflicts, but regretfully, among these are many of the worst offenders.Distrust of novelty may not always be wholly irrational; new beliefs and behaviours may be incompatible with the consensus necessary for social stability, and premature release of insufficiently untested information may lead to unwanted consequences. Undisseminated knowledge, however, may be no more than latent information not influential moving neither people nor governments. Knowledge flowing through a mass information system, however, resembles a current of electricity, with power to shock, destroy, fuse, energize, empower, illuminate, and sometimes assuage.

Some closely held knowledge may enhance personal power, but to change people, knowledge through information is now carried throughout society by broadly diffusing processes such as the Internet. The effects of this flow of information on beliefs and behaviours raise questions of social and individual responsibility, ethics, and the role of institutions and practices of governance and hence public administration.

As all information, notably scientific knowledge, expands, and as the media of its dissemination expand also, suppression becomes more difficult. Knowledge more than ever becomes a pervasive, impersonal force, sometimes designated as the noo¨spherea term given currency by the Russian mineralogist V. I. Vernadsky (1945) and the French Jesuit scientist Pierre Teilhard de Chardin (1961) describing the realm of knowledge existing independently of the personal knowledge possessed by specific individuals. This also affects the responsibilities of public administration in numerous areas of policy.

In high-information-level societies today, especially in the more developed democracies, functional boundaries between public and non-governmental public interest organizations are increasingly interlapping. In the advancement and custody of knowledge, private or non-governmental public institutions, including museums, libraries, universities, technical schools, medical schools, advocacy research institutions, and for-profit industrial organizations, interact with government through contracts, grants, and collaborative efforts and the news media. The outsourcing of services previously public to private sectorsfrom trash collection and disposal to legal analysis and public/private social initiatives is indicative of a much larger question. How much larger, more inclusive, more complex, and more dynamic can modern society and its governance become before human capacity to comprehend and manage is exceeded? To believe that human mental capacity is unlimited is an assumption not confirmed (or refuted) by human experience or objective evidence. If mental growth occurs, can its development parallel the growth of the managerial necessities?

MANAGING INFORMATION IN A HIGHLY INFORMED SOCIETY

Knowledge may be potentially available for application to the problems of society and yet be unusable when uninterpreted, misinterpreted, unfocused, or offensive to well-organized political interests. Whatever their limitations, environmental impact analysis and technology assessment provide information that can reveal the single purpose and narrowly selective factual bases upon which too many large and costly public and private enterprises have been undertaken. Use of these information-gathering techniques are now required on many occasions for administrative planning and decision making.

Environmental impact analysis, technology assessment, and when necessary, fact finding for arbitration of disputes, are intended to mobilize and evaluate all relevant information and to discover probable consequences of proposed actions, both positive and negative. The objective of these assessments is essentially preventive, corrective, or conciliatory. In advanced societies today, certain critical information is managed through monitoring of changes in the environment inimical to public health and safety. In some countries, and notably in the United States, environmental and health protection provisions in statutory law invoke regulations when, for example, certain levels of toxic pollution or atmospheric ozone levels are detected. Information thus automatically triggers the administrable application of government regulations.

Governmental policy making characteristically has involved conflict among interests, and perhaps it always will, but advances in information and understanding have influenced assumptions and behaviour. While no one should be confident that the politics of the future will differ fundamentally from the past, the expansion of information and information technology suggests the probability of more rational policies and procedures in public administration, although desirable progress towards more effective governance is likely to be incremental. Old expectations and habits in bureaucracies are often resistant to change.

Nevertheless, it is not unreasonable to conjecture that in scientifically advanced countries there may be informational and behavioural changes as great in the next 100 years as in the ten centuries between 1000 and 2100 a.d. The evolution of information technology and substantive information (*e.g.*, derived from the human genome project) might lead to yet unforeseen consequences for governance. This could happen if science-based information, particularly in the biobehavioural sciences, led to increased popular comprehension and consensus on policy priorities and even to alterations in human behaviour that, for example, might induce changes in the administration of criminal justice and provide alternatives to incarceration in prison.

The processes of policy making and public administration seem certain to be affected by new popular attitudes (and conflicts) engendered by applicable advances in the biobehavioural sciences that might uncover findings many people would rather not know but with which the medical sciences, government, and public administration will have to cope. People have generally become aware of the rising level, scope, and transmission of information, and to the techniques of analysis and forecasting. Not everyone welcomes this development or has confidence in its reliability.

The present dominant expectation is for indefinite expansive growth in the global economy, driven by population growth and continuing developments in information technology, notably in computerized artificial intelligence and the expanding use of the Internet. Recent reports, however, on the deteriorating quality of global environmental and social conditions have also shown that the impacts of many technologies are yielding negative consequences that need to be addressed if these developments are to advance unimpeded.

NEW PUBLIC ADMINISTRATION AND ETHICS

Globally the concept of privatization has been promoted in new public administration. It is seen that this concept is related to the measures which promote establishment of efficiency and efficacy leading to development of quality deliverance of public services. In the research conducted by Savas (2000), the concept of "privatization in new public management", is promoted. Further identified by Walsh *et al.* (1997) introduction of new market mechanisms which promote effective implementation of public services in organizations is identified. Walsh in his research has identified that privatization in governance in the United Kingdom has resulted in a new paradigm, which has promoted transformation of both organizational and cultural needs.

The purpose of these reforms include reduction of cost relating to the actions of the governments, identification of measures to reduce the direct impact of action of public employees and bringing about a variation in the overall views of the government by the public.

This type of privatization manoeuvre not only challenged the current realities associated with ethics in public administration, wherein administrators were considered as technical professionals, but also identified the type of functioning that does not take into account good judgement on the part of employees. Accordingly, intellectual proponents of the ethical perspective were responsible for the first noteworthy approach of public administrators' ethical obligations and the importance of citizen participation in administrative decisions. This has long been in place in developed countries across the world as seen with the NPM concepts promoted by Ronald Reagan in USA and Margaret Thatcher in the UK.

INFLUENCE OF NEW PUBLIC ADMINISTRATION PARADIGMS ON ETHICS

The paradigms of New Public Management and more recently Reinventing Government provided a crucial mutation in the parameters and concepts of the public administration role. For that reason, not only ethics became an important area of concern, as its conception needed to adapt to the new formulations of governance and public service. Therefore, in order to define the correct interaction among these models, public administration and ethics, it is vital to provide an advance to these theories. We are now aware that the satisfaction of citizens' needs is essential when we refer to Public Services. This is a significant subject for Managerial School supporters, who have been debating the ways that governments should produce and deliver public services. They pinpoint that every element that involves public production is more expensive and inefficient than those of private production. Because of that assumption, the Managerial School promotes a modification in the delivery of public services. Consequently, the State must constantly endorse the provision of public goods or services, while third parties can supply production. Managerial School approach also maintains that large public services organizations should be broken down into independent units (the agency approach), with enough independence to function on a relatively free basis. This school integrates two major movements, namely New Public Management and Reinventing Government.

New Public Management Globally speaking, NPM supports that privatisation is the adequate mechanism to establish efficiency, efficacy and quality in the delivery of public services, mainly because private practices are more qualified and accurate. In fact, as Emanuel Savas underlines "privatisation is the New Public Management". Kieron Walsh defines that the central characteristic of this movement is "the introduction of market mechanisms to the running of public services organizations: the marketisation of the public service". This author demonstrates that the main principle in the use of privatisation mechanism in the United Kingdom was the alteration in the delivery of public services through the organizational and cultural transformation of the Public Sector.

The reform purposes were to:

- Reduce the costs of government action,
- Reduce the number of public employees and action,
- Change organizational public values.

Within the ethical area, this movement challenged the ancient understandings of administration, believing that administrators worked as technical professionals, without making much use of good judgement according to the desires of their political masters. The NPM denied ideas of administration as ethically neutral instrumental thinkers apart from the electorate. Accordingly, intellectual proponents of this perspective were responsible for the first noteworthy approach of public administrators' ethical obligations and the importance of citizen participation in administrative decisions.. This movement gained impact with Ronald Reagan's administration in the United States of America and Margaret Thatcher in the United Kingdom.

Reinventing Government

The movement emerges from Osborne and Gaebler´s work, and becomes relevant with Bill Clinton's administration. RG supports that Public Administration must consider two features: mission and improving productivity. Its mission is to satisfy the needs of the customers. Improving productivity is achieved by means of a distinction between the results and the quantity of resources implied. It is unavoidable to point out results (and not only rules) and objectives (not only the resources). The customers requests must also be fulfilled, since "the purpose of a business is to create a customer".

This perspective is not drastic and radical as the previous one, primarily because it defends that in order to make the productivity progress possible in Public Administration, hierarchical structures must be flexible, and opposite to concentration and centralisation. Privatisation can be an answer if the alterations in the hierarchical structure do not have any influence on productivity. If it is not possible, delegation mechanisms can be a solution. Concerning ethical position, the authors of this movement, advocate that the use of privatisation devices does not alter the fact that the State has the responsibility as the organizer. It has to supervise and control all the process, bearing in mind the satisfaction of citizens, and the execution of efficiency, effectiveness and accountability.

The Present Impact of these Paradigms on Ethics

These two movements, in spite of their clear difference in methods, believe that administrative reform is an evolutionary process. In sum, they shaped important aspects that had consequences on nowadays ethics. The transition from the Weberian model to the present one also brought new ethical concerns. To be exact, the Government becomes a partner among others, public and private; therefore the delimitation between public and private is imprecise. New forms of public delivery are available. The activities of Government are distributed through organizations that involve numerous actors and decentralisation is expanding, achieving flexibility and responsiveness. With more and more autonomous new units and networks, it is obviously difficult to define responsibilities and to control them.

The NPM formulates an unambiguous distinction between state bureaucracy and market modes of organization. The implementation of the notion of business and competition in managerialism intensifies the idea of customer orientation. This idea promotes government transparency, denying the old close bureaucracy. The introduction of a market type mechanism signifies innovating forms like contracting out, agentification and privatisation, among others. The performance of public servants is evaluated and controlled, chiefly because the service to the public (and its quality) has become a core value in public administration. Public service users are now faced as clients or costumers. Otherwise, "While in the traditional Weberian bureaucracy the responsibility of public servants is restricted to the execution of orders given by the legitimate power, public servants now have a broad spectrum of responsibility". As Parsons highlights, "In this Weberian world there was a place for everything and everything was in its place. Civil servants knew their place and parliaments knew where things were and who was responsible for them". In fact, public servants turn out to be more accountable, sustained by audit mechanisms. When the Weberian hierarchical forms become more elastic, it is difficult to define unbending roles.

The key words of this new reality are diversity and complexity, against the consistency and predictability of the older bureaucratic model. These postulations carry an expected increase in the diversity of modus operandi, procedures and actions. In the same way, this diversity acts also in the field of values. It is also relevant to refer that the managerialist notions of government are not neutral, they imply an ideology, a defined conception, and largely that, "The rapid spread of NPM practices has been their utility and acceptability to dominant political elites.".

In effect, it seems clear that managerial reforms brought new ethical problems and doubts; however, it is undisputable that the paradigms that support these reforms have made an open space for ethics awareness and discussion possible. Actually, not only has ethical conduct become an important issue, but also the widening ideas of governance include "democratic and participative values which give greater weight to accountability than efficiency, while recognizing that citizens want government to be efficient too.". In fact, the common problem of corruption may be a symbol of the insufficiencies of a poor public management. The new focus on ethics derives then, not only from fresh interest, but also represents a double sign: of the evolution and improvement of society and of the declining public reliance in government.

The Portuguese Case

In our Portuguese framework, two historical events shaped public management reform. The first was the Revolution of 1974, which ended over 40 years of dictatorial and corporatist regime. The second was the integration as a member of the European Union in 1986. This latter membership involved a "fundamental transformation from a closed, highly controlled, inward-looking, state-oriented, oligarchical society to an open, outwardlooking, citizen-oriented, democratic society that places high value on individual freedoms and initiatives.". In effect, public management reform was a real movement in Portugal, mostly because notwithstanding the political changes and party lines, the modernization process continued, engaged by roughly the same frame of officials, without drastic changes of policies. Therefore, ""dynamic continuity" constitutes the strength of the Portuguese administrative modernization". This "dynamic continuity" means that reformers proceeded with their mission, always learning from experience and mistake; by balancing actions; adapting to new environments or situations through new strategies and tools. One of the major results of this perspective was the evolution of reform strategies, from a global focus to selective and flexible guidelines. According to the OECD paper about Portugal, "selective radicalism" is an original feature of the strategy shift. "A selective radical approach concentrates reform efforts on a single issue or area that, if radically changed, can have a deep impact on all other issues and areas, and create a chain reaction". Therefore, in Portugal "citizen-orientation" was the source of this approach. Still, we cannot forget that it is a long-term process. As Caiden refers, "Administrative reform is difficult and fraught with problems".

The reformation process began with the application of the "Intercalary Foment Plan" and the preparation of the "III Foment Plan" that promoted the forming of "Working Group 14", accountable for Administrative Reform. This group was responsible for a major delegation of competences and the proposal for the establishment of the "Secretariat for Administrative Modernisation" (23rd November 1967). Their aim was to solve the Welfare-State crisis, amplified by the enormous increase of costs in a difficult context of economical crisis. The model failed in the achievement of an equal society; effectively only the middle class took advantage of Welfare-State actions. This paradigm was also condemned by a prevalent anti-bureaucratic feeling. Therefore, "professional administration" (1945-1975) was replaced by politics and governance. The Weberian bureaucracy was not able to carry out the implementation of new public politics, and their professionals (Simon and behaviourists) did not have the conditions to execute their tasks. Thus, the environment was set up for the development of a different form of Public Administration.

The Public Choice and Managerial Models generate contradictory principles and distinct styles of management. The differences are underlined in the following image. The managerialism solution pleases politicians and professional managers to be exact because politicians can now blame other groups for public service bad functioning, and the managers can impose their professional values and interests. The outcomes represent the exponential growth of public costs, without any increase for quality and quantity of service.

THE IMPORTANCE OF ETHICS IN PUBLIC ADMINISTRATION

Ethics (or "morality") is a branch of philosophy that attempts to define right from wrong, and provide guidance on how an ethical person should behave. Today, ethics is often divided into three subfields: meta-ethics, normative ethics, and applied ethics. Meta-ethics addresses big questions such as whether ethical claims can be proven or disproven, and if so, what is their reach beyond the present situation? Normative ethics tries to articulate practical moral standards that can be used to determine right from wrong, and help individuals live morally correct lives. This may involve specifying good habits, duties to follow, and whether our actions should be guided by their content or consequences. Applied ethics is the application of ethical theory to specific issues such as abortion, euthanasia, human rights, the death penalty, the sanctity of life, and matters of personal integrity such as lying, stealing, and shirking responsibility. Maintaining high ethical standards in government is obviously very important. In fact, it can be argued that the ethical bar is set somewhat higher in government than in business or personal life. This is because government has the authority to demand obedience from individuals and compel them to act in desired ways. Government finances its operations by levying taxes on the public; thus, taxpayers expect honesty and integrity in government. Public administrators are instruments of the state; their actions are extensions of government institutions, laws, and policies. Moreover, public administrators exercise discretion when sizing up problems, formulating courses of action, and meting out justice. Top-level executives wield enormous power in their spheres of influence; street level bureaucrats are the face of government in their communities and to their clientele.

Public servants are expected to have high ethical standards for several other reasons. First of all, it is the law. The most basic forms of ethical conduct are prescribed in statutes, regulations, ordinances, etc. Second, ethical behaviour is essential for maintaining public trust in government. Citizens must know that public officials have integrity and will deliver critical public services on time. High levels of trust translate into greater legitimacy, which is government's license to operate. Third, moral reasoning is required to balance the competing values and demands of government. Public administrators often make hard decisions based imperfect information; the administrator's ethical values inform these decisions. Finally, ethics is a central element in the long running debate over administrative responsibility, responsiveness, and accountability.

As a result, the American Society for Public Administration (ASPA) (2006) has an ethical code with five important touchstones: (1) serve the public interest; (2) respect the Constitution and the Law; (3) demonstrate personal integrity; (4) promote ethical organizations; and (5) strive for professional excellence. In addition, ASPA has a special membership section devoted to ethics which includes a subscription to the journal Public Integrity. There are several other journals specializing in ethics in political science and public administration, and the more general journals frequently host symposiums and publish individual articles on ethics and related topics. In addition, there are a variety of mainstream ethics textbooks, readers, and edited works in public administration. Concern about ethical behaviour in government – and its antithesis "corruption" – has become a hot-button issue for international organizations such as the

United Nations, World Bank, International Monetary Fund, and Organization for Economic Cooperation and Development. Many member nations are similarly concerned, and have placed special emphasis on stamping out corruption and encouraging ethical behaviour in government. The concern for ethical behaviour has also focused on government contractors of late. The disconnect between government institutions that authorize and fund public programmes, and private contractors who implement them, spotlights the wide gap in ethical standards between the sectors. This concern for ethical behaviour extends beyond the halls of government in other ways. Some years ago, Rest and Narvaez (1994) pointed out that approximately 10,000 applied ethics courses were taught annually in U.S. colleges and universities. In all likelihood this number has increased. The recent financial collapse of the banking, automobile, and insurance industries in the late 2000s, and reports of departing executives receiving huge bonuses while stockholders lose their investments and employees lose their pensions raise nagging questions about corporate and business ethics. As government underwrites these industries, it is expected to instill greater integrity and ensure more ethical behaviour.

This discussion raises important questions about the sources of ethical behaviour in government, and the specific ethical standards that apply to public administrators. Terry L. Cooper (2006 and elsewhere) presents five theoretical accounts for a normative foundation of public service ethics: connection to regime values, constitutional theory, and founding thought; citizenship theory which can be thought of as an ethical obligation; social equity, which can also be thought of as an ethical principle; the virtue approach which suggests that public administrators should cultivate a balanced set of virtues that include ethicalness and integrity; and finally, the notion of protecting and defending the public interest.

Similarly, Van Wart (1996) identified five sources of ethical behaviour in government: the public interest, legal interests, personal interests, organizational interests, and professional interests. Yet Van Wart noted the slippery nature of ethics in the public sector: "Administrators' decisions cannot be determined to be ethical simply based on the content of their final actions but by the thorough consideration that they give all legitimate values in formulating the best possible decision when various values compete."

Garofalo and Geuras (2005) go a step further. The authors examine the public and private roles of the individual citizen as a moral agent and contend that this agent should recognize morality as a motive for action, follow moral principles, and acknowledge that morality is his or her principal. The authors argue that public administration is a fundamentally moral enterprise that exists to serve the values that society considers important, broadly conceived. Thus, public administration's moral nature makes it a prototype for other professions to emulate, and a model of moral governance in society.

A final example helps to cement this point. It is well known how some German public officials participated in and helped to implement the atrocities of World War II. It is also well known how some German citizens and members of resistance groups in occupied countries refused to comply with these orders. In fact, some openly aided and harboured Jews and other persecuted groups. As an example, Frederickson and Hart (1985) cite the Dutch resistance and its aid to Anne Frank and other Jews during the German occupation of Holland in World War II. Frederickson and Hart (1985) explain that patriotism alone (*i.e.*, love of one's country) is an inadequate basis for ethical behaviour. Such behaviour must be founded on knowledge of, and belief in, democratic values, and it must include an intentional inculcation and practice of benevolence (the extensive and non-instrumental love of others).

The authors refer to this as a "patriotism of benevolence". Moreover, Adams and Balfour (2009) argue that there is a tendency towards administrative evil woven into the identity of public affairs and other fields and professions in public life. This tendency can be manifested in acts of dehumanization and genocide wherein ordinary people, acting within their normal professional and administrative roles, engage in acts of evil without being aware that it is wrong. Adams and Balfour (2009) argue that under conditions of moral inversion, people may even view their evil activity as good.

This example connects directly to a well-known series of experiments conducted by the experimental psychologist Stanley Milgram. Milgram tried to understand why so many people are obedient to authority when ordered to commit unethical or immoral acts. His work was eventually discredited because he subjected experimental subjects to traumatic conditions, but his central research question – to what extent are people obedient to authority – was worthy, and his findings – that more than three-fourths of the experimental subjects would harm other experimental subjects if ordered to do so – were quite surprising. The take-home point here is that intuition is not a sufficient basis for ethical conduct, and it cannot be grounded in governments, regime values, laws, or management edicts, as history has shown. Rather, ethical conduct must be grounded in more universal and deliberative values as Frederickson and Hart (1985) suggested.

AN ETHICAL DIMENSION OF PUBLIC SERVICE MOTIVATION

Much of the theoretical and empirical research on PSM has been heavily laden with ethical concerns and moral issues. For example, Elmer Staats said: "In the broadest sense, 'public service' is a concept, an attitude, a sense of duty – yes, even a sense of public morality." Brewer and Selden (1998) first connected PSM with an important behavioural outcome – willingness to blow the whistle on corruption, graft mismanagement, and wrongdoing. Mosher (1968) said the nature of public employment is presumed to demand, on the part of individual employees, a unique sense of loyalty, both to duty and to the government as a whole. Wamsley and colleagues add: "... a public administrator's sense of calling is to the public service and is rooted in the U.S. Constitution and subsequent historical experiences. One powerful idea is that of a commitment to something: the public service, the client, or the broadest possible definition of the public interest." But as I have argued, patriotism, organizational commitment, and compliance with the law is not enough. Lilla argued for a more balanced set of virtues: "...the balance of virtues which officials in different positions in government must display.

Those virtues are rather obvious: a respect for the law, a concept of the public interest, courage, tenacity, and prudence, to name a few." One nagging question is whether an ethical dimension of PSM is distinctive, or whether it is subsumed by existing bases or dimensions of the construct. This question must be answered with a combination of theoretical and empirical evidence. Theoretically, Perry and Wise (1990) began their effort to operationalize PSM by building on Knoke and Wright-Isak's (1982) three fundamental bases for motivation: rational, norm-based, and emotional. Perry (1996) further developed these three bases into four dimensions of PSM: public policy-making, public interest, compassion, and self-sacrifice. Since inception, scholars have noted that these bases of motivation and dimensions of PSM are quite slippery and overlapping, which is not necessarily a fatal problem. It does, however, set the bar low for additional candidate dimensions of PSM. Such dimensions need not be theoretically distinctive. Individuals may, for example, render moral judgements that are rational and achievable through the policy-making process, norm-based and related to patriotism, or emotional in nature and evoking compassion towards others. Many other variations are possible.

Most motivation scholars acknowledge that individuals have mixed motives. An ethical dimension of PSM, like other existing dimensions, can draw from all three motivational bases – rational, norm-based and emotive. It can also partially overlap those dimensions, which include: public policy making, public interest, compassion, self-sacrifice, and possibly democratic governance. Ultimately, however, a proposed ethical dimension of PSM must have some unique content and it must independently contribute to PSM's explanatory power.

PUBLIC ADMINISTRATORS' ROLE IN SOCIETAL KNOWLEDGE MANAGEMENT

PA functions in the modern, democratic society are complex. Ideally, but unrealistically, civil servants should possess the best expertise and collaborate with experts with the most advanced state-of-the-art understanding. While at times being experts, they should also be lead facilitators and knowledge management moderators. However, communication difficulties in societal knowledge management may make it difficult to walk the narrow line between:

(a) having deep and special insights into how to proceed and (b) involving the public and special needs groups in a collaborating process. PAs must provide initiatives, leadership, and coordination to implement the most effective approaches and to ascertain that society as a whole is served appropriately.

The role of guiding and governing society's agendas for public IC falls to PAs. The conceptual leadership for knowledge management must in part reside with PA but must also be shared with all stakeholders. Broad knowledge management practice must ultimately be the responsibility of each public agency and each civil servant.

Without broad agreement on concepts knowledge management will not be effective. A separate, but small PA entity or office should be created to support the knowledge management practice. Its function must be supportive, innovative, and collaborative. It must avoid being prescriptive and needs to operate on several levels. Part of its work needs to be on the policy level with responsibility to coordinate knowledge management activities in accordance with society goals and objectives. It must also communicate with legislatures and public agencies to secure resources required to pursue the knowledge agenda. It must collaborate with citizen groups and the business community to facilitate joint programmes, determine capabilities, opportunities, needs, and constraints (CONC) analysis.

The office must maintain the broad vision for comprehensive knowledge management and facilitate its adoption across all society's entities. It must secure shared resources that individual agencies cannot justify and provide methodological leadership with ensure common standards to allow interoperability, uniform access, collaboration, and knowledge sharing.

These demands lead to needs for specialized expertise in several areas and the knowledge management office staff should have considerable expertise in areas like public policy. In addition they should have – or have access to – knowledge management expertise such as Knowledge Engineering, Management Sciences, Cognitive Sciences, Social Sciences, Library Sciences, Philology or Linguistics, Artificial Intelligence, and Advanced Computer Sciences.

PA entities have broad responsibilities in pursuit of societal objectives. PA governs and facilitates public aspects of operations and life of public and private organizations and individual citizens. When considering knowledge-related issues, such responsibilities cover not only knowledge-related functions within PA. Responsibilities extends to govern and facilitate other knowledge-related and affected areas, particularly preparing effective policy partners, building and leveraging societal IC, and building and maintaining a capable and competitive workforce. Furthermore, the responsibility also includes creating and governing the overall vision, perspective, and strategy for the society's general knowledge management practice.

PREPARE EFFECTIVE POLICY PARTNERS

PAs help the public understand needs and direction of public activities, programmes, and projects. They inform the public about planned or proposed actions through hearings, town meetings, and informative news programmes. Unfortunately, these may be marginally effective. Often, they do not provide in-depth dialogue to correct wrongful understandings that many citizens have of proposed actions. Citizens are faced with being engaged in "informed decision making" while having limited understanding of implications. They are not prepared to participate as knowledgeable decision makers on their own behalf. Much resistance against public actions has resulted from public ignorance or misunderstanding. Also, inappropriate public actions may be approved by a public that does not understand its negative sides. Effective and efficient transfer of deep knowledge and understanding can improve the public's insight by use of knowledge management methods. Public governance is more effective when citizens have understanding of directions, options, issues, and opportunities. It is particularly value if value systems and 'models of the world' are shared with PAs.

That, however, does not mean that everyone should agree! No society can expect all its citizens to build deep and shared insights. Nowhere will the complete citizenry be fully educated or of one mind. There will always be legitimately different opinions, knowledge sparse misunderstandings, and value-based disagreements. To have the desired results, communications must be knowledge-effective and preferably closed loop with feedbacks through dialogue.

In dealings with the public, many problems are caused by the wide difference in mental models and resulting understandings that exist in the general population. The public's insights often are different from those of PAs. PAs may have developed extensive knowledge of proposed actions, although at times from narrower perspectives than those available in the public-at-large which will be aware of circumstances not known to PA. The administration's views are not always right. In a democracy, special interests may pursue undesirable public actions which rightfully should be modified extensively or defeated by the citizenry as better understandings are developed. Knowledge management methods provide opportunities to prepare the citizenry to be more effective policy partners – for conceptualizing, planning, deciding, and implementing public actions as well as for providing general support. To be effective policy partners, citizens need to have breadth of knowledge and understanding of consequences.

PUBLIC AND PRIVATE INTELLECTUAL CAPITAL

A country's viable success depends upon its leveragable resources. Public and private IC of all kinds create significant opportunities for success and PA influences both creation and leveraging of IC. Also, in today's global economy technology is important. Hence, public support to creation technology and research parks and knowledge flow clusters is important for building environments where world class expertise can congregate and provide environments of synergy.

In addition, knowledge-related actions often are complemented with other actions to facilitate the desired results. For example, tax or import-export restrictions may have to be eased to attract external industry that can benefit from a well educated domestic workforce. On a national level, PA influences knowledge-related mechanisms for building and leveraging IC assets in many ways.

These include patent policies and legal support for value realization and protection enforcement of IC. Other interventions include international trade agreements and targeted support of individual export or import contracts. On both national and local levels public projects provide direct support to create and leverage public and private IC. Societies benefit from knowledge-related activities in several ways. Some result in increased trade and economic activity. In particular, developments of IC assets such as world-competitive expertise and knowledge-based products can result in valuable economic and trade changes.

Larger economic activity leads to increased employment, trade, and area payroll with associated positive economic impacts. However, as for other societal developments, many of these impacts take time to realise. Numerous mechanisms are available to PAs to create IC assets directly or to facilitate their creation in the private sector. In the private sector, public knowledge management need to be governed by the desired national or regional strategy. IC asset development must be related to available resources and current conditions. Governments frequently allocate resources to create capabilities to obtain specific results. While providing the desired primary results, such actions often also develop highly valuable secondary IC assets and capabilities.

6

Theory of Policymakers

INTRODUCTION

In addition to the three kinds of public policy and the three arenas in which to make policy, there are three kinds of public officials, who see their role as policymakers quite differently.

DELEGATE

The first kind of policymaker is a Delegate. Delegates believe themselves to be representative of their neighbourhood or district; they see their role as reflecting and representing the views and values of their constituencies. They are very sensitive to the polls and are always trying to understand the prevailing public opinion in their specific districts.

These public officials take the concept of "representative" literally, working hard to reflect the interests and values of their neighbours. Delegates are acutely aware of public opinion and polls and, consequently, tend to be more followers than leaders. Delegates make up the majority of elected officials serving in most elected bodies.

TRUSTEE

The second kind of policymaker is a Trustee. The trustee is someone who advocates a specific ideology, principle, or value that they believe best serves the public and is less interested in the prevailing public opinion. Trustees place a high value on principle and their particular world view and are often seen as uncompromising and rigid. A liberal Democrat and a conservative Republican would view themselves as trustees, as would pro-choice or right-to-life advocates, even environmental advocates. The key idea here is that trustees are concerned about public opinion and may be persuaded by information or research that reflects their particular world views. Trustees see themselves as leaders and enjoy policy as it relates to their world views. Trustees generally make up 10 to 15 per cent of public bodies, clearly a minority but an important factor in policymaking.

POLITICO

The third kind of policymaker is the Politico. This person is more interested in the campaign, trappings, and benefits of office than the particulars of public policy. Politicos are always looking for the next office, always campaigning, and focus little time on public policy, except as it impacts their ability to seek and achieve another office. As one considers impacting public policy and approaching public officials, it is important to know how they each view themselves. One approaches a delegate differently than one approaches a trustee. With a delegate, one would want to demonstrate broad public support for the issue they are advocating.

One would want to approach the delegate with petitions, polls, and letters of support from important individuals. When one approaches a trustee, however, it is more important to have data that support that individual's philosophical orientation and enhance the public good as they see it. One approaches the politico with an eye on the next campaign and how the issue you advocate will be impacted by the next election. The politico will also be very sensitive to current polls. One easy way to remember these introductory comments is to think of three Ps—policy, politics, and personality—as all three interact in this dynamic process.

BODIES MAKE POLICY

Public policy is traditionally made in elected bodies. Most people believe that the lawmaking process is the beginning and end of policymaking, but it is important to understand that there are five separate and distinct ways that public bodies make policy.

LAWMAKING

The first and most obvious is Lawmaking itself. On the national level, Congress enacts laws. On the state level, the legislature enacts laws. On the local level, elected bodies pass resolutions and ordinances that have the force of law but are secondary to the state and federal laws. The lawmaking process itself is one of compromise and consensus building. Any lawmaker can introduce any bill at any time in the legislative session. These sessions are two-year cycles in which proposals are considered and either become law or not. Most state legislatures consider about 4,000 bills in a two-year legislative cycle. On average, 90 per cent of the bills introduced will fail and only 10 per cent will become law.

This is true on the national, state, and local level. What distinguishes those ideas and bills that become law from those that fail is two fold—aligning good policy with good politics and the effective participation of multiple constituencies, which creates power. The average time it takes an idea to become a law, if it's not too controversial, is three to five years. It takes time to convince the leadership that your ideas have broad enough support to make it to the agenda. The proposal is then sent to committee to be studied and refined. Input is received from every sector, and the bills are examined and approved a line and a page at a time. In Congress and State Legislatures (with the exception of Nebraska which has a one-house legislature), the same versions of a bill must pass both the House and Senate. As difficult and time consuming as it is to have an idea become a law and get the bill signed by the governor, it is important to understand that you've actually just begun the policymaking process.

BUDGET PROCESS

A law without a Budget is simply rhetoric. The budget-making process is as critical as the lawmaking process. The budget process generally is an annual process that runs independently of the lawmaking process. Each year the president, governor, mayor, school superintendent, or township supervisor presents their annual proposed budget to their respective elected bodies. The entire body does not consider the budget; it is referred to an appropriations (or budget) committee. These budget committees are generally not as representative demographically as the entire elective body, but tend to be made up of the more senior members of the legislature.

These senior members have more experience, seniority, and power. The appropriations committees themselves are broken into subcommittees, which parallel the Cabinet departments on the national, state, and even local levels. So, you'll have a House subcommittee on education and a Senate subcommittee on education. You'll have a House subcommittee on state police, a Senate subcommittee on state police, and on it goes until the entire cabinet is covered. The subcommittees are organised along partisan lines with the majority party controlling the subcommittee in the same ratio that it controls the particular chamber. The subcommittees and the subcommittee chairs are extraordinarily powerful because the members are usually experts on the particular department and have considerable influence on the policies and budget of that particular department. It is absolutely critical to know who those subcommittee members are and to follow their actions as the budget moves through the process.

Most subcommittees hold hearings, seek public input, and operate transparently in the initial phases of the budget process, which generally occurs early in the year. The budget bills get full consideration by both chambers and eventually end up in a joint House Senate Conference subcommittee to resolve all policy differences. Those final decisions are made in the middle of the night on the last night before the Legislature adjourns for its summer recess, generally the night before the Fourth of July holiday.

These complex multimillion-dollar budgets are generally negotiated between the chairperson of the House subcommittee and the chairperson of the Senate subcommittee in the middle of the night, without anyone else knowing the details and actual line items in each bill. The chair of the subcommittee briefs the leadership, and then the modified bill is considered by the full Legislature and, again, enacted late in the night without the non-appropriations members understanding the detail or the complexity of the budget they are voting on.

This is why it's important to be informed and engaged in the hearings, so that you understand your relative position going into this initial period. It is also imperative to meet with and understand the policymakers themselves, whether they see themselves as trustees or delegates, and to get your idea or programme understood by these influential policymakers as they consider the budget options late into the night before the summer recess. While you will not be there in person, you can still have an impact if you have met with, informed, and persuaded the key leaders of the merits of your programme or policy. Generally speaking, governors will not support funding a new programme at 100 per cent in the first year. More than likely, the governor will recommend a modest beginning and incrementally increase the programme over a period of years. It is important to follow the budget process over time as well.

KINGMAKER

Kingmaker is a term originally applied to the activities of Richard Neville, 16th Earl of Warwick — "Warwick the Kingmaker" — during the Wars of the Roses in England. The term has come to be applied more generally to a person or group that has great influence in a royal or political succession, without being a viable candidate. Kingmakers may use political, monetary, religious, and/or military means to interfere in the succession. They may also be assigned as Minister of State without Portfolio.

Examples include:

- Chanakya in the Mauryan Empire.
- Vidyaranya in the Vijayanagara Empire.
- Ricimer in the Late Western Roman Empire.
- Richard Neville, 16th Earl of Warwick in the Wars of the Roses.
- Nogai Khan, Mamai Khan, and Edigu Khan in the Golden Horde.
- Baron Carl Otto Mörner in the House of Bernadotte.
- Wiremu Tamihana in the Mâori King Movement.

Citizens of West Africa's sub-national monarchies often use the word *kingmaker* to refer to the members of the electoral colleges that choose their sovereigns because they also usually officiate during the coronation rituals and rites of purification, the word in this particular case taking on a literal meaning *i.e.*, a *Maker* of the king.

IN GAME THEORY

In game theory, a kingmaker is a player who lacks sufficient resources or position to win at a given game, but possesses enough remaining resources to decide which of the remaining viable players will eventually win.

CONTEMPORARY USAGE

By analogy, "Kingmaker" is also used in some countries to refer to those individuals with the ability to influence the selection of political leaders. The term though always unofficial, has tended to gain more importance in places of power struggle *e.g.* politics, sports organizations etc. Consequently, bestowement of such a title is looked upon significantly and more often as a means of indirect gratification for individuals wanting to silently dictate the affairs of the organization. The term is also occasionally used in a pejorative sense during elections, where a small number of independent political candidate who hold a sizeable sway in the 'vote bank', can most likely decide the course of an outcome.

Instead of referring to an individual, the term can also be applied to an institution or think tank whose opinions are held in great regard by the interested organization. The influence of the religious orders like the Roman Catholic Church in running the affairs of the state during medieval times is a well known example. Kingdoms and Empires in the Indian sub-continent often relied on their religious heads. Besides religious orders, even countries can fit into this terminology when they can dicate the affairs of the other country.

In current political scenarios across the world the term can expand its scope to include powerful lobbying groups, whose role is often seen as a defining factor on major issues.

Modern Kingmakers

Modern politicians known as "Kingmaker" include:

- Mohandas Karamchand Gandhi - a pre-eminent political and ideological leader of India during the Indian independence movement under whose influence were all the major political leaders of the Indian freedom struggle including Jawaharlal Nehru and Sardar Vallabhai Patel.
- James Farley - orchestrated the gubernatorial and presidential elections of Franklin D. Roosevelt.
- K. Kamaraj - instrumental in making Lal Bahadur Shastri and Indira Gandhi as Prime Ministers of India in the year 1964 and 1966 respectively.
- Sonia Gandhi - seen to many the *de facto* Prime Minister of India; named as a kingmaker on numerous occasions, *Time* magazine named her as such and called her India's leader in all but title.
- Dick Morris - orchestrated the gubernatorial and presidential elections of Bill Clinton.

- Girija Prasad Koirala - described as a kingmaker in Nepal with the election of Madhav Kumar Nepal.
- Fred Malek - described as a kingmaker for the Republican Party in the United States.
- David Axelrod - described by *U.S. News and World Reports* as a "reporter turned kingmaker" with respect to the ascendancy of Barack Obama.
- Bakili Muluzi - described as a kingmaker in Malawi.
- Stefan Cardinal Wyszyñski - was highly instrumental in the papal election in 1978 of Karol Wojty³a, Archbishop of Kraków, as John Paul II.
- Rupert Murdoch - a successful media tycoon who has consistently backed every winning United Kingdom Prime Minister since 1979.
- Nick Clegg - described as a kingmaker in the 2010 UK general election as the leader of the Liberal Democrats following a hung parliament result.
- Sarah Palin - During the 2010 midterm elections, Sarah Palin endorsed 64 Republicans nationwide. Out of 64 Palin-endorsed politicians, 33 won the republican nomination and later the general election. Along with this, her endorsement helped fx. Karen Handel and Nikki Haley to take the lead in the Republican gubernatorial primaries in Georgia and South Carolina. This trend, that a candidate went from being in obscurity to leading the primary polls through Sarah Palins endorsement, caused some to claim that Palin is a kingmaker in Republican politics.

IN FICTION

The character Leon Fortunato from the *Left Behind* series of novels is often described as a kingmaker.

Marcus Jefferson Wall, the antagonist of much of the Matador series by Steve Perry is called the Kingmaker, and controls the President of the Galactic Federation.

The character Mayvar Kingmaker from the *The Saga of the Exiles* series of novels tests the ability of aspirants before they can be proclaimed king of the Tanu.

IRON TRIANGLES

The closed, mutually supportive relationships that often prevail in the United States between the government agencies, the special interest lobbying organizations, and the legislative committees or subcommittees with jurisdiction over a particular functional area of government policy. As long as they hang together, the members of these small groups of movers and shakers tend to dominate all policy-making in their respective specialized areas of concern, and they tend to present a united front against "outsiders" who attempt to invade their turf and alter established policies that have been worked out by years of private negotiations among the "insiders".

The middle-level bureaucrats who run the agencies may use their special friends in Congress to block the efforts of a new President or a new Congressional majority leadership bent on reforming or reducing the size of their agencies. The Congressmen and Senators on the oversight committees can count upon their friends in the agencies to continue "pet" programmes and pork-barrel projects important to their local constituencies or even to do special favours for their political supporters and financial backers. Lobbying organizations provide useful information to the committees and the agencies, provide campaign support for the relevant Congressmen, and often help to mobilize public opinion in favour of larger appropriations and expanded programmes for "their" part of the government bureaucracy.

In return, they tend to be consulted and carefully placated when new laws or administrative regulations or important appointments affecting their special interests are being made. These triangles are said to be "strong as iron" in that these mutually supportive relationships are often so politically powerful that representatives of the more general interests of society are usually effectively prevented from "interfering" with policy-making altogether whenever their concept of the general interest runs counter to the special interests of the entrenched interest groups, bureaucrats and politicians.

RATIONAL-COMPREHENSIVE

A theoretical model of how public policy decisions are taken. All possible options or approaches to solving the problem under study are identified and the costs and benefits of each option are assessed and compared with each other. The option that promises to yield the greatest net benefit is selected. The main problem with rational-comprehensive approaches is that it is often very costly in terms of time and other resources that must be devoted to gathering the relevant information. Often the costs and benefits of the various options are very uncertain and difficult to quantify for rigorous comparison. The costs of undertaking rational-comprehensive decision-making may themselves exceed the benefits to be gained in improved quality of decisions.

RATIONAL PLANNING MODEL

The rational planning model is the process of realizing a problem, establishing and evaluating planning criteria, creating alternatives, implementing alternatives, and monitoring progress of the alternatives. It is used in designing neighbourhoods, cities, and regions. The rational planning model is central in the development of modern urban planning and transportation planning. The very similar rational decision-making model, as it is called in organizational behaviour is a process for making logically sound decisions. This multi-step model and aims to be logical and follow the orderly path from problem identification through solution.

Method

Verifying, Defining and Detailing the Problem

This step includes recognizing the problem, defining an initial solution, and starting primary analysis. Examples of this are creative devising, creative ideas, inspirations, breakthroughs, and brainstorms. The very first step which is normally overlooked by the top level management is defining the exact problem. Though we think that the problem identification is obvious, many times it is not. The rational decision making model is a group-based decision making process. If the problem is not identified properly then we may face a problem as each and every member of the group might have a different definition of the problem. Hence, it is very important that the definition of the problem is the same among all group members. Only then is it possible for the group members to find alternate sources or problem solving in an effective manner.

Generate All Possible Solutions

This step encloses two to three final solutions to the problem and preliminary implementation to the site. In planning, examples of this are Planned Units of Development and downtown revitalizations. This activity is best done in groups, as different people may contribute different ideas or alternative solutions to the problem. Without alternative solutions, there is a chance of arriving at a non-optimal or a rational decision. For exploring the alternatives it is necessary to gather information. Technology may help with gathering this information.

Generate Objective Assessment Criteria

Evaluative criteria are measurements to determine success and failure of alternatives. This step contains secondary and final analysis along with secondary solutions to the problem. Examples of this are site suitability and site sensitivity analysis. After going thoroughly through the process of defining the problem, exploring for all the possible alternatives for that problem and gathering information this step says evaluate the information and the possible options to anticipate the consequences of each and every possible alternative that is thought of. At this point optional criteria for measuring the success or failure of the decision taken needs to be considered.

Choose the Best Solution Generated

This step comprises a final solution and secondary implementation to the site. At this point the process has developed into different strategies of how to apply the solutions to the site. Based on the criteria of assessment and the analysis done in previous steps, choose the best solution generated. These four steps form the core of the Rational Decision Making Model.

Implement the Preferred Alternative

This step includes final implementation to the site and preliminary monitoring of the outcome and results of the site. This step is the building/ renovations part of the process.

Monitor and Evaluate Outcomes and Results

This step contains the secondary and final monitoring of the outcomes and results of the site. This step takes place over a long period of time.

Feedback

Modify the decisions and actions taken based on the evaluation:

- Planner defines the problem
- Planner considers several alternatives and analyses each
- Preliminary choices of the alternative for best fit considering feedback and impact of the client group
- Planner designs and implements course of action in the form of an experiment
- Evaluation of effects of the course of action. Did it alleviate the problem? Any feedback from course of action?
- On the basis of the feedback should the project or course of action be continued, changed, etc. If effective institutionalize the course of action.

Requirements and Limitations

However, there are a lot of assumptions, requirements without which the rational decision model is a failure. Therefore, they all have to be considered. The model assumes that we have or should or can obtain adequate information, both in terms of quality, quantity and accuracy. This applies to the situation as well as the alternative technical situations. It further assumes that you have or should or can obtain substantive knowledge of the cause and effect relationships relevant to the evaluation of the alternatives. In other words, it assumes that you have a thorough knowledge of all the alternatives and the consequences of the alternatives chosen. It further assumes that you can rank the alternatives and choose the best of it.

The following are the limitations for the Rational Decision Making Model:

- Requires a great deal of time
- Requires great deal of information

- Assumes rational, measurable criteria are available and agreed upon
- Assumes accurate, stable and complete knowledge of all the alternatives, preferences, goals and consequences
- Assumes a rational, reasonable, non-political world

Current Status

While the rational planning model was innovative at its conception, the concepts are controversial and questionable processes today. The rational planning model has fallen out of mass use as of the last decade.

MUDDLING THROUGH

Suppose an administrator is given responsibility for formulating policy with respect to inflation. He might start by trying to list all related values in order of importance, *e.g.*, full employment, reasonable business profit, protection of small savings, prevention of a stock market crash. Then all possible policy outcomes could be rated as more or less efficient in attaining a maximum of these values. This would of course require a prodigious enquiry into values held by members of society and an equally prodigious set of calculations on how much of each value is equal to how much of each other value. He could then proceed to outline all possible policy alternatives. In a third step, he would undertake systematic comparison of his multitude of alternatives to determine which attains the greatest amount of values.

In comparing policies, he would take advantage of any theory available that generalized about classes of policies. In considering inflation, for example, he would compare all policies in the light of the theory of prices. Since no alternatives are beyond his investigation, he would consider strict central control and the abolition of all prices and markets on the one hand and elimination of all public controls with reliance completely on the free market on the other, both in the light of whatever theoretical generalizations he could find on such hypothetical economies. Finally, he would try to make the choice that would in fact maximize his values.

An alternative line of attack would be to set as his principal objective, either explicitly or without conscious thought, the relatively simple goal of keeping prices level. This objective might be compromised or complicated by only a few other goals, such as full employment.

He would in fact disregard most other social values as beyond his present interest, and he would for the moment not even attempt to rank the few values that he regarded as immediately relevant. Where he pressed, he would quickly admit that he was ignoring many related values and many possible important consequences of his policies.

As a second step, he would outline those relatively few policy alternatives that occurred to him. He would then compare them. In comparing his limited number of alternatives, most of them familiar from past controversies, he would not ordinarily find a body of theory precise enough to carry him through a comparison of their respective consequences. Instead he would rely heavily on the record of past experience with small policy steps to predict the consequences of similar steps extended into the future.

Moreover, he would find that the policy alternatives combined objectives or values in different ways. For example, one policy might offer price level stability at the cost of some risk of unemployment; another might offer less price stability but also less risk of unemployment.

Hence, the next step in his approach—the final selection-would combine into one the choice among values and the choice among instruments for reaching values. It would not, as in the first method of policymaking, approximate a more mechanical process of choosing the means that best satisfied goals that were previously clarified and ranked. Because practitioners of the second approach expect to achieve their goals only partially, they would expect to repeat endlessly the sequence just described, as conditions and aspirations changed and as accuracy of prediction improved.

BY ROOT OR BY BRANCH

For complex problems, the first of these two approaches is of course impossible. Although such an approach can be described, it cannot be practiced except for relatively simple problems and even then only in a somewhat modified form. It assumes intellectual capacities and sources of information that men simply do not possess, and it is even more absurd as an approach to policy when the time and money that can be allocated to a policy problem is limited, as is always the case. Of particular importance to public administrators is the fact that public agencies are in effect usually instructed not to practice the first method. That is to say, their prescribed functions and constraints-the politically or legally possible-restrict their attention to relatively few values and relatively few alternative policies among the countless alternatives that might be imagined. It is the second method that is practiced.

Curiously, however, the literatures of decision-making, policy formulation, planning, and public administration formalize the first approach rather than the second, leaving public administrators who handle complex decisions in the position of practicing what few preach. For emphasis I run some risk of overstatement. True enough, the literature is well aware of limits on man's capacities and of the inevitability that policies will be approached in some such style as the second. But attempts to formalize rational policy formulation—to lay out explicitly the necessary steps in the process—usually describe the first approach and not the second.

The common tendency to describe policy formulation even for complex problems as though it followed the first approach has been strengthened by the attention given to, and successes enjoyed by, operations research, statistical decision theory, and systems analysis. The hallmarks of these procedures, typical of the first approach, are clarity of objective, explicitness of evaluation, a high degree of comprehensiveness of overview, and, wherever possible, quantification of values for mathematical analysis. But these advanced procedures remain largely the appropriate techniques of relatively small-scale problem-solving where the total number of variables to be considered is small and value problems restricted. Charles Hitch, head of the Economics Division of RAND Corporation, one of the leading centers for application of these techniques, has written:

I would make the empirical generalization from my experience at RAND and elsewhere that operations research is the art of sub-optimizing, *i.e.*, of solving some lower-level problems, and that difficulties increase and our special competence diminishes by an order of magnitude with every level of decision making we attempt to ascend. The sort of simple explicit model which operations researchers are so proficient in using can certainly reflect most of the significant factors influencing traffic control on the George Washington Bridge, but the proportion of the relevant reality which we can represent by any such model or models in studying, say, a major foreign-policy decision, appears to be almost trivial.'

I propose in this thesis to clarify and formalize the second method, much neglected in the literature. This might be described as the method of *successiue limited comparisons. I* will contrast it with the first approach, which might be called the rationalcomprehensive method. More impressionistically and briefly-and therefore generally used in this object—they could be characterized as the branch method and root method, the former continually building out from the current situation, step-by-step and by small degrees; the latter starting from fundamentals anew each time, building on the past only as experience is embodied in a theory, and always prepared to start completely from the ground up. Let us put the characteristics of the two methods side by side in simplest terms. Assuming that the root method is familiar and understandable, we proceed directly to clarification of its alternative by contrast. In explaining the second, we shall be describing how most administrators do in fact approach complex questions, for the root method, the "best" way as a blueprint or model, is in fact not workable for complex policy questions, and administrators are forced to use the method of successive limited comparisons.

INTERTWINING EVALUATION AND EMPIRICAL ANALYSIS

The quickest way to understand how values are handled in the method of successive limited comparisons is to see how the root method often breaks down in *its* handling of values or objectives. The idea that values should be clarified, and in advance of the examination of alternative policies, is appealing. But what happens when we attempt it for complex social problems? The first difficulty is that on many critical values or objectives, citizens disagree, congressmen disagree, and public administrators disagree. Even where a fairly specific objective is prescribed for the administrator, there remains considerable room for disagreement on sub-objectives.

Consider, for example, the conflict with respect to locating public housing, described in Meyerson and Banfield's study of the Chicago Housing Authority-disagreement which occurred despite the clear objective of providing a certain number of public housing units in the city. Similarly conflicting are objectives in highway location, traffic control, minimum wage administration, development of tourist facilities in national parks, or insect control. Administrators cannot escape these conflicts by ascertaining the majority's preference, for preferences have not been registered on most issues; indeed, there often are no preferences in the absence of public discussion sufficient to bring an issue to the attention of the electorate. Furthermore, there is a question of whether intensity of feeling should be considered as well as the number of persons preferring each alternative. By the impossibility of doing otherwise, administrators often are reduced to deciding policy without clarifying objectives first.

Even when an administrator resolves to follow his own values as a criterion for decisions, he often will not know how to rank them when they conflict with one another, as they usually do. Suppose, for example, that an administrator must relocate tenants living in tenements scheduled for destruction. One objective is to empty the buildings fairly promptly, another is to find suitable accommodation for persons displaced, another is to avoid friction with residents in other areas in which a large influx would be unwelcome, another is to deal with all concerned through persuasion if possible, and so on.

How does one state even to himself the relative importance of these partially conflicting values? A simple ranking of them is not enough; one needs ideally to know how much of one value is worth sacrificing for some of another value. The answer is that typically the administrator chooses—and must choose—directly among policies in which these values are combined in different ways. He cannot first clarify his values and then choose among policies.

A more subtle third point underlies both the first two. Social objectives do not always have the same relative values. One objective may be highly prized in one circumstance, another in another circumstance. If, for example, an administrator values highly both the dispatch with which his agency can carry through its projects *and* good public relations, it matters little which of the two possibly conflicting values he favours in some abstract or general sense. Policy questions arise in forms which put to administrators such a question as: Given the degree to which we are or are not already achieving the values of dispatch and the values of good public relations, is it worth sacrificing a little speed for a happier clientele, or is it better to risk offending the clientele so that we can get on with our work? The answer to such a question varies with circumstances.

The value problem is, as the example shows, always a problem of adjustments at a margin. But there is no practicable way to state marginal objectives or values except in terms of particular policies. That one value is preferred to another in one decision situation does not mean that it will be preferred in another decision situation in which it can be had only at great sacrifice of another value. Attempts to rank or order values in general and abstract terms so that they do not shift from decision to decision end up by ignoring the relevant marginal preferences. The significance of this third point thus goes very far. Even if all administrators had at hand an agreed set of values, objectives, and constraints, and an agreed ranking of these values, objectives, and constraints, their marginal values in actual choice situations would be impossible to formulate.

Unable consequently to formulate the relevant values first and then choose among policies to achieve them, administrators must choose directly among alternative policies that offer different marginal combinations of values. Somewhat paradoxically, the only practicable way to disclose one's relevant marginal values even to oneself is to describe the policy one chooses to achieve them. Except roughly and vaguely, I know of no way to describeor even to understand-what my relative evaluations are for, say, freedom and security, speed and accuracy in governmental decisions, or low taxes and better schools than to describe my preferences among specific policy choices that might be made between the alternatives in each of the pairs.

In summary, two aspects of the process by which values are actually handled can be distinguished. The first is clear: evaluation and empirical analysis are intertwined; that is, one chooses among values and among policies at one and the same time. Put a little more elaborately, one simultaneously chooses a policy to attain certain objectives and chooses the objectives themselves. The second aspect is related but distinct: the administrator focuses his attention on marginal or incremental values. Whether he is aware of it or not, he does not find general formulations of objectives very helpful and in fact makes specific marginal or incremental comparisons. Two policies, X and Y, confront him. Both promise the same degree of attainment of objectives a, b, c, d, and e. But X promises him somewhat more of f than does Y, while Y promises him somewhat more of g than does X. In choosing between them, he is in fact offered the alternative of a marginal or incremental amount of f at the expense of a marginal or incremental amount of g. The only values that are relevant to his choice are these increments by which the two policies differ; and, when he finally chooses between the two marginal values, he does so by making a choice between policies.

As to whether the attempt to clarify objectives in advance of policy selection is more or less rational than the close intertwining of marginal evaluation and empirical analysis, the principal difference established is that for complex problems the first is impossible and irrelevant, and the second is both possible and relevant. The second is possible because the administrator need not try to analyse any values except the values by which alternative policies differ and need not be concerned with them except as they differ marginally. His need for information on values or objectives is drastically reduced as compared with the root method; and his capacity for grasping, comprehending, and relating values to one another is not strained beyond the breaking point.

RELATIONS BETWEEN MEANS AND ENDS

Decision-making is ordinarily formalized as a means-ends relationship: means are conceived to be evaluated and chosen in the light of ends finally selected independently of and prior to the choice of means. This is the means-ends relationship of the root method. But it follows from all that has just been said that such a means-ends relationship is possible only to the extent that values are agreed upon, are reconcilable, and are stable at the margin. Typically, therefore, such a meansends relationship is absent from the branch method, where means and ends are simultaneously chosen.

Yet any departure from the means-ends relationship of the root method will strike some readers as inconceivable. For it will appear to them that only in such a relationship is it possible to determine whether one policy choice is better or worse than another. How can an administrator know whether he has made a wise or foolish decision if he is without prior values or objectives by which to judge his decisions? The answer to this question calls up the third distinctive difference between root and branch methods: how to decide the best policy.

THE TEST OF "GOOD" POLICY

In the root method, a decision is "correct," "good," or "rational" if it can be shown to attain some specified objective, where the objective can be specified without simply describing the decision itself. Where objectives are defined only through the marginal or incremental approach to values, it is still sometimes possible to test whether a policy does in fact attain the desired objectives; but a precise statement of the objectives takes the form of a description of the policy chosen or some alternative to it. To show that a policy is mistaken one cannot offer an abstract argument that important objectives are not achieved; one must instead argue that another policy is more to be preferred.

So far, the departure from customary ways of looking at problem-solving is not troublesome, for many administrators will be quick to agree that the most effective discussion of the correctness of policy does take the form of comparison with other policies that might have been chosen. But what of the situation in which administrators cannot agree on values or objectives, either abstractly or in marginal terms? What then is the test of "good" policy? For the root method, there is no test. Agreement on objectives failing, there is no standard of "correctness". For the method of successive limited comparisons, the test is agreement on policy itself, which remains possible even when agreement on values is not. It has been suggested that continuing agreement in Congress on the desirability of extending old age insurance stems from liberal desires to strengthen the welfare programmes of the federal government and from conservative desires to reduce union demands for private pension plans. If so, this is an excellent demonstration of the ease with which individuals of different ideologies often can agree on concrete policy. Labour mediators report a similar phenomenon: the contestants cannot agree on criteria for settling their disputes but can agree on specific proposals. Similarly, when one administrator's objective turns out to be another's means, they often can agree on policy.

Agreement on policy thus becomes the only practicable test of the policy's correctness. And for one administrator to seek to win the other over to agreement on ends as well would accomplish nothing and create quite unnecessary controversy.

If agreement directly on policy as a test for "best" policy seems a poor substitute for testing the policy against its objectives, it ought to be remembered that objectives themselves have no ultimate validity other than they are agreed upon. Hence agreement is the test of "best" policy in both methods. But where the root method requires agreement on what elements in the decision constitute objectives and on which of these objectives should be sought, the branch method falls back on agreement wherever it can be found. In an important sense, therefore, it is not irrational for an administrator to defend a policy as good without being able to specify what it is good for.

NON-COMPREHENSIVE ANALYSIS

Ideally, rational-comprehensive analysis leaves out nothing important. But it is impossible to take everything important into consideration unless "important" is so narrowly defined that analysis is in fact quite limited.

Limits on human intellectual capacities and on available information set definite limits to man's capacity to be comprehensive. In actual fact, therefore, no one can practice the rational-comprehensive method for really complex problems, and every administrator faced with a sufficiently complex problem must find ways drastically to simplify.

An administrator assisting in the formulation of agricultural economic policy cannot in the first place be competent on all possible policies. He cannot even comprehend one policy entirely. In planning a soil bank programme, he cannot successfully anticipate the impact of higher or lower farm income on, say, urbanization- the possible consequent loosening of family ties, possible consequent eventual need for revisions in social security and further implications for tax problems arising out of new federal responsibilities for social security and municipal responsibilities for urban services. Nor, to follow another line of repercussions, can he work through the soil bank programme's effects on prices for agricultural products in foreign markets and consequent implications for foreign relations, including those arising out of economic rivalry between the United States and the U.S.S.R.

In the method of successive limited comparisons, simplification is systematically achieved in two principal ways. First, it is achieved through limitation of policy comparisons to those policies that differ in relatively small degree from policies presently in effect. Such a limitation immediately reduces the number of alternatives to be investigated and also drastically simplifies the character of the investigation of each. For it is not necessary to undertake fundamental enquiry into an alternative and its consequences; it is necessary only to study those respects in which the proposed alternative and its consequences differ from the *status quo*. The empirical comparison of marginal differences among alternative policies that differ only marginally is, of course, a counterpart to the incremental or marginal comparison of values.

Relevance as Well as Realism

It is a matter of common observation that in Western democracies public administrators and policy analysts in general do largely limit their analyses to incremental or marginal differences in policies that are chosen to differ only incrementally. They do not do so, however, solely because they desperately need some way to simplify their problems; they also do so in order to be relevant. Democracies change their policies almost entirely through incremental adjustments. Policy does not move in leaps and bounds.

The incremental character of political change in the United States has often been remarked. The two major political parties agree on fundamentals; they offer alternative policies to the voters only on relatively small points of difference. Both parties favour full employment, but they define it somewhat differently; both favour the development of water power resources, but in slightly different ways; and both favour unemployment compensation, but not the same level of benefits.

Similarly, shifts of policy within a party take place largely through a series of relatively small changes, as can be seen in their only gradual acceptance of the idea of governmental responsibility for support of the unemployed, a change in party positions beginning in the early 30's and culminating in a sense in the Employment Act of 1946. Party behaviour is in turn rooted in public attitudes, and political theorists cannot conceive of democracy's surviving in the United States in the absence of fundamental agreement on potentially disruptive issues, with consequent limitation of policy debates to relatively small differences in policy. Since the policies ignored by the administrator are politically impossible and so irrelevant, the simplification of analysis achieved by concentrating on policies that differ only incrementally is not a capricious kind of simplification. In addition, it can be argued that, given the limits on knowledge within which policy-makers are confined, simplifying by limiting the focus to small variations from present policy makes the most of available knowledge. Because policies being considered are like present and past policies, the administrator can obtain information and claim some insight. Non-incremental policy proposals are therefore typically not only politically irrelevant but also unpredictable in their consequences.

The second method of simplification of analysis is the practice of ignoring important possible consequences of possible policies, as well as the values attached to the neglected consequences. If this appears to disclose a shocking shortcoming of successive limited comparisons, it can be replied that, even if the exclusions are random, policies may nevertheless be more intelligently formulated than through futile attempts to achieve a comprehensiveness beyond human capacity. Actually, however, the exclusions, seeming arbitrary or random from one point of view, need be neither.

Achieving a Degree of Comprehensiveness

Suppose that each value neglected by one policy-making agency were a major concern of at least one other agency. In that case, a helpful division of labour would be achieved, and no agency need find its task beyond its capacities. The shortcomings of such a system would be that one agency might destroy a value either before another agency could be activated to safeguard it or in spite of another agency's efforts. But the possibility that important values may be lost is present in any form of organization, even where agencies attempt to comprehend in planning more than is humanly possible.

The virtue of such a hypothetical division of labour is that every important interest or value has its watchdog. And these watchdogs can protect the interests in their jurisdiction in two quite different ways: first, by redressing damages done by other agencies; and, second, by anticipating and heading off injury before it occurs.

In a society like that of the United States in which individuals are free to combine to pursue almost any possible common interest they might have and in which government agencies are sensitive to the pressures of these groups, the system described is approximated. Almost every interest has its watchdog. Without claiming that every interest has a sufficiently powerful watchdog, it can be argued that our system often can assure a more comprehensive regard for the values of the whole society than any attempt at intellectual comprehensiveness. In the United States, for example, no part of government attempts a comprehensive overview of policy on income distribution. A policy nevertheless evolves, and one responding to a wide variety of interests. A process of mutual adjustment among farm groups, labour unions, municipalities and school boards, tax authorities, and government agencies with responsibilities in the fields of housing, health, highways, national parks, fire, and police accomplishes a distribution of income in which particular income problems neglected at one point in the decision processes become central at another point. Mutual adjustment is more pervasive than the explicit forms it takes in negotiation between groups; it persists through the mutual impacts of groups upon each other even where they are not in communication. For all the imperfections and latent dangers in this ubiquitous process of mutual adjustment, it will often accomplish an adaptation of policies to a wider range of interests than could be done by one group centrally.

Note, too, how the incremental pattern of policy-making fits with the multiple pressure pattern. For when decisions are only incremental- closely related to known policies, it is easier for one.group to anticipate the kind of moves another might make and easier too for it to make correction for injury already accomplished.

Then partisanship and narrowness, to use terms, will sometimes be assets to rational decision-making, for they can doubly insure that what one agency neglects, another will not; they specialize personnel to distinct points of view. The claim is valid that effective rational coordination of the federal administration, if possible to achieve at all, would require an agreed set of valuess-if "rational" is defined as the practice of the root method of decision-making. But a high degree of administrative coordination occurs as each agency adjusts its policies to the concerns of the other agencies in the process of fragmented decision-making I have just described.

For all the apparent shortcomings of the incremental approach to policy alternatives with its arbitrary exclusion coupled with fragmentation, when compared to the root method, the branch method often looks far superior. In the root method, the inevitable exclusion of factors is accidental, unsystematic, and not defensible by any argument so far developed, while in the branch method the exclusions are deliberate, systematic, and defensible. Ideally, of course, the root method does not exclude; in practice it must. Nor does the branch method necessarily neglect long-run considerations and objectives. It is clear that important values must be omitted in considering policy, and sometimes the only way long-run objectives can be given adequate attention is through the neglect of short-run considerations. But the values omitted can be either long-run or short-run.

SUCCESSION OF COMPARISONS

The final distinctive element in the branch method is that the comparisons, together with the policy choice, proceed in a chronological series. Policy is not made once and for all; it is made and re-made endlessly. Policy-making is a process of successive approximation to some desired objectives in which what is desired itself continues to change under reconsideration. Making policy is at best a very rough process. Neither social scientists, nor politicians, nor public administrators yet know enough about the social world to avoid repeated error in predicting the consequences of policy moves. A wise policy-maker consequently expects that his policies will achieve only part of what he hopes and at the same time will produce unanticipated consequences he would have preferred to avoid. If he proceeds through a *succession* of incremental changes, he avoids serious lasting mistakes in several ways.

In the first place, past sequences of policy steps have given him knowledge about the probable consequences of further similar steps. Second, he need not attempt big jumps towards his goals that would require predictions beyond his or anyone else's knowledge, because he never expects his policy to be a final resolution of a problem. His decision is only one step, one that if successful can quickly be followed by another. Third, he is in effect able to test his previous predictions as he moves on to each further step. Lastly, he often can remedy a past error fairly quickly-more quickly than if policy proceeded through more distinct steps widely spaced in time.

Compare this comparative analysis of incremental changes with the aspiration to employ theory in the root method. Man cannot think without classifying, without subsuming one experience under a more general category of experiences. The attempt to push categorization as far as possible and to find general propositions which can be applied to specific situations is what I refer to with the word "theory.~' Where root analysis often leans heavily on theory in this sense, the branch method does not. The assumption of root analysts is that theory is the most systematic and economical way to bring relevant knowledge to bear on a specific problem. Granting the assumption, an unhappy fact is that we do not have adequate theory to apply to problems in any policy area, although theory is more adequate in some areas-monetary policy, for examplethan in others. Comparative analysis, as in the branch method, is sometimes a systematic alternative to theory.

Suppose an administrator must choose among a small group of policies that differ only incrementally from each other and from present policy. He might aspire to "understand" each of the alternatives—for example, to know all the consequences of each aspect of each policy. If so, he would indeed require theory.

In fact, however, he would usually decide that, for policy-making purposes, he need know, only the consequences of each of those aspects of the policies in which they differed from one another. For this much more modest aspiration, he requires no theory, for he can proceed to isolate probable differences by examing the differences in consequences associated with past differences in policies, a feasible programme because he can take his observations from a long sequence of incremental changes.

For example, without a more comprehensive social theory about juvenile delinquency than scholars have yet produced, one cannot possibly understand the ways in which a variety of public policies-say on education, housing, recreation, employment, race relations, and policing-might encourage or discourage delinquency. And one needs such an understanding if he undertakes the comprehensive overview of the problem prescribed in the models of the root method. If, however, one merely wants to mobilize knowledge sufficient to assist in a choice among a small group of similar policies-alternative policies on juvenile court procedures, for examplehe can do so by comparative analysis of the results of similar past policy moves.

THEORISTS AND PRACTITIONERS

This difference explains-in some cases at least-why the administrator often feels that the outside expert or academic problem-solver is sometimes not helpful and why they in turn often urge more theory on him. And it explains why an administrator often feels more confident when "flying by the seat of his pants" than when following the advice of theorists. Theorists often ask the administrator to go the long way round to the solution of his problems, in effect ask him to follow the best canons of the scientific method, when the administrator knows that the best available theory will work less well than more modest incremental comparisons. Theorists do not realise that the administrator is often in fact practicing a systematic method. It would be foolish to push this explanation too far, for sometimes practical decision-makers are pursuing neither a theoretical approach nor successive comparisons, nor any other systematic method.

It may be worth emphasizing that theory is sometimes of extremely limited helpfulness in policy-making for at least two rather different reasons. It is greedy for facts; it can be constructed only through a great collection of observations. And it is typically insufficiently precise for application to a policy process that moves through small changes. In contrast, the comparative method both economizes on the need for facts and directs the analyst's attention to just those facts that are relevant to the fine choices faced by the decision-maker.

With respect to precision of theory, economic theory serves as an example. It predicts that an economy without money or prices would in certain specified ways misallocate resources, but this finding pertains to an alternative far removed from the kind of policies on which administrators need help. On the other hand, it is not precise enough to predict the consequences of policies restricting business mergers, and this is the kind of issue on which the administrators need help. Only in relatively restricted areas does economic theory achieve sufficient precision to go far in resolving policy questions; its helpfulness in policy-making is always so limited that it requires supplementation through comparative analysis.

SUCCESSIVE COMPARISON AS A SYSTEM

Successive limited comparisons is, then, indeed a method or system; it is not a failure of method for which administrators ought to apologize. None-the-less, its imperfections, which have not been explored in this thesis, are many. For example, the method is without a built-in safeguard for all relevant values, and it also may lead the decision-maker to overlook excellent policies for no other reason than that they are not suggested by the chain of successive policy steps leading up to the present. Hence, it ought to be said that under this method, as well as under some of the most sophisticated variants of the root method-operations research, for examplepolicies will continue to be as foolish as they are wise.

Because it is in fact a common method of policy formulation, and is, for complex problems, the principal reliance of administrators as well as of other policy analysts. And because it will be superior to any other decision-making method available for complex problems in many circumstances, certainly superior to a futile attempt at superhuman comprehensiveness. The reaction of the public administrator to the exposition of method doubtless will be less a discovery of a new method than a better acquaintance with an old. But by becoming more conscious of their practice of this method, administrators might practice it with more skill and know when to extend or constrict its use.

One of the noteworthy incidental consequences of clarification of the method is the light it throws on the suspicion an administrator sometimes entertains that a consultant or adviser is not speaking relevantly and responsibly when in fact by all ordinary objective evidence he is. The trouble lies in the fact that most of us approach policy problems within a framework given by our view of a chain of successive policy choices made up to the present. One's thinking about appropriate policies with respect, say, to urban traffic control is greatly influenced by one's knowledge of the incremental steps taken up to the present.

An administrator enjoys an intimate knowledge of his past sequences that "outsiders" do not share, and his thinking and that of the "outsider" will consequently be different in ways that may puzzle both. Both may appear to be talking intelligently, yet each may find the other unsatisfactory. The relevance of the policy chain of succession is even more clear when an American tries to discuss, say, antitrust policy with a Swiss, for the chains of policy in the two countries are strikingly different and the two individuals consequently have organized their knowledge in quite different ways.

If this phenomenon is a barrier to communication, an understanding of it promises an enrichment of intellectual interaction in policy formulation. Once the source of difference is understood, it will sometimes be stimulating for an administrator to seek out a policy analyst whose recent experience is with a policy chain different from his own.

This raises again a question only on the merits of like-mindedness among government administrators. While much of organization theory argues the virtues of common values and agreed organizational objectives, for complex problems in which the root method is inapplicable, agencies will want among their own personnel two types of diversification: administrators whose thinking is organized by reference to policy chains other than those familiar to most members. of the organization and, even more commonly, administrators whose professional or personal values or interests create diversity of view so that, even within a single agency, decision-making can be fragmented and parts of the agency can serve as watchdogs for other parts.

RULE MAKING

As elected bodies consider legislation, they have the option of writing a complex, comprehensive, and detailed bill that tackles all of the issues and offers specific answers to the multiple policies involved. This strategy has the advantage of offering clarity, but the disadvantage is that the bill is considered a page and a line at a time and must pass both chambers exactly the same. The longer and more complex the bill, the higher the likelihood of adding years to the process. An alternative legislative strategy is to pass a simple, two- or three-page bill that creates a policy framework, but leaves the detail to be worked out later. More and more legislatures are choosing the second option because it is simpler and faster and leaves some of the tougher decisions to the state bureaucracy. The process of formulating the specific policy growing out of this generalised brief legislation is called the Administrative Procedures Process or promulgating Rules and Regulations. Most states have enacted an elongated, transparent, and painfully precise process of formulating rules and regulations that clarify the policy.

These processes require public hearings, extended public comment, and a guarantee of a written response to every individual who testifies over the period of review. Unfortunately, consumers and advocates, who are traditionally active and engaged in the lawmaking process and somewhat in the budget-making process, generally stay away from the rules and regulation process because it is so intimidating and precise. Special interest groups have lobbyists, research resources, and budgets to fully engage in the complex and precise rule-making process. While citisen advocates feel comfortable dealing with broad policy issues and are willing to talk to their elected officials, they generally are less comfortable with the nitty-gritty detail. Special interest groups often succeed in reversing or significantly modifying the intent of original legislation because they have the time and resources to shape the details.

OVERSIGHT

Another policy-making arena in elected bodies is the Oversight Committee.

These time-limited committees are created to look at a specific problem or issue and make recommendations to the full body. Oversight committees have the advantage of cross-fertilisation with members from multiple standing committees and the appropriations committees of the legislative body. The process of creating an oversight committee involves simply finding enough interested legislators to commit the time and effort involved in the process—and convincing the leadership of either the House and Senate, or both, to create, staff, and provide resources so that oversight can be effective. Once created, their task is to define a problem, look at alternative solutions, hold public hearings, create public awareness, and make recommendations to the full body; then to advocate and follow through, getting those recommendations adopted as policy. (Examples of policy issues that have been effectively addressed by oversight committees include the medical malpractice insurance crisis, homelessness, environmental contamination, and lead paint extraction.)

SUNSET OPTION

The final way that elected bodies make policy is through Sunset, referring to the concept that some kind of automatic review or termination is built into a policy. For example, the first mandatory seatbelt legislation had a provision that the bill would terminate after five years, giving the legislature the option to reenact it only if it were proven to be successful. (The final version excluded that provision but it was an important part of the early discussion of the policy.) Legislatures often enact laws that expire after a given number of years. The idea is to give the policy a chance, then re-enact it only if proven successful. Another sunset strategy is to create a new programme and an automatic review, but not termination, after five years. The idea behind the review is to create some kind of evaluation and accountability within the policy-making process.

While accountability is important, it should be noted that many constitutional offices and their departments are exempt from sunset (*e.g.*, secretary of state, attorney general); the politics are that you're not going to sunset the state police or the prison system or popular established programmes. The tendency is to focus the sunset process on more vulnerable, less popular human service programmes.

Nevertheless, sunset is an important policy tool. To recap, then, we have a Lawmaking process that is open, participatory, and consensual, taking three to five years; a less participatory, annual Budget process; a five- to seven-year Rule- Making process; an Oversight process that allows for an evaluation and judgement on the effectiveness of the law, budget, and rules; and the potential to Sunset a programme or policy. Conceptually, these legislative processes fit together. Ideally, a lawmaker helps formulate the law, participates in the budget, helps provide oversight, and is engaged in any serious sunset review of the policy or programme. This happens when you have an extraordinarily talented and fully engaged policymaker who is committed to follow through during this extensive process. (Term limits, enacted in many states, severely hamper the ability of elected officials in playing this role. So, more than likely, a special interest group ends up providing continuity and advocacy over time. Power clearly has shifted to the special interests and the bureaucracy.)

KEY TRENDS TODAY

Now that we understand the three different kinds of policy, the three arenas around which policy is made, the three different ways that policymakers view themselves, and the five different ways that elected bodies make policy, let's look at some key trends that are impacting policymakers on the national, state, and local level.

THE FUTURISTS

Let's begin with the observations of many futurists.

Adapting to Change

Basically, futurists are saying that everything is changing and that change is accelerating. All institutions (*i.e.*, business, social, political, educational, and even the family) are being challenged and must change, innovate, and adapt. The institutions that survive and thrive will have several things in common: they will be organised around the autonomy of the individual; provide customised, flexible programmes and services; and be committed to self actualisation, eliminating barriers and enabling people to participate at the level that facilitates their potential. Workers engaged and empowered to undertake bottom-up decision making will fully embrace adaptability and innovation. This is the essence of Deming's work and the continuous, quality improvement process.

New Definitions of "Community"

The futurists are also saying that the nexus of power, the center of decision making, has shifted or devolved from the federal government, where it was pervasive in the 1940s through the 1960s; it then shifted to the states in the 1970s, 1980s, and even 1990s. Today, new regions are evolving that are defined by labour markets, not political boundaries, and led by the business community, not the political leadership. These new regional configurations are engaged with universities and are arranged through non-governmental organisations (both for-profit and non-profit). This is a significant change and a common element of those communities that are thriving in America today.

AGING POPULATION AND LEGACY COSTS

One of the overriding trends is the aging of America's population.

The Aging and "Baby-Boom Generation" Factors

The economic and political implications of the aging of America are best understood when one focuses on how dramatically this has developed in the last few decades. In the middle of the last century, you were considered old if you were 50 or older. Today, those 65 to 75 are called the "young old"; those 75 to 85 are the "middle old"; and those 85 and older are the "old old." The fastest growing portion of our population today is the "old old" category, increasing at a rate of four times the national average.

Health Care Costs

Health care costs are the fastest growing segment of all state budgets. Medicaid is a stateadministered programme that provides health insurance for the poor, the blind, and disabled; it receives a lot of attention as legislatures wrestle to control those cost. But states also pay public employee and retiree insurance, school teachers' insurance, and provide health care for prisoners and those in mental facilities.

Taken together, these costs are squeesing all state budgets and causing cuts in education and other human services. The burden of increased health care cost is not limited to state budgets. Congress is struggling with the uncontrolled growth of Medicare and trying to figure out how to serve 45 million Americans who are currently uninsured. Nationally, health care represents 15 per cent of America's GNP, almost double the rest of the world. Annual health care cost increases have been averaging 12 to 15 per cent, double and triple the rate of inflation.

This cost crunch will require the attention of policymakers for years to come. On the positive side of the pending Baby Boomers' retirement is the fact that 50 per cent of the current workforce will be eligible to retire in the next ten years, creating enormous employment opportunities for those who have the necessary skills. As Boomers age and spend more on health care, the impact will be felt in the economy as well. The health care industry is one of the most rapidly growing sectors of the economy. Health care jobs will be plentiful, with most specialties experiencing shortages. In many communities, if not most, health care is already the single largest employer. Furthermore, our mature manufacturing sector is at a significant disadvantage internationally as it competes against foreign competitors from countries that have tax-supported, national health insurance and therefore no health care cost associated with their products.

ECONOMIC COSTS

While the legacy cost associated with the aging workforce burdens the manufacturing sector, there are three other trends impacting the overall economy.

Shift to Information and Service Economy

First, the U.S., is shifting from a manufacturing to an information and service economy. In 1950, 60 per cent of jobs were available to the unskilled; by 2000 only 15 per cent of jobs were available to the unskilled. Today, even the most basic employment requires higher math, science, and social skills. Manufacturing, the mainstay of the twentieth-century economy, is not going to disappear; but, through increased use of technology, it takes far fewer workers to produce more and higher-quality products. Manufacturing productivity increased dramatically in the last decade, while manufacturing employment continued to decline; that trend will continue. Additionally, the economy is becoming much more technological and workers more highly skilled. Having post-high school training, whether it be through a university, community college, or some skilled training, has become an absolute necessity. We have now added a new dimension to participation in our economy, dual literacy.

You must be functionally literate—able to read, write, understand basic math—and technologically literate, meaning that you are comfortable with computers, robots, and other forms of technology. No longer will one be able to be a high school dropout and get a good job in the new and ever-changing, technological economy. The flip side of this new equation is the possibility of being dually illiterate, meaning that you are neither functionally literate—able to read and write—nor technologically literate, comfortable with computers, robots and technology. This dual illiteracy phenomenon is something we must come to understand and solve. With the aging of America and the pending retirement of an additional 77 million baby boomers, it is imperative that anybody who is able to work have the skills necessary to participate fully in the economy.

New Learning Fundamentals

Will Daggett, an international expert on education and the workforce, calls for "future basics." Professor Daggett believes that every student coming out of high school must have three years of technical reading and writing, at least two years of applied physics, a year of statistics, a year of logic, and at least one foreign language. These future basics are currently the norm in European and Asian high schools. These countries place a premium on science and math and have clear policies that encourage emerging and technical training in areas that America has lost ground in over the last few decades. This has serious policy implications for us all.

An International Workplace

A third way our economy is changing is that it is becoming international. In auto manufacturing, the Big Three are no longer General Motors, Ford, and Chrysler; the Big Three employers in Michigan are McDonald's, Wendy's, and

Kentucky Fried Chicken. Toyota has already overtaken DaimlerChrysler and Ford and is challenging General Motors as the number-one automaker in the world. One out of six American workers currently works for a foreign-owned company.

Thomas Friedman's hot selling book, *The World Is Flat*, is required reading in every Board Room in America and should be required reading for every American. So, key trends impacting policymakers on the national, state, and local levels are the aging of America and an economy that is shifting from manufacturing to one that is international, technological, and service based. While we have traditionally looked to the federal government for solutions to the complex problems facing our society, the locus has shifted to new regional configurations led by business leaders through non-governmental organisations. This last feature creates enormous opportunities for participation, engagement, and impact on the local level.

SECONDARY TRENDS

Two other trends need to be highlighted.

Prison Growth

The first is the enormous growth in prison populations across America. The Department of Corrections has the fastest-growing budget in most states and is taking up a larger share of state spending. While it is good politics to be "tough on crime" and put more people in prison, the consequences must be understood. Policymakers are confronted with either raising taxes or making deep cuts in higher education, revenue sharing, health care, and other discretionary human service programmes. Prisons are becoming a major public policy debate, which takes on a special edge when one considers that the people going to prison are basically young, poor, minority males.

It is a national disgrace that more young, minority males are in prison or on parole than are enrolled in our institutions of higher education. It's cheaper to send a young person to Harvard than it is to send them to prison, yet the prison building goes on unabated. From a policy viewpoint, we know that these young, minority males have three things in common: they dropped out of school, have substance abuse problems, and, most importantly, were abused as children. With that knowledge, we ought to be able to develop public policy initiatives that reduce the crime rate, drop-out rate, substance-abuse rate, and child abuse rate. We must invest in these young people instead of destroying their ability to work and participate in this economy by putting them in prison.

Which category of public policy do you think the prison debate revolves around? Good policy/good politics? Good policy/bad politics? Or bad policy/good politics? Knowing that 77 million baby boomers will retire in the next decade makes it imperative that we intervene early and make sure that everyone who is able gets the skill sets they need to participate in this increasingly complex, technological, and international economy. We simply cannot afford to have a generation of minority youth in prison and unproductive.

Growth of Tax Expenditures

The other trend that is going on in most legislative bodies across America is the growth of tax expenditures. Tax expenditures are special provisions enacted into the tax code that create special incentives, or loopholes, to exempt a particular service, business, or industry from the tax burden. While these tax expenditures can promote good policies—installing solar energy on your home, encouraging hydrogen cars, and facilitating home ownership, each loophole forfeits tax collection for that particular service or product, which means that the federal, state, or local budget must absorb cuts in other areas to make up for these lost revenues. Tax expenditures are second to prisons as the fastest growing part of state spending. Most importantly, they are not subject to periodic review nor to the annual budget process that we discussed earlier.

MAKING OF PUBLIC POLICY

The making of public policy for a country as large, populous and diverse as India is intrinsically a more complex task than in a smaller political unit. This makes a study of the institutions which make policy all the more important. Measured by economic growth or attainment of human development objectives, India remains not only an underdeveloped country but one which is usually regarded as an under-performer, which could do better. If it is taken as given that India is an under-performer, the question then arises as to why is this the case.

A priori, under-performance vis-a-vis potential could be due to:

- Adopting the wrong public policies
- Poorly implementing the right public policies.

There can, of course, be valid disagreements as to what is the "right" policy in a given sector, in a given situation. It can be argued that merely because there are errors, changes or postponements in policies, one cannot conclude that policy-making suffers from weakness. Success is often the result of trial and error. Disagreements, often strong ones, are common and, in a democratic society, both inevitable and healthy. Vigourous debate prior to policy-making and adaptation in response to debate is good, not bad. Flexibility in policymaking to respond to evolving exogenous factors is good, not bad. And the phenomenon of political considerations intervening in decisions otherwise well taken, is inevitable in a fractious but genuinely democratic polity like India.

A survey of some recent and not-so-recent examples of policy-making in India suggests however, that there may indeed be something wrong with the policymaking process:

- *Policy on Private Power*: In 1991, in the wake of the then newly-launched liberalisation process, the Central Government decided to permit private participation in the power sector by "Independent Power Producers". The 1991 policy allowed states to enter into Memoranda of Understanding with individual promoters without following open or competitive tendering. A number of states entered into these MOUs, and the Central Government also committed itself to providing 'counter-guarantees' to the project promoters of these so-called "fast track" projects. The nowdefunct Enron plant in Dabhol was the biggest of these projects. As is now known, the Dabhol project was a disaster, and indeed the 1991-5 approach is now almost universally acknowledged to have been severely faulty. There has been a lot of criticism of the detailed terms of the agreements on the Dabhol project and other individual MOU/fast track projects. However, the most important cause of the independent power fiasco was the poorly crafted policy, which (among other things) failed to take account of the problems in the distribution and supply side of the industry, the scope for mispricing in a non-competitive process and the lessons learnt in other countries in private power development.

- *Grounding of Airbus aircraft*: In 1990, a newly purchased Airbus A 320 aircraft of Indian Airlines crashed killing many passengers. The Central Government decided to ground all the newly acquired aircraft on suspicion that a design defect in the aircraft might be the cause of the crash. In the initial aftermath of the crash, the decision could be considered an understandable short-term precaution, but the decision was allowed to stand for several months. The grounding forced Indian Airlines to lease aircraft from charter operators and caused crippling losses from which it did not fully recover for many years. Eventually the planes were allowed to fly without any modification. With hindsight, the long stoppage was a serious policy error, which could have been avoided by a better policymaking process.
- *Value Added Tax (VAT)*: There have been repeated postponements of the introduction of VAT despite years of preparation. Till late March 2003, it was assumed that VAT would be introduced on April 1st 2003. This was then postponed to June 1st. Eventually this too was deferred, for a variety of reasons, and the target date has been extended to April 1st 2005. Last minute changes have been made to policy decisions (for example on retaining exemptions for new industries which were taken after long deliberation. Uncertainties about scope remained and reached a stage where a strike by truckers listed exemption from VAT as a demand, when in fact they were never within its scope—a fact which was clarified later.
- *Fiscal Responsibility Bill*: A Fiscal Responsibility and Budget

Management Bill was tabled in Parliament in 2000 to be enacted that year. It was eventually enacted only in 2003 in a greatly modified form.

- *Reservation of Parliamentary Seats for Women*: Two attempts to introduce the Women's Reservation Bill over a three year period have failed. Both the main national political parties claim to be in support of the objective. Surprisingly alternatives to some of the specific policy provisions of the Bill, or the fundamental philosophical questions of the desirability or otherwise of reservation for women, do not seem to have been adequately explored or debated either before or after the first attempt at its introduction, or in the interregnum before the first and second attempt.
- *Telecom Interconnection Charges*: The Telecom Regulatory Authority of India introduced a new policy on interconnection charges for private operators in April 2003. Within ten days of its introduction, after criticism from some of the affected quarters, it indicated that the policy would be changed.
- *Conditional Access System (CAS)*: The government decided in early 2003 to introduce a Conditional Access System for cable television in the metro cities with effect from July 15th 2003. The date was announced well in advance and due publicity given. All parties concerned were told that the policy was firm and as late as June 30, it was asserted that the date would not be changed. Various sections of the cable industry argued for or against various aspects of the policy. Among other things a shortage of set-top boxes was feared. Eventually, just a few days before July 15th, the implementation was postponed to September and it was decided to go for a phased implementation. After the postponement of the implementation to September, a Parliamentary Committee recommended even further postponement (this was not accepted by the Government). In September 2003, it was implemented in Chennai alone, but not in Delhi, Kolkata or Mumbai. As of mid-2004, the system continues to operate in Chennai alone (despite Chennai residents' judicial attempts to reverse it) but nowhere else.

In each of the examples:

- Debate has occurred *after* policy-making, instead of before
- Views of one or other important party affected by a decision seem to have not been adequately considered or canvassed before policy was made
- Considered decisions on relatively apolitical issues have been reversed at the last minute even where no new information or circumstances have arisen

- Factors which were endogenous to the problem, which were known or could have been foreseen while making policy, appear to have not been anticipated or considered.

These features are symptomatic of a poor policy-making process and in particular of "executive policy unreliability". Barring the Women's Reservation case, politics was not the prime reason for delays or changes in most of the examples. Even where politics appears to be the reason, there is often more to it. While it is quite possible for purely political considerations to derail a well-structured policy-making process, in many cases *weaknesses in the policy-making process exacerbated political interference*. Indeed political "interference" was often (though by no means always) just a manifestation of factors ignored or missed in the policymaking process. Good policy-making structures and processes do matter and can overcome political bickering, as apparent from the evidence of other countries which are democracies. To cite one instance, a good part of the credit for the post-1945 Japanese economic miracle goes to the processes which enabled Japan to come out with coherent and well-implemented policies.

ATTRIBUTES OF A GOOD POLICY-MAKING PROCESS

It is interesting, and indeed revealing, that the literature on the public policymaking *process* is far less copious than the literature on *substantive* policy issues. The following part on the attributes of a good policy-making process draws on the literature, and on the authors' own experience in the policy making process. One way of describing a "good" policy-making process is one that "is committed to producing a high quality decision—not any particular decision" and that "invests any decision made with a high degree of legitimacy, power and accuracy".

What features or characteristics should a policymaking process have which, if present, would lead to high quality decisions? First, to start with the most obvious, a good policy-making process would involve *due consideration of up-to-date available subject-matter knowledge and relevant data, and the use of available analytical tools*. Second, policies made ostensibly for one sector often have significant impacts on other sectors: a transport policy (*e.g.*, expansion of national highways in lieu of investment in rail) affects the environment; an environmental policy (stricter pollution norms) affects industrial development; a revenue enhancement measure intended to develop one sector can adversely affect another (*e.g.*, the cess to fund the National Highway Development Project reduces the competitiveness of road transport).

Policy-making therefore nearly always means trade-offs, the giving up of something to get something else, losses to one group or section in exchange for (hopefully larger) gains for another. *Policy-making processes and structures should ensure the gathering of information on such inter-sectoral impacts, the analysis of trade-offs, and fully informed choices between alternatives after a proper consideration of effects on different sectors*. Many analytical techniques have been evolved to assist policy-makers in dealing with these issues, coming broadly under terms like policy analysis, programme evaluation, cost-benefit analysis, etc.

These techniques are not without their critics, and their effect on policy–making has been less than their protagonists would like to think. Nevertheless, these techniques are generally judged to have a positive effect on the quality of decisions made. Third, especially in a democratic polity, such *analysis should invariably include an assessment of the "winners" and "losers" from a given policy and a strategy for dealing with likely opposition from losers to what has been determined to be the "right" policy*. Fourth, theory and practice both show that decisions which are seen to have 'legitimacy' are far more likely to be successfully implemented.

Legitimacy is both procedural and substantive:

- Procedural legitimacy is sometimes narrowly viewed as meaning that the *decision is made by an authority legally authorised to make it*, but in practice *consultation of those affected is crucial to perceived legitimacy*. Procedural legitimacy can often be more important in securing the implementation of a policy, than its substantive merits.
- *Substantive legitimacy is achieved when the persons and groups who have knowledge and expertise in the field affected by a policy are involved in formulating the policy*. Note that this point is about the legitimacy—not efficacy—of a policy. The question is not whether the policy was substantively correct, but whether persons who are publicly known or perceived to have subject matter knowledge were involved in making it.

Fifth, a good policy-making process should produce policies which can be executed swiftly and successfully. *This requires the close involvement, during formulation, of the persons who actually have to implement a policy on the ground*, and implies a degree of 'decentralisation' of policymaking. At the same time, a *degree of centralised control is necessary, so that the priorities and interests of implementers do not supplant the public interest*. Whether this central control should be confined to "process control" (*i.e.*, control over how the decision is made) or should extend to "quality control"(control over the substance of the decision) is the subject of debate but the choice is partly a factor of the kind of organisation and the kind of policy being made. On the whole, while policy-making must remain in touch with reality and be conscious of implementation issues, it should not be a prisoner of the current short-term priorities, time constraints and conveniences of implementers.

A good policy making structure should, therefore, provide for appropriate separation between the policy and implementation functions Finally, in order to make the (often difficult) decisions on trade-offs and make them without undue delay, information, analysis and good procedures alone are insufficient. *Those charged with making, or advising on, policy, must possess certain skills (e.g., in coordination, synthesis and integration) and attributes (such as freedom from bias)* which increase the likelihood of quick and sound decisions.

To recapitulate, a "good policy-making process" would meet the following criteria:

- The problems and issues confronting a sector are subjected to expert analysis;
- Information on overlaps and trade-offs with other sectors is systematically gathered and made available to policy-makers;
- Opposing points of view within and between sectors, are properly articulated, analysed and considered and those likely to benefited or harmed are identified and their reactions anticipated;
- Decisions are made with due legal authority, after consultation of those likely to be affected, and with the involvement of knowledgeable persons in the sector(s) concerned;
- Those responsible for implementation are systematically involved in the process, but are not allowed to take control of it;
- Policy-makers and/or their advisers have the honesty, independence, intellectual breadth and depth to properly consider and integrate multiple perspectives and help arrive at optimal policy choices within a reasonable time.

MANAGING THE TRADE-OFFS

Unfortunately the application of these theoretical principles in designing a real-world structure is not simple. There are trade-offs. Criterion—expert analysis of a given sector—is usually achieved by specialists in a field. The pursuit of specialised expertise often leads, quite logically, to fragmentation, *i.e.*, the creation of more and more specialised organisations—ministries, departments, directorates, etc. The narrower the specialisation, the greater the potential for depth in knowledge of that field. For example, instead of one Department of Science and Technology, one can have separate departments for Space, Ocean Development, etc. Instead of an Education Department one can divide it into Primary Education, Secondary Education, Collegiate Education, Technical Education, etc. In the years since, Independence, the Central Government has created an ever-increasing number of more-specialised departments in place of more-generalised departments. However, narrow specialisation diminishes knowledge of the larger picture, of overlaps and trade-offs.

Thus, excessive pursuit of criterion:

- Reduces the attainment of criterion.
- Improved analysis may come at the cost of reduced synthesis — a

weakness as prevalent in the private sector as in the public sector. Besides, specialists in a real-world bureaucracy begin to acquire an interest in the pursuit of their specialism or ministry—expansion of that sector means more departments and hence, more top jobs, faster promotion, greater responsibility, more prospects of public recognition, etc.,—thereby diminishing their independence and thus attainment of criteria.

- (consideration of opposing points of view) and.
- (independence and lack of bias).

Besides, while fragmentation improves specialised knowledge, it:

- Reduces communications between the fragmented units, both formal and informal, and
- Reduces coordination and integration

Integration of different functions is intrinsically difficult and costly. Officers in the same department interact frequently at meetings (formal communication) and may even meet daily for lunch (informal communication). Disagreements between them may be quickly resolved by referral to their common superior. Officers in different departments interact less frequently and more formally, reducing the quantity and quality of information- and idea-sharing. Thus as a corollary of the preceding criteria, a good policy-making structure must *neither be so wide as to militate against specialisation, nor be so fragmented as to affect integration*. What then is the 'right' or 'optimal' degree of fragmentation? Two general principles are suggested. While policy in any sector can theoretically affect any other, in practice the number of interconnections is greatest among related sectors. Thus the interconnections or trade-offs between road transport and rail transport are greater than between road transport and space technology, while the interconnections between information technology and rail transport are less than between, say, information technology and telecommunications.

This leads to the conclusion that:

- As a general principle, related sectors (meaning sectors with significant policy interactions between them) should be grouped together so as to maximise policy coordination.

The lower down the hierarchy one operates, the greater the value of specialised knowledge. Thus the sanitary engineer operating a sewage pumping station needs very specific knowledge about the working of his pumps, a level of detail which his utility's chief executive does not need to know. By contrast, the chief executive has to have a basic level of awareness of every facet of the utility's operations. A heart surgeon in a teaching hospital needs highly specialised knowledge—but the Director of Medical Education needs a very different set of skills and information.

The corollary is that:

- As a general principle, fragmentation needs to diminish as one goes higher up the hierarchy.

Finally at the apex, namely the Prime Minister, one person becomes responsible for everything.

THE DEVELOPMENT SETTING: MANY SLIPS BETWEEN POLICIES AND GOALS

The strategy and policies for rural development are in the nature of interventions in rural communities—to provide resources, infrastructures and development services—to achieve development goals. It is useful to divide the full range from policymaking to achievement of goals into two phases. The first phase consists of policy making, translation of policies into concrete programmes, targets specified for the programmes and the actual outcomes. The assessment of this phase needs to be in terms of these targets and outcomes. The second—and more critical—phase is the response of rural communities to the outcomes of programmes, the benefits derived by them and the enduring improvement in status and life style resulting from the programmes cumulatively over time. Such enduring improvement will depend not merely on the outcomes of individual programmes but, even more, on the total impact of mutually inter-linked and reinforcing package of programmes. Let me elaborate the framework with an illustration. Consider the goal of providing food security to the rural poor.

The two phases of policymaking to achieve this goal are:

1. First Phase:
   - Formulation of Strategy, Policy, Priorities and Time Frame
   - Designing of the Programme with eligibility criteria, targets, subsidy, etc.
   - Putting in Place Infrastructures, Personnel and Procedures
   - Targets?
   - Supporting Policies
   - Outcomes?
2. Second Phase:
   - Response from the Poor?
   - Situational Constraints?
   - Linkages with Other Goals?
   - Achievement of Food Security?

What are the implications of this framework for the contextual limitations on quantitative approaches to policymaking? This needs looking at this framework from two points of view— policymaker's and quantitative researcher's. A policymaker would find himself in a fairly familiar and manageable situation so long as he moves through the first four steps in the first phase. He would actively look for help from quantitative researcher to find out why targets are not fully achieved. There is a question mark against targets to indicate that taking the first three steps does not guarantee achievement of targets. Targets refer to intended first set of results of a policy like expenditure incurred, beneficiary coverage and extension to new areas and groups. In the case of food security, these can be subsidies disbursed, number of poor covered by PDS, increase in the number of Fair Price Shops.

This research area could be regarded as having been fairly adequately covered by collaboration between the policymaker and quantitative researcher leading to fruitful research and better achievement of targets. I distinguish between targets and outcomes reserving the latter term for features which are critical in ensuring the benefits of a policy. In the case of food security, the outcomes would include easy and dependable accessibility of FPSs, adequate availability of food grain stocks with them, good quality of food grains and subsidy large enough to make food grains economically accessible to the poor. There is a question mark against outcomes to indicate that achievement of targets does not ensure that outcomes are satisfactory.

Outcomes are also affected by other policies. For example, policies for agricultural and food grain growth, trade policies, policies for income support like employment generation would all have a bearing on the interface between outcomes and the actual impact on the poor. My impression is that the research area between targets and outcomes and linkages among policies is still to be adequately explored. The quantitative researcher is active but I doubt whether the policymaker has really any time or interest in looking beyond targets. It may be mentioned here that recently Planning Commission brought o ut a massive annual report on outcomes of programmes. The exercise was abandoned the very next year as, apparently, it turned out to be too complex to manage! I am afraid that much of research in this area circulates among the academics but is neglected by the policymaker. As regards the second phase, it covers a complex and only partially charted area in which policy outcomes get processed into achievement of development goals.

All the steps in this phase— response from the poor, situational constraints and the status of linkages among goals— carry question marks indicating that they are not amenable to control, regulation or prediction by the policymaker. In fact, a common feature of Indian development scenario is that even when programmes achieve or even over-achieve the targets, the corresponding goal remains as distant as ever. For example, regarding food security, the subsidies have increased substantially over recent years and the government claims that they have adequate stocks of food grains for distribution, but hunger and malnutrition persist widely and India is nowhere near ensuring food security to the poor. This is the case with other critical goals like universalisation of school education, health for all, etc.

One clue is that goals have to be achieved as a package and not singly. For example, food security needs employment/income security, institutional credit to meet basic consumption needs, etc. Development is indivisible—either the whole package is achieved or none of the goals at all! Hence, it is of utmost importance that the policy maker and the researcher take up the challenge of exploring the area covered by the second phase. I believe that single disciplines like Economics would find their theories and models inadequate to cope with the complexity of processes in this area. Academics not only tend to be confined to single disciplines but they also choose narrow areas of specialisation within single disciplines.

They usually operate with quantitative approaches specific to their areas o f specialisation. It would not be unfair to assume that the academics would find the area covered by the second phase difficult to penetrate and colonise. Without help from academics, the policymaker will be even more hesitant to venture beyond their familiar territory of playing with targets. However, quantitative approaches to policymaking would add little of value if they retreat from the area of the second phase. I offer two guesses about how to begin exploration of the area of second phase. One line o f investigation could be to pursue the outcomes of a single policy as they move through the second phase towards achievement of the policy goal.

This would still need taking into account linkages among policies and goals besides response from the poor and situational constraints. The second line is to look at the system as a whole focusing on development as a package of goals. The emerging phase of globalisation makes the system vulnerable to shocks originating outside as shown by the current recession emanating from the developed countries. The writing on the wall is clear. Even the giants like General Motors and Citibank beg for help! Another recent development in developing countries like India is political agitations which suddenly erupt resulting in widespread interruptions, destruction and breakdown of law and order for long periods.

An even more worrisome trend is that only a dozen or so determined individuals aided by high-tech can challenge the policymaker at the highest level and compel him to yield. It is obvious that the system as unstable as the one which is emerging now makes effective implementation of policies for development, democratisation and better governance infinitely more difficult than in the past.

A keen observer of Indian scene has come out recently with the following assessment:

- "Having many parties in power at the centre is in one respect a reflection of democracy's deepening, a product of the representation of groups and regions previously excluded from government. At the same time, the satisfaction of so many different interests leads to short-term rent-seeking rather than to rational policy. Smaller parties covet the most lucrative ministries, and the larger parties, simply to stay in power, are obliged to concede these to them. Like the 14 others that preceded them, the Indian elections of 2009 will be marked by colour, intensity and a mass involvement of individuals in democracy unmatched elsewhere in the world. But unless governance itself becomes more transparent and accountable, India will continue to be plagued by corruption and inefficiency of a scale unacceptable in a modern state presuming to speak for and serve the people".

We give below two recent perspectives on hunger in India:

1. " The decline in calorie consumption in rural areas is associated with a steady downward drift of calorie Engel curve...it would be difficult to attribute the decline in calorie consumption to declining per capita income, or to changes in relative prices". This is a typical perspective from an academic which misses the seriousness of the problem of hunger
2 Compare this with the perspective of activists who trace the widespread incidence of hunger in India to the structural features of the system.

"The experience of chronic hunger in distant villages as much as on city streets is one of intense avoidable suffering; of self-denial; of learning to live with far less than the body needs; of minds and bodies stymied in their growth; of the agony of helplessly watching one's loved one's—most heartbreakingly children—in hopeless torment; of unpaid, arduous devalued work; of shame, humiliation and bondage; of the defeat and the triumph of the human spirit. Such high levels of hunger and malnutrition are a paradox, because they stubbornly survive surging economic growth and agricultural production which outpaces the growth of population. The riddle deepens because the State in India runs some of the largest and most ambitious food schemes in the world.

The persistence of widespread hunger is the cumulative outcome of public policies that produce and reproduce impoverishment; of failures to invest in agriculture especially in Central and Eastern India and for rain-fed and small farmers; of unacknowledged and unaddressed destitution; of embedded gender, caste, tribe, disability and stigma which construct tall social barriers to accessing food; but in the last analysis it is the result of a profound collapse of governance

THE SOCIETAL SETTING: POLICYMAKER, ADMINISTRATOR AND RESEARCHER

The characterisation of the system given above is incomplete in an important respect. "Policies that produce impoverishment" and "tall social barriers...a profound collapse of governance" do not just happen when the society sleeps. They come into being because the few privileged in the society obtain disproportionate control over resources and the rest suffer from severe deprivations. This can happen, as India shows, even in a functioning democracy. One feature which may make a difference in the medium and long run is that trickle-down from growth and growing political awareness and mobilisation among the vast numbers suffering from deprivation could build up pressures in both economy and polity for more equitable sharing of resources and benefits of development.

Until these processes gain enough strength and spread, the system will remain stuck at the stage described in the Report quoted above. The advocates of excellence who believe that a hundred incorruptible people, if given an opportunity to rule, will solve all problems show profound ignorance of how societies change, develop or disintegrate. Corruption needs to be eliminated. Incorruptible people are invaluable assets. However, overcoming India's problems is a far tougher task than one which a few clean and determined people of "excellence" can tackle. Incidentally, such people hardly carry a tag by which they can be identified.

The point is that our problems need to be traced to systemic features and not to actors who would seem to be responsible if we do not look at the actors in the context of the societal setting in which they operate. We should view the policymakers and researchers from this perspective. Three groups need to be considered—politicians who are at the apex; senior administrators who provide expertise and organise and supervise implementation and monitor achievement of targets and outcomes; and researchers who carry out evaluations and, also, carry out independent academic analyses of the system and policies as a watchdog taking care of national and societal interests. These three groups are not mere collection of individuals functioning independently of each other and each guided by his own norms and criteria for behaviour. In fact, the groups are closely networked and hierarchical with a strong sense of group identity and pride.

They have numerous links with global networks, have strong motivation for upward mobility. They also function as lobbies to protect their interests and improve their status. It is equally relevant to note that three kinds of distances intervene between them and rural areas and community—physical, life style and cultural. Few among them might have lived in villages or have active links with those in villages, leave alone the rural poor. This makes for alienation and poor capacity for rapport with the rural areas and communities. When these groups are placed in the broader political context sketched by Ramachandra Guha—"Having many parties in power at the centre is in one respect a reflection of democracy's deepening... At the same time, the satisfaction of so many different interests leads to short-term rent-seeking rather than to rational policy.. unless governance itself becomes more transparent and accountable, India will continue to be plagued by corruption and inefficiency of a scale unacceptable in a modern state", it becomes clear that they would be severely handicapped in policymaking for rural development because of the broader political context and, also, their own biases and shortcomings. In fact, it is these groups which defeated Gandhi whose vision for rural India was based on fundamental structural reforms like land reforms, cooperative village management and Panchayati Raj Institutions to empower the poor. The interesting point to note is that most members in these groups would not approve the way policymaking functions.

There are also rebels who register their protest. However, despite these attitudes of members, the groups continue to operate the way they do and, still, retain the loyalty and support of enough members to sustain and even enhance the power wielded by the groups. A little reflection will show that the Indian democracy has many such instances. For example, everyone agrees that cities like Bangaloe are caught up in an irreversible process of explosive construction activities, severe traffic congestion and spreading and deepening pollution of air and water. Yet they remain helpless witnesses without any credible move to heal the city. I give below eminent propositions indicative of serious weaknesses in policymaking for rural development and its implementation, monitoring and evaluation.

I treat the three groups—policymaker, administrator and researcher—as one combined entity called policymaker for this purpose:

- Policymaking for rural development needs an extensive, reliable and periodically updated data base. This is particularly important given the distances separating the policymaker from rural areas and communities. The position in this respect is unbelievably sad for a developing country in which village and agriculture ought to be at the centre of policymaking.
- Database:
  - Consider the database for land. The evaluations of land reforms carried out in mid 1950s and 1990s have pointed out glaring weaknesses, unreliability and carelessness in updating records. The database continues to be in the same state even today. If one goes by this database, there is no scope for any substantial redistribution of land. On the other hand, villagers can readily identify those with large ownership evading the law with the provisions existing within the law itself! Recently, a minister in the Union government publicly called the land records as garbage!
  - As regards irrigation, the present irrigated area is only about a half of the potential estimated by experts. I have yet to see any concrete plan about when the full potential will get utilised. Meanwhile, there are persistent gap between irrigation statistics given by the two different ministries of the Government of India! If half of the irrigation potential remains unutilised after six decades of development planning in a country suffering from periodic severe droughts, the policymaker would indeed have a lot to explain.

  - Regarding human development, consider the following observation by Deaton and Dreze.

- *Perspective*: There are numerous clues that the policymaker's perspective extends only up to providing a modest measure of relief to rural communities and not their development. The wide range of programmes with ambitious targets do give the impression of development as the goal of policy making. But reading between the lines indicates that the policymaker treats the rural poor in exactly the same way as we as individuals treat the beggar. We do not ask the beggar how he was reduced to his present state nor what he will do tomorrow. We indulge in a bit of charity in giving alms to the beggar without any intention to help him acquire a better status. This is how the employment programmes and PDS work. The policymaker proudly announces the amounts spent and the poor who benefitted, but there are no arrangements at all to ensure food security and employment security to the poor. Let me cite another clue. Elimination of poverty needs to be identified with attainment of economic viability and political empowerment. Yet, in practice, crossing of poverty line based on the calorie norm is the most quoted magic number identified with poverty elimination! The policymaker has no better norm nor a more adequate accounting of reduction in poverty.
- *Reach*: The thrust of policies for rural development depends on the targets achieved and outcomes of numerous schemes implemented in pursuance of these policies. Since, the schemes are implemented in an uncoordinated manner and their outcomes vary widely, the combined thrust delivered by them to the second phase would be far too modest to achieve the development goals. This is true of even the United Nations Millennium Development Goals which are unable to achieve the modest target of reducing hardcore poverty by half by 2015. This has three implications. First, elites by their own efforts cannot reach development to rural areas and communities. Second, the changes that we see in rural areas and communities are attributable not so much to policies as to other factors like "trickle down', spread of markets, growing ruralurban linkages and breakdown of "self-sufficient villages". Third, the reach of the policies improves substantially where local leaders and activists organise people for development, institutions like panchayats and self-help groups get activated and the poor come together to demand their due. Improvement in the reach of policies depends crucially on the spread of these processes at the grassroots. It is only fair to recognise that these processes are now confined to a few pockets. A word of caution.

If political mobilisation of the poor gains momentum without active panchayats and SHG to channel their energies into productive endeavors, the result would be explosive naxalism and disruptions in development.

- *Countering Vulnerability*: Observers from the developed countries view the prospects for developing countries like India with a noticeable measure of pessimism. We may not agree with them, but one must admit that placing the developing countries in the emerging global context does bring out their vulnerability to tsunami like shocks and reverses.

7

Democratising Policy Making

THEORETICAL CONTEXT OF POLICY MAKING

GOVERNANCE—A POLICY STRATEGY FOR DEVELOPMENT

In the field of development policy, the focus on institutions has led to an ambitious agenda of governance reforms aimed at overcoming the inefficacy of neo- liberal reforms that rely heavily on liberalisation, privatisation, and stabilisation. These notions of governance have evolved in tandem with the theories on development. Much of development has been understood as economic growth and such reforms of governance are seen to as necessary restructuring in order to advance economic growth in developing countries. In the 1960s, and through the 1980s, development policy of countries was state led within a planning framework.

In this framework the notion of governance lay in strengthening public administration for the implementation of state led development plans. With the advent and assertion of multilateral organisations as the World Bank and UNDP in developing countries and their agendas of economic liberalisation, the idea of governance included all the apparatus that were conducive to the implementation of economic reform programmes that aided liberalisation, privatisation, and stabilisation. This "good governance" agenda of 1990s was focused on creating efficient institutions and rules that aided development by making markets work and ensuring that public services were effectively managed. With priorities on increasing economic efficiency and growth, the key aspects of governance included emphasis on rule of law, such as the enforcement of contracts and property rights; eliminating corruption and other rent-seeking activities; transparency in public services to ensure efficiency and effectiveness; reducing uncertainties and instability in the economic and political environment; and ensuring efficient public services for basic social services such as schools and health care centers.

Thus, the governance agenda at this time was predicated on assisting economic growth and efficiency. Within the "good governance" reforms, decentralisation is promoted as a major policy prescription for development, economic growth and poverty reduction. In the governance literature, definitions and clarifications regarding the concept of decentralisation abound, yet there seems to be significant agreement that largely there are three distinct forms of decentralisation—political, administrative and fiscal. More often than not and in the experience of most developing countries like Mexico, Brazil, China, India, the three types of decentralisation occur under the framework of devolution of power. This is the strongest form of decentralisation, with the clearest attributes, as it involves transfer of powers, resources and administrative responsibility from central to sub-national authorities.

Since, the advent of decentralisation as a governance reform and its predominant form as the devolution of power, much is documented on the challenges that decentralisation faces. The wave of governance reforms in the form of decentralisation efforts in countries as Brazil, India, Argentina, Colombia and South Africa reveal that decentralisation as understood by western countries does not translate well to the institutional context of developing countries. *Decentralisation of Governance and Development*, Bardhan emphasises the difficulties that arise with decentralisation in developing and transition economies, predominantly as a result of differences in the structural and institutional contexts from that of the US and European Union contexts. Unsworth claims that the development community has conceived of governance and its tools in terms of models that have worked relatively well in developed countries, *i.e.*, a merit-based bureaucracy, an independent judiciary, and programmatic political parties.

The focus is on formal institutions rather than on the informal relationships that shape the way institutions work. Unsworth argues that the failure of governance reforms is due to an ahistorical approach in conceiving and implementing reforms and that while imposing governance reforms, little effort was made to understand the processes whereby current institutional models in developing countries were negotiated, or the social, economic and political circumstances in which they evolved. Bardhan highlights that "political agency problems" resonate more in the context of developing and transition economies; therefore in understanding the effects of decentralisation, there is need to take account of the political and economic issues of institutional process and accountability at both the local and central level. Evans uses the term "institutional monocropping" to explain the dominant method of imposing uniform institutional reform on developing countries as a way to build institutions and governance that promote development.

There are strong analytical arguments as to why institutional monocropping is unlikely to improve the developmental performance of the individual countries on which it is imposed. O'Donnell contends that in the area of delivery of public services, institutional monocropping has largely imposed an ineffectual proposition that the solution to inefficient governance is less governance; the result being the persistence of ineffective governance, polarised power among the citisenry, and political paralysis. Dani Rodrik points out the flaws in the strategy of imposing "one best way" or governance recipe based on the experiences of western developed countries, and suggests that to make decentralisation practices effective, efforts should be made towards strategies that foster institutions that improve citisens' ability to make their own choices; the use of democracy, especially participatory politics is the tool towards furthering effective policies. On similar grounds, Hoff and Stiglitz argue that imposing formal rules without simultaneously reshaping the distribution of power that underlies prior institutional arrangements is a dubious policy strategy.

The evidence provided in the literature is divided on the impact of decentralisation on poverty reduction; however, scholars like Evans, Rodrik, and Jette observe that it is the participatory element in the implementation of governance reforms that makes decentralisation effective in poverty reduction. Dethier notes that decentralisation when accompanied by participation, empowerment, transparency and accountability is likely to have a more positive impact on service delivery and poverty reduction. The rationale for decentralisation being weakening of centralised authority and making local level governance more responsive to needs of citisens, Bardhan claims that "for decentralisation to be really effective, it has to accompany serious attempts to change existing power structures within communities and to improve the opportunities for participation and voice and engaging the hitherto disadvantaged or disenfranchised in the political process"..

Thus, the new way forward in reinventing governance towards reduction in poverty is the democratisation of decentralisation with strong links of accountability emerging from the "effective participation of citisens in transparent processes of determining public policy priorities and managing public resources in a manner that assures collective action in support of the set policy priorities". Democratic decentralisation is thus defined as an institutionalised form of participatory approach to development where powers and resources are transferred to authorities not only representative of but also accountable to local populations and decentralisation processes require more power for people with regard to decision making.

Thus the discourse on decentralisation and governance emphasises that rather than technocratically imposing one best institutional way for governance reform, a better strategy lies in "democratisation of decentralisation" which involves creating and sustaining participatory political institutions that elicit and aggregate local knowledge and thus emphasise the role of civil society in governance. Carothers studies the nexus between donor agencies, the good governance agenda and civil society and observes that "democracy promoters" often start with the same "democracy template", which includes a standard recipe of support for elections, state institutions and civil society. However, the practice of participation/ democratisation in decentralisation as it has been currently conceived in mainstream thinking has served to maintain, if not increase the dichotomy between the state and "non-state" actors.

The participatory methods employed in decentralisation efforts tend to define and operationalise civil society narrowly, *i.e.*, in terms of consultations with community based organisations, non-government organisations and professionals with technocratic expertise, knowledge and skills. It is possible that the efforts in democratising governance have led to a greater role of civil society as an autonomous countervailing power against the state rather than focusing on deepening democratic engagement through participation of citisens in the processes of governance with the state. Fukuda Parr suggests a contrast to good governance—the concept of "humane governance" developed by Richard Falk to reflect a governance agenda not just for economic growth and efficiency but human development and equity.

The concept of "humane governance" was developed in an attempt to make governance people oriented, focused on human rights and global security, redress "inhumane governance" reflected in five persistent global problems:

1. The failure to meet basic needs;
2. Discrimination and denial of human rights to women, indigenous people and others;
3. Failures to protect the environment and to safeguard the interests of future generations;
4. Lack of progress in abolishing war; and
5. Failure to achieve the spread of "transnational democracy".

A policy agenda for "humane governance" was developed in the report "Human Development in South Asia – the crisis of governance" by Mahbub ul Haq, which aimed at securing:

- Structures and processes that support the creation of a participatory, responsive, and accountable polity;
- A competitive, non-discriminatory, and equitable economy; and
- A society in which people are given the ability to self organise.

Fukuda Parr argues that this shift in the agenda of governance being the promotion of human development was elaborated as "democratic governance".. Democratic governance thus provides space for democratic processes and institutions, securing of political and civil rights and freedoms as human rights into the notion of good governance. Thus the reform agenda for democratic governance is not solely about creating institutions and rules that allow for efficient production and economic development but more about fair institutions that are developed through a democratic process in which all people are engaged and have a real political voice.

MAKING GOVERNANCE WORK

Recent work on democratic governance proposes that "the best way to tap into the energy of society is through 'co-governance', which involves inviting social actors to participate in the core activities of the state". Some scholars argue that participatory reform of governance and decentralisation must require citisens to deliberate and co-govern and provide for "direct roles in public choices or at least for citisens to engage more deeply with substantive political issues and be assured that officials will be responsive to their concerns and judgements". Building public discussion and exchange directly into processes of governance can be loosely labeled "deliberative democracy" where citisens deliberate as reasonable equals and this is a prerequisite for the legitimate exercise of authority and as a way of transforming the preferences and intentions of citisens..

Deliberative democracy transforms the "democracy of voters" to the "democracy of citisens"; rather than relying on traditional avenues for political participation, in the deliberative democratic sphere "citisens address public problems by reasoning together about how best to solve them ... The ambitious aim of deliberative democracy, in short, is to shift from bargaining, interest aggregation, and power to the common reason of equal citisens as a dominant force in democratic life". Fung and Olin Wright have studied experiments in deliberative decision making and governance where "ordinary people can effectively participate in and influence policies which directly affect their lives". Their study suggests that this model of Empowered Participatory Governance has the "potential to be radically democratic in its reliance upon the participation and capacities of ordinary people; deliberative because it institutes reason-based decision-making; and empowered since, it attempts to tie action to discussion".

An "empowered participatory governance" orientation is based on principles of bottom-up participation, starting with a pragmatic orientation to solve concrete problems. At the same time, it seeks to foster deliberation in which "participants listen to each other's positions and generate group choices after due consideration". For the role of the government in decentralisation, Bardhan has argued that rather than playing a minimalist role, the state does at times have to play an 'activist role' in mobilising people in local participatory development, neutralising power of local oligarchs, etc.

To that end, the key design properties of the EPG model are:

- A focus on devolution, but to mechanisms which have public authority;
- Coordination and supervision by a strong central body to insure quality and to diffuse learning, and
- An attempt to harness state power.

Finally, the EPG approach also recognises the importance of countervailing forms of power which help to open the public spaces and insure they do not become captured by existing power holders.

AN APPROACH TO DEVELOPMENT THEORY AND OUTCOMES

For a long time, under the aegis of the Washington Consensus and the neo-liberal model of development, poverty reduction was predicated on economic growth and its trickle down effects. Under the traditional economics-based approach, poverty was measured based solely on consumption or income level. For example, the standard poverty measure for developing countries is the proportion of population below income poverty line of $1 or $2 a day. However, the capability approach proposed by Amartya Sen provides a paradigm shift in the international discourse on development theory and poverty reduction.

Sen argues for an interdisciplinary and multi-dimensional approach to poverty in that "poverty must be seen as the deprivation of basic capabilities rather than merely as lowness of incomes...... which is the standard criterion of identification of poverty". This paradigm shift in the understanding of poverty and human development was noted in mainstream policy world when the Human Development Report of 1990 stated "The basic objective of development is to create an enabling environment for people to enjoy long, healthy and creative lives. This may appear to be a simple truth. But it is often forgotten in the immediate concern with the accumulation of commodities and financial wealth".

Therefore rather than evaluate poverty reduction in terms of income, expenditure, consumption, or utility maximisation, the capability approach focuses on what are a person's functioning, *i.e.*, are her beings and doings and her capabilities. Therefore, in the field of development policy, the agenda is no longer just about economic growth but more directly focused at improving human well being of the poor, in other words, human development. "Development can be seen, as a process of expanding the real freedoms that people enjoy". In his book *Inequality Re-examined,* Sen proposes that social arrangements should be evaluated in terms of "a person's capability to achieve functionings that he or she has reason to value"; therefore development or poverty reduction occurs when people have greater freedoms or capabilities Alkire notes that Sen's significant contribution lies in defining capabilities in terms of both freedom and valuable beings or doings.

Sen states that capability is the "various combinations of functionings that the person can achieve. [It] is, thus, a set of vectors of functionings, reflecting the person's freedom to lead one type of life or another...to choose from possible livings"; he argues that functionings are constitutive of a person's being, *i.e.*, "the various things a person may value doing or being". Therefore functionings may be related to goods and income but describe more what people are able to do or be as a result. In Sen's writings, freedoms are termed as "agency" which refers to a person's ability to pursue and realise goals that he or she values or has reason to value. Alkire clarifies that the aspect of freedom is intrinsic to the understanding of capabilities and it is both functionings and freedoms that are elements of the capability approach. Robeyns notes that other than highlighting the difference between substantive freedoms and outcomes the capability approach also distinguishes between the means and ends of well being and development.

While means are instrumental to goals of increased well being, justice and development, only the ends have intrinsic importance and should be conceptualised in terms of "people's capabilities to function; that is, their effective opportunities to undertake the actions and activities that they want to engage in, and be whom they want to be". In operationalising the capability approach, a key point of contention in the literature is whether or not there are specific capabilities that should be promoted as part of the approach. To further develop the capability approach, Nussbaum has proposed ten central human capabilities that she argues should provide the basis for "constitutional principles that should be respected and implemented by the governments of all nations."

Sen has steered away from prescribing a set of focal functionings and capabilities as he argues that the exercise of selecting capabilities does not lie with the theorist, but has to be a "democratic process of public discussion and reasoning, where capabilities that people value will be set and reset, depending on the purpose of the exercise". In *Inequality Re-examined* Sen notes, "The primary claim is that in evaluating well-being, the value-objects are the functionings and capabilities. That claim neither entails that all types of capabilities are equally valuable, nor indicates that any capability whatsoever—even if totally remote from the person's life—must have some value in assessing that person's well-being.... The relative valuation of different functionings and capabilities has to be an integral part of the exercise." Nussbaum has, however, always stressed that the list generated by her is a list of highly general capabilities, which should be made more specific by the local people. Since, the inception of the capability approach, in mainstream development policy circles capabilities have been operationalised in the form of the Human Development Index (HDI) that could serve as dimension of universal basic capabilities for intercountry comparisons.

The UNDP required a somewhat crude index of human development that was a better indication of well being and quality of life other than income (GNP per capita) alone. Thus the current HDI includes income, literacy and education, and life expectancy not because they are the most important, but because they capture indicators of well being (other than income) that can be measured.

However, "human development approach to development has fallen victim to the success of its human development index". Though the HDI emerged from the normative framework of the capability approach, it has not been able to exploit its potential. As a result of the construction of the index, the HDI reinforces a narrow idea of human development as dimensions related to education, health, living standards and life expectancy and has obscured the inclusion of more complex indicators of human development and capabilities for reasons that have more to do with measurement, than importance to human development..

However there is some scope for expanding the definition of human development in that the Millennium Development Goals for halving income poverty in the world also include achievement of a number of human development outcomes that relate to "first-order" needs, such as food and health, that are basic to life; and "second order" needs that improve the quality of life and the capacity for agency. Within the capability approach, the concern for agency requires that participation, public debate, democratic practice, and empowerment are fostered alongside well-being and also should be the process for valuing and selecting capabilities that are to be advanced.

It can be argued that the aspect of public debate and agency as outlined in the capability approach is being tested by mainstream researchers and theorists who are beginning to elicit and emphasise the perception of the poor concerning their situations, and also on their own desires for and priorities in improving livelihood conditions. In preparation for the World Development Report 2000/2001, a Voice of the Poor survey, interviewing 60,000 poor people in 60 countries across the developing world, was carried out to determine how the poor view their living conditions, what restrictions and barriers they face, and what goals they have. The voices were drawn from 81 participatory poverty studies.

The field studies used participatory and open-ended methods, and were carried out mainly by local research institutes and NGOs, under the supervision of the World Bank. This survey provided an unprecedented detailed understanding of their lives and had a great impact in expanding the definition of poverty, revealing as it did the resulting vulnerability of livelihoods and the powerlessness/voicelessness of the poor in sociopolitical relations. Importantly such research efforts viewed the poor as active participants, or actors, in remedying their situations, not as passive aid recipients.

PARTICIPATORY AND DELIBERATIVE GOVERNANCE AND THE CAPABILITY APPROACH

Till very recently the two literatures on Capability Approach and Deliberative Democracy have existed independently; most of the work on bridging the literature has been on a normative level about how deliberative democracy contributes to the ideal of democracy and public action that is alluded to in the capability approach. Sen's work in *Development as Freedom*, *Democracy as a Universal Value*, *India: Development and Participation*, and *The Argumentative Indian: Writings on Indian History, Culture and Identity* clearly envisions democratic practice conceived of as public discussion and democratic decision-making.

As has been indicated earlier, with regard to the question on selecting and valuing capabilities, Sen has argued that groups and communities have the primary responsibility to evaluate relevant capabilities in question and do so through public discussion, democratically and deliberatively. Emphasising social choice as the basis of development, Sen claims "There is thus a strong methodological case for emphasising the need to assign explicitly evaluative weights to different components of quality of life and then to place the chosen weights for open public discussion and critical scrutiny... A proper understanding of what economic needs are – their content and their force- requires discussion and exchange. ...Processes of participation have to be understood as constitutive parts of the ends of development in themselves". Democracy as "the exercise of public reason" Sen advises that public discussion as an attribute of democracy enables a groups or community to collectively examine and improve their individual and shared values.

Furthermore, Sen portrays democracy as a "demanding system" of governance, and not just a "mechanical condition". On the level of nation-state governance, Sen argues that democratic governance is important for intrinsic, instrumental, and what he calls "constructive" reasons. Scholars like Crocker and Bohman argue that the literature on deliberative democracy could provide direction to understanding and implementing democratic procedures and principles – 'for deriving practical policies from the norms which the capability approach has provided'. While linking Sen's intent to the practice of deliberative democracy in a normative way, Crocker contends that the theory and practice of deliberative democracy strengthens Sen's democratic turn and the capability orientation.

In his forthcoming normative work on *Capabilities. Development and Democracy*, Crocker explores the work of deliberative democrats like Guttman and Thompson, Bohman, Drysek and Deneulin to argue how deliberative democracy advances the notion of democratic practice emphasised by the capability approach. In operationalising deliberative democracy within the framework of the capability approach, Crocker suggests the Empowered Participatory Governance model of Fung and Olin Wright that "extends the application of deliberation from abstract questions over value conflicts and principles of justice to very concrete matters such as street paving, school improvement, and habitat management."

As said earlier, most of the work on the capability approach and deliberative democracy has been theoretical and some insights on empirical work can be gained from Alkire's work—*Valuing Freedoms: Sen's Capability Approach and Poverty Reduction*. The book elaborates Alkire's work on applying the capability approach and participatory development to local development projects implemented by aid agencies in Pakistan. Alkire provides a unique approach to the evaluation of income generation and community building projects and decisions on continuation of their funding. Alkire's approach involves using local yet external facilitators to assess and elicit from beneficiaries of the project the impacts and outcomes of the project in terms of types of valued functionings and capabilities that have changed during the course the project. Crocker studies Alkire's work and suggests that Alkire's participatory assessment of the project could be improved by the theory and practice of deliberative democracy.

Having studied the two literatures with an interest in the synergy between the capability approach and deliberative decision making processes, I propose empirical work that assesses the Empowered Participatory Governance Model from the framework of the capability approach to explore the potential, role and practice of the EPG model in advancing capabilities and freedoms of people in India. Such research can be justified for dual reasons of practice and theory. At the level of democratic practice and governance, the deliberative decision-making model is being studied and promoted as an institutional arrangement and its value in addressing equity and power issues in policy making and bridging closer institutions and citisens.

Though advocated at a normative level, little has been studied about the policy outcomes of such models, especially not from the capability approach. In the conclusion of his book *Development as Freedom*, Sen reminds us about "the implications of this approach for policy analysis as well as for the understanding of general economic, political and social connections. A variety of social institutions—related to the operation of markets, administrations, legislatures, political parties, non-governmental organisations, the judiciary, the media and the community in general—contribute to the process of development precisely through their effects on enhancing and sustaining individual freedoms". Therefore it becomes appropriate to evaluate the EPG model on human capabilities and freedoms as within the capability approach it is reasonable to propose evaluating the social arrangement of EPG in terms of "a person's capability to achieve functionings that he or she has reason to value".

At the theoretical level, such an empirical evaluation of a deliberative democracy model will provide insight on the linkages between deliberative democratic practice and the capability approach and thus add to the just emerging literature on operationalising the capability approach and deliberative democracy, *i.e.*, "processes such as public debate or democratic deliberation, where alternatives are discussed and value judgements made or revised".

'PUBLIC POLICY MAKING': CONCEPTS AND THEORIES

In its simplest sense, 'policy' refers to a broad statement that reflects future goals and aspirations and provides guidelines for carrying out those goals. Hill defines 'policy' as 'the product of political influence, determining and setting limits to what the state does'. To be more precise, when a government takes a decision or chooses a course of action in order to solve a social problem and adopts a specific strategy for its planning and implementation, it is known as public policy. Policy scientists argue that public policy is best conceived in terms of a process. This is because policy decisions are not 'something confined to one level of organisation at the top, or at one stage at the outset, but rather something fluid and ever changing'.

Rose also made a similar argument when he said, 'policy making is best conveyed by describing it as a process, rather than as a single, once-for-all act'. This process involves negotiation, bargaining and accommodation of many different interests, which eventually give it a political flavour. These political interactions happen within the network through which decisions flow, programmes are formulated and implemented and inter organisational dependencies and interactions take place. Thus 'policy making' is not a simple rather a complex dynamic process involving series of actions and inactions of varieties of groups with varieties of interests at different stages.

Here it is important to note that public policy making not only involves the public bodies or public officials as policy actors; rather, private or non-official groups also play a very active role in policy making. This public private interaction constitutes the structure of the political system within which policy actors influence the policy process. The structure of the political system greatly differs from the developed and developing countries. This makes the existing theories or models of public policy making derived from the developed countries inadequate to explain the policy making process of developing countries. In the existing literature, policy making has been viewed from varieties of approaches like rational approach, incremental approach, mixed scanning model, group theory, elite theory, pluralist theory and political system model.

Of these approaches, it is popularly believed that Easton's 'Political System Model' can be employed to explain the policy making process of developing countries. Easton's 'political system' model views the policy process as a 'political system' responding to the demands arising from its environment. The 'political system' as defined by Easton is composed of those identifiable and interrelated institutions and activities in a society that make authoritative decisions that are binding on society. He explains that the environment provides inputs to the decision process/political system in the form of demands and supports. Inputs into the system are provided through outside interests particularly from pressure groups, consumer groups and interest groups.

These environmental inputs are converted through the political system into outputs or policies. Easton's model was originated from the studies of a developed country like the United States. In the American context along with other developed countries, although the interactive stages of policy making, input-throughput-output-feedback, are quite practical, it is highly variable in developing countries. In these countries policy making does not always follow the chain of actions identified by Easton. Particularly, presence of feedback mechanisms is very infrequent in policy making of developing countries. Moreover, the nature of the influence of demands, supports and resources that generate policy as argued by Easton widely varies from the American society along with other developed countries to the developing countries.

Compared to the developed countries, policies of developing countries are less responsive to the demands of the environment. On the other hand, support from the society as input for decision making is also less significant in the developing country context. Walt rightly observes that in developing countries, there exist huge examples of retaining power by the governments without popular support. While support from social groups is given considerable importance in the developed countries. Therefore, without studying the particular policy context, it can not be argued that the policy making process, particularly in developing countries, always follows the stages suggested by Easton. Thus although the existing theories of policy making provide broad outlines for studying the policies of developing countries, for a minute or a comprehensive analysis, they are less adequate. Conceiving it a very broad, general conclusion, the following parts of the chapter give a very precise example of this particular phenomenon through undertaking the theory of 'health policy making' as a case and its application in Bangladesh as a developing country.

THEORY OF HEALTH POLICY MAKING

Health policy' can be conceived and interpreted in different ways. One of the simplest ways of defining 'health policy' is as 'authoritative statements of intent, probably adopted by governments on behalf of the public, with the aim of altering for the better the health and welfare of the population'. Thus health policy consists of a series of governmental decisions about what type of care is to be provided for the betterment of the health of its population and how it will be done. Heidenheimer in identifying the components of health policy say that it is about the 'choice of Governments, direct or indirect, regarding which kinds of personnel may provide what kinds of medical care'. But health policy should not be narrowed down only to health care provision. Along with health care provision, health policy is concerned with social, economic and organisational effects on health.

Walt focuses on these aspects in her definition of health policy:

- 'Health policy embraces courses of action that affect the set of institutions, organisations, services, and funding arrangements of the health care system. It goes beyond health services, however, and includes actions or intended actions by public, private and voluntary organisations that have an impact on health.'

This definition provides a broader view about health policy by indicating the involvement of different actors and factors in achieving the policy goal.

Government assumes a major responsibility of making health policy. But Paton argues that seeking a strategy for health implies policy and action from a wide range of government and non-government agencies. Along with the state actors, various interest groups like professional organisations, health insurance companies, political parties, and the community have influence over the process. The health policy of a country is the product of a diverse range of conflicts, interests and demands from these varieties of groups.

These groups and institutions and their interactions form the 'political system' as termed by Easton. We see, therefore, that like the policy process in general, the health policy process involves a wide and complex range of interests, actors and institutions. Focusing on the power struggle amongst the interest groups within the structure of the health care system, Alford presented his theory of structural interests in the context of the U. S. health care system. His theory has been widely accepted as a very comprehensive and realistic approach to studying the relative power of interest groups and their interrelationships within the structure of a health care system.

Alford's theory of structural interests in health care has proved influential and has been identified as a useful heuristic device by several authors. Supporting the importance of this theory, Wistow notes that 'it remains of considerable value as a framework both for identifying the essential interests of the three main categories of participant in health service policy making and for analysing the changing balance of their respective influences over time'.

ALFORD'S THEORY OF STRUCTURAL INTERESTS IN HEALTH CARE

Alford views the total health care system as a network involving different structural interests. His theory of structural interests determines which group within the structure is powerful and to what extent and what is the interest of particular groups within the health service structure and how they are interdependent with each other. By using the term 'structural interests' he means the interests that gain or lose from the form of organisation of health services. In this regard, he identifies three different types of structural interests termed as dominant interests, challenging interests and repressed interests.

Dominant Interests

Alford has portrayed the interests of the medical profession as the 'dominant structural interest' in health care policy. Alford argues that the medical profession is in a dominant, exclusive and monopolistic position within the health sector. He states that professional autonomy is represented by a diverse nature of professionals involving physicians in private or group practice, salaried physicians, and those in other health occupations holding or seeking professional privileges and status. Amongst all these groups 'physicians are the most important interest group representing professional monopoly'. All of these groups have different interests and are related to the health system in different ways.

As a result, Alford says, 'their interests are thus affected differently by various programmes of reform. But they share an interest in maintaining autonomy and control over the conditions of their work, and professional interest groups will— when that autonomy is challenged— act together in defence of that interest'. Explaining the source of such hegemony of the professionals, Alford argues 'these interests are at present the dominant ones, with their powers and resources safely embedded in law, custom, professional legitimacy, and the practices of many public and private organisations'. Thus the existing socio-political institutions provide the source of power to the professionals. Society depends on doctors due to special knowledge they have and the state depends on medical profession in order to implement its health programmes. By virtue of special knowledge, the profession enjoys clinical autonomy as well as self regulation. Due to their self-regulatory capacity, the profession controls their own income and career prospects.

Thus along with the clinical autonomy, the physicians also do have economic autonomy. State dependency also gives power to the medical profession by enacting laws/medical acts legitimising their self-regulating authority. Thus the professional monopoly derives from the society and state policy rather than their interest group organisation. All these reasons explain why, as long ago as 1975, Alford identified doctors as the dominant interests.

Challenging Interests

Professionals exercise autonomy and dominance within an institutional set-up which in turn challenges their power. Alford argues, 'the changing technology and division of labour in health care production and distribution and the shifting rewards to social groups and classes are creating new structural interests which I label corporate rationalisation'. The structure within which professionals function is termed by Alford as 'corporations'. By its definition, 'corporation' refers to 'a group of people producing goods and services under clearly defined legal structures'.

Health service is produced and managed by large scale organisations or corporations like hospitals, medical schools and public health agencies at all governmental levels and health planning agencies. These large-scale organisations represent an increasingly powerful structural interest, which Alford calls 'corporate rationalisation'. Professionals are subject to the rules, plans and priorities of these organisations. Professionals are never challenged by the existing laws, customs and society rather they are most often challenged by persons occupying the top positions in large scale health organisations like hospital administrators, government health planners or bureaucrats, directors of city health agencies who represent the structural interests of corporate rationalisers. Alford calls their interests as 'challenging interests'. Although each of these organisations compete with each other for power and resources, they share a common goal of maintaining and extending their control 'over the work of the professionals whose activities are key to the achievement of organisational goals'. Professionals work within the boundary of rules, job descriptions and priorities of the hospitals.

They are free to diagnose and prescribe but the types and numbers of cases they handle are controlled by the hospital management and their performances are appraised by internal audit. The economic autonomy of professionals is challenged when they are paid by hospitals/government. Apart from the micro level challenge, Alford argues that the medical profession is also challenged at the macro level in terms of control over hospitals through licensing, accreditation and certification. Another example of attempted corporate rationalisation at the macro level is the state requirements that 'expansion of health care facilities need to be approved by an administrative decision'. The role of the state in health care leads to an apparent diminution of the profession's privileged status in health policy decisions at the centre.

Repressed Interests

Alford has termed the 'repressed interests' as 'negative structural interests', 'because no social institutions or political mechanisms in the society insure that these interests are served'. Repressed interests are heterogeneous with respect to their health needs, ability to pay, and ability to organise their needs into effective demands. Interests of the community population are portrayed as 'repressed interests' as they are not organised as are the other interest groups.

Although they are not organised, they share a common interest 'in maximising the responsiveness of health professionals and organisations to their concerns for accessible high quality health care'. Access of this group to the health services is also restricted. This is the central thesis of Alford. Alford's theory encompasses almost all the key interest groups influencing the health care system. This theory provides an understanding of the changing balance of influence within the policy network through examining to what extent are the professional monopolisers under challenge, by whom and to what effect, whether the corporate rationalisers challenge them on particular issues or at particular periods; and how far the community interests remain repressed. Thus Alford identified three distinct structural interests in health care but he cautioned against overemphasising the difference between the dominant and challenging interests as both of them are the modes of organising health care.

Alford's theory is considered very useful in identifying the principal actors/ interest groups, the nature of their interactions influencing the health policy process of a country and above all, to examine the health policy network of Bangladesh. But due to contextual variations, full employment of this theory in case of a developing country like Bangladesh, is a more complex task. Poor economic condition, political instability and other common phenomena of developing countries generate different types of health care systems, which widely vary from the health system of the USA dealt by Alford. Therefore, it is not sensible to employ Alford's theory to analyse a case of developing country like Bangladesh without substantive modifications.

The next part points out the major determinants of contextual variations between the developing and developed countries along with the United States from where Alford's theory was originated and how this theory is inadequate to explain the case of Bangladesh as a developing country. Inadequacies of the Theory of 'Health Policy Making' in Explaining the Case of Bangladesh This paper considers Alford's theory useful to analyse the health policy making process of Bangladesh through identifying the structural interests in health care systems. But this theory is very closely influenced by the political and economic trends in the world's richest and most advanced country, *i.e.*, the United States, which reduces the suitability of employing them directly for studying the health policy of a developing country like Bangladesh because of their widely different policy contexts. Certain distinct features of the American society that influenced Alford's theory can be identified. Firstly, American society is basically a pluralist society. Decentralised political structure of the USA has created multiple sources of power and has contributed to shape a 'pluralist' society. Paton describes how a decentralised political system has originated a pluralist American society.

He states:

- 'The fact that many areas of jurisdiction provide a greater scope for 'democracy', in that one's life is not in the hands of only one government or tier of government, is rather academic compensation for the fact that many 'power centres' are thereby rendered powerless in many ways.'

Thus pluralism which dismisses the monopoly of the ruling class has provided the source of power to the structural interests. For instance, neglecting the state as a source of power by pluralist theorists reflects the influence of the political tradition of a less powerful state in the USA. Alford's theory has also been influenced by this less powerful state, which helps make the professionals excessively dominant in the health care arena. Mead agrees that American politics is reluctant to impose ironclad control over groups or individuals through authority and America's health system's freedom from public control is unusual compared to other advanced countries.

He adds that both the market and the government leave the professionals remarkably free to determine the price and supply of health services by themselves. Such a political context influenced Alford labeling in the professionals as 'dominant interests' in health care system. Secondly, the market economy is another dominant feature of the American society as well as of the developed countries which has influenced Alford's theory. Alford categorised the management power as 'corporate rationalisers' from the capitalist context of America. The US health system is mostly a corporate health system where large for-profit hospitals/public health agencies compete with each other and employ the doctors and tend to control their activities to attain their goals.

These types of competitive large-scale organisations in the health sector are less evident in developing countries due to weak economic structure. Thus Alford's theory of health policy making contains profound influence of the industrially developed society of the United States, which makes it difficult to apply in explaining the cases of developing countries. There are certain common socio-political and economic features of developing countries that lead to a quite different policy context from the developed countries. These features are the following: Firstly, in contrast to the American society, pluralism is least practised in developing countries.

In these countries, societies are not well organised to place their demands as there exists a persistent lack of interest among the citisens about the national policies. Paarlberg observes that 'in the developing countries, and especially where imperial rule has suddenly been withdrawn, state elites frequently find themselves facing weak and disorganised societies. Their own autonomous preferences can thus play a large role—at least initially'. In addition to a colonial legacy, illiteracy, poverty might be the reasons for such disorganised society. Less organised interest groups thus cannot become dominant over the state machinery and in the same way, professionals in developing countries are less dominant than their counterparts in the developed countries.

Secondly, decision making in developing countries is highly centralised. In developing countries the state assumes the key role in policy making. Grindle and Thomas rightly note that the state actors in developing countries are 'frequently the most important actors in placing issues on an agenda for government action, assessing alternatives and superintending implementation'. As a result, decision making is highly centralised in the hands of the state and the societal forces get lesser scope to voice their demand.

This trend also reduces the power of professionals. Walt states that professionals in the developing countries particularly in India and Latin America, appear to have much less power than their Western counterparts due to the absence of control over recruitment, training and regulation of their members. Thirdly, in most developing countries, health sector has not yet emerged as a corporate system as it is in the capitalist society of America and in most of the developed countries. As economy of developing countries is mostly agrarian and informal, market is less developed in these countries. Due to poor economic condition also, people are less able to provide a market. In absence of a strong market, the state has emerged as the key player. This is because in most of the developing countries, despite the predominant role of the private sector in providing services, the health sector is mostly controlled by the state.

The governments of developing countries, particularly in Africa and Asia, 'have a major role in directly providing health care, in owning facilities, and in employing health staff'. As a result, mainly the government health planners instead of diverse nature of 'rationalisers' challenge professionals in developing countries. Fourthly, scarcity of financial resources in developing countries has made donor agencies another dominant policy actor which is non-existent in developed countries. Health systems of developing countries are significantly dependent on foreign aid, which influences policy priority, allocation of resources and creates scope to the donor agencies to emerge as important policy actors. In addition, due to the unavailability and inaccessibility of health services provided by the government, voluntary agencies emerge as another policy actor in developing countries, which is not evident in developed countries. These voluntary agencies popularly known as NGOs (Non-governmental Organisations) play important role in providing health services to the poor. Although almost all the developing countries share the above mentioned common policy environment in general, the nature of their implication is highly variable among countries again. Likewise, the Bangladeshi policy context also has certain special features that are distinguishable from other developing countries. They are the following: Firstly, the legacies of long history of British colonial rule and subsequent military rule have left the political system of Bangladesh mostly autocratic.

Consequently, national decision making including the health sector decisions has become highly centralised compared to neighbouring India and Srilanka. The Ministry of Health is responsible for the formulation and implementation of the national health policy as well as for the organisation and management of the delivery of health services. While in India the Ministry of Health is mainly responsible for policy formation and regulatory functions and the policy is carried out by the states. The centralised decision making system in Bangladesh leaves lesser scope to the professionals and other interest groups to be dominant over the policy. Secondly, professionals in Bangladesh are mostly challenged by the government as most of them are government employees.

As the health system is centralised, professionals are accountable to higher level government instead of local level managers. This system contrasts to the Srilankan system as well as the Chinese system where health professionals are accountable to local bodies for their performance who act as the challengers of their interests. Thus the composition of challenging interests of Bangladesh also varies from other developing countries. Although the health sector of Bangladesh is almost privatised, most of the private practitioners are the government employees and as the private sector is managed by small-scale carers, interests of private employers as 'corporate rationalisers' are less prominent here. Thirdly, resource scarcity and incapacity of government to provide quality service have generated two significant policy actors in Bangladesh: NGOs and the donor agencies. Influence of donors over the health policy of Bangladesh is highly pervasive compared to even in neighbouring India. This is because India is much less dependent on foreign aid than Bangladesh. On the other hand, in Bangladesh, hundreds of NGOs are playing the key role in providing health services in contrast to another neighbouring country Pakistan.

In Pakistan, Roemer notes that there are a small number of non-government but non-profit health activities performed by religious missions and voluntary agencies. The World Bank has also termed the Bangladeshi NGOs as 'unusually strong'. Given these differences of policy contexts of developed and developing countries and also of Bangladesh from other developing countries, it is seen that theories derived from the studies of industrially developed countries can not be instantly applied for studying the health policies of developing countries. As even the contexts of developing countries also vary from each other, it is argued that it would not be useful to apply the existing theories to the case of Bangladesh without a factual study of the Bangladeshi system. Varieties of socio-political and economic forces peculiar to every single country shape a specific nature of policy context which in turn, produces a different kind of health policy.

As a result, although Alford's theory as well as other theories of policy making derived from the studies of developed countries can provide the basis of a systematic analysis of the health policy of a developing country like Bangladesh, they can not be utilised directly without an empirical study of the Bangladeshi system.

WEAKNESSES IN INDIA'S PUBLIC POLICY MAKING

EXCESSIVE FRAGMENTATION IN THINKING AND ACTION

One of the main problems with policy-making in India, is extreme fragmentation in the structure. For example, the transport sector is dealt with by five departments/Ministries in the government of India whereas in the US and UK it is a part of one department (Department of Transport and Public Works in the US and Department of Environment, Transport and Regions in the UK). Similar examples exist in the energy, industry and social welfare sectors as well. Such fragmentation fails to recognise that actions taken in one sector have serious implications on another and may work at cross purposes with the policies of the other sector. Besides, it becomes very difficult, even for closely related sectors, to align their policies in accordance with a common overall agenda.

Excessive Overlap between Policy Making and implementation

Another problem is the excessive overlap between implementation, programme formulation and policy making which creates a tendency to focus on operational convenience rather than on public needs. Policy-making in Indian ministries occurs at the levels of Director and above, but the most important level (crucial for consideration of cross-cutting impacts) is that of the Secretaries to the Government of India, who are their Ministers' "policy advisers-in-chief".

However, the very same Secretaries spend a large part of their time bogged down on routine day-to-day administration of existing policy. Time is spent anticipating and answering parliamentary questions, attending meetings and functions on implementation issues, etc. Partly the problem is symptomatic of over-centralisation—excessive concentration of implementation powers at the higher levels of the Ministries. Partly, it is also due to such officers being more comfortable with implementation matters than with policy making. The result is that sub-optimal policies, where adequate attention has not been paid to citisen needs, tend to emerge. The diagram attempts to depict both, the fragmented policy making structures in India and the low degree of separation between policy-making and implementation.

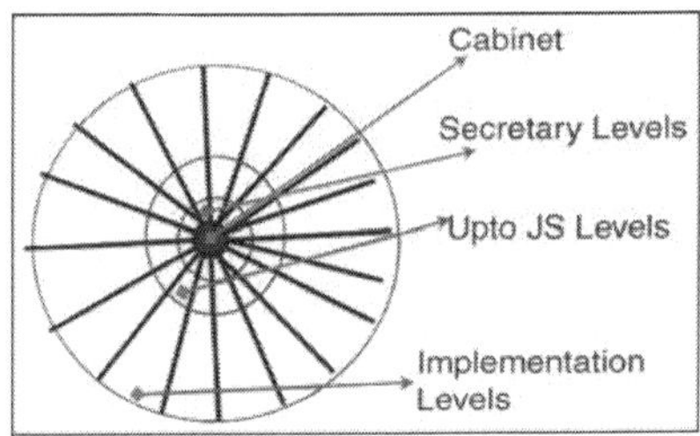

Fig. Current Structure.

Points nearer the centre of the circle represent higher levels of authority, the centre of the circle being the Cabinet. The black radii represent departmental divisions and their thickness denotes the relative lack of communication between departments. The two thin concentric circles denote the separation between implementation and policy making levels. They have been depicted as thin circles (as opposed to the thick radii) to signify that there is little effective separation between policy and implementation. The principle of gradual diminution in fragmentation as one goes up the hierarchy is not followed, a clear indicator that fragmentation at policy levels is excessive. (This is in contrast to the early years after Independence, when there were far fewer Secretaries.).

Fragmentation has often occurred for reasons not directly connected with the design of an optimal structure. Indeed there is a widespread belief that fragmentation has been driven more by the compulsion to accommodate a larger council of ministers, in coalition politics, as well as the bureaucratic desire for more top level posts. Recent experience suggests that inter-sectoral issues and trade-offs are becoming very difficult to address. The truck owners' strike of April 2003 is a case in point: the road transport department had great difficulty dealing with the strike because many of the issues raised pertained to policy decisions of other ministries. Indeed the immediate triggers of the strike—diesel price increases, the mistaken apprehension of VAT on truckers' services—were totally beyond that department's purview. Yet the major impact of those decisions was on the road transport sector.

Lack of Non-governmental Inputs and Informed Debate

Often public policy is made without adequate input from outside government and without adequate debate on the issues involved. The best expertise in many sectors lies outside the Government. Yet the policy processes and structures of Government have no systematic means for obtaining outside inputs, for involving those affected by policies or for debating alternatives and their impacts on different groups. Most developed countries have a system of widespread public debate before a policy is approved. For example, in the US, the legislature subjects a new policy initiative to extensive debate not only in Committees but also in the Senate and House. Such debates not only enable an assessment of different viewpoints but also help build up a constituency in support of the policy through sound arguments. Probably the only example of fairly systematic consultation of outside expertise in India is in the process of formulating the Central Budget, where there is a long tradition of pre-budget confabulations with chosen members of industry, labour and academia.

There are several reasons for a poor pre-policy consultative process. *Firstly*, structures for consulting outsiders either do not exist or if they do, are moribund. *Secondly*, in the absence of good consultative structures, outsiders who do make themselves heard in the policy-making process are often single issue advocates. This makes them liable to the charge of having vested interests, and their views lose credibility. Even if a receptive civil servant were to take their views seriously, he would run the risk of appearing to do an illegitimate favour. *Thirdly*, outsiders involved in policy are usually allowed to make spasmodic or single issue inputs but are not required to sustain their interaction, to confront trade-offs or to meet the objections of other outsiders with opposite views. This makes it easy for outsiders who were indeed consulted, to then disclaim any responsibility for the final decision by protesting that their advice was only partially followed.

Fourthly and as a result of the first three, there is a lack of identification of stakeholders with any policy. In countries like the USA, there are often strong advocates on both sides of a policy question—for example pro- and anti-abortion, pro- and anticapital punishment. In India, judging by the public reaction to many policy announcements, it would appear that almost every new policy announced by Government has "only opponents". This is because the 'winners' from a Government policy rarely feel involved in it, and hence, rarely stand up and support it.

Lack of Systematic Analysis and Integration Prior to Policy-making

Policy decisions are often made without adequate analysis of costs, benefits, trade-offs and consequences.

There are several underlying causes for this:

- *Excessive fragmentation*: This has already been referred to. Fragmentation has led to a widespread prevalence of the 'blind men and the elephant' syndrome in policy-making.
- *Inadequate time spent on policy-making*, mainly due to excessive overlap of policy-making and implementation and to overcentralisation of implementation authority.
- *Inadequate professionalism of policy-makers and advisers*: Debates have been common in India about the pros and cons of 'generalists' vs. 'specialists' in Government. There is a school of thought which suggests that the excessive involvement of poorly informed generalists is the main cause of poor policy-making and implementation. However, when it comes to the realm of policymaking and the making of trade-offs, experience in government and the private sector suggests that this is usually best handled by an intelligent, well-informed person who has a wide rather than narrow perspective. This person could be termed the "intelligent and informed generalist" who, though not a specialist in any one field, is in fact a specialist in analysis, integration and synthesis—i.e identifying problems, trade-offs and solutions. His strength and training lie in being well-informed about a variety of related subjects, in incisive analysis, and in intelligent use of information provided by specialists to frame policy options and assess their consequences. Note that many successful businesses in India and abroad are headed by generalists (MBAs for instance) and the Tata conglomerate continues to operate through the generalist "Tata Administrative Service" to man key positions—an approach regarded as a great success. The problem currently encountered is that the civil servants (who act as key policy advisers) often *are not sufficiently well informed or trained to act in this manner*. This could be described loosely but conveniently as "inadequate professionalism"
- *Inadequate consultation of in-house specialists:* Even conceding that

public policy-making might not be improved by insisting on specialists becoming the policy-makers, it is nevertheless crucial that specialist knowledge be fully consulted and utilised in arriving at policy. For reasons ranging from 'generalist arrogance' to interservice rivalries between groups of specialists, the available expertise of specialists within the Government is often under-utilised.

- *Mediocrity of in-house specialists:* While there are many outstanding specialists working for the Government, there is a widespread feeling that many in-house specialists are not on top of their specialisms. This perception of mediocrity vis-à-vis outside experts tends to worsen the problem of inadequate consultation of even the good in-house specialists who get tarred with the same brush. It also promotes an undue respect for outside specialists and the error of accepting poorly formulated prescriptions from outsiders simply because they have a more professional or expert image.

Reforming the Policy-Making Process

The foregoing analysis attempted to identify the shortcomings in India's policy-making processes. This leads to the question: What can we do to improve policy-making?

The problems highlighted in the analysis can broadly be divided into two types. The first of these is *structural*—too much fragmentation, too much implementation work load on policy-makers, poor structure and process for involving outside experts and stakeholders. The second kind of problem lies with the *competence of the people who man the structure*—inadequate professionalism of the policy-making staff, and inadequate competence of the specialists.

CURRENT CHALLENGES TO MONETARY POLICY MAKING IN INDIA

Perhaps the most distinguishing feature of recent domestic developments is the pace at which economic activity is expanding. On February 7, 2007 the advance estimates of the Central Statistical Organisation (CSO) placed India's real GDP at 9.2 per cent in 2006-07 on top of 9.0 per cent in 2005-06 and reaffirmed the robust optimism that has been building around India's macroeconomic performance. In retrospect, it is evident that there has been a pervasive sense of the gathering momentum of growth, reflected in the direction of revisions in projections by various forecasters during the year. For instance, real GDP growth projections of the Reserve Bank were raised from 7.5-8.0 per cent in the Annual Policy Statement of April, 2006 to 8.0 per cent in the Mid Term Review of October and further to 8.5-9.0 per cent in the Third Quarter Review.

Similar revisions have also been made by various international observers and agencies. But actual growth has turned out to be ahead of all forecasts. Business confidence has been rising in successive rounds of surveys conducted by various agencies and there is considerable optimism on the outlook as reflected in order books, employment and profit margins. Viewed in an international perspective, the Indian economy seems to be well ahead of the synchronous global economic cycle that has enabled the world economy to record four per cent plus growth in an unprecedented run of five years to 2006. There is growing evidence that the step-up in India's growth which set in during 2003-04 is strengthening into an upward shift in the underlying trend. This acceleration of growth has been accompanied by a significant moderation of volatility, particularly in the period 2003-07.

There are also indications of small but important shifts in the composition of growth. The services sector continues to be the main stay of the economy, contributing 73 per cent of overall growth; however, services led growth is getting reinforced by a sustained resurgence in industrial activity after a long hiatus of slow down and restructuring during the period 1996-2003. The buoyancy in industrial performance has been the most heartening feature of India's growth story. Industry's contribution to overall growth has improved noticeably from the 1990s. While the services sector has been the most stable despite high growth, the recent acceleration in industrial growth has also displayed lower volatility than in preceding years.

Table. Patterns of Growth: Average Growth Rates.

(Per cent)

	Agriculture	Industry	Services	Overall
1970s	0.6	4.7	4.1	2.9
1980s	4.4	7.4	6.4	5.8
1990s	3.0	5.9	7.4	5.8
2000-05	1.4	6.0	7.8	5.9
2005-06	6.0	8.0	10.3	9.0
2006-07	2.7	10.2	11.0	9.2
Memo				
2000-03	-0.2	5.2	6.6	4.6
2003-07	4.2	8.1	10.2	8.5

Table. Patterns of Growth: Coefficients of Variation.

	Agriculture	Industry	Services	Overall
1970s	13.65	0.80	0.53	1.42
1980s	1.38	0.36	0.18	0.39
1990s	1.30	0.71	0.27	0.32
2000-05	4.71	0.35	0.25	0.33
Memo				
2000-03	–26.21	0.47	0.13	0.22
2003-07	1.24	0.18	0.11	0.10

Table. Patterns of Growth: Weighted Contribution.

	Agriculture	Industry	Services	Overall
		Weighted Contribution		
1970s	39.7	21.5	38.8	100.0
1980s	19.5	27.0	53.5	100.0
1990s	10.7	18.1	71.1	100.0
2000-05	0.1	21.5	78.3	100.0
2005-06	13.5	17.5	69.0	100.0
2006-07	5.8	21.4	72.7	100.0
Memo				
2000-03	-6.2	23.8	82.4	100.0
2003-07	9.7	18.7	71.6	100.0

Corporate balance sheets have strengthened considerably in an unprecedented run spanning seventeen quarters which began in the second half of 2002-03. Buoyant domestic demand and overseas markets have enabled corporates to scale up production and sales. Profitability (net profits) has recorded growth consistently in the range of 25-60 per cent on a year-to-year basis. Internally generated resources have powered a massive expansion in investments in existing capacity as well as in building up new capacity, while economising on borrowings from the banking system. Interest burden (interest to sales ratio) has tended to fall.

Table. Corporate Financial Performance.

(Growth Rates in Per cent)

Item	2003-04	2004-05	2005-06	2005-06	2006-07			2005-06		2006-07	
				April-September		Q1	Q2	Q3	Q4	Q1	Q2
1	2	3	4	5	6	7	8	9	10	11	12
Sales	16.0	24.1	16.9	17.2	27.4	18.5	16.4	13.2	19.5	25.6	29.2
Expenditure	14.4	22.9	16.4	16.6	25.6	18.0	16.3	12.7	18.9	24.6	26.6
Gross Profits	25.0	32.5	20.3	26.7	39.8	32.0	19.1	21.2	16.6	33.9	45.9
Interest	–11.9	–5.8	1.9	–10.3	20.8	-13.5	–8.0	4.6	3.8	19.9	18.0
Profits After Tax	59.8	51.2	24.2	41.3	41.6	54.2	27.55	27.0	15.1	34.7	49.4
Memo: Interest to Sales Ratio	3.4	2.6	2.0	2.2	2.2	2.2	2.1	2.1	1.7	2.2	2.0

Note:

1.Growth rates are percentage change in the level for the period under reference over the corresponding period of the previous year.

2.Data in column (2) and (3) are based on audited balance sheets while those in column (4) onwards are based on the un audited/audited abridged results of the non- Government non-financial companies.

The optimism generated by India's recent macroeconomic performance has been somewhat marred by the setback to agriculture which has suffered substantial deceleration and instability. Shortfalls in key crops such as wheat (accompanied by depleting stocks), oilseeds and pulses have emerged and the supply situation in respect of these crops is further endangered on account of weather related adverse international conditions. The decline in the global production of wheat in 2006 has turned out to be the largest in ten years. Apart from poor harvests in key producing countries, their carry over stocks are declining and cereal acreage is losing out to the fast growing demand for bio-fuel production. Alongside, in the domestic economy, infrastructural bottlenecks are tightening.

Managing the supply situation is emerging as a formidable challenge. In the current scenario, limitations on the supply response to the momentum of growth are showing up as excess demand pressures. Monetary and financial conditions are reflecting these demand supply gaps as well as the onset of a durable pick-up in aggregate spending. Banks' non-food credit is expanding above 30 per cent for the fourth year in succession, driving up money supply and squeesing overall liquidity. The growth of bank credit has favoured retail lending, particularly housing, real estate, trade transport and professional services and non-banking financial companies – sectors which hitherto were not priced into the credit market.

While banks' exposures to these new sectors is still relatively small, given the low base, the high rates of growth have raised worries about the quality of these assets and potential non-performance. Default rates in regard to credit card receivables and personal loans have been rising. While buoyant deposit growth has, to an extent, alleviated the financial constraints on banks, credit deposit ratios remain high and investments in gilts have been drawn down to close to the statutory minimum of the SLR. These developments are likely to pose challenges to banks in managing liquidity. Financial markets have, by and large, remained stable. Money markets experienced generally orderly conditions along with spells of tightening of liquidity in November and again from mid-December. During these episodes, contrasting conditions have often been observed when short-term interest rates have firmed up despite LAF absorptions but long-term rates have declined in the Government securities market. In December, there was an inversion of the yield curve and a narrowing of yield spreads.

Forward premia have firmed up in November and December across the board in concert with the hardening of short-term interest rates in the domestic money market segments. On the other hand, asset prices, particularly equity prices, have risen to record highs. Another significant feature of recent domestic developments is the firming up of inflation through the year. Currently hovering above 6 per cent, inflation, in terms of the wholesale price index, is ruling above indicative projections and represents a key concern in the evolving macroeconomic outlook. In terms of consumer prices, inflation is even higher in the range of 7-8 per cent.

In crafting appropriate monetary policy in these conditions, it is important to undertake a careful assessment of the manner in which inflation is evolving. Primary articles, unlike in recent years, have contributed significantly to WPI during 2006-07. Accounting for a third of headline inflation, they can be interpreted to originate from supply side pressures. Furthermore, in 2006, there has been a surge in the international prices of cereals. International futures prices of foodgrains have climbed to record levels due to substantial reductions in crop production estimates. At the same time, prices of manufactured products account for over half of current headline inflation. Domestic prices are firming up in sympathy with international prices. Metal prices have risen by 53.6 per cent in 2006. Low stock levels and continuing demand has kept most metal prices high and elevated levels are likely to persist in the near term. In conjunction with emerging strains on capacity, elevated asset prices and the surging demand for bank credit, the rising prices of manufactures constitute the demand pressures on inflation.

Table. Wholesale Prices and Constituents.

(Year-on-year Changes in Per cent)

	Commodity	2005-06 (March 25)			2005-06 (Jan.14)		2006-07 (Jan.13)	
		Weight	Inflation	WC	Inflation	WC	Inflation	WC
	1	2	3	4	5	6	7	8
All	Commodities	100.0	4.1	100.0	4.2	100.0	6.0	100.0
1.	Primary Articles	22.0	5.4	28.3	5.6	28.7	9.3	34.1
	Food Articles	15.4	6.6	24.2	7.4	26.5	8.5	22.0
	Non-food Articles	6.1	–1.9	–2.7	–2.4	–3.3	9.6	8.9
	Minerals	0.5	43.6	6.8	34.8	5.7	20.6	3.0
2.	Fuel, Power, Light and Lubricants	14.2	8.9	47.9	7.9	41.1	3.7	14.0
3.	Manufactured Products	63.8	1.7	23.2	2.2	29.9	5.6	52.3
	Memo:							
	Food Items (Composite)	26.9	4.2	26.5	4.6	28.6	6.2	26.8
	WPI Excluding Food	73.1	4.0	73.5	4.0	71.4	5.9	73.2
	WPI Excluding Fuel	85.8	2.7	52.1	3.2	58.9	6.6	86.0

Note:

WC: Weighted Contribution.

The silver lining to the cloud is the improvement in public finances and the decline in international crude prices, and consequently in domestic prices of petroleum products. Excluding the beneficial effect of this softening of fuel prices results in inflation exceeding the headline in terms of wholesale prices. Globally too, headline inflation has been moderating mainly on account of the decline in international crude prices, while core inflation has generally remained firm and is likely to shape inflation expectations. India's interface with the global economy has been another distinguishing feature of macroeconomic developments.

The strength and resilience reflected in India's balance of payments has to be assessed in the context of global economic and financial developments. Global real GDP growth on a purchasing power parity basis is expected to have accelerated to above 5 per cent in 2006 but with a shift away from the US and towards Europe, Japan and the emerging world, all of which have distinctive features. In China, for instance, there are concerns that high levels of growth might be unsustainable and that some parts of the economy are becoming overheated. In Korea, there are concerns about a relatively rapid growth in house prices along with a rise in household indebtedness. In Thailand, concerted efforts have been taken to stem strong capital inflows into the economy over the past few months. Global financial markets have been reasonably stable while re-pricing risks. Short-term interest rates have firmed up since, October, but long-term bond yields have fallen, translating into a steeper inversion of the yield curve. Foreign exchange markets have been recording lower levels of volatility in recent weeks than before. Global equity markets have posted steady gains. In line with developments in the major markets, emerging equity markets in Asia and Latin America have continued to recover from the May-June sell-off.

The markets which suffered the largest losses have more than recouped earlier losses. Against this backdrop, India's merchandise export growth has resumed strongly from a dip in October, 2006. At the same time, imports of POL increased siseably, but reflecting a sharp increase in import volume in the current year. Non-oil import growth, which remained subdued in the early months of 2006-07, has picked up during the third quarter in consonance with industrial activity. There are also reports of a substantial pick up in bullion imports in October-November. While the merchandise trade deficit has consequently widened, the sustained surplus on account of invisibles is expected to contain the current account deficit at well under two per cent of the GDP. The capital flows to India have recovered from the moderation during May-June 2006. The current account deficit is expected to be comfortably financed in the remaining part of the year. To sum up the assessment, global growth continues to be strong but is exhibiting mixed patterns. In the global financial markets, current indications suggest that the risks remain underpriced and more diversified. Consequently, there is an increasing discomfort of the possibility of tail risk materialising. Geo-political risks remain significant. There is a growing recognition of the need to contain extreme volatility in capital flows. More importantly, on the domestic front, demand pressures appear to have intensified alongside robust growth and there are increased supply side pressures in evidence. Macroeconomic management will be constrained by the lagged response of productive capacity and infrastructure to the ongoing expansion in investment.

THE CHALLENGES

The foregoing analysis provides some evidence, though still formative, that a structural change could be taking place in the Indian economy. There is a gathering confidence that the economy is possibly poised on the threshold of a step-up in the growth trajectory. The central theme of the Third Quarter Review is the challenge of managing the transition to higher growth path, accompanied by low and stable inflation and well anchored inflation expectations. The objective is to firmly entrench potential output and productivity and thereby create the conditions for a further acceleration of growth. The role of monetary policy is to continue to maintain stability and so contribute to growth on an enduring basis. It is in the context of sensitising the public to the dilemmas and trade-offs involved in managing this change that the Mid Term Review of October, 2006 explained the concept of overheating, *i.e.*, a situation in which current output is running above potential output. In the current environment, and in the presence of structural change, the task of identifying overheating becomes difficult for the monetary authority. For the conduct of monetary policy, however, it is crucial to monitor all available information for signs of overheating with a view to keeping inflation expectations stable and ensuring that the gains from high growth are consolidated. Sensing how close is the economy to its potential growth is the vital judgement that has to be made to set the timing and direction of monetary policy. What is potential growth is thus the question that holds the key. There is general agreement among policy makers that the level and pace of potential growth is becoming increasingly difficult to diagnose. Open trade has expanded the supply potential of several economies. Moreover, for a country undergoing structural transformation with large unemployment/ under employment of resources, the concept of potential growth becomes even more fuzzy. For instance, the Economist observes: "India is undergoing a paradigm shift and so backward-looking historical data are now irrelevant for assessing future growth".

Nevertheless, monetary policy decisions have to be made and the closest approximation of potential growth must be identified in terms of a rate of growth which is associated with non-accelerating inflation. At the current juncture, the challenge facing us is to judge the compatibility of the current pace of growth with non-accelerating inflation. In this context, I would like to draw your attention to the new estimates of gross domestic saving and capital formation in India in 2005-06, released on January 31, 2007, the same day as the Third Quarter Review. Close analysis of these numbers reveals the underpinnings of the recent growth experience. The rate of gross domestic saving (GDS), which was earlier estimated at 29.1 per cent of GDP in 2004-05, has been revised upwards by a clear 2 per cent of GDP. The rate of gross domestic investment (GDI) for that year has also been raised by 1.4 per cent of GDP to 31.5 per cent. The significant improvement in GDS in 2004- 05 is attributable mainly to a distinct increase in saving by the corporate sector.

The revision is consistent with the observed improvement in corporate profitability and internally generated resources that has been sustained over the period 2003-07, and to which we have been drawing attention for some time. Corporate profitability has remained strong despite a sharp rise in input costs and in interest payments.

There is some evidence to suggest that the corporate sector performance is being powered by rising productivity. The increase in corporate saving during 2004-05 can be expected to be the onset of a longer trend, supporting high rates of GDS on a sustained basis.

Table. Non-Government Non-financial Public Limited Companies.

(Per cent)

	1990-95	1996-2000	2001-05
Gross profits to total net assets	10.00	8.54	8.62
Gross profits to sales	11.80	11.90	10.72
Profits after tax to net worth	12.04	8.68	10.14
Tax provision to profits before tax	29.22	27.68	30.54
Profits retained to profits after tax	63.74	60.10	53.3
Dividends to net worth	4.26	3.20	4.2
Ordinary dividends to ordinary paid-up capital	19.14	18.70	21.64

Household saving remains the predominant component of domestic saving and would increase even further as incomes grow and social security reforms take shape. The improvement in GDS has particularly benefited form the turnaround in public sector saving. After turning negative between 1998-99 and 2002-03, public sector saving has turned positive from 2003-04 onwards, mainly reflecting the ongoing fiscal consolidation. Public sector saving will continue to have a significant role in further improvement in the GDS. The CSO's estimates for 2005-06 indicate that these signs are firming up with GDS placed above 32 per cent of GDP and GDI close to 34 per cent.

Table. Domestic Saving Rates in India.

(Per cent)

Period/Year	Household Sector	Private Corporate Sector	Public Sector	Total
		Saving		
1970s	12.2	1.6	3.7	17.5
1980s	14.6	1.8	3.0	19.4
1990s	18.5	3.7	1.0	23.2
2000-05	22.2	4.8	-0.2	26.8
Memo				
2004-05	21.6	7.1	2.4	31.1
2005-06	22.3	8.1	2.0	32.4

Table. Domestic Investment Rates in India.

(Per cent)

Period/Year	Household Sector	Private Corporate Sector	Public Sector	Total
		Investment		
1970s	7.6	2.4	8.2	17.6
1980s	7.8	4.2	10.0	21.2
1990s	8.5	6.7	7.8	24.5
2000-05	11.6	6.8	6.6	26.3

Memo				
2004-05	11.4	9.9	7.1	31.5
2005-06	10.7	12.9	7.4	33.8

Against the background of these developments, it is plausible that GDS could rise to a range of 34-35 per cent of GDP by 2007-08. With a current account deficit of below 2 per cent of GDP, GDI could rise to a range of 36-37 per cent. Given an incremental capital output ratio – a summary measure of the productivity of capital – of around 3.5 to 4.3, sustaining real GDP growth rates in the range of 8 to 9 per cent in the medium term appears eminently realisable. The Mid Term Appraisal of the Tenth Five Year Plan provides interesting estimates of assessed capacity or potential output in various sectors of the economy. The existence of high excess capacity in agriculture and allied activities, registered manufacturing, electricity, storage, public administration and other services suggests that the focus needs to shift from an 'investment only' approach to a more comprehensive one.

In all these sectors capacity utilisation has undoubtedly improved but there remains ample scope for high growth. Under capitalisation, which has traditionally characterised the services sector, is beginning to change with the emergence of more organised service activities. Yet another factor that needs to be taken into account in the assessment of potential growth is the trends in productivity. While the empirical evidence remains somewhat ambiguous, there are indications that trade liberalisation has had a positive impact on total factor productivity since, 1991. At the sectoral level, there is evidence of improved productivity for exporting sectors relative to non-exporting sectors. Some studies also throw up evidence of an increase in the growth of labour productivity.

Thus, it is clear that micro structural reforms undertaken over the years have enabled continuing productivity gains, particularly in the manufacturing sector, with enhanced access of Indian business to technology, increased competition, greater attention to research and development and other productivity enhancing activities. Widening and deepening of the financial sector, along with improved regulation and supervision, has also contributed to improvement in productivity.

An important challenge for the monetary policy authority is to judge the durability of the recent upsurge in growth. While there is some evidence, as documented, that the acceleration of growth has been supported by structural factors such as improvement in gross domestic saving and investment rates, productivity gains, the demographic dividend and capital accumulation including skill formation, it is important to disentangle the structural and cyclical components underlying the growth process. It is necessary to note that a cyclical upswing is also underway in India since, 2003- 04 after a prolonged trough which began in 1996.

There is also some sense that this upturn is part of a synchronised global economic cycle which has seen five consecutive years of accelerated global growth. In the event of a judgement that the current growth momentum is more cyclical than structural, the stance of monetary policy would need to reflect a sensitivity to the inevitability of a downturn. On the other hand, the judgement that structural factors predominate would warrant a different policy stance. An overriding concern faced by the Reserve Bank is the persistently high growth of bank credit, with attendant worries relating to the quality of bank credit. In this context, the Reserve Bank has consistently emphasised diligent monitoring of the health of credit portfolios and non-performing assets, the need for counter-cyclical provisioning and sensitivity to risks.

The sharp increase in credit to sectors such as housing, commercial real estate and retail loans have also been worrisome on account of the vulnerability of banks to credit concentration risks. The important question however relates to the sustainability of the credit expansion and its compatibility with the overall acceleration of growth. Credit penetration in India remains low even by emerging economy standards

Table. Cross Country Comparisons of Bank Credit Indicators.

							(Per cent)
	Average Growth Rate (Real)		Domestic Credit as % of GDP		Real Bank Credit Growth to Private Sector		
	1995-99	2000-04	1999	2005	1995-99	2000-04	2005
1.Latin America	3.6	4.5	42	45	–0.2	–1.1	18.4
2. China	17.1	13.3	130	169	16.0	12.5	9.4
3. India	6.1	14.6	51	65	6.9	13.5	30.0
4. Hong Kong SAR, Singapore	1.4	3.4	130	122	0.6	2.2	–3.2
5. Other Asia	–0.3	4.7	89	80	4.0	5.9	8.2
6. Central Europe	9.6	8.1	40	42	8.8	3.8	8.0
Total	7.8	9.6	78	92	6.9	8.9	15.8
Memo							
United States	10.1	3.3	80	92	5.6	5.1	10.9

Consequently, growing financial intermediation could possible be reflected in high credit growth. The Mid Term Review of October 2006 reported empirical evidence of a structural break in the evolution of the elasticity of bank credit with respect to output with an upward shift since, the end of the 1990s. Faster credit growth is also a reflection of the wider dispersal across the economy. Viewed in a holistic perspective, it is difficult to arrive at a clear judgement as to what rate of credit growth is too high in relation to potential growth. Even when the macro availability of resources is adequate to fund the increase in demand arising from both consumption and investment, there could be micro imbalances that lead to observation of excess demand and overheating.

It is in this context that monetary management has to also look at imbalances that could be transitional. The challenge before us at the present time is to manage the transition to a higher growth path, in the presence of some structural rigidities, in such a way that actual inflation and inflation expectations are contained and do not become mutually reinforcing. Our assessment is that while expansion of capacity is underway, the realisation, particularly in sectors like infrastructure could be constrained over the next two years. Indeed, the difficulties with improving the supply response are more complex and challenging than aggregate demand management. Supply management will need to encompass wide areas including labour markets, land laws and the content of regulation in each sector. As long as supply responses are less than elastic, they could show up as excess demand, causing inflationary pressures and raising inflation expectations.

To reiterate, managing structural change while keeping inflation low without dampening the growth momentum is the quintessential challenge to monetary policy in the period ahead. Illustratively, given the growth in consumption demand, rising incomes and high growth in sectors such as information technology (IT), it is not surprising that there is a huge actual demand for housing, retail activity and office space from the burgeoning services sector. It is also not surprising that there would be associated problems on the supply side including availability of land, zoning and other land regulations, and social concerns about the conversion of land from agricultural purposes to other uses. Therefore, monetary policy has to be creative in addressing these problems in a non-disruptive manner. It is in this context that prudential and other measures such as provisioning and risk weights on bank loans to specific sectors are being used so as to enhance the sensitivity to risks emanating from these sectors rather than standard monetary policy responses that address aggregate demand. The task before monetary policy is thus rendered complex, requiring that both macro issues and sectoral problems be addressed in a specific manner.

THE MONETARY POLICY RESPONSE

It is well known that monetary policy operates cumulatively and with lags that can range between 12 to 18 months, depending on the specifics of the economy. It is in this context that beginning in mid 2003, the Reserve Bank started a graduated withdrawal of accommodation. Since, September, 2004 repo/ reverse repo rates have been increased by 125/150 basis points, the CRR has been raised by 100 basis points, risk weights have been raised in the case of housing loans (from 50 per cent to 75 per cent), commercial real estate (from 100 per cent to 150 per cent) and consumer credit (from 100 per cent to 125 per cent) and general provisioning requirement for standard advances in specific sectors has been raised to 1.0 per cent of standard advances. At the time of the Third Quarter Review, the combination of macroeconomic developments embodied in high growth and firming inflation, escalating asset prices and the enduring strength of capital flows, a three-pronged approach was envisaged.

A measured increase in policy interest rates to assuage demand pressures was considered necessary in conjunction with some modulation of capital flows and the need to fortify banks' balance sheets by precautionary provisioning and a greater sensitivity to underlying risks. It was decided to increase the fixed repo rate under the liquidity adjustment facility (LAF) of the Reserve Bank by 25 basis points to 7.50 per cent. The LAF reverse repo rate, the Bank rate and the cash reserve ratio were kept unchanged. Furthermore, the provisioning requirement in respect of standard assets in the real estate sector, outstanding credit card receivables, loans and advances qualifying as capital market exposure, personal loans and systemically important non-deposit taking non-banking financial companies (NBFCs) was raised to 2 per cent. Risk weights for banks' exposure to such NBFCs was increased from 100 per cent to 125 per cent.

Interest rates on non-resident deposit schemes, which have been recording siseable inflows, were reduced by 50 basis points for rupee deposits and by 25 basis points for foreign currency deposits. Banks were also restrained from granting fresh loans in excess of ₹.20 lakhs against non-resident deposits. The Reserve Bank has indicated that over the remaining part of the year, liquidity management would receive the highest priority. All policy instruments would be deployed to ensure appropriate modulation of liquidity.

The stance of monetary policy was set out as:

- To reinforce the emphasis on price stability and well-anchored inflation expectations while ensuring a monetary and interest rate environment that supports export and investment demand in the economy so as to enable continuation of the growth momentum.
- To re-emphasise credit quality and orderly conditions in financial markets for securing macroeconomic and, in particular, financial stability while simultaneously pursuing greater credit penetration and financial inclusion.
- To respond swiftly with all possible measures as appropriate to the evolving global and domestic situation impinging on inflation expectations and the growth momentum.

It is important to note that monetary policy authorities all over the world over are expressing similar sentiments in terms of an uncertain outlook, concerns about persistent underlying inflation and some nervousness about visitations of financial volatility. Several central banks have shown a readiness to respond asymmetrically to any signs of price and financial instability. The ECB, the Bank of England, the Reserve Bank of Australia, the People's Bank of China and the Bank of Korea raised policy rates. In order to contain financial market volatility arising from large liquidity flows, several central banks have tended to tighten monetary policy, even at relatively low current inflation rates, as in Thailand, Turkey, Saudi Arabia and Iceland. On the other hand, some central banks have paused in their policy cycles, particularly the US Fed, the Bank of Canada, the Bank of Japan, Bank Negara Malaysia and the Banco de Mexico.

Some other central banks have cut back their policy rates in recent months. In India, it is recognised that inflation is a tax on the poor against which there are no hedges available. Consequently, ensuring price stability is a societal compulsion to which monetary policy as a arm of public policy must be committed. The measures taken in the Third Quarter Review needs to be seen as sustaining and supporting the growth process while ensuring a minimum social insurance by delivery of a tolerable rate of inflation.

IMPROVING THE COMPETENCE AND SKILLS OF POLICY-MAKING MANPOWER

It was observed that policy-making is usually best supervised by the "informed and intelligent generalist". There is however a very big difference between a mere "generalist" and an "informed and intelligent generalist".

Being "informed and intelligent" requires certain skills, namely the ability to:

- Structure a problem,
- Assess what kinds of issues are likely to arise,
- Know where to look for appropriate information and expert opinion,
- Speak and understand the "language of the specialists" so as to communicate effectively with them and be able to interpret expert opinion.

Currently, the extent to which a generalist civil servant acquires these vital policy skills is left partly to the individual (his own efforts to acquire them) and partly to chance (the postings he holds). Despite sporadic efforts by the Department of Personnel to promote a degree of broad specialisation, little has actually been achieved.

The key reform which would greatly improve the policy-making competence of India's senior civil servants—and improve the competence of specialists in Government— is implementation of a well-designed career path which has strong incentives for the progressive acquisition of expertise and professional skills. Experience abroad, including in developing countries, shows this to be a significant contributor to good policy making.

The key requirement is the design of a career path which:

- Creates incentives to learn, and to acquire and apply the right skills.
- Strengthens links between academia and the administration.
- Identifies and weeds out poor performers.
- Ensures that only those with the requisite knowledge and intelligence make it to the top policy levels.

The following is an approach designed to achieve these results in the specific context of the Indian Administrative Service (IAS—the premier generalist civil service cadre in India, which accounts for the largest number of policy level positions):

- All IAS officers should spend their first 10-12 years in general management, largely in field assignments. This will provide them with a thorough grounding in field realities and in basic managerial skills, which are crucial for making the right policy-choices.

- All officers would undergo an evaluation by an independent body. About 90 per cent of the officers should be cleared for the next level with about 10 per cent (relatively poor performers) continuing to remain in the general management stream without further promotion for a further 5-7 years before early retirement.
- Officers clearing the selection process would be assigned a broad specialisation, and undergo a specific training programme leading up to a Masters and/or M.Phil Degree. The area of specialisation would be determined fairly and transparently based on educational background, demonstrated aptitude, performance in training programmes, sectoral manpower needs, and individual preferences. An illustrative list of broad specialisms would be: economic and commercial management, financial management, personnel management, infrastructure management, Internal Security and Defence, Social sector management, Rural development and local administration, Health sector management, Education sector management, General management, regulatory matters and Governance.
- During the next 15 years, officers would work in their chosen broad specialism, and (if they desire) work towards a Ph.D, taking up spells of research in suitably timed sabbaticals.
- The academic qualifications acquired (M.Phil., Ph.D etc) would give academic endorsement and credit for an officer's achievements, provide a transparent and objective input for career progression, reduce complacency, inculcate a culture of continuous learning, and strengthen officers' self-confidence and ability to deal with peers in other countries and international institutions.
- Around the 27th year, they would, after a rigourous selection process, be assigned to a policy-making position. Selection would be done through the UPSC or another credible agency. This would be a substitute for the "empanelment" process. Only about 30 per cent of the opening cohort should make it to this level. Those not selected will retire at the age of 55.

Similar career paths can be designed for other quasi-generalist services (like the Revenue Services, Accounts Services) and a suitably modified version for specialists (Economic Service, Engineering services, Scientific services).

The emphasis on academic qualifications in the proposed career path has the advantages that it would:

- Give academic endorsement and credit for an officer's achievements,

- Provide a transparent and objective input for career progression,
- Reduce complacency,
- Inculcate a culture of continuous learning, and,
- Strengthen officers' self-confidence and ability to deal with peers in other countries and international institutions.

However, it also has some limitations and disadvantages. Mediocrity is widespread in Indian academia. This would reduce many of the theoretical advantages unless the choice of institutions was also tightly and centrally prescribed. The process of such prescription may well invite challenge from individuals or institutions left out.

The skills required for academic success are not necessarily the same as those required for success in public management and public policy making; the services are replete with academically brilliant officers who are poor managers or policy-makers. There are also a few instances of superb administrators with just a Bachelor's degree.

This limitation can be overcome by ensuring that academic achievement is only one factor in the selection process, but it does mean that the benefit of a 'transparent basis for career progression' is diminished to that degree.

FEASIBILITY OF THE PROPOSALS

India has no dearth of reform proposals, but a poor record of actual reform. This concluding part of the chapter attempts to assess the practicability of these proposals and the chances of their actually getting implemented. The first set of proposals involves structural reform of the Central Government. On closer examination though, it would be clear that it affects primarily the higher echelons of the civil service. It hardly touches the political executive, except to the extent that lesser fragmentation makes it necessary to divert sub-cabinet (Minister of State/ Deputy Minister) berths to head Agencies and Boards. What it would do is diminish the number of posts of Secretary to the Government of India—-and this might attract opposition from the most senior levels of the bureaucracy.

Ultimately however, since, the impact is primarily on the bureaucracy, it is a reform which is *politically highly feasible*. The second—personnel— reform is more problematic. It is likely to find opponents within the bureaucracy, since, it implies weeding out 10 per cent and 50 per cent per cent respectively at around the 15th and 30th years of service. However, part of the likely resistance, especially from the 50 per cent left out at the 30th year of service, can be overcome by allowing them to continue in service, with all attendant benefits, but keeping them out of top policy making positions. They could be placed in equivalent positions elsewhere or even asked to stay at home and draw their full pay. The narrowing of choice for the political executive in bureaucratic appointments at the Centre (to a narrower and exogenously selected pool) may be a potential source of political resistance, though this is not likely to be very strong. The State governments may not comply with central "guidance" on career paths as it would blunt the use of transfer as a weapon to secure obedience.

However, non-compliance at the state level would not mean a death blow and implementation of this even in the senior postings at the Central government level would be enough to start with. More problematically however, the concept of 'weeding out deadwood" is likely to be judicially challenged. Even if the concept is upheld, individuals who are dropped out of the selections may challenge decisions, obtain stays and or secure re-appointment and even promotion. The approach of the Indian courts on matters of this kind has been strongly pro-employee, and the constitutional "doctrine of pleasure" has been greatly eroded. Existing provisions for "compulsory retirement without disciplinary action" have been greatly circumscribed and made virtually unimplementable. However, this has partly been due to the absence of transparent criteria for weeding out officers who fail to perform.

This is also compounded by a performance appraisal system where grade inflation is rampant. If transparent criteria are established and clear indicators of inadequate performance are put in place, it would become legally more tenable to screen deadwood. Recent judgements on points of administrative law have widened the scope of judicial review to include the concept of "proportionality" and it would be open to the court to hold, for instance, that the decision not to select for the next level is, for instance, not proportionate to the deficiency in performance. While there may be many such difficulties, the pay-offs to the nation from the implementing a professionalisation of the civil service would be very high in terms of far better policies and better implementation.

Therefore, even if this proposal seems unlikely to find immediate acceptability, it would be worth canvassing academic and public opinion in its favour so that a gradual change of heart in both the political executive and the judiciary results. The change in India's economic policy post-1991 is illustrative of how policies which seemed political anathema earlier became widely accepted. Similarly the evolving approach of the Supreme Court on various issues in response to changing circumstances and changes in public opinion (for example the upholding of the Government's right to formulate economic policy in the BALCO case even though it seemed "anti-socialist", the overturning of the Unnikrishnan judgement in the T.M.A.

Pai case in 2002 in which the Supreme Court declared its own earlier ruling to be unconstitutional) show that judicial opinion too is not immutable. Greater dissemination of these and other reform ideas would eventually make them feasible.

Bibliography

A.K. Singh: *Gender and Digital Economy : Perspectives from Developing World*, M.D. Publications, Delhi, 2011.

Aanchal Sarkar: *Gender and Development*, Pragun Publication, Delhi, 2006.

Amita Sahaya, Sunita Kaistha and Vibhuti Patel: *Gender and Development*, The Women Press, 2011.

Anu Saksena: *Gender and Human Rights : Status of Women Workers in India*, Shipra Publication, Delhi, 2004.

Anuradha Mathu: *Gender and Development in India : The Indian Scenario*, Kalpaz Publication, Delhi, 2008.

B. Ratna Kumari: *Gender and Globalization : A Comparative Perspective Between Europe and India*, Kanishka Publication, Delhi, 2010.

Bina Agarwal: *Gender and Green Governance : The Political Economy of Women's Presence Within and Beyond Community Forestry*, Oxford University Press, Delhi, 2010.

Bishnu C. Barik, Pushpesh Kumar and Usha S. Sarode: *Gender and Human Rights : Narratives on Macro-Micro Realities*, Rawat Publication, Delhi, 2010.

Brinda Bose: *Gender & Censorship*, Women Unlimited, 2006.

Deboshruti Roychowdhury: *Gender and Caste Hierarchy in Colonial Bengal : Inter-Caste Interventions of Ideal Womanhood*, Stree Publication, Delhi, 2013.

Gupta, K R.: *Gender : Problems and Policies*, Atlantic Publication, Delhi, 2009.

Himanshu Sekhar Rout and Prasant Kumar Panda: *Gender and Development in India : Dimensions and Strategies*, New Century Publication, Delhi, 2008.

Indu Grover and Puspita Das: *Gender Analysis in Agriculture : Grassroot Realities*, Supriya Books, Delhi, 2011.

J.B. Flueckiger: *Gender and Genre in the Folklore of Middle India*, Oxford University Press, Delhi, 1996.

Kanwar Sonali Jolly-Wadhwa: *Gender : A Cross-Cultural Perspective*, Gyan Publication, Delhi, 2000.

Lalima Chakraverty: *Gender and Culture in the Works of Indian Subcontinents Select Women Novelists*, Atlantic Publication, Delhi, 2012.

Lisa D. Brush: *Gender and Governance*, Rawat Publication, Delhi, 2007.

M. Suriya, S. Balakrishnan, L.N. Umadevi, V. Ganesh and Vijay Arumugam: *Gender And ICT* , A.P.H Books, Delhi, 2011.

Madhu Nagla: *Gender and Health*, Rawat Publications, Delhi, 2013.

Manoranjan Pal, Premananda Bharati, Bholanath Ghosh and T.S. Vasulu: *Gender and Discrimination : Health, Nutritional Status, and Role of Women in India*, Oxford University Press, Delhi, 2009.

Mondira Dutta: *Gender and Human Development in Central and South Asia*, Pentagon Press, Delhi, 2013.

Rekha Choudhary: *Gender : In Decision Making*, Ritu Publication, Delhi, 2007.

Sachidananda Mohanty: *Gender and Cultural Identity in Colonial Orissa*, Orient Longman, Delhi, 2008.

Seema Chandra: *Gender and Development*, ALP Books, Delhi, 2013.

Siddhartha Sarkar and John V Mensah: *Gender and Development : An Afro-Indian Study*, Arise Publication, Delhi, 2008.

Simon Brodbeck and Brian Black: *Gender and Narrative in the Mahabharata*, Manohar Publication, Delhi, 2007.

Triveni Goswami: *Gender and Conflict Transformation : Nagaland and Egypt*, Akansha Publication, Delhi, 2007.

U. Kalpagam: *Gender and Development in India : Current Issues*, Rawat Publication, Delhi, 2011.

V Geetha: *Gender*, Stree Publication, Delhi, 2002.

Yubaraj Sangroula and Geeta Pathak: *Gender and Laws : Nepalese Perspective*, Pairavi Prakashan, Delhi, 2002.

Index